# Culture, Self, and Motivation

## Essays in Honor of Martin L. Maehr

# Culture, Self, and, Motivation

## Essays in Honor of Martin L. Maehr

*Edited by*

**Avi Kaplan**
*Ben Gurion University of the Negev*

**Stuart A. Karabenick**
**Elisabeth De Groot**
*University of Michigan*

**INFORMATION AGE PUBLISHING, INC.**
Charlotte, NC • www.infoagepub.com

**Library of Congress Cataloging-in-Publication Data**

Culture, self, and, motivation : essays in honor of Martin L. Maehr / edited
by Avi Kaplan, Stuart A. Karabenick, Elizabeth De Groot.
  p. cm.
  Includes bibliographical references and index.
  ISBN 978-1-60752-107-5 (pbk.) – ISBN 978-1-60752-108-2 (hardcover)
1. Motivation in education. 2. Motivation (Psychology)–Social aspects.
3. Educational sociology. 4. Maehr, Martin L. I. Kaplan, Avi. II.
Karabenick, Stuart A. III. Groot, Elizabeth de.
  LB1065.C87 2009
  370.15'4–dc22
                                         2009011495

Printed in the United States of America

# CONTENTS

PART I

## MOTIVATION AND SELF

PART II

## CULTURE AND MOTIVATION

# CULTURE, SELF, AND MOTIVATION

## The Contribution of Martin L. Maehr to the Fields of Achievement Motivation and Educational Psychology

**Avi Kaplan, Stuart A. Karabenick, and Elisabeth De Groot**

Martin L. Maehr is, without question, one of the most influential contributors to achievement motivation theory over the past several decades. Marty was a leading architect of the paradigmatic shift that characterized motivational theorizing during the second half of the 20th century. His significant theoretical, empirical, and practical contributions have become cornerstones in the development of the fields of motivation and educational psychology more generally. In the 1960s, Marty was one of the early and vocal critics of the behaviorist practices of reinforcement and rewards (Maehr, 1968). In the 1970s, his was the preeminent voice challenging David McClelland's and John Atkinson's personality theory of motivation (Maehr & Sjogren, 1971; Maehr, 1974a). In the 1970s and 1980s, he championed the importance of including *contextual* socio-cultural processes in motivational theorizing (Maehr, 1974a; Maehr & Nicholls, 1980). In the 1980s, he was one of the founders of the currently dominant perspective—achievement goal theory (Maehr, 1984, 1989), and in the 1990s, Marty and colleagues in-

*Culture, Self, and Motivation: Essays in Honor of Martin L. Maehr,* pages vii–xxi
Copyright © 2009 by Information Age Publishing
**vii**

troduced an influential model for the methodical transformation of school cultures guided by motivational theory (Ames & Maehr, 1989; Maehr & Midgley, 1991, 1996).

In addition to the influence of his own research, Marty's impact on the field of motivation was also due to his decades-long editorship of the prestigious book series, *Advances in Motivation and Achievement* (JAI Press and Elsevier). Throughout his career, Marty held fast to three prominent ideas, which he promoted in all of his work:

a.    contexts and situations have a primary effect on people's motivation and quality of engagement;

b.    leaders and educators can transform organizational cultures and thus facilitate more adaptive motivation among students and workers; and

c.    adaptive motivation is a valued outcome in and of itself.

These ideas are now taken for granted in theories of academic motivation, and are beginning to take ground in other domains in educational psychology.

Marty Maehr's interest in motivation began when he was still a student at Concordia Seminary, St. Louis, Missouri, pursuing his B.A. (1955) and then his M. Div (1958). This interest resulted in his M.A. thesis, which he completed at the University of Nebraska (1959) on *The Value Patterns of Persisting and Non-persisting Seminary Students*. After a brief diversion from this interest into researching *The Effect of Food Deprivation in Binocular Conflict* among inmates for his Ph.D. dissertation at the University of Nebraska (1960), Marty took a faculty position at Concordia Senior College in Fort Wayne, Indiana (1960–1967) and returned to pursue his interest in understanding and affecting effortful and meaningful engagement.

Although Marty's religious background is likely to have had an influence on his theoretical interests, it was clearly his fascination with the writing and ideas of Kurt Lewin and other social psychologists of the 20th century's early decades such as Cooley and Mead that led him to pursue the Self as an important topic of research (Maehr et al., 1962)—a concept that would become central in his later theorizing (Maehr & Simmonds, 2004). The focus on self, its dynamic and social nature, and its role in motivation and engagement, led Marty to question and criticize behaviorist motivational concepts and practices commonly accepted at the time, such as reinforcement (Maehr & Videbeck, 1968). And, in what already was a characteristic of his scholarship, which continues until today, Marty readily translated his criticism of behaviorism and his emphasis on the social origins of motivation into practical applications to education (Maehr, 1964, 1968). However, behaviorism was not the least of his targets at the time. The focus on the social and situational processes that underlie self and motivation, and his stance that theory should inform educational practice, led Marty to recognize and point to the limits of the other predominant motivational theory of the period: John Atkinson's theory of achievement motivation and its emphasis on relatively stable personality attributes (Maehr & Sjogren, 1971).

A transfer to the faculty of the University of Illinois, Urbana-Champaign in 1967 provided Marty opportunities, which he used with tremendous rigor and talent, for constructing his own innovative theory of academic motivation. Then, as today, the University of Illinois was home to scholars conducting cutting-edge theoretical and empirical work, and the two decades that Marty spent at Illinois were immensely formative of his theoretical views of achievement motivation. His interest in the social-contextual origins of motivation already established, Marty engaged in a research project in the Chicago schools, aiming to facilitate students' motivation. This experience led him to become intrigued by the contextual influences on the motivation of African-American students (Rubovits & Maehr, 1973). Anecdotes from the schools and conversations with Harry Triandis (1972) about "subjective culture," led to systematic research. The findings from this research led Marty to fiercely criticize David McClelland's widely-accepted personality perspective on the relations between culture and achievement motivation (Maehr, 1974a). Spending a year in Iran as a visiting professor at the Faculty of Education in the University of Tehran also helped to solidify Marty's ideas. At the same time that Clifford Geertz was promoting a parallel shift in American anthropology, Marty proposed his perspective on the role of culture in the *socio-cognitive meaning* of action and its implications for motivation and engagement (Maehr, 1974b).

However, Marty's perspective on the sociocultural origins of motivation and achievement did not divert him from his primary concern with promoting the adaptive motivation of individual students. His strong conviction that adaptive motivation is crucial for achievement, but even more importantly, for optimal development and well-being, led him to propose that adaptive motivation itself—in school and beyond—should be a desired outcome of the educational project (Maehr, 1976). And it was the responsibility of the school and its leaders to change the educational environment—the school's organization *culture* (Baden & Maehr, 1986; Maehr & Willig, 1982)—in order to facilitate among students more adaptive motivation in school and "continuing motivation" after school (Maehr & Lysy, 1978). His theoretical perspective on culture, context, and motivation provided Marty with a lens through which to examine and comment on several important educational issues that plagued American education and about which he felt strongly, including desegregation (Hartman & Maehr, 1984; Maehr, Hartman & Bartz, 1984), and the achievement of boys and girls in science (Maehr, 1983; Steinkamp & Maehr, 1983, 1984).

Marty's concern with the motivation of individual students, while recognizing the effect of context and culture, was strengthened by interactions with educational psychology colleagues at the University of Illinois, most particularly, Carole Ames, John Nicholls, and Carol Dweck. These researchers were pursuing somewhat different projects; however, they all recognized the convergence of their perspectives in the emphasis on the central role of the *subjective meaning* of achievement situations for students' motivation and engagement. The collaboration among these researchers was a watershed for motivation theory, as it led to the formation of what is now known as *Achievement Goal Theory* (Ames, 1984; Dweck, 1986; Maehr, 1984; Nicholls, 1984). Marty continued to engage in cross-cultural research (e.g., Fyans & Maehr, 1982; Fyans, Salili, Maehr, & Desai, 1983; Shwalb, Shwalb, Harnisch, Maehr, & Akabane, 1992), but his interest in cultural processes became the bedrock for a more comprehensive theory of individuals' achievement motivation—the Theory of Personal Investment (Maehr & Nicholls, 1980; Maehr, 1984; Maehr & Braskamp, 1986)—Marty's version of achievement goal theory.

Marty's belief in the power of contexts over individuals' motivation was clearly based on personal experience. Contexts, such as the Chicago schools and the culture of Iran, often had an influence on his interests and research questions. This was also the case when he assumed administrative responsibilities at the University of Illinois as Associate Dean for Graduate and International Programs (1975–1977), Associate Director and Director of the Institute for Child Behavior and Development (1977–1986), and Director of the Institute for Research on Human Development (1986–1988)—experiences that triggered his interest in employee motivation. This led to a set of studies and the development of instruments that applied the theory of Personal Investment to workers and business organizations (Maehr & Braskamp, 1986; Maehr, 1989a). Similarly, a short stint as the Acting Director of the Office of Gerontology and Aging Studies (1980) led to the consideration of motivation among the elderly (Maehr & Kleiber, 1980, 1981).

But Marty's diversions from educational settings were brief. His primary interest in student motivation continued to pull him back to focus on enhancing students' quality of motivation and engagement. Again, a change in context seemed to provide an opportunity when Marty was invited to transfer to the University of Michigan to assume the position of Director of the Combined Program in Education and Psychology (1989-1992). The move to Michigan introduced Marty to Carol Midgley, a motivational researcher interested in the role of context in the change of students' motivation across the transition from elementary to middle school. Marty's theoretical perspective appealed to Midgley, and the two formed a productive partnership. Basing their intervention on Ames' (1990) contributions to classroom interventions, Marty Maehr and Carol Midgley focused on the school as a whole. Their collaboration resulted with a quasi-experimental school-transformation research project, which became to be known as the "coalition" project (Maehr & Midgley, 1996), and afforded Marty the opportunity to test his theories in practice. The contribution of this project to motivational theory, research, and practice has been tremendous and included elevating the importance of the school context in students' achievement goals (Maehr, 1991; Anderman & Maehr, 1994); the development of what has become the most widely used instrument to assess students' motivational orientations, the Patterns of Adaptive Learning Survey (PALS) (Midgley et al., 1998) as well as the articulation of a model for the theoretically-informed transformation of the school culture (Maehr & Midgley, 1991, 1996).

In the years that followed, Marty continued to pursue his theoretical and research interests in culture, self, and motivation and to emphasize the central role of school contexts in the motivational patterns of students. He continued to serve as co-Principal Investigator on funded projects focusing on motivation and achievement in groups (Spencer Foundation with Paul Pintrich), motivational evaluation and consultation to Math and Science Partnerships (NSF with Stuart Karabenick and Paul Pintrich), and the motivation of Middle-Eastern students in the US (Spencer Foundation with Revathy Kumar and Stuart Karabenick). Towards his retirement, Marty even returned to visit his early interest in religion and motivation through a PEW fellowship at the University of Notre Dame (Maehr, 2005), integrating his well-developed notions of culture, self, meaning, and motivation with religious life; and with editing Volume 14 (2005) of the *Advance* series on Motivation and Religion (with Stuart Karabenick). Marty retired and assumed emeritus faculty status on May 31, 2005.

## THE CURRENT VOLUME

The authors of the chapters in this volume—past and present collaborators of Marty Maehr, and a few of his former graduate students along the years—are motivational researchers who conduct research using diverse methods and perspectives, and in different parts of the world. All, however, see their intellectual roots in Marty's theoretical and empirical work. The chapters in this book are divided into two sections: *Motivation and Self* and *Culture and Motivation*. Clearly, the distinctions between these two sections are very blurry, as they are in Marty's work. And yet, when the authors were asked to contribute their chapters, the research questions they addressed seemed to have formed two foci, with personal motivation and socio-cultural processes alternating as the core versus the background in the two sections.

*Motivation and Self*

The section on *Motivation and Self* concerns three of Marty's main contributions to the field of achievement motivation: the theory of Personal Investment (Maehr & Braskamp, 1986; Maehr & McInerney, 2004); the concept of continuing motivation (Maehr, 1976); and most prominently, Achievement Goal Theory (Maehr, 1989b, 1991; Maehr & Midgley, 1991, 1996). The chapters span these issues and include theoretical reviews, empirical research, personal application to practice, as well as a description of a national-scale practice-oriented research and intervention project in which Marty was also involved.

In the first chapter, Larry Braskamp, a researcher and high-level university administrator who was one of Marty's collaborators in developing the theory of Personal Investment (Maehr & Braskamp, 1986), describes how he applied it in his university administrative practice. Braskamp begins by stating the two main tenants of the theory of Personal Investment:

1.   that motivation can only be inferred from observed behavior, or personal investment of resources; and
2.   that this personal investment is based in the meaning that students construct in contexts.

He then describes at length the psychological components that the theory suggests interact to result with the meaning of action:

1.   sense of self;
2.   sense of purpose; and
3.   the sociocultural environment.

For each component, Braskamp describes how he applied it, at times extending it, to fit the developmental stage and context of college students. His review highlights the strong emphasis in the theory on the contextual nature of motivation. He follows by describing how he used the perspective he developed for understanding the personal investment of college students as well as for enhancing these students' motivation and facilitating their holistic development through research and counseling.

The second chapter addresses the notion of *continuing motivation*—a concept that Marty introduced to the field over three decades ago. In this chapter, Eric Anderman and Jennifer Weber follow Marty's steps in noting that one of the most important goals of education is to facilitate engagement in learning and adaptive behavior beyond the school context. They then point to the fact that it was Marty Maehr, in his important 1976 article in *Review of Educational Research*, who coined this concept and argued for its importance as an educational outcome. In the chapter, Anderman and

Weber review the definition of continuing motivation as well as its contemporary permutation—life-long learning. While pointing to its importance, Anderman and Weber also lament the fact that continuing motivation has mostly remained a theoretical concept, and that its potential as an important educational outcome has not been pursued. In order to promote such an agenda, Anderman and Weber review two research projects—Eccles' and colleagues' Expectancy-Value model to facilitate future course enrollment, and Anderman and Johnston's use of achievement goal theory to explain engagement in news-seeking behavior—as examples of research that concerned continuing motivation as an outcome, even if not labeled as such. They then review various education interventions, ranging from structuring *Small Learning Communities* to school-based motivational interventions, that may potentially enhance continuing motivation. They conclude by voicing again Marty's contention to consider students' adaptive motivation as an important outcome in and of itself of the educational project.

In the third chapter, Glyn Roberts, Frank Abrahamsen, and Nicolas Lemyre, provide a comprehensive review of the theoretical and empirical application of achievement goal theory to the sport domain. Roberts et al. note the discrepancy between the commonly-held beliefs of coaches, who equate motivation with arousal, and who create competitive climates in order to motivate their athletes, and the findings from over 25 years of research that suggest quite strongly that athletes' persistence, effort, satisfaction, self-esteem, sportspersonship, cooperation, well-being, and performance are higher when they focus on personal mastery rather than on demonstrating their superiority over others. The authors do note, however, the important findings that point to the moderating role of perceived competence on both the relations of task-involvement or mastery goals with positive outcomes, and the relations of ego-involvement or performance goals with negative outcomes. Still, research in the sport domain supports Marty's perspective on achievement goal orientations—that they constitute different meaning systems within which athletes interpret competition, winning and losing, set different objectives, and employ different strategies. Roberts et al. point to the rather scant attempt to intervene to enhance athletes' motivation through mastery-oriented environmental goal structures and call for more intervention research in this direction.

In the fourth chapter, Avi Kaplan, Hanoch Flum, and Keren Kemelman pursue Marty's notion of motivation as the meaning of engagement. In the chapter, they report on a study that sought to describe the process by which students who are enrolled in a college introductory course that emphasized mastery goals construct the meaning of engagement in a specific task. The study included manipulating a task in the course to emphasize mastery or performance-approach goals and involved in-depth interviews of the students about their experiences at the university, department, course, and specific task. The analysis of the interviews revealed the dynamics of meaning-making of engagement, and how students' personal histories and dispositions sensitized them to different aspects of the educational environment, which in turn influenced the meaning of engagement in the course. Moreover, the analysis also highlighted the role of specific meaningful events in eliciting alternative meanings and the cognitive and emotional strategies that students employed in order to integrate different meanings into a purpose of engagement.

In the fifth chapter, a group of researchers from the University of Rochester headed by Andy Elliot pay tribute to Marty's contribution to achievement goal theory and describe one of the most influential developments in this literature in the past decade: the integration of the mastery versus performance goals distinction and approach and avoidance motivation. Beginning with the definition of approach and avoidance motivation, the chapter follows with a historical review of the approach-avoidance distinction starting with the Greek philosophers, its manifestation in the theories of early psychological thinkers, through the period of the cognitive revolution to the present when the distinction between approach and avoidance motivation is prominent in several motivational perspectives. The chapter then provides a parallel review of the concept of "goals," from Aristotle through the work of Kurt Lewin to its prominent status in contemporary motivational theory. Here the chapter turns to review the emergence of the achievement goal approach, reviewing the work of Marty and his colleagues in facilitating the achievement goal framework: John Nicholls, Carol Dweck, Carole Ames and their collaborators. The authors then highlight the important integration of the achievement goals approach with the approach-avoidance distinction, precipitated by Elliot and his colleagues, and the resultant trichotomous model, and then the 2 x 2 model, of achievement goals. The chapter ends with the authors' perspective of the hierarchical model of achievement motivation that includes motives and goals, and which views the operation of these constructs in a goal-complex: achievement goals that serve a certain motive. The authors emphasize the contribution of the goal-complex notion to the understanding of various ways that combinations of motives and achievement goals may affect outcomes in different contexts.

In the sixth and final chapter in the section, a team of researchers from the University of Michigan, headed by Stuart Karabenick, describe the "Math and Science Partnership-Motivation Assessment Program (MSP-MAP)"—a *very* large scale, NSF funded project that provided motivational consultation and evaluation to partnerships between universities and school systems, which were designed to improve math and science education. The project emerged from the realization that, whereas many science researchers and educators acknowledge the important role of motivation in science learning and achievement, they are generally unfamiliar with the theoretical, methodological, and practical knowledge in the motivational domain. Focusing particularly on their collaboration with two large scale academic-school system partnerships having students with markedly different demographics (Latino/a students in California and African American and Caucasian students in Alabama), Karabenick et al. describe how the MSP-MAP program provided these partnerships with the conceptual and empirical tools to assess motivational processes of students and teachers, statistical consultation, and professional development workshops to facilitate change in educational practices and, in turn, students' motivation and engagement. The authors then describe developments in motivational assessment that took place as a result of these projects, most notably, the introduction of the systematic application of Cognitive Pretesting (Karabenick et al., 2007) that contributes to the validity of motivational scales among different groups of respondents. Finally, the authors describe some of the research findings that emerged from the data collected through the MSP-MAP, including the complex interaction of motivational processes and contextual factors in predicting achievement and adaptive help-seeking,

## Culture and Motivation

The second section of the book—*Motivation and Culture*—addresses the role of culture and socio-cultural processes in motivational processes, which was earlier described as one of Marty's most influential lines of research (Maehr, 1974; Maehr & Nicholls, 1980). The chapters in this section range from a quantitative, empirical investigation of the role of school cultures in students' motivation, through reviews of decades-long research projects that examined cultural processes and achievement motivation, to recent critiques of contemporary perspectives and of Marty's own position in his famous debate with David McClelland (McClelland, 1961; Maehr, 1974a; McClelland, 1985) on the role of culture in motivation.

In the first chapter of the section, chapter seven, Lennia Matos, Willy Lens, and Maarten Vansteenkiste report research that followed Marty's emphasis on the role of school culture in students' motivation. These authors sought to investigate whether students distinguish between the school's emphasis on mastery and performance goals and their classroom teachers' emphasis on mastery and performance goals, how these two perceptions were related to students' own personal achievement goals, and whether perceived teachers' emphases mediated the influence of school culture on students' motivation. Conducting their study among high-school students in Peru—a context and population not commonly studied in achievement-goal theory—Matos et al. found partial support for their predictions. Students do indeed perceive their school culture as emphasizing mastery and performance goals, and their teachers as emphasizing different achievement goals. Moreover, perceived teacher emphasis on mastery goals partially mediated the relations between a school culture emphasizing mastery goals and students' adoption of their mastery goals orientation. Interestingly, whereas perceived teachers' emphasis on performance-approach goals was related to the overall school's emphasis on performance goals, it was the school performance goal culture, and not teachers' emphases, that was related to students' adoption of performance-approach goal orientation. Matos et al.'s study highlights the theoretical and empirical work needed to conceptualize and investigate the complex ways by which norms, values, and practices at different organizational units of analysis integrate to result in students' patterns of motivation and engagement.

In chapter eight, Farideh Salili reviews early research, conducted by herself, Marty Maehr and others, that challenged McClelland's conception of achievement motivation as a stable personality characteristic, and how cultures influence children to be more or less achievement motivated. During the 1970s and 1980s, Salili, Maehr, and their colleagues conducted cross-cultural research demonstrating that achievement had different meanings in different cultural groups, focusing most notably on Iran and the US, and hence, that achievement motivation may be based in different psychological processes among people from different cultures. Salili then goes on to describe her more recent research with Chinese students, and compares the meaning of success and achievement among Chinese and British students in Hong Kong. Using techniques such as the Repertory Grid and Semantic Differential, Salili noted that whereas both groups considered success as important and were highly motivated to achieve in the social and academic domains, the meaning of success and failure, the more particular goals they pursued, the attributions for success and failure, and the means for achieving goals were somewhat different in the two groups. She also noted changes in these cultural constructions of achievement and success among these cultural groups from the 1960s to the 2000s. The limitations of current models of achievement motivation in accounting for these cultural differences led Salili to develop a model that depicts both the similarities and the differences in processes of achievement motivation between these two cultural groups.

In chapter nine, Dennis McInerney and Arief Liem highlight Marty Maehr's contribution to cross-cultural perspectives on achievement motivation. McInerney and Liem begin by reviewing the problematic practice of investigating phenomena in one culture with the uncritical use of concepts and methods derived from a different culture. They note that this was the case with David McClelland's theory of achievement motivation, which emphasizes the individual as the standard—a focus that ill-suited collectivist cultures. The emergence of the cross-cultural perspective in psychology in the 1970s challenged this perspective and called for verifying the relevance of constructs across cultures. Marty Maehr and his colleagues engaged in such research into the meanings of achievement in different cultures. Their findings suggested that there was much that is similar in cross-cultural conceptions of achievement. However, the relevance of these conceptions to people's lives across cultures was quite different. This research formed an important foundation for the theory of Personal Investment, which the authors describe at some length. They follow by describing the results of research that is based on Personal Investment Theory, most particularly findings that accumulated over decades of research by McInerney and his colleagues. These results pointed to remarkable similarities in motivational structures among such diverse cultural groups as Europeans, Asians, Aborigines, Middle Easterners, Africans, and Native Americans (Navajo). However, the findings also pointed to differences among the groups, for example in the importance of motivational predictors. An important outcome of this rigorous research was the development of cross-culturally valid and reliable scales of the various aspects of Personal Investment Theory: the Inventory of School Motivation (ISM) and the Facilitating Conditions Questionnaire (FCQ). Finally, the authors describe qualitative research that is based on Personal Investment Theory. The findings point to similarity in motivational concerns across students from different cultural groups, but also to the immense complexity of motivational processes. These understandings led to the development of yet another quantitative instrument—the GOALS-S—which aspires to capture the complexity and multi-dimensional nature of students' motivation. The authors end the chapter with an emphasis on the importance of employing motivational models, such as Personal Investment Theory, that allow to capture the motivational phenomenon in its complexity.

In chapter ten, Julie Turner and Helen Patrick pay tribute to Marty's sociocultural perspective on motivation and critique the still prevalent emphasis in motivation theory and research on enduring, de-contextualized, individual characteristics. Turner and Patrick note that current perspectives of motivation conceive of persons' engagement as separated from the contexts within which they engage. This is manifested in the predominance of intra-psychological beliefs in motivational explanations, and the heavy reliance on surveys in operationalizing motivational processes. All this, Turner and Patrick claim, is in contrast to much evidence supporting the dynamics of contexts and situations and the embedded nature of behavior in social situations. Turner and Patrick then go on to describe examples of situated motivation from their respective mixed-method research projects. Patrick describes how different kindergartens and kindergarten science teachers create different learning environments that result in very different conceptions of what science and engagement in science mean. Turner describes the change that one math teacher went through—simultaneously in beliefs and in instructional practice—during one year of collaborative intervention, that had marked effects on her students' motivation and achievement. They conclude by emphasizing the insights from these studies to the nature of motivational change and to the role of situations in this change.

Finally, in the last chapter of the book, Tim Urdan provides a critique of Marty Maehr's ideas on the relations of culture and achievement motivation in light of contemporary understandings and research evidence. Urdan begins by reminding readers of the danger of hindsight dismissal of ideas that are taken for granted today, yet were groundbreaking and innovative at the time of their writing. With a sense of appreciation for Marty's work, Urdan goes on to present a summary of Marty's challenges of the McClelland-Atkinson personality approach to culture and motivation, where he argued that

1.  the perspective of achievement motivation as a primarily stable individual difference personality trait is misguided;
2.  a focus on contextual and situational effects on motivation is empowering to educators; and
3.  that there are cultural differences in the definition of achievement and, hence, in people's decisions concerning where and how to invest their effort.

Urdan follows by highlighting Marty's focus on contextual influences on the individual's decision-making about investing their resources. He further points to the way these ideas developed into an emphasis on the role of organizational culture in the motivation of ethnically diverse students. Urdan ends the chapter with an eye-opening scrutiny of Maehr's major claims in light of empirical and practical understandings. He presents McClelland's response to Maehr's challenge of achievement motivation as a stable personality trait, which proposed the existence of different motivational systems—an affective one that is more stable and a cognitive one that is more influenced by context. He also discusses the difficulties that educators experience when they consider incorporating theoretical understandings about the role of culture and context in motivation into their practice. Finally, while acknowledging its theoretical validity, he raises a question concerning the practical benefit of viewing achievement motivation as based in cultural meanings. Urdan's critique of Maehr's claims provides an important challenge to the field of academic motivation: how to create motivational concepts and theories that can be useful for practitioners while accounting for the current understandings of the cultural, situated, dynamic, multi-faceted, and multi-dimensional nature of motivational processes.

## REFERENCES

Ames, C. A. (1984). Competitive, cooperative, and individualistic goal structures: A motivational analysis. In R. E. Ames & C. Ames, (Eds.), *Research on motivation in education,* (Vol. 1, pp. 177–207). New York: Academic Press.

Ames, C. (1990, April). *The relationship of achievement goals to student motivation in classroom settings.* Paper presented at the Annual Meeting of the American Educational Research Association, Boston.

Ames, C., & Maehr, M. L. (1989). *Home and school cooperation in social and motivational development.* (Contract No. DE-H023T80023). Research funded by the Office of Special Education and Rehabilitative Services. Technical Report.

Anderman, E. & Maehr, M. L. (1994). Motivation and schooling in the middle grades. *Review of Educational Research, 64,* 287–309.

Baden, B., & Maehr, M. L. (1986). Confronting culture with culture: A perspective for designing schools for children of diverse sociocultural backgrounds. In R. Feldman (Ed.), *Social psychology applied to education.* New York: Academic Press.

Dweck, C. S. (1986). Motivational processes affecting learning. *American Psychologist, 41,* 1040–1048.

Fyans, L. J., Jr., & Maehr, M. L. (1982). A comparison of sex differences in career and achievement motivation in Iran and the U.S. *International Journal of Intercultural Relations, 6,* 355–367.

Fyans, L. J., Jr., Salili, F., Maehr, M. L., & Desai, K. (1983). A cross-cultural exploration into the meaning of achievement. *Journal of Personality and Social Psychology, 44,* 1000–1013.

Hartman, A., & Maehr, M. L. (1984). In search of a remedy: Desegregation and achievement motivation. In D. E. Bartz (Ed.), *Advances in motivation and achievement, Vol. 1: School desegregation, motivation and achievement.* Greenwich, CT: JAI Press.

Karabenick, S. A., Woolley, M. E., Friedel, J. M., Ammon, B. V., Blazevski, J., Bonney, C. R., De Groot, E., Gilbert, M. C., Musu, L., Kempler, T. M., & Kelly, K. L. (2007). Cognitive processing of self-report items in educational research: Do they think what we mean? *Educational Psychologist, 42,* 139–151.

Maehr, M. L. (1964). Programmed learning and the role of the teacher. *Journal of Educational Research, 57,* 554–556.

Maehr, M. L. (1968). Some limitations of the application of reinforcement theory to education. *The Education Digest, 34,* 23–25.

Maehr, M. L. (1974a). Culture and achievement motivation. *American Psychologist, 29,* 887–896.

Maehr, M. L. (1974b). *Sociocultural origins of achievement.* Monterey, CA: Brooks-Cole.

Maehr, M. L. (1976). Continuing motivation: An analysis of a seldom considered educational outcome. *Review of Educational Research, 46,* 443–462.

Maehr, M. L. (1978). Sociocultural origins of achievement. In D. Bar-Tal & L. Saxe (Eds.), *Social psychology of education: Theory and research.* New York: Wiley.

Maehr, M. L. (1983). On doing well in science: Why Johnny no longer excels—Why Sarah never did. In S. Paris (Ed.), *Learning and motivation in the classroom.* Hillsdale, NJ: Lawrence Erlbaum.

Maehr, M. L. (1984). Meaning and motivation: Toward a theory of personal investment. In R. Ames & C. Ames (Eds.), *Research on motivation in education, Vol. 1: Student motivation* (pp. 115–144). New York: Academic Press.

Maehr, M. L. (1989a). Building job commitment among employees. In R. Rubin (Ed.), *Critical issues in library personnel management.* Urbana-Champaign: Graduate School of Library and Information Science.

Maehr, M. L. (1989b). Thoughts about motivation. In C. Ames & R. Ames (Eds.), *Research on motivation in education* (Vol. 3). New York: Academic Press.

Maehr, M. L. (1991). The "psychological environment" of the school: A focus for school leadership. In P. Thurston & P. Zodhiatas (Eds.), *Advances in Educational Administration* (Vol. 2). Greenwich, CT: JAI Press.

Maehr, M. L. (2005). The meaning that religion offers—and the motivation that may result. In W. R. Miller & H. D. Delaney (Eds.), *Human nature, motivation and change: Judeo-Christian perspectives on psychology.* American Psychological Association.

Maehr, M. L., & Braskamp, L. (1986). *The motivation factor: A theory of personal investment.* Lexington, MA: D. C. Heath.

Maehr, M. L., Hartman, A. & Bartz, D. E. (1984). Metropolitan solutions to desegregation problems: The social psychological harm of an administrative remedy. In D. E. Bartz & M. L. Maehr (Eds.), *Advances in motivation and achievement, Vol. 1: School desegregation, motivation and achievement.* Greenwich, CT: JAI Press.

Maehr, M. L., & Karabenick, S. (Eds.), (2005). *Advances in motivation and achievement, Vol. 14: Motivation and religion* (pp. 107–152). Oxford, UK: Elsevier Press.

Maehr, M. L., & Kleiber, D. (1980). The graying of America: Implications for achievement motivation theory and research. In L. J. Fyans, Jr. (Ed.), *Achievement motivation.* New York: Plenum Press.

Maehr, M. L., & Kleiber, D. A. (1981). The graying of achievement motivation. *American Psychologist, 36,* 787–799.

Maehr, M. L., & Lysy, A. (1978). Motivating students of diverse sociocultural backgrounds to achieve. *International Journal of Intercultural Relations, 2,* 38–69.

Maehr, M. L., & McInerney, D. M. (2004). Motivation as personal investment. In D. M. McInerney & S. Van Etten (Eds.), *Research on sociocultural influences on motivation and learning. Big theories revisited.* (Vol. 4). Greenwich, CT: Information Age.

Maehr, M. L., Mensing, J., & Nafzger, S. (1962). Concept of self and the reaction of others. *Sociometry, 25,* 353–357.

Maehr, M. L. & Midgley, C. (1991). Enhancing student motivation: A school-wide approach. *Educational Psychologist, 26,* 399–427.

Maehr, M. L., & Midgley, C. (1996). *Transforming school cultures.* Boulder: Westview Press/Harper& Collins.

Maehr, M. L., & Nicholls, J. (1980). Culture and achievement motivation: A second look. In N. Warren (Ed.), *Studies in cross-cultural psychology* (Vol. 3, pp. 221–267). New York: Academic Press.

Maehr, M.L., & Simmonds, P. (2004) Achievement motivation: It may be all about self after all. In Marsh, H. (Ed.), *Proceedings of the SELF conference.* Berlin, Germany: Max Planck Institute and Sydney, Australia: Self Research Centre, University of Western Sydney.

Maehr, M. L., & Sjogren, D. (1971). Atkinson's theory of achievement motivation: First step toward a theory of academic motivation? *Review of Educational Research, 41*, 143–161.

Maehr, M. L., & Videbeck, R. (1968). Predisposition to risk and persistence under varying reinforcement-success schedules. *Journal of Personality and Social Psychology, 9*, 96–100.

Maehr, M. L., & Willig, A. C. (1982). Expecting too much or too little: Student freedom and responsibility in the classroom. In H. Walberg & R. Luckie (Eds.), *Improving educational productivity: The research basis of school standards.* Chicago: NSSE Series in Contemporary Issues in Education.

McClelland, D. C. (1961). *The achieving society.* New York: The Free Press.

McClelland, D. C. (1985). How motives, skills, and values determine what people do. *American Psychologist, 40*, 812–825.

Midgley, C., Kaplan, A., Middleton, M., Maehr, M. L., Urdan, T., Hicks Anderman, L., Anderman, A., & Roeser, R. (1998). The development and validation of scales assessing students' achievement goal orientations. *Contemporary Educational Psychology, 23*, 113–131.

Nicholls, J. G. (1984). Achievement motivation: Conceptions of ability, subjective experience, task choice, and performance. *Psychological Review, 91*, 328–346.

Rubovits, P. C., & Maehr, M. L. (1973). Pygmalion black and white. *Journal of Personality and Social Psychology, 25*, 210–218.

Shwalb, D. W., Shwalb, B. J., Harnisch, D. L., Maehr, M. L., Akabane, K. (1992). Personal investment in Japan and the U.S.A.: A study of worker motivation. International *Journal of Intercultural Relations, 16*, 107–123.

Steinkamp, M. & Maehr, M. L. (1983). Affect, ability and science achievement: A quantitative synthesis of correlational research. *Review of Educational Research, 53*, 369–396.

Steinkamp, M., & Maehr, M. L. (1984). Gender differences in motivational orientations toward achievement in school sciences: A quantitative synthesis. American Educational *Research Journal, 21*, 39–59.

Triandis, H. C. (1972). *The analysis of subjective culture.* New York: John Wiley.

# BRIEF BIO

Martin L. Maehr is currently Professor Emeritus, The Combined Program in Education and Psychology, at The University of Michigan. He was previously Chair of the program. Prior to coming to the University of Michigan he was Director and Professor at the Institute for Child Behavior and Development and Professor of Educational Psychology at the University of Illinois, Urbana-Champaign. He received his PhD at the University of Nebraska and later was granted an NIMH fellowship for pursuing his research with fellow scholars at Syracuse University. He has also been granted research support from the NIH, USOE, NSF, and from various other federal, state, and private funding agencies. His research is currently supported by NSF and the Spencer Foundation. He maintains an enduring interest in multiple fields, including most especially a special interest on culture, motivation, and achievement.

*Culture, Self, and Motivation: Essays in Honor of Martin L. Maehr,* pages xxiii
Copyright © 2009 by Information Age Publishing

# PART I

MOTIVATION AND SELF

CHAPTER 1

# CONTINUING MOTIVATION REVISITED

## Eric M. Anderman and Jennifer A. Weber

In 1976, Martin Maehr published an inspirational and influential article in *Review of Educational Research*. The title of that article was "Continuing motivation: An analysis of a seldom considered educational outcome" (Maehr, 1976). Maehr defined continuing motivation as "the tendency to return to and continue working on tasks away from the instructional context in which they were initially confronted" (p. 443). Back in 1976, Maehr argued that although continuing motivation is a construct that is valued in most societies, it is seldom studied by researchers as an outcome variable. Indeed, researchers knew relatively little in 1976 about why some students continue to be motivated to learn outside of the classroom and why for others, learning ended with the classroom bell. Regardless of the amount of attention continuing motivation has received, the construct remains intensely important today.

Continuing motivation is highly regarded among educators, policy-makers, and parents. Today, continuing motivation is often discussed using the phrase "life-long learning." An individual who continues to be motivated to engage in a task or activity beyond initial instruction or required comprehension would be considered a "lifelong learner" in that particular domain. Put simply, a "lifelong learner" is an individual who continues to be motivated to engage in learning activities past the intended scope of academic performance.

*Culture, Self, and Motivation: Essays in Honor of Martin L. Maehr,* pages 3–19

Much evidence suggests that "life-long learning" is highly valued in contemporary society. For example, in 2005, United States Secretary of Education Spellings, in testimony given to the U.S. Senate Committee on Health, Education, Labor, and Pensions, thanked the committee for its diligent "focus on lifelong learning." Tony Blair, Prime Minster of the United Kingdom, recently stated to Newsweek.com,

> ...more important today than ever, [successful countries] need sustained investment in science, education and lifelong learning to make the most of the skills and talents of all their people—to create, in fact, true knowledge economies" (Tyre, 2006).

Lifelong learning is also espoused by many influential institutions of higher education. A host of universities have programs and centers promoting lifelong learning among its faculty, students, and alumni. For example, Washington University established a Lifelong Learning Institute (http://www.lli.wustl.edu/), offering "not-for-credit, peer-learning groups," where participants must be members of the Institute and age 55 or older. Ohio University has offered programs in Lifelong Learning since 1919 (http://www.lifelong.ohio.edu/). Tufts University offers alumni the opportunity to study on campus and through online distance education courses via the Osher Lifelong Learning Institute at Tufts University (http://www.tufts.edu/alumni/ed-learn.html).

In some locations, state-wide organizations also emphasize lifelong learning as a critical movement. The vision of various "Lifelong Learning" centers, scholarships, and organizations touch upon Maehr's depiction of continuing motivation, which is closely related to with the concept of intrinsic motivation.

## CONTINUING MOTIVATION, "LIFELONG LEARNING," AND INTRINSIC MOTIVATION

Small (1997) argues that the overarching goal of educators has always been the development of intrinsically motivated, lifelong learners. Three decades ago, Maehr (1976) captured the picture of a lifelong learner as he described the concept of continuing motivation. Undoubtedly to the disadvantage of researchers and educators throughout the world, the concept developed by Maehr has become little more than that—a concept in theory rather than one used in daily educational practice. Much of the recent research and news media coverage utilizes phrases such as "Lifelong Learning" and "Lifelong Learners" to describe traditional modes of education; indeed, these expressions have become catch-phrases, rather than terms that are based on empirical or theoretical research foundations.

Although institutes referred to as Lifelong Learning centers are appearing in diverse settings throughout the United States and the rest of the world, many of the programs do not seem to follow the original tenets of Maehr's 1976 review of the topic. Today, academic achievement gains remain the primary focus of school initiatives and reform efforts, with academic assessment of cognitive learning used as the yardstick for how well schools are meeting the needs of students and progressing toward educational success. A review of Maehr's depiction of continuing motivation may improve such school initiatives and reforms by providing a better sense of their purpose.

## Maehr's Definition of Continuing Motivation

Maehr noted that "continuing" motivation is a unique and important psychological construct. In particular, he noted that continuing motivation differs from other psychological constructs that were prominent in the literature at the time (e.g., persistence, the Zeigarnik effect, and intrinsic motivation) (Maehr, 1976). Particularly important is the distinction between continuing motivation and intrinsic motivation.

Maehr (1976) observed that the concept of continuing motivation as similar to intrinsic motivation, but not identical. Although work by Deci and his colleagues was relatively new at that time (Deci, 1975), Maehr distinguished continuing motivation from intrinsic motivation, indicating that continuing motivation referred specifically to behaviors associated with learning and education as opposed to the social psychological processes studied by Deci and his colleagues. Maehr offered a specific definition for continuing motivation (CM). Specifically, he noted:

> CM must in some sense be viewed as a domain of behavior, like achievement. That is, it refers to a class of behaviors and not necessarily to just one variable. But it can be dealt with very specifically for research purposes, and in this regard it is proposed here that it be defined as (1) a return to a task (or task area) at a subsequent time, (2) in similar or varying circumstances, (3) without visible external pressure to do so, and (4) when other behavior alternatives are available. (Maehr, 1976, p. 448)

Thus, although continuing motivation is broad in scope, it has specific qualities as a psychological construct. Most notably, individuals display continuing motivation when they return to activities in the future, without any constraints or external incentives or pressures. To illustrate with an example, a child who chooses to read a novel during his or her free time might be described as displaying continuing motivation for reading if

1.     the child chooses to read in the future,

2. across a variety of contexts (e.g., at home and while visiting the child's grandparents),

3. without receiving any rewards for reading or punishments for not reading, and

4. when other alternative activities (e.g., watching television, playing video games) are also available choices.

### Influences on Continuing Motivation

Maehr noted that continuing motivation is affected by a host of predictable variables. Most remarkably, continuing motivation is likely to be undermined in the presence of extrinsic incentives, similar to effects found for intrinsic motivation (Deci, Koestner, & Ryan, 1999, 2001; Lepper, Greene, & Nisbett, 1973). More specifically, extrinsic incentives that control and restrict individual learners' choices are most likely to negatively impact continuing motivation. However, Maehr noted that extrinsic incentives such as verbal reinforcement and approval do not necessarily reduce intrinsic motivation; additional research from studies of intrinsic motivation confirms this finding (Deci, 1975; .Deci & Ryan, 1987). Thus extrinsic incentives that control and restrict individual learners' choices are most likely to negatively impact continuing motivation.

### Culture and Continuing Motivation

One particularly important point Maehr emphasized about continuing motivation is that social context and culture play important roles in predicting continuing motivation. Indeed, the norms and values of individual cultures certainly affect individuals' choices of free-time activities. Consideration of the effects of cultural variables on continuing motivation is important at international, national, and local levels. On an international level, certainly different nations express different values, wherein certain types of behaviors are more valued in some nations. At the national and local levels, the variation in activities considered to be valuable is extremely important. Some children may display continuing motivation for a particular task or activity because it represents a valued behavior in their subculture, whereas others may not choose to engage in the same activity because that task is not as highly valued in their subculture. Thus, educators must accommodate for cultural diversity in their instruction.

Instructional techniques representing the values of diverse students will lead to more adaptive educational outcomes for those students. As noted by Gay (2000),

> If educators continue to be ignorant of, ignore, impugn, and silence the cultural orientations, values, and performance styles of ethnically different stu-

dents, they will persist in imposing cultural hegemony, personal denigration, educational inequality, and academic underachievement upon them. Accepting the validity of these students' cultural socialization and prior experiences will help them to reverse achievement trend. It is incumbent upon teachers, administrators, and evaluators to deliberately create cultural continuity in educating ethnically diverse students. (p. 25)

Therefore, as educators work to enhance continuing motivation in students, it is important to consider that continuing motivation will differ for students from diverse backgrounds. The importance of this type of differentiated instruction is further enhanced due to discontinuities between home cultures and classroom practices, particularly for minority students (Boykin, Tyler, & Miller, 2005). The assumption that "one size fits all" in terms of instructional practices that promote continuing motivation simply does not work.

Thus, teachers need to accept, promote, and value those differences if they are to promote continuing motivation in diverse students. Several examples of such attempts are evident in today's research and school reform initiatives.

## CONTEMPORARY EXAMPLES OF CONTINUING MOTIVATION

Although the phrase "continuing motivation," as originally defined by Maehr, is not often used in current research or practice, there are some significant areas of research and development that still emphasize continuing motivation as an important educational outcome. Some researchers and policy-makers value concepts that are highly similar to continuing motivation; unfortunately, examples of these are few.

In the next section of this chapter, we review two fairly recent examples of ways in which continuing motivation has been emphasized in recent efforts. First, we review a recent program of research conducted by Jacquelynne Eccles, Allan Wigfield, and their colleagues, regarding students' motivation to enroll in academic courses when they become optional, using an expectancy X value framework. Second, we review research examining adolescents' continuing motivation to engage in news-seeking behaviors outside of school. Both of these examples represent efforts to consider continuing motivation as a valued outcome.

### Achievement Values and Continuing Motivation

Expectancy-value theories of motivation have a long history in educational and social psychology (Atkinson, 1957, 1964; Lewin, 1935). However, the program of study receiving the most attention in recent years is Eccles and Wigfield's expectancy-value model (Eccles, Adler, Futterman, Golf,

Kaczala, Meece, et al., 1983; Eccles & Wigfield, 2002; Wigfield & Eccles, 1992, 2000, 2002). Briefly summarized, Eccles and Wigfield argue that an individual's motivation to engage in a particular task is a function of (a) expectancies for success at the task and (b) perceived value of the task.

The "value" component is of particular interest as it relates to continuing motivation. Studies indicate that value breaks down into four sub-components: attainment value, intrinsic value, utility value, and cost. Attainment value refers to the perceived importance of an academic subject or task, particularly as it relates to the learner's self-concept. Intrinsic value refers to the learner's interest in the domain or task. Utility value refers to the perceived extrinsic usefulness of engagement in a particular task. Cost refers to beliefs about what an individual has to give up (and if it is worth the sacrifice) in order to engage in a task (Eccles & Wigfield, 1995; Wigfield & Eccles, 1992).

For example, consider a student who "values" reading mystery novels. The student would have attainment value for the reading of mystery novels if the student felt that reading such novels is important; this is particularly true if reading mystery novels validates some part of the student's self concept (e.g., the student might want to become a detective in the future; therefore, reading the novels supports this aspect of the student's self-concept). The student would have intrinsic value for reading mystery novels if the student simply enjoyed reading the novels; the only perceived benefit that the student accrues from intrinsic value is enjoyment of the activity. In contrast, the student would have utility value for reading if the student gets some type of useful, extrinsic benefit from reading the novels; for example, the student might know that he or she needs additional practice with reading, so the extra time spent reading the novels would be useful to the student in achieving this goal. Finally, the "cost" dimension comes into play if the student believes that it is worth his or her time to read the novels. The student actually does a cost-benefit analysis, and if the student decides that it is "worth" reading these novels (instead of engaging in some other activity), then there is little cost involved with reading the mysteries.

*Relating Achievement Values to Continuing Motivation*

The study of students' achievement values parallels the study of continuing motivation in a number of ways. On a general level, achievement values are similar to "continuing motivation" because individuals will most likely exhibit continuing motivation toward activities which they value. For instance, a student who displays continuing motivation for reading mystery novels probably chooses to read such novels at least in part because reading the novels is interesting, useful, personally important, and worth the time. Support from an empirical level also exists for the relation between continuing motivation and achievement values. One way in which continuing motivation has been operationalized empirically is through future course enrollment, as individuals make decisions about whether or not to enroll in classes when the classes become optional. For example, if a student *chooses* to enroll in a mathematics class when the class is not necessarily required for a degree or for graduation, that choice represents a form of continuing motivation to study mathematics; the student is choosing to spend time in the future engaged with mathematics, when participation in a mathematics course is not required.

Future enrollment in a math class meets Maehr's description of the characteristics of continuing motivation (Maehr, 1976). First, by enrolling in a subsequent math course, the learner is returning to the "task" of mathematics at a later time; second, by taking another course, the learner is returning to the task in similar or varying circumstances (depending on where the learner takes the next course); third, since the learner is participating when enrollment is not a requirement, there is no "external pressure" to enroll; and finally, the learner is enrolling in the course when other options (courses) are available. Thus Eccles and Wigfield's studies of future enrollment mirror Maehr's conception of continuing motivation.

One of the most important findings from Eccles' and Wigfield's work is that achievement values predict intentions to enroll and subsequent enrollment in courses in the future (Eccles et al., 1983; Meece, Wigfield, & Eccles, 1990; Wigfield & Eccles, 1992). Specifically, when learners value academic material (i.e., they find it important, useful, and interesting), they are more likely to intend to and ultimately to choose to enroll in subsequent courses in the same content area.

Consequently, students who value certain topics may be likely to display and actualize continuing motivation, in the form of future course enrollment. The fact that achievement values predict subsequent behaviors provides empirical support for the importance of continuing motivation as an outcome. The cultivation of positive achievement values may be a particularly useful means of enhancing continuing motivation in disciplines where enrollment is on the decline. For instance, given the attention that is being paid to lack of enrollments in STEM (science, technology, engineering, and mathematics) disciplines, more positive achievement values can be nurtured in the mathematical and scientific domains to increase student interest and enrollment in STEM-related courses.

## News-Seeking Behavior and Continuing Motivation

Individuals obtain information about current events in a variety of manners. Nevertheless, the formal study of current events in schools has not been common (Shaver, 1989). Whereas some schools require students to study and learn about current events via in-school television news programming, many do not (Johnston, Brzezinski, & Anderman, 1994).

An area in which continuing motivation can be assessed in adolescent learners is in the domain of current events knowledge. Since students often are not required to follow the news, engagement in news-seeking behaviors outside of school represents a form of continuing motivation. If students choose to watch the news, read the newspaper or a news magazine, or read the news on an internet website when this is not required for school, students are displaying continuing motivation to engage in news-seeking behaviors.

We have conducted some research examining motivation and news-seeking behaviors in adolescent populations. In a longitudinal study of 582 adolescents (Anderman & Johnston, 1998), we found that after controlling for prior knowledge of current events, TV news viewing in school, and demographic variables, the strongest predictor of news-seeking behaviors outside of schools was holding mastery goals toward understanding the news (Anderman & Johnston, 1998). Specifically, when students reported that they truly wanted to understand the news, and to understand why events occur throughout the world, those students actually reported greater autonomous news-seeking behaviors (i.e., continuing motivation to engage with the news) outside of school. Similar results were obtained in another correlational study with college students (Griessinger & Anderman, 1997).

The Anderman and Johnston (1998) study considered continuing motivation to engage in news-seeking behaviors as a valued outcome. Whereas current events knowledge was also an outcome (dependent) variable in that study, it was not the only outcome of interest. We argued and strongly believe that an important outcome of social studies education is the production of learners who want to continue to seek information about social issues; results of this study indicated that such learning occurs when mastery goals are salient. Interestingly, mastery goals did not have direct effects on knowledge in that study; rather, the effects of mastery goals were indirect, through self-reported news-seeking behaviors. Thus students who reported being mastery oriented were more likely to autonomously seek news outside of school, and those news-seeking behaviors ultimately were predictive of current events knowledge.

## SMALL LEARNING COMMUNITIES: A WAY OF BUILDING CONTINUING MOTIVATION

One of the most important questions that emanates from discussions of continuing motivation is the question of how schools can foster continuing motivation to learn in their students. In the United States, since the passage of the No Child Left Behind legislation in 2002, test scores have become increasingly important outcomes in evaluations of successful education programs (Nichols & Berliner, 2007). Consequently, students' autonomous engagement in non-required learning activities has not been a salient issue in American educational policy.

Nevertheless, there is one federally-funded program in the United States that has, in many ways, adopted the tenets of continuing motivation. The "small learning communities" movement represents an initiative to improve both student motivation and achievement. The movement is based on solid research, and has had and may continue to have important effects on instructional practices that affect continuing motivation. Small learning communities are particularly common at the secondary level; the concern over continuing motivation is particularly salient at the secondary school level, due to research indicating that positive forms of motivation decline as students move through the adolescent years (Anderman & Maehr, 1994; Anderman, Maehr, & Midgley, 1999; Anderman & Mueller, in press).

*What Are "Small Learning Communities (SLCs)"?*

The nation-wide trend of breaking down large high schools into smaller schools has been well supported and fueled by various funding agencies. The United States Department of Education and the Bill and Melinda Gates Foundation alone have funded numerous initiatives with hundreds of millions of dollars annually; the intent of these initiatives has been to transform large comprehensive schools into smaller schools that operate separately (Copland & Boatwright, 2004). In cases where larger schools have not been physically divided, school reformation has included the development of schools-within-schools, or S*mall Learning Communities (SLCs).*

SLCs are the result of restructuring large public schools into smaller autonomous subunits within the same building, yielding individualized learning units with small class sizes and often a separate identity. The SLC initiative has provided educators and administrators across the United States with new strategies for student advising to ensure individual student attention; more productive classroom scheduling; and a more integrated, as well as differentiated curriculum (Noguera, 2004). Essential SLC components have been identified in the literature and include: student and teacher teams; teacher collaboration on an integrated curriculum; separate space within the school; distinctive focus; and autonomy and flexibility (Heath, 2005).

One of the most important qualities of SLCs is that they often are based on a common focus or "theme," emphasizing the importance of motivation in this endeavor. One of the primary rationales for theme-based schools is that students will learn about centralized topics from multiple perspectives, and ultimately will want to become lifelong learners in the topic area (i.e., they will display continuing motivation to learn about the SLC theme).

More specifically, SLCs often tend to be focused around an identified theme such as ninth-grade academies and career academies, where particular career paths are highlighted and guidelines for curriculum help students structure their high school coursework requirements around a particular area of concentration. The vision for many SLC initiatives is to transform larger high schools into academies that focus on career development, with the intent of involving all students rather than particular subgroups within schools (Wilder, 2006).

*Why Do We Need SLCs?*

Over the past two decades, secondary educators and policy makers have attempted to implement the suggestions from researchers who have shown the positive impact of small school size on students when compared to high schools of larger size. There has been abundant research indicating that smaller schools and smaller class sizes (typical of SLCs) are related to greater achievement in learners (Grissmer, Flanagan, Kawata, & Williamson, 2000; Lee & Smith, 1995). Reported advantages of small schools (student populations of only 200 to 400) have included better attendance records, higher grade-point averages, fewer disciplinary problems, more positive student perceptions of their school experiences, lower drop-out rates, and more rapid progress toward graduation (McMullan, Sipe, & Wolf, 1994; Stockard & Mayberry, 1992; Pittman & Haughwout, 1987; Wasley, Fine, King, Powell, Holland, Gladden, & Mosak, 2000). The academic, social, and financial benefits of SLCs are similar to those of small schools, and have been shown to create safer, more pleasant school environments for students (Oxley, 2001).

*Are SCLs Effective?*

Overall, evaluations of SLCs have yielded positive results for students, teachers, and communities. Assessment of SLC implementation and impact has included quantitative measures such as student, teacher, and parent surveys, as well as student records of attendance, dropout rates, test scores, grades and progress toward graduation. Qualitative measures have captured information gathered through student and teacher focus groups, along with interviews and school observations. Early reviews of student outcomes provides evidence of higher levels of achievement, lower dropout rates, and an increase in student participation (Raywid, 1996). In addition, SLCs may be particularly helpful for students enrolled in special education, since those students may accrue additional motivational, social, and cognitive benefits from learning in more intimate environments (Dukes & Lamar-Dukes, 2006). Some research also suggests that SLCs may be particularly effective for minority students (e.g., Conchas & Noguera, 2004).

Strides have yet to be made at all schools, however. Noguera (2004) has reported that some schools' implementation of SLCs have not been entirely successful. For example, one of the goals of SLCs is that all students have an adult in whom they can confide; however, many students in schools that have only partially implemented SLC initiatives, still believe they do not have an adult to turn to at school. Nevertheless, a recent examination of the advantages of SLCs indicates an overall increase in student learning, personalized student-teacher relationships, safety, efficiency, attendance, graduation rates, student participation, and quality of curricula (Cotton, 2001). Although enhanced motivation is suggested by the benefits of SLCs such as increased student participation and academic success, outcome variables indicative of motivation have been less of a priority in formal SLC evaluation processes. The preeminence of the No Child Left Behind legislation in the United States and its focus on cognitive outcomes has made the assessment of motivation an even lower priority.

One area that has received relatively little attention, but of extreme importance, is the study of intervention strategies to enhance continuing motivation. Although little intervention research exists wherein motivation is operationalized in terms of continuing motivation, some research supports the notion that motivation can be enhanced to increase students' continuing motivation to engage in a task or activity.

## ENHANCING CONTINUING MOTIVATION THROUGH INTERVENTIONS

Several interventions have been designed to enhance motivation, some with significant success. A typical goal of motivation-focused interventions treats motivation variables, like continuing motivation, as valued outcomes. Interventions leading to significantly positive effects on levels of motivation have had multiple components. Midgley and Urdan (1992) suggest that motivational interventions in schools should emphasize

1.   grouping students by topic, interest and student choice,
2.   cooperative learning among students,
3.   alternative measures of achievement such as student portfolios,
4.   inclusion of students in the assessment of progress,
5.   learning for the sake of learning,
6.   allowing for student choice, decision-making, and self-regulation,
7.   a thematic approach to curriculum where students are encouraged to take risks and redo work,
8.   raising expectations while provide encouragement for problem-solving, and
9.   utilizing peers for tutoring and interpersonal support.

A review of the literature indicates researchers have implemented interventions into schools as school- and/or classroom-wide strategies. The content of many interventions has been centered on the use of multiple intelligences, cooperative learning, use of Web-based learning environments (Wang &

Reeves, 2006), student choice (control and collaboration), and an emphasis on task-focused goals (Anderman & Maehr, 1994). Alternative assessment measures have been developed and utilized as an addition to or replacement of standardized testing in some of these interventions. Interventions and use of alternate assessments have generally produced positive changes in student motivation, as reported by parents, teachers, and students themselves (Margolis & McCabe, 2006). Although not always across classrooms or longitudinal, evidence supports increased levels of engagement, participation, and interest (Cluck & Hess, 2003). Wentzel and Wigfield (2007) suggest that successful motivational interventions should be based on theory, reflect the needs of minority students, emphasize the importance of positive social interactions and relationships, incorporate strong research designs, and consider developmental issues.

Maehr, Midgley, and their colleagues worked with elementary and middle school teachers and parents in order to change school policies toward the goal of enhancing the quality of student motivation (Maehr & Midgley, 1996). Using a quasi-experimental design, positive changes in student motivation were evident at both the elementary and middle school levels, thus demonstrating that interventions can be used to enhance and improve positive forms of motivation, such as mastery goals, intrinsic motivation, and continuing motivation (Anderman, Maehr, & Midgley, 1999; Maehr & Midgley, 1996). Examples of such interventions involve both academic and social education and include, for instance, HIV and pregnancy preventions among school-aged children.

*Interventions to Enhance Motivation Toward Preventing HIV and Pregnancy*

In some of our recent work, we have adapted Maehr's views of the importance of continuing motivation in studies of HIV and pregnancy prevention. Specifically, we have been involved in large-scale school-based interventions aimed at enhancing students' motivation to avoid risky situations and behaviors that could result in HIV infection or pregnancy.

Our work is described in detail elsewhere (e.g., Anderman, Cupp, Zimmerman, Land, & Phebus, in press; Anderman, Noar, Zimmerman, & Donohew, 2004; Noar, Anderman, Zimmerman, & Cupp, 2004). Briefly summarized, we conducted several studies in which we randomly assigned classrooms to be in intervention or control conditions. In the intervention conditions, teachers were trained in a variety of techniques aimed at improving students' motivation to avoid engaging in risky behaviors in the future. The outcome variables of interest have been motivation constructs (e.g., mastery and performance goals, achievement values, self-efficacy beliefs). Preliminary analyses indicate that some of these interventions have successfully improved positive indicators of motivation over time.

## CONCLUSIONS AND DISCUSSION

In 1976, Maehr noted that "continuing motivation" was not a valued outcome in education, although it should be. More than thirty years later, researchers and policy-makers continue to espouse the importance of continuing motivation. In reality, however, little research or active policy emphasizes the importance of continuing motivation. Rather, we live in an age of high stakes accountability, where, to our disadvantage, continuing motivation does not fit largely into the equations used to measure the successes or failures of schools. Ultimately, scores on standardized achievement examinations are used to determine the effectiveness of schools, teachers, and curricula.

Maehr's work has been inspiring, because it has continually reminded us that motivation should be considered as an outcome variable, and not just as a predictor. Indeed, his early work on "continuing motivation" was followed by important intervention work with Carol Midgley in the 1990s. Maehr and Midgley's intervention studies were initiated in order to enhance student motivation, wherein motivation was valued as a meaningful and important outcome in the studies (Maehr & Midgley, 1996). In those studies, improvements in achievement were important and valued, but they were not the ultimate goals of the studies. Instead, the goals involved changing the policies, practices, and procedures of schools in order to enhance student motivation.

In this paper, we reviewed two more contemporary exemplars of continuing motivation. Eccles and Wigfield's work on achievement values provides an example of a program of research that has empirically identified predictors of continuing motivation in student populations. The longitudinal nature of these studies indicates that students' prior achievement values influence their subsequent motivation to engage in optional coursework. The implications of this work for practitioners are important. As educators can do more to enhance positive achievement values in students, continuing motivation to engage in certain activities also may be enhanced. For example, if curricula can be developed to enhance the development of positive achievement values for the learning of chemistry, perhaps more students would choose to enroll in subsequent optional chemistry courses (or even become chemists) in the future.

We also reviewed research examining students' motivation to learn about current events outside of school. This is a particularly compelling example, since the study of current events is not formally included in many curricula, and is not formally evaluated in most standardized tests. Thus students who seek news information during their free time are truly demonstrating continuing motivation toward learning about the news. Research indicates that holding mastery goals toward the acquisition of current events knowledge is a strong predictor of continuing motivation to learn about current events.

Also in our review, we identified the SLC movement as a large-scale school reform effort, aimed at improving both the achievement and motivation of adolescent learners. Although motivational variables have not been measured as outcomes in many evaluations of small learning communities, the thematic nature of these communities emphasizes the importance of motivation in this initiative, since these "communities" are organized around central themes, designed to motivate students to learn across subject areas. Goals of SLCs include both enhanced achievement and greater continuing motivation, particularly in the thematic area emphasized within the SLC. Thus, SLCs can and should be studied as school-wide interventions designed to produce lifelong learners. Furthermore, investigation into Lifelong Learning institutes and organizations could reveal the missing links between school instruction and the drive of individuals to continue learning long past graduation.

## Concluding Thoughts

Maehr reminded us in 1976 that continuing motivation should be considered as a valued outcome in educational research. Those words ring true today. In an era of high-stakes accountability and assessment of knowledge, it is important to remember that learning isn't just about memorizing facts.

Success in education can be defined in many ways. Whereas we know that Maehr and other motivation researchers clearly want students to gain useful and important knowledge, students' continuing motivation should not be ignored or treated as a second class outcome in education.

It would be particularly interesting to assess student learning in a particular domain (e.g., social studies) at the end of the eighth grade, and then to give the students the identical assessment one year later, at the end of the ninth grade, and compare the scores; simultaneously, it would *also* be interesting to assess the students' engagement in further non-required learning about similar social issues one year later. Which outcome would be more valuable one year later—the retention of knowledge, or engagement in additional learning?

## REFERENCES

Anderman, E. M., Lane, D. Cupp, P. C., Zimmerman, R., & Phebus, V. (in press). Comparing the Efficacy of Permanent Classroom Teachers to Temporary

Health Educators for Pregnancy/HIV Prevention Instruction. *Health Promotion Practice.*

Anderman, E. M., & Johnston, J. (1998). Television news in the classroom: What are adolescents learning? *Journal of Adolescent Research, 13,* 73–100.

Anderman, E. M., & Maehr, M. L. (1994). Motivation and schooling in the middle grades. *Review of Educational Research, 64*(2), 287–309.

Anderman, E. M., Maehr, M. L., & Midgley, C. (1999). Declining motivation after the transition to middle school: Schools can make a difference. *Journal of Research and Development in Education, 32,* 131–147.

Anderman, E.M., & Mueller, C. (in press). Middle school transitions and adolescent development. In J. Meece & J. Eccles (Eds.), *Handbook of Research on Schools, Schooling, and Human Development.* Mahwah, NJ: Lawrence Erlbaum Associates.

Anderman, E. M., Noar, S., Zimmerman, R. S., & Donohew, L. (2004). The Need for Sensation as a Prerequisite for Motivation to Engage in Academic Tasks. In M. L. Maehr & P. R. Pintrich (Eds.), *Advances in motivation and achievement: Motivating students, improving schools: The legacy of Carol Midgley* (Vol. 13). Greenwich: JAI Press.

Atkinson, J. W. (1957). Motivational determinants of risk taking behavior. *Psychological Review, 64,* 359–372.

Atkinson, J. W. (1964). *An introduction to motivation.* Princeton: Van Nostrand.

Boykin, A. W., Tyler, K., & Miller, O. A. (2005). In search of cultural themes and their expressions in the dynamics of classroom life. *Urban Education, 40*(5), 521–549.

Cluck, M., & Hess, D. (2003). *Improving student motivation through the use of the multiple intelligences.* Unpublished Master's thesis, Saint Xavier University and Skylight Professional Development Field-based Master's Program.

Conchas, G. Q., & Noguera, P. A. (2004). Understanding the exceptions: How small schools support the achievement of academically successful black boys. In N. Way & J. Y. Chu (Eds.), *Adolescent boys: Exploring diverse cultures of boyhood* (pp. 317–337). New York: New York University Press.

Copland, M. A., & Boatwright, E. E. (2004). Leading small: Eight lessons for leaders in transforming large comprehensive high schools. *Phi Delta Kappan, 85*(10), 762–769.

Cotton, K. (2001). *New small learning communities: Findings from recent literature* (Contract No. ED-01-CO-0013). Portland, OR: Northwest Regional Educational Lab.

Deci, E. (1975). *Intrinsic motivation.* New York: Plenum.

Deci, E., & Ryan, R. M. (1987). The support of autonomy and the control of behavior. *Journal of Personality and Social Psychology, 53,* 1024–1037.

Deci, E. L., Koestner, R., & Ryan, R. M. (1999). The undermining effect is a reality after all—Extrinsic rewards, task interest, and self-determination: Reply to Eisenberger, Pierce, and Cameron (1999) and Lepper, Henderlong, and Gingras (1999). *Psychological Bulletin, 125*(6), 692–700.

Deci, E. L., Koestner, R., & Ryan, R. M. (2001). Extrinsic rewards and intrinsic motivation in education: Reconsidered once again. *Review of Educational Research, 71*(1), 1–27.

Dukes, C., & Lamar-Dukes, P. (2006). Special education: An integral part of small schools in high schools. *High School Journal, 89,* 1–9.

Eccles, J. S., Adler, T. F., Futterman, R., Goff, S. B., Kaczala, C. M., Meece, J. L., & Midgley, C. (1983). Expectancies, values and academic behaviors. In J. T. Spence (Ed.), *Achievement and achievement motivation* (pp. 75–146). San Francisco: W.H. Freeman.

Eccles, J. S., & Wigfield, A. (1995). In the mind of the actor: The structure of adolescents' achievement task values and expectancy-related beliefs. *Personality and Social Psychology Bulletin, 21*(3), 215–225.

Eccles, J. S., & Wigfield, A. (2002). Motivational beliefs, values, and goals. *Annual Review of Psychology, 53*(1), 109–132.

Gay, G. (2000). *Culturally responsive teaching: Theory, research, and practice.* New York: Teachers College Press.

Griesinger, T., & Anderman, E.M. (1997). Motivation to learn about current events. *Peace and Conflict: Journal of Peace Psychology, 3,* 193–211.

Grissmer, D., Flanagan, A., Kawata, J., & Williamson, S. (2000). *Improving Student Achievement: What State NAEP Test Scores Tell Us.* Santa Monica, CA: RAND.

Heath, D. (December, 2005). Small Learning Communities 2000–2003. *Education Brief,* 1–5.

Johnston, J., Brzezinski, E.J., & Anderman, E. M. (1994). *Taking the measure of Channel One: A three year perspective.* Ann Arbor: University of Michigan Institute for Social Research.

Lee, V. E., & Smith, J. B. (1995). Effects of high school restructuring and size on early gains in achievement and engagement. *Sociology of Education, 68*(4), 241–270.

Lepper, M. R., Greene, D., & Nisbett, R. E. (1973). Undermining children's intrinsic interest with extrinsic reward: A test of the "overjustification" hypothesis. *Journal of Personality and Social Psychology, 28,* 129–137.

Lewin, K. (1935). *A dynamic theory of personality: Selected papers* (D. K. Adams & K. E. Zener, Trans.). New York: McGraw-Hill.

Maehr, M. L. (1976). Continuing motivation: An analysis of a seldom considered educational outcome. *Review of Educational Research, 46*(3), 443–462.

Maehr, M. L., & Midgley, C. (1996). *Transforming school cultures.* Boulder, CO: Westview Press.

Margolis, H., & McCabe, P. P. (2006). Improving self-efficacy and motivation: What to do, what to say. *Intervention in School and Clinic, 41*(4), 218–227.

McMullan, B. J., Sipe, C. L., & Wolf, W. C. (1994). *Charters and student achievement: Early evidence from school restructuring in Philadelphia.* Philadelphia: Center for Assessment and Policy Development.

Meece, J. L., Wigfield, A., & Eccles, J. S. (1990). Predictors of math anxiety and its influence on young adolescents' course enrollment intentions and performance in mathematics. *Journal of Educational Psychology, 82*(1), 60–70.

Midgley, C., & Urdan, T. (1992). The transition to middle school: Making it a good experience for all students. *The Middle School Journal, 24,* 5–14.

Noar, S., Anderman, E. M., Zimmerman, R. S., & Cupp, P. (2004). Fostering student motivation in health education: Are we applying relevant theory to school-based HIV prevention programs?

Noguera, P. A. (2004). Transforming high schools. *Educational Leadership, 61*(8), 26–31.

Oxley, D. (2001). Organizing schools into Small Learning Communities. *NASSP Bulletin, 85*(625), 5–16.

Pittman, R., & Haughwout, P. (1987). Influence of high school size on dropout rate. *Educational Evaluation and Policy Analysis, 9*, 337–347.

Raywid, M. A. (1996). *Taking stock: The movement to create mini-schools, schools-within-schools, and separate small schools.* New York: ERIC Clearinghouse on Urban Education, Teachers College, Columbia University (ERIC Document Reproduction Service No. ED396045).

Shaver, J.P. (1989). Lessons from the past: the future of an issues-centered social studies curriculum. *Social Studies, 80*, 192–196.

Small, R. V. (1997). *Motivation in instructional design.* Syracuse, NY: ERIC Clearinghouse on Information and Technology (ERIC Document Reproduction Service No. ED 409 895).

Stockard, J., & Mayberry, M. (1992). *Effective educational environments.* Newberry Park, CA: Corwin Press.

Tyre, P. (2006). *The new first grade: Too much too soon?* Retrieved February 7, 2007, from Newsweek.com. Available at: http://www.msnbc.msn.com/id/14638573/site/newsweek/from/ET/

Wallis, C., & Steptoe, S. (December 10, 2006). *How to bring our schools out of the 20th century.* Retrieved February 8, 2007, from Time.com. Available at: http://www.time.com/time/magazine/article/0,9171,1568480-6,00.html

Wang, S. K., & Reeves, T. (2006). The effects of a Web-based learning environment on student motivation in a high school earth science course. *Educational Technology Research Development, 54*(6), 597–621.

Wasley, P. A., Fine, M., King, S. P., Powell, L. C., Holland, N. E., Gladden, R. M., & Mosak, E. (2000). *Small schools: Great strides: A study of new small schools in Chicago.* New York: Bank Street College of Education.

Wentzel, K.R., & Wigfield, A. (2007). Motivational interventions that work: Themes and remaining issues. *Educational Psychologist, 42*, 261–271.

Wigfield, A., & Eccles, J. S. (1992). The development of achievement task values: A theoretical analysis. *Developmental Review, 12*(3), 265–310.

Wigfield, A., & Eccles, J. S. (2000). Expectancy-value theory of achievement motivation. *Contemporary Educational Psychology, 25*(1), 68–81.

Wigfield, A., & Eccles, J. S. (2002). The development of competence beliefs, expectancies for success, and achievement values from childhood through adolescence. In A. Wigfield & J. S. Eccles (Eds.), *Development of achievement motivation. A volume in the educational psychology series* (pp. 91–120). San Diego, CA: Academic Press.

Wilder, D. (May, 2006). Reinventing America's high schools: A wall-to-wall approach. *Techniques Connecting Education and Careers, 81*, 21–23.

# CHAPTER 2

# APPLYING PERSONAL INVESTMENT THEORY TO BETTER UNDERSTAND STUDENT DEVELOPMENT

**Larry A. Braskamp**

## INTRODUCTION: PERSONAL INVESTMENT THEORY AS A CONCEPTUAL FRAMEWORK

Over the past two decades and more, I have used Personal Investment Theory (PI) (Maehr & Braskamp, 1986) to better understand holistic development of college students, one of my primary interests, both as a researcher and administrator. PI Theory, as Marty and I worked on it over two decades ago, primarily grew out of Marty's interest and expertise in motivation. In our work, we developed an instrument, (coinciding with my interests and background in assessment) primarily based on a conceptualization of motivation that was appealing and made sense to me. It highlighted both the person as a unique human being and the community and communities in which one lives. His perspective of motivation extended beyond achievement motivation and holistic student development, fitting nicely into my view and area of research for the past decade that college is an ideal place

*Culture, Self, and Motivation: Essays in Honor of Martin L. Maehr*, pages 21–37
Copyright © 2009 by Information Age Publishing
**21**

to develop the whole student. Thus, in this chapter, I will first outline how I have used and interpreted PI theory to describe and understand the holistic development of college students. My use and adaptation of the PI conceptual framework has helped me in organizing my view of college student development which includes the role of the college or campus environment. PI theory has given me the concepts to see human development within community. In all of my adaptations, I have built them around the core concept of Personal Investment, which Marty labeled and embellished over the last three and more decades. Within higher education, the concept of meaning is emerging as a central theme in understanding human learning and development, something that Marty conceptually struggled with over three decades—and is still interested in updating PI theory to make it even more relevant today.

*Personal Investment Theory*

Personal Investment Theory is built on the centrality of meaning and on persons having the ability to make choices in their lives depending on the meaning the choices have for them (Maehr & Braskamp, 1986). I have used the three major elements of PI theory to understand the development of students—a person's sense of self, sociocultural environment, and patterns of behavior and engagement. The major elements of my adaptation of the PI theory are presented in Figure 1.

PI theory is based on several propositions. First, since no one can observe motivation per se, it can only be inferred. "The behavioral patterns associated with motivation are collectively referred to as personal investment" (Maehr & Braskamp, 1986, p. 45). What one does, such as performance, intensity of behavior, persistence of patterns of behavior, and results of choices to become engaged in specific activities is what we called personal investment. It is what anyone can observe in college students, but neither I nor others desire to only describe what students do. Using PI theory I have attempted to better understand these patterns of behavior—the reasons why students are so engaged. I have used the two major antecedents of these patterns of behavior as outlined in PI theory—sense of self and sociocultural environment—to understand the lives of students.

Second, I have built on the proposition that persons—students—act within the context of their giving meaning to the situation. Thus cognition and affect are a part of the motivational process.

> We have asserted that meaning and motivation are inextricably linked—that the meaning of the situation to the individual determines personal investment, and knowing the meanings individuals hold allows us to predict how

**Figure 1.** Application of PI Theory to College Student Development

and when they will invest their time and energy—in their jobs or in other activities (Maehr & Braskamp, 1986, p. 125).

In short, "People invest themselves in certain activities depending on the meaning these activities have for them." (Maehr & Braskamp, 1986, p. 62) Thus thinking, being, and doing are intricately related. The inner and outer life—the interior and exterior life—are connected and reinforce each and thus need to be studied in concert.

## SENSE OF SELF

I have divided sense of self into three major dimensions. Sense of self generally has been referred to as a student's self-identity, a term common among college student affairs administrators and campus leaders. Students in college begin to achieve self-authorship, which Baxter Magolda defines as "the capacity to define their own beliefs, identity, and relationships internally" (2002, p. 3). Astin's definition of sense of self includes

values that one holds most dear, our sense of who we are and where we come from, our beliefs about why we are here—the meaning and purpose that we see in our work and our life—and our sense of connectedness to each other and to the world around us. (2004, p. 1)

The three dimensions adapted from the original list are: personal goals and values, sense of purpose, and abilities and strengths.

*Personal Goals*

People have personal goals, "what the person perceives to be attractive or unattractive" (Maehr & Braskamp, 1986, p. 50), at that moment of their life. They have a sense of what is important to them, in what they like to invest their time, talents, and treasures. Goals are what persons find rewarding and of interest to them—their priorities in life. In our earlier work we referred to them as personal incentives (Maehr & Braskamp, 1986). The four original major categories of personal goals (Maehr & Braskamp, 1986) are presented in Table 1.

In subsequent years I have adapted these four categories by renaming them "personal motivators" to make them more attractive for college students in their thinking and planning about their future. I portrayed them in terms of a broad category of reasons students may invest their time, talents, and energy into activities of their choosing. The four personal motivators are portrayed in terms of continuum whereby a student receives a score not in terms of how much one indicates the importance of an incentive (e.g., power) but in terms of a position in a continuum with two attractive endpoints. This adaptation makes the scale more useful to college students. They previously expressed disappointment when they scored low on the originally-named scales, assuming that a high score was always more desirable. By making both ends of the continuum an attractive option, the students interpreted their scores less defensively. The renamed scales are listed below. Appendix A includes a summary of these scales and how they are presented to students in the interpretative guide.

- Striving/Accepting
- Directing/Collaborating

**TABLE 1. Four Primary Goals that Influence Motivation**

| Intrinsic | | Extrinsic | |
|---|---|---|---|
| Task Focused | Ego Focused | Social Solidarity | Extrinsic Rewards |
| Understanding Something | Doing better than others | Pleasing others | Earning a prize |
| Experiencing Adventure/Novelty | Winning | Making others happy | Making money |

- People-Oriented/Socially Independent
- Recognition-Oriented/Inner Reliant

## Sense of Purpose

Sense of purpose is the second dimension of sense of self. One seeks and derives meaning from their investment in part from their purpose in life. Maehr (2004) has argued that that "purpose in life" may be one, if not the most important, factor in influencing one's investment of their time and efforts. Persons invest their time, talent, and treasures to fulfill their perceived purpose in life.

I have used the concept of vocation as a way to define finding purpose and meaning in life (Braskamp, Trautvetter, & Ward, 2006; Braskamp & Wergin, 2008). One can think of vocation in many ways, for example, as "The Dream," (Parks, 2000, p. 146) or as good work, (Gardner, Csikszent-mihalyi, & Damon, 2001. Vocation is not an activity or event but rather a life-long encounter of becoming who one is and expressing oneself in life. Neafsey (2004) argues that vocation includes both self-discovery and self-expression. One tries to understand oneself in the midst of one's current situations and realities of life and then acts within the moment. One does not need to be religious or have a distinct faith tradition to have a vocation. I have incorporated three major questions to reflect the notion of vocation. They are:

1. How do I know?
2. Who am I? and
3. How can I best serve others?

The first two questions reflect one's inner self; that is, self-identity and self-identification—developing a sense of self. This focuses on self-knowl-edge, "to know thyself," a common phrase used in advocating the value of a liberal education. The second question refers to how we respond: How do I relate to others? It reflects the exterior side of one's life and has a social and interpersonal dimension. The third refers to the focus of the response to the calling; that is, how I can use my potential strengths, abilities, and contributions in terms of my relationships with others and benefit to society in general. "True vocation joins self and service" (Palmer, 2000, p. 16). In sum, vocation includes an understanding of oneself in relationships with others, which may include a relationship with a God, supreme being, other-ness, etc.

The focus on finding meaning in life is often connected to faith devel-opment, and one that has strong historical roots. The majority of colleges founded by church denominations have historically stressed character, moral, and faith development as important ends of a college education. The good life includes personal meaningfulness, not just career success Today colleges are debating once again this responsibility and opportunities to foster character, moral and ethical responsibility, religious, faith and spiritual development as a part of their mission. Recently many leaders in higher education have stressed the importance of college as the place to foster the holistic development of young people (Braskamp et al., 2006; Dalton, 2001; Gomes, 2002; Hartley, 2004; Parks, 2000). (This is consistent with Marty's personal values and background, having grown up as a Lutheran and attending and teaching at Lutheran colleges. It is also consistent with my Calvinist leanings, given my personal life experiences.)

*Talents and Strengths*

Educators in higher education have a deep desire and commitment to assist students in their personal and professional development during their collegiate years. College students come to college with potential—talents and gifts—and a willingness to explore, develop, and grow (Astin, 1999). But they need assistance in their collegiate journey to discover, develop, and apply their strengths so they can reach their potential in their personal lives and in their careers.

Within the PI theory, the concept of strengths can be interpreted in terms of a key characteristic in the sense of self. It is related to both personal values and purpose in life, As I have interpreted PI theory, students make choices to engage given the meaning they give to the engagement at the time. Thus I include self-knowledge and awareness of one's strengths as an important antecedent to personal investment.

Persons who build on their strengths are more apt to be successful in what they pursue. Developing talents and strengths has a theoretical foundation that is closely linked and exemplified by the positive psychology perspective (Seligman & Csikszentmihalyi, 2000). The Gallup Organization has concluded from its study of over two millions adults from virtually every profession, career, and field of achievement that top achievers understand their talents and strengths, and build their lives upon them. That is, persons are more apt to perform at levels of excellence if they are using and applying their strengths in their engagement. "The best of the best build their lives around their talents," and "The best of the best invent ways of developing and applying strengths in areas where they want to improve, achieve, and become more effective" (Anderson, 2004, p. 7).

I focus on talents and strengths based on the argument that students who discover and develop their talents into strengths are able to live and perform at a high level of excellence—career success and a fulfilling life. "In a sense, the development and application of strengths generates a feeling that you are fulfilling your personal destiny" (Clifton & Anderson, 2003, p. 9). Achieving at a level of excellence is hard work and challenging, but can be made more fulfilling and meaningful if one builds a life on her unique talents and gifts and systematically and consistently develops them. Thus it reinforces my perspective of student development in terms of investing oneself—one's talents, time, and talents—to becoming the person one desires and chooses to become. In short, college is the place where students are to discover, develop, and apply their strengths to become the whole persons they are meant to be.

## SOCIOCULTURAL CONTEXT

Personal investment (PI) theory is not only focused on the person but also the environment. As Marty has often stated in our conversations that one's personal investment does not exist and change in a vacuum. To him—and to me—one's community can have a powerful impact on one's sense of self and actions. Marty has always been intrigued with the concept, "perceived options" which reflects the centrality of the environment in one's life.

> It is obvious that people who are members of different cultures often view life and work quite differently. They also define success, failure, achievement, and happiness in different ways—they live by different rules and are guided by different expectations. (Maehr & Braskamp, 1986, p. 183)

Maehr (2005) further argues,

> The roles we play, the norms to which we conform, the options that we perceive as possible, allowable, and worthy are established by and set within a community, or multiple communities. These communities are often created around belief systems, and while individuals play special and important roles, these roles are enacted within the community. (p. 140)

I have portrayed the collegiate environment as a place that provides a set of expectations and opportunities for students. The mores and norms of a campus (sociocultural) environment influences what students focus on and do in their days as a student. In our research on the potential influence of the sociocultural environment on student development, we used a framework, called "4 Cs"—culture, curriculum, co-curriculum, and communities within and beyond the campus—to classify the major influencers of student development. (Braskamp et. al., 2006). In other chapters my colleagues and I have reviewed the research literature on the effects of these four dimensions of the college environment on the faith, religious, and spiritual development of students (Braskamp & Hager, 2005; Braskamp, 2008). The literature on college impact is extensive (e.g., Pascarella & Terrenzini, 2005). In this chapter I will briefly summarize the findings of our qualitative study of the ten colleges in our study.

## Culture

The mission of a college provides a sense of direction and vision and reinforces its distinct identity and character (Association of Governing Boards, 2003). In our study of ten church-related colleges, they relied on the mission to determine college priorities and set the culture and identity of the campus. The current strength of the college's legacy influences how the colleges commit themselves to fostering the various dimensions of student development—intellectually, morally, and spiritually and/or religiously. In the colleges we studied, the culture is reflected by and reinforced strong personal relationships among the members of the campus community, including deep student-faculty relationships. Faculty and staff feel invested in the students, and have a shared commitment to develop the student holistically.

## Curriculum

The curriculum is the academic enactment of a college's culture and identity and its mission.

> The curriculum is bedrock to the college. It represents what a college values students to learn and experience. The curriculum is shaped by what and how faculty members teach. Colleges in our study focus on the liberal arts to prepare students not just for careers, but to lead meaningful lives....Colleges vary in how purposeful they are in integrating faith and learning in and out of the classroom....Given the relatively strong church-related missions of some colleges in the study, the curriculum is an important vehicle for these campuses to articulate their church's worldview and integrate faith and learning. (Braskamp et. al., 2006. p. 127)

In our study, colleges intentionally create safe and open classroom settings and social environments to foster student learning and development. Many colleges use variations of the pedagogy of engagement—service learning, community based service and research, January and May terms, study abroad, and student research opportunities—to accomplish their curricular goals about student learning and development. Participation in service learning, for example, enhances community responsibility, civic engagement, and political activity (Colby et al., 2003; Zlotkowski, 1998).

*Co-Curriculum*

Students develop holistically to a larger extent when expectations of ethical, social, or spiritual development permeate the entire campus environment (Colby et al., 2003). This conclusion, which is in accord with PI theory, contradicts the general trend in American higher education in which co-curricular experiences are largely the province of student affairs and campus ministry professionals. In our study we found that the co-curricular environment represents places to interact—resident halls, faculty offices—and people to interact with—including faculty as well as professional staff in Student Affairs, coaches, and campus ministers. We concluded that all staff including faculty make a difference in assisting students connect the co-curricular context with other aspects of the undergraduate experience.

We found that faculty develop significant relationships with students through their time with them during office hours (formal and informal), meeting with students in their homes and other off campus locations, going with students on study abroad programs where the curriculum and co-curriculum intersect naturally, accompanying students on service and immersion trips, and directing research experiences where one-to-one interactions between faculty and students are created. The focus on creating a viable environment for students to develop holistically can be summed up by the phrase, "It takes a whole campus of whole persons to develop whole students."

*Communities—The Campus and Beyond*

One of the major themes of PI Theory is the saliency of the sociocultural context in which a person lives. For college students it involves the community, or many different types of communities, such as colleagues in one's major field of study, residence halls or apartments, social clubs, church, political and social organizations (Lee, 2002a; Pascarella & Terenzini, 2005). Community includes faculty, student affairs professionals, ministry, administrators, and students at the local college as well as organizations and participants beyond the campus walls. Student-faculty relationships are very important to foster student development Pascarella and Terrenzini (1991; 2005).

In our study we found that students at church-related colleges, especially those with a strong evangelical mission, often develop strong personal relationships with faculty and discussed their personal lives with the faculty and other professionals. Faculty also see themselves as mentors and role models, and accept this responsibility as a part of their work and contributions (Braskamp, Trautvetter, & Ward, 2006). We found that the campuses in the study all desire to create communities that are open, hospitable, and caring of all members. They also recognize the importance of the college community meaningfully engaging in interactions with communities beyond the campus. They recognize that students have multiple communities of which they are members, and not all have the same set of shared values and expectations of their members. Faculty, in particular, value pluralism on campus, and all are deliberate in including multiple and diverse viewpoints.

*Student Engagement as Patterns of Behavior*

Patterns of behavior refer to the observable actions of a person—what a person does that is visible to others. It can include levels of performance and persistence of behavior under changing conditions. From a motivational perspective it is what we make inferences of motivation from, a point that Marty stressed in all of our thinking about PI. Within PI Theory it signifies that the person has made choices in what he wishes to be engaged in depending on the meaning the engagement has for him. An authentic and purposeful life requires one to select activities that reflect one's sense of self and purpose. PI theory stresses the linkage between commitment and behavior. Thus introspection, reflection, and knowing oneself are important antecedents to investing one's talents, time and energy into activities. Thinking, being, and doing—the inner and exterior life—are all necessary for holistic development (Braskamp & Braskamp, 2007; Braskamp, 2008).

In my adaptation of PI Theory, I refer to the patterns of behavior in terms of student engagement, student involvement, and performance. Student engagement is now widely used to denote how students spend their time in college (Kuh, Kinze, Schuh, Whitt, & Associates, 2005).

> What students do during college counts more in terms of what they learn and whether they persist in college than who they are or even where they go to college…the time and energy students devote to educationally purposeful activities is the single best predictor of their learning and personal development. (pp. 17–18)

Students need to be involved in effective educational programs and practices to develop and learn in desired ways. They need to integrate their behavior with their sense of self. A connection is implied between engagement and growth. For example, if developing student leaders is an important goal for students, then students will more likely be involved if the college provides these opportunities to the students, rewards them for this engagement, and helps them better understand themselves as leaders in this world, linking it to the concept of a vocation or calling. In our study, we observed ways that colleges designed their curriculum and co-curricular activities that linked being and doing. For example, faculty taught capstone courses by focusing on the relevance of the material to the personal lives of students and worked with other professionals on campus to engage them in activates that would give them an opportunity to apply their values and knowledge. They were guided in reflecting on how their views of themselves and the world matched their behavior. Some used service learning as the medium to help students practice the skill of good citizenship while learning the shared values of a community, nation, or society in general.

## USING PI THEORY IN STUDYING STUDENT DEVELOPMENT

PI theory has provided me with a framework that is similar to that of many others who study student development. PI is closely related to such concepts as talent development. Astin (1999) argues we should use the term "talent development" since it encompasses a broad range of abilities, skills, and interests and values that should be considered in understanding and assessing student growth and development. Earlier he wrote, "involvement refers to the investment of physical and psychological energy in various objects" (1984, p. 298). More recently Astin wrote

> Putting more emphasis on students' interior development has enormous implications on how we approach student learning and development. In most institutions today the primary focus is on what students do: how well they perform on classroom exercises and examinations, whether they follow the rules and regulations, how many credits they receive and so on. (2004, pp. 1–2)

The perspective of Baxter Magolda and King (2004) on students' development toward self-authorship is similar to PI theory in that they argue that students incorporate three dimensions of development—epistemological, intrapersonal, and interpersonal—in their journey to selfhood. In short, a student's sense of purpose, self-knowledge, identity, and values as well as skills and competencies acquired during college are important conceptual elements in theories of student development.

PI theory has also provided me with a perspective from which to analyze and understand a holistic view of student development. From my perspective, PI theory emphasizes that students develop holistically. Students act purposefully based on their self-reflection, seeking purpose and meaning in life, and knowledge of their strengths and abilities in their development. In this theory, what students do—student engagement—is put into a larger context incorporating the important dimensions of being as well as doing. Students become and remain involved in their learning, and achievements—their personal investments—and are an important part of their total developmental pattern. They act however by connecting to their sense of identity and are influenced by their sociocultural environment. I have also been able to incorporate the concept of purpose into our view of student development. In my adaptation of PI theory, the concepts of vocation and personal values are important elements in interpreting how students become engaged. For some students, their collegiate experiences may reinforce and build on their commitment and purpose in life, but for other students the experiences may be opportunities that can lead to commitment. College experiences are considered a critical part of a developmental process by which students develop meaning, become holistic and authentic in their choices and actions, cultivate spirituality, and further develop their talents.

## USING PI THEORY TO FOSTER
## HOLISTIC STUDENT DEVELOPMENT

Based on PI theory, students engage in activities in part out of their sense of identity, a common theoretical position of many who study college student development (e.g. Chickering & Reiser, 1993; Baxter Magolda, 2002). We have concluded that the environment of college students in and outside the classroom does foster a student's sense of self and a sense of meaning and values (Braskamp et al, 2006). For example, we highlighted faculty in a senior capstone course who design courses that challenge students to integrate what they learn with what they consider to be of high personal value and meaning, often around the study of religion and values.

Theorists in college student development have always recognized the importance of the college environment (Sanford, 1952; Parks, 2000). Theorists, especially those who favor a psychosocial perspective, have stressed the importance of the interaction between the college environment and students' development of a sense of self, often couched in terms of identity formation (Lee, 2002b). We learned that colleges are effective to the extent to which they can create a challenging and supportive environment, and encourage students to be involved in campus life, a finding shared by others (Astin, 1984; Light, 2001).

We have argued for an environment—a combination of the 4 Cs—that puts students first and builds on close relationships among student affairs, ministry, and faculty to create programs (e.g., service learning in urban areas and third world countries, volunteer programs, and chapel) and a community that supports holistic student development (Baxter Magolda & King, 2004; Braskamp & Braskamp, 2007; Chickering, 2003; Parks, 2000; Zlotkowski, 1998). I found that PI theory provides a useful theoretical and conceptual framework for researchers and practitioners to study and interpret these complex interactions between students and their environment. I have argued that a collegiate environment, which stresses both challenge and support will assist students in their journey throughout their college days, a theme that has been stressed for many decades (Sanford, 1952). For educators, the journey begins with helping students gain a better, deeper and richer understanding of who they are and can become.

## SUMMARY

I have been able to use PI theory to help understand that students are continuously investing themselves in activities depending on the meaning they find in the involvement and engagement. Equally important, campus leaders have created environments, through the 4 Cs—culture, curriculum, co-curriculum, and community within and beyond the campus—to influence student growth and development. They have begun to see the importance of a focus on educating students for purpose and meaning since it helps influence students to invest in ways that are consistent with one's sense of self and helping students to use their abilities, talents, and strengths to make this world a better place to live.

In sum, in my writing, research, and consultation in the area of student development, I have used PI theory as a conceptual framework to study and interpret the development of students during college. PI theory as portrayed in our book, *The motivation factor*, now over twenty years old, still is highly relevant and even more relevant given the recent interest in the role of meaning and learning and development. And, I have tried to use it as a heuristic device to help others create effective campus environments. Faculty and administrators can use PI theory to understand the significance of educating students holistically and as a framework to create environments that foster holistic student learning and development.

## REFERENCES

Association of Governing Boards, Association of Catholic Colleges and Universities, & Association of Jesuit Colleges and Universities (2003). *Mission and identity.* Washington DC: Association of Governing Boards.

Astin, A. W. (1985). *Achieving educational excellence.* San Francisco: Jossey-Bass.

Astin, A. (1999). Student involvement: A developmental theory for higher education. *Journal of College Student Development, 40*(5), 518–530.

Astin, A. W. (April 2004). Why spirituality deserves a central place in higher education. *Spirituality in Higher Education Newsletter. 1*(1), www.spirituality.ucla.edu/newsletter

Baxter Magolda, M. B. (2002). Helping students make their way to adulthood. *About Campus, 6*(6), 2–9.

Baxter Magolda, M. B. & King, P. M. (2004) (Eds.). *Learning partnerships; Theory and models of practice to educate for self-authorship.* Sterling, VA: Stylus.

Braskamp, D. C. & Braskamp, L. A. (1989). *The use of personal incentives in understanding student development.* Paper presented at annual meeting of American Educational Research Association, San Francisco.

Braskamp, L. A., Trautvetter, L. C., & K. Ward. (2006). *Putting students first: How colleges develop students purposefully.* Bolton, MA: Anker Publishing.

Braskamp, L. A., & D. C. Braskamp (Fall, 2007). Fostering holistic student learning and development of college students: A strategic way to think about it. *The Department Chair, 18*(2), 1–3.

Braskamp, L. A., & J. F. Wergin (Winter, 2008). Inside-out leadership. *Liberal Learning,* AAC&U, 30–35.

Braskamp, L. A. (2008). The religious and spiritual journeys of college students. In Jacobsen, D.& Jacobsen, R. (Eds.) *The American university in a postsecular age: religion and higher education.* New York: Oxford University Press.

Chickering, A. W., & Reisser, L. (1993). *Education and identity* (2$^{nd}$ Ed.) San Francisco: Jossey-Bass.

Colby, A., Ehrlich, T. Beaumont, E., & Stephens, J. (2003). *Educating citizens: Preparing America's undergraduates for lives of moral and civic responsibility.* San Francisco: Jossey Bass.

Dalton, J. C. (2001). Career and calling: Finding a place for the spirit in work and community. In Jablonski, M. A. (Ed.). *The implications of student spirituality for student affairs practice* (pp. 17–25). New Directions for Student Services, no. 95. San Francisco: Jossey-Bass.

Gardner, H. M. Csikszentmihalyi, M., & Damon, W. (2001). *Good work: When ethics and excellence meet.* New York: Basic Books.

Gomes, Peter J. (2002). *The good life: Truths that last in times of need.* San Francisco: Harper.

Hartley, H. V., III (Spring 2004). How colleges affects students' religious faith and practice: A review of research. *Faith, spirituality and religion on campus., 23,*(2), 111–129.

Kuh, G. D. Kinze, J., Schuh, J. H., Whitt, E. J., & Associates. (2005). *Student success in college: Creating conditions that matter.* San Francisco: Jossey-Bass and American Association for Higher Education. .

Lee, J. J. (2002a). Changing worlds, changing selves: The experience of the religious self among Catholic collegians. *Journal of College Student Development, 43,* 341–356.

Lee, J. J. (2002b). Religion and college attendance: Change among students. *Review of Higher Education, 25,* 369–384.

Light, R. J. (2001). *Making the most of college.* Cambridge: Harvard University Press.

Maehr, M. L. (2005). The meaning that religion offers and the motivation that may result. In W. R. Miller & H. D. Delaney (Eds.) *Judeo-Christian perspective on psychology.* Washington, DC: American Psychological Association

Maehr, M. L., & Braskamp, L. A. (1986). *The motivation factor: A theory of persona investment.* Lexington, MA: Heath & Co.

Neafsey, J. P. (2004). Psychological dimensions of the discernment of vocation. In J. Haughey, S.J. (Ed.). *Revisiting the idea of vocation: Theological explorations.* Washington, DC: The Catholic University of America Press.

Palmer, P. P. (2000). *Let your life speak.* San Francisco: Jossey-Bass

Parks, S.D. (2000). *Big questions, worthy dreams: Mentoring young adults in their search for meaning, purpose, and faith.* San Francisco: Jossey-Bass, Inc.

Parscarella, E. T., & Terenzini, P. T. (2005). *How college affects students.* Vol. 2. San Francisco: Jossey-Bass.

Sanford, N. (1952) (Ed.) The *American college.* New York: John Wiley

Zlotkowski, E. (Ed.). (1998). *Successful service-learning programs: New models of excellence in higher education.* Bolton, MA: Anker Publishing.

## APPENDIX A:
## DESCRIPTIONS OF THE FOUR PERSONAL MOTIVATORS

*Personal Motivator –Striving/Accepting*

### Striving
- You want your life to be challenging.
- You become involved in what you do.
- Generally you feel most comfortable and proud of yourself when you do things others can't.
- You may often feel dissatisfied when your freedom to explore new solutions to problems is restricted.
- You desire variety.
- You are strongly goal oriented.
- You may often find yourself working extra and putting in time when others don't.

### Accepting
- You can often be counted on to get the job done, regardless of the interest it holds for you personally.
- You generally take a more relaxed approach to life.
- You are aware of others when you are working and playing.
- You thrive in situations with established routines and procedures, and expectations.
- You do not need to find novelty or excitement in everything you do.

*Personal Motivator –Directing/Collaborating*

### Directing
- You like to be the one in charge.
- You seek status and leadership positions in which you can influence others.
- You often feel that the best way you can help others is to get them to follow you.
- You enjoy competing and winning.
- You identify with people who work hard to get ahead.

### Collaborating:
- You think of yourself as a team player.
- You generally have a collaborative approach to life.
- You identify with people who do not need to take large risks in life.
- At times you are comfortable following directions from others.
- You are cooperative in your relating to others.

*Personal Motivator – People-Oriented/Socially Independent*

### People-Oriented
- You like to be around other people continually.
- You need the stimulation of other people to work at your best.
- You generally trust people and are able to relate warmly to them.
- You frequently can be counted to be generous of your time to help others.
- You feel a strong commitment to social, civic, or religious concerns.
- You spend a significant portion of your time involved in directly helping others.

### Socially Independent:
- You are comfortable being by yourself.
- You usually prefer to work alone rather than part of a team.
- You identify with self-sufficient people.
- You are responsive to those around you or to the needs of society in a quiet way rather than in a highly public manner.
- You can sustain yourself without support from others.
- You don't need to share with others.

*Personal Motivator – Recognition-Oriented/Inner Reliant*

### Recognition-Oriented

- You are likely to do your best when you have encouragement and support of others.
- You generally work harder when you receive acknowledgement for your achievements.
- You often think of financial rewards as a significant indicator of your success and status.
- You are apt to work harder for salary increases and other visible symbols of success.
- You care about what others think of you. put earlier see Carla about outward directed

### Inner Reliant

- Your rewards come from within yourself or from the task or work itself.
- You are more likely to judge your own behavior against your expectations rather than expectations of others.
- You don't need constant reassurance by others that you are doing well.
- You don't need prestige and status to feel good about yourself.
- You participate in activities and work that doesn't provide large financial returns.

# CHAPTER 3

# MOTIVATION IN SPORT AND PHYSICAL ACTIVITY

## An Achievement Goal Interpretation

**Glyn C. Roberts, Frank Abrahamsen, and P. Nicolas Lemyre**

At the outset, it must be confessed that despite its obvious importance to sport and other physical activities, exemplified by the newspaper column inches and television "air time" devoted to motivational issues in sport, motivation is a poorly-understood concept in the "trenches" (the gymnasium, the exercise setting, the playing field, the dance studio, the broadcasting booth, and so on). Motivation is often assumed to be the concern of the coach and is considered to be synonymous with arousal (witness the "locker room" pre-game and half-time pep talks). Coaches and teachers often use questionable arousal tactics in the quest for motivation. As examples of the "twilight zone" of sport psychology, the coach of Mississippi State University football team, Jackie Sherrill, had a Longhorn bull castrated in front of his players in order to "motivate" them prior to taking the field against the University of Texas "Longhorns" (Sherman, 1992)! And, the football coach of Libertyville High School in Illinois, Dale Christensen, staged a fake shooting in the school to "motivate" his players to be "combat ready" for an upcoming game (Sakamoto & Parsons, 1993)! Fortunately, most coaches do not go to such extremes. Despite coaching folklore to the contrary, motivation and arousal are separate constructs.

*Culture, Self, and Motivation: Essays in Honor of Martin L. Maehr,* pages 39–67
Copyright © 2009 by Information Age Publishing
**39**

Most coaches and teachers also assume that positive thinking (often described as "confidence," "a winning attitude," or "being competitive") has immense motivational attributes. The belief is that if you are confident and can "see" yourself winning, or achieving success you will be more motivated to realize the dream. But expectations have to be realistic to have motivational properties; otherwise they can be demotivating (see Locke & Latham, 1985). Finally, many coaches and teachers believe that motivation is genetically endowed. Thus, if a coach believes an athlete is "motivated," it is considered to be a desirable stable entity, and the athlete is expected to display motivation all the time. But if an athlete is adjudged to be low in motivation, the same coaches do not believe this can or will change and often cut such players from the team, or display their disapproval so that the athlete feels uncomfortable and eventually drops out. Although all the beliefs above are grounded on certain beliefs, and even research evidence, such simplistic assumptions do not begin to capture the complexity and richness of the process of motivation.

Over the past twenty years, research in sport, physical education, and exercise contexts focusing on motivation has adopted a social cognitive approach (see Roberts, 1984; Roberts, Treasure, & Conroy, 2007). In particular, the achievement goal approach has become an important conceptual avenue to address motivation in physical activity. The approach evolved from the collaborative and independent classroom work of Ames (e.g., 1992), Dweck (e.g., 1986), Maehr (e.g., Maehr & Braskamp, 1986) and Nicholls (e.g., 1989) and their respective colleagues, and from the sport and exercise work of Duda (e.g., 1992; 2001) and Roberts (e.g., 1984; 1992; 2001; Roberts, et al., 2007) and their respective colleagues. This framework is well known to the contributors of this book, and most of the readers. We will not explain the theory here. Briefly, the approach assumes the individual is an intentional, goal-directed organism operating in a rational manner, and that achievement goals govern achievement beliefs and guide subsequent decision making and behavior in achievement contexts. It is argued that in order to understand the motivation of individuals, the function and meaning of the achievement behavior to the individual must be taken into account, and the goal of action understood. By so recognizing the meaning of behavior, it becomes clear that there are multiple goals of action, not one (Maehr & Nicholls, 1980; Maehr & Braskamp, 1986). Thus, variation of behavior may not be the manifestation of high or low motivation per se, but the expression of different perceptions of appropriate goals. An individual›s investment of personal resources such as effort, talent, and time in an activity then becomes dependent on the achievement goal of the individual in that activity.

The first publications using achievement goal theory (AGT) in sport were in 1981, mostly from the University of Illinois. Since then, there have been over 300 refereed publications in sport psychology journals, and motivation papers in meetings and congresses of sport and exercise psychology over the past 25 years that have been hugely biased in favor of achievement goal theory. As one would expect, the research focus has been along two avenues. The first dealt with dispositional goal orientations (task and ego) and looked at the emotional, cognitive, and behavioral implications of being task- and/or ego-oriented. The second avenue, one that has become even more popular of late, deals with the motivational climate (mastery and performance) and the implications of coaches, teachers, and parents using mastery or performance criteria of success and failure in sport contexts. The remainder of this chapter will address the focus of those research efforts and review the literature in sport and physical activity.

## UNDERSTANDING MOTIVATION AND ACHIEVEMENT BEHAVIOR IN SPORT

*The Motivational Implications of Task- and/or Ego-Involvement*

The most popular approach, especially in the early years was to investigate the implications of being task- and/or ego-oriented. It was argued that individuals were oriented to demonstrate competence in one of two ways:

1. to demonstrate mastery (task-involved), or
2. to demonstrate superiority (ego-involved).

To measure the goal orientations, researchers have typically created questionnaires that are assumed to assess ego and task goal orientations (e.g., Nicholls, Patashnick, & Nolen, 1985). Although Dweck and Leggett (1988) conceptualize and measure the achievement goals as dichotomous, it has been more usual for researchers to assume that the two goals are conceptually orthogonal and measure them accordingly (Duda & Whitehead, 1998; Roberts, Treasure, & Balague, 1998).

Nicholls (1989) argued that in order to assess personal achievement goals, individuals should be asked about the criteria that make them feel successful in a given situation, rather than noting their definition of competence. In line with this suggestion, Roberts and colleagues (Roberts & Balague, 1989; Roberts et al., 1998; Treasure & Roberts, 1994b) and Duda and colleagues (1989; Duda & Nicholls, 1992; Duda & Whitehead, 1998) have developed the POSQ and TEOSQ scales, respectively, to measure task and ego goal orientations in sport. Both have demonstrated acceptable reliability and construct validity (Duda & Whitehead, 1998; Marsh, 1994; Roberts et al., 1998). While other scales exist, the POSQ and the TEOSQ are the scales that best meet the conceptual criteria of measuring orthogonal achievement goals in sport (Duda & Whitehead, 1998; Roberts et al., 2007).

Most AGT research has focused on the antecedents and the consequences of goal orientations. But whether one is in a state of task or ego involvement is not only dependent on one's personal goal of achievement. The context also has an important influence on one's state of involvement.

One of the most fundamental tenets of AGT is the central role the situation plays in the motivation process (e.g., Ames, 1992; Maehr & Braskamp, 1986; Nicholls, 1989). Research from an achievement-goal perspective examined how the perceived criteria of success and failure extant in the environment can make it more or less likely that achievement behaviors, thoughts and feelings associated with a particular achievement goal are adopted. This is then assumed to affect the achievement behaviors, cognition, and affective responses through the perception of the participants of the behaviors necessary to achieve success (e.g., Roberts et al., 1997, 2007). This area of research has become very popular of late in the sporting world with the growing recognition that the way coaches coach affects not only the beliefs and perceptions of athletes, but also the outcomes of the competitive experience.

Adopting the term motivational climate, Ames (e.g., 1992b) argued that two dimensions of the motivational climate, namely mastery and performance, are crucial to understand achievement cognitions and behaviors in achievement contexts. Mastery (or task involving) climates refer to structures that support effort, cooperation, and an emphasis on learning and task mastery, while performance (or ego-involving) climates refer to situations that foster normative comparisons, focus on intra-team competition, and a punitive approach by teachers and coaches to mistakes committed by participants.

Research from an achievement goal perspective in sport and physical education demonstrated that goal orientations and perceptions of the motivational climate are relevant to the ongoing stream of achievement behavior, cognition, and affect. We will briefly review this research in the following section, paying special attention to the relationship between achievement goals and cognitive, affective, and outcome variables.

### Perceptions of Competence

An essential distinction between task- and ego-oriented athletes is how they construe and define the demonstration of competence in achievement settings. A task-oriented athlete will use self-referenced criteria to evaluate success and failure, and is, above all, concerned with mastery and learning of new skills and activities. Thus, task-oriented athletes, compared to ego-oriented athletes, are expected to develop more perceived competence over time (Elliott & Dweck, 1988). Ego-oriented athletes on the other hand, demonstrate competence when they compare favorably to others. Consequently, high perceived competence is less likely to be maintained over time. Past research has generally supported this prediction (e.g., Boixadós, Cruz, Torregrosa, & Valiente, 2004; Chi, 1994; Cury, Biddle, Sarrazin, & Famose, 1997; Kavussanu & Roberts, 1996; Nicholls & Miller, 1983, 1984b; Reinboth & Duda, 2004, 2006; Vlachopoulos & Biddle, 1996, 1997).

Taken together, the evidence suggests that being task-oriented enhances resilience of perceived competence. The implications of these findings are particularly important in learning contexts. For example, for individuals who are beginning to learn a new physical skill, holding a task orientation may be instrumental in facilitating perceptions of competence, effort and persistence, and, consequently, success in the activity. Boixadós and colleagues (2004) reported that a task-involving climate, as perceived by young football players, was positively related with both satisfaction in practice and self-referenced perceived ability. The task-involving climate was also inversely associated with rough play attitudes and perceived normative ability. Rienboth and Duda (2004) found that athletes with low perceived ability in a performance climate had low self-esteem, whereas those athletes that perceived a task-involving environment had high self-esteem regardless of their perceived athletic competence. Vazou, Ntoumanis, and Duda (2006) found that the only predictor of physical self worth was a perception of a task-involving peer climate in various sports. Finally, in a study with Dutch male soccer players Van Yperen and Duda (1999) reported that athletes high in task orientation possessed greater soccer skills from pre- to post-season, as deemed by their coaches.

Not surprisingly, a task orientation promotes possibilities for competence and success experiences for athletes that are either high or low in perceived competence, as well as encouraging the exertion of effort. On the other hand, an ego orientation may lower perception of success and competence, and lower perceived effort, in particular with athletes unsure of their ability. As evident from the above, the positive effects of being task-involved might trickle down to more global psychological characteristics such as self-esteem.

### Beliefs About the Causes of Success

Nicholls (1989, 1992) suggests that one's goal in conjunction with one's beliefs about the causes of success in a situation comprise an individual's personal theory of how things work in achievement situations. For the low perceived ability individual, a belief that ability causes success will most likely result in frustration, a lack of confidence, and even lead to dropping out as these individuals feel they do not possess the natural ability required to be successful. In the physical activity domain, where practice and hard work are so essential for improvement especially at the early stages of learning, the belief that effort leads to success is the most adaptive belief for sustaining persistence (Roberts et al., 2007).

Research on young athletes (e.g., Hom, Duda, & Miller, 1993), high school students (Duda & Nicholls, 1992; Lochbaum & Roberts, 1993), British youth (Duda, Fox, Biddle, & Armstrong, 1992; Treasure & Roberts, 1994a), young disabled athletes participating in wheelchair basketball (White & Duda, 1993), and elite adult athletes (Duda & White, 1992; Guivernau & Duda, 1995; Roberts & Ommundsen, 1996; Pensgaard & Roberts, 2003) has consistently demonstrated that a task-goal orientation is associated with the belief that hard work and cooperation lead to success in sport. In general, ego orientation has been associated with the view that success is achieved through having high ability and using deception strategies such as cheating and trying to impress the coach. A similar pattern of results emerged in the physical-education context (Walling & Duda, 1995) as well as in research with college students participating in a variety of physical activity classes (e.g., Kavussanu & Roberts, 1996; Roberts, Treasure, & Kavussanu, 1996).

### Purposes of Sport

In classroom-based research, ego orientation has been associated with the belief that the purpose of education is to provide one with wealth and social status, which is evidence of superior ability. Task orientation, on the other hand, has been linked to the view that an important purpose of school education is to enhance learning and understanding of the world, and to foster commitment to society (Nicholls et al., 1985; Thorkildsen, 1988). Similar findings have been reported in the athletic arena (e.g., Duda, 1989; Duda & Nicholls, 1992; Roberts & Ommundsen, 1996; Roberts, Hall, Jackson, Kimiecik, & Tonymon, 1995; Roberts et al., 1996, 1997; Treasure & Roberts, 1994a; White, Duda, & Keller, 1998) indicating that world views cut across educational and sport contexts.

Task orientation has been linked with the belief that the purpose of sport is to enhance self-esteem, advance good citizenship, foster mastery and cooperation (Duda, 1989), to encourage a physically active lifestyle (White et al., 1998), and to foster pro-social values such as social responsibility, cooperation, and the willingness to follow rules, as well as lifetime skills (Roberts, et al., 1996; Roberts & Ommundsen, 1996). Likewise, task orientation is associated with the view that the purpose of physical education is to provide students with opportunities for improvement, hard work, and collaboration with peers (Papaioannou & McDonald, 1993; Walling & Duda, 1995). In contrast, ego orientation has been linked to the view that sport should provide one with social status (Roberts et al., 1996; Roberts & Ommundsen, 1996), enhance one's popularity (Duda, 1989; Roberts & Ommundsen, 1996) and career mobility, build a competitive spirit (Duda,

1989), enhance status, and teach superiority and deceptive tactics (Duda, 1989; Duda & White, 1992). Ego orientation is also associated with the view that the purpose of physical education is to provide students with an easy class and teach them to be more competitive (Papaioannou & McDonald, 1993; Walling & Duda, 1995).

### Affect and Intrinsic Interest

One of the most consistent findings in achievement goal research in the athletic arena has been the link between task orientation and experienced enjoyment, satisfaction, and interest during participation in physical activity for high school students (Boixadós et al., 2004; Duda, Chi, Newton, Walling, & Catley, 1995; Duda & Nicholls, 1992), athletes competing in international competition (Walling, Duda, & Chi, 1993), and college students enrolled in a variety of physical activity classes (e.g., Duda et al., 1995; Kavussanu & Roberts, 1996). A positive relationship has also been reported between task orientation and flow, an intrinsically enjoyable experience in college athletes (Jackson & Roberts, 1992). In the above studies, ego orientation was either inversely related or unrelated to intrinsic interest, satisfaction, or enjoyment.

Participants with a high task orientation, either in combination with a high or low ego orientation, experience greater enjoyment than those participants who are high in ego orientation and low in task orientation (Biddle, Akande, Vlachopoulos, & Fox, 1996; Cury, Biddle, Famose, Goudas, Sarrazin, & Durand, 1996; Goudas, Biddle, & Fox, 1994; Vlachopoulos & Biddle, 1996, 1997). A task orientation seems to be especially important for continued participation in physical activity as it is associated with enjoyment, and this occurs regardless of one's perceived success (Goudas, et al., 1994) or perceived ability (Vlachopoulos & Biddle, 1997), and intrinsic interest (Goudas, Biddle, Fox, & Underwood, 1995).

Another interesting finding of previous research is the different sources of satisfaction that are associated with goals. Ego-oriented athletes glean satisfaction when they demonstrate success in the normative sense and please the coach and friends, whereas task-oriented individuals feel satisfied when they have mastery experiences and perceive a sense of accomplishment during their sport participation (Roberts & Ommundsen, 1996; Treasure & Roberts, 1994a). Spray and colleagues (2006) reported that athletes perceiving ability to be an entity and therefore firmly set were more likely to endorse performance goals, whereas athletes with incremental sport ability conceptions were more likely to adopt learning goals. These associations were stronger when the athletes faced adversity. After failure, the athletes with an entity belief made stronger ability attributions. Taken together, the above findings implicate that having a fixed conception of ability and focusing on normative goals might undermine self-confidence in the long run, because the success criterion is inflexible.

Probably the most significant study to illustrate the association of goals with affect was conducted by Ntoumanis and Biddle (1999). They conducted a meta-analysis with 41 independent samples and found that task orientation and positive affect were positively, and moderately to highly, correlated. The relationship between ego orientation and both positive and negative affect was small. In essence, being task-involved fosters positive affect in physical activities.

### Anxiety

In 1986, Roberts suggested that an athlete was prone to experience anxiety as a function of whether or not the athlete believed it was possible to demonstrate competence in an achievement context. Task-oriented athletes were predicted to be less anxious, because self-worth was not threatened when competence was self-referenced. Research supports these predictions (see Roberts, 2001; Roberts et al., 2007).

Most of the research has supported the tenets of AGT in a theoretically coherent manner. Task orientation has been negatively associated with precompetitive anxiety (Vealey & Cambell, 1988), cognitive anxiety with young athletes (Ommundsen & Pedersen, 1999), somatic and cognitive anxiety (Hall & Kerr, 1997), task-irrelevant worries and the tendency to think about withdrawing from an activity (Newton & Duda, 1993), and concerns about mistakes and parental criticisms (Hall & Kerr, 1997; Hall, Kerr, & Matthews, 1998). Further, a task orientation has been associated with higher global self-esteem (Hein & Hagger, 2007), with keeping one's concentration and feeling good about the game (Newton & Duda, 1993), and with effective use of coping strategies in elite competition (Kristiansen et al., 2006; Pensgaard & Roberts, 2003). Pensgaard and Roberts reported that female athletes high in ego orientation reported less use of active coping, and planning strategies, and more use of denial as coping strategies. Task orientation has been associated with more use of social support (Kristiansen et al., 2006), which is regarded to be an important stress buffer strategy (e.g., Smith, 1989; Smith et al., 1995). An ego orientation, on the other hand, has been positively related to state and trait anxiety (Boyd, 1990; Newton & Duda, 1993; Vealey & Campbell, 1988; White & Zellner, 1996), cognitive anxiety in the form of worry (White & Zellner, 1996), getting upset in competition, and concentration disruption during competition (Newton & Duda, 1993; White & Zellner, 1996).

Most studies have been conducted with very young athletes (Hall & Kerr, 1997) or with recreational or physical education students (Hall, et al., 1998, Ommundsen & Pedersen, 1999, Papaioannou & Kouli, 1999). However, research with elite athletes also suggest that being ego-involved might increase performance anxiety (e.g., Abrahamsen et al., 2007a). Abrahamsen and colleagues found that the interaction of ego orientation and performance climate perceptions predicted more performance worries for female athletes, but not males. Perceived ability mediated the results of the female players. In a similar vein, Ommundsen and Pedersen (1999) remind us that simply stating that being task-involved is beneficial in terms of anxiety is not necessarily sufficient. Ommundsen and Pedersen found that being task-involved did decrease cognitive trait anxiety, while low perceived competence increased both somatic and cognitive anxiety. This suggests that being task-involved is beneficial, but that perceived competence is an important predictor of anxiety, too. Being task-oriented and perceiving one's competence to be high are both important antecedents to reduce anxiety in sport (Abrahamsen et al., 2007). Abrahamsen and colleagues found that the interaction term of ego orientation and performance climate perceptions were positively related to performance anxiety with female elite team handball players, but that perceived competence mediated this relationship. Similarly, while Hein and Hagger (2006) found that ego orientation had a direct effect on self-esteem, they also found that autonomous motivation, which correlates highly with perceived ability (i.e., individuals with high perceived competence are likely to have high autonomous motivation toward their activity), mediated the effect of achievement goals on general self-esteem.

The above has looked at the emotional, cognitive, and behavioral antecedents and consequences of being task- and/or ego-oriented. However, the most interesting aspect of the recent work with AGT has been the attention paid to outcome variables, especially adopted achievement strategies, performance, exerted effort, overtraining and burning out, peer relationships, dropping out, and cheating in sport. AGT and research in educational and sport settings suggest that personal theories of achievement comprise different beliefs about what leads to success, or how Nicholls used to put it: "about how things work" (Nicholls, 1989).

### Achievement Strategies

Lochbaum and Roberts (1993) were the first to report that the emphasis placed on more problem-solving and adaptive learning strategies was tied to a task orientation in a sport setting. Research (Lochbaum & Roberts, 1993; Roberts et al., 1995; Roberts & Ommundsen, 1996; Ommundsen & Roberts, 1999) demonstrated that task orientation is associated with adaptive achievement strategies, such as being committed to practice, being less likely to avoid practice, learning, and trying hard. Typically, in these investigations, ego orientation corresponds to a tendency to avoid practice and to a focus on winning during competition. Goals also differentiate athletes in terms of the perceived benefits of practice. Thus, ego-oriented athletes consider practice as a means to demonstrate competence relative to other athletes, whereas their task-oriented counterparts view practice as a means to foster team cohesion and skill development (Lochbaum & Roberts, 1993; Roberts & Ommundsen, 1996). In an elegant experiment by Reinboth and Duda (2006), they created both a task-involving and an ego-involving condition in a cycling task. In line with AGT predictions, those who lost in the ego-involving condition both performed worse and felt less satisfied and interested in the task when compared to winners in the same condition, and importantly, to both losers and winners in the mastery environment.

When choosing post-climbing task feedback strategies, high ego-oriented climbers who were low in perceived ability were more likely to reject task-related and objective performance feedback than task-oriented climbers (Cury, Sarrazin, & Famose, 1997). In addition, Cury and Sarrazin (1998) found that high-ego and high-ability athletes selected normative feedback and rejected task-relevant information. High ego-oriented athletes with low ability requested no feedback and discarded objective information. Research has shown that an ego orientation is related to other unacceptable achievement strategies such as the use of aggression (Rascle, Coulomb, & Pfister, 1998).

These studies demonstrate that the achievement strategies endorsed by physical activity participants are meaningfully related to their goal perspective. Across the studies, task orientation was coupled with adaptive learning strategies; practice was valued in order to learn new skills and improve, and to seek task-relevant information. In contrast, ego-oriented athletes endorsed avoiding practice as an achievement strategy, and avoided task-relevant information preferring normative feedback (but only when high in perceived ability).

### Exerted Effort and Performance

There is not much research to date investigating exerted effort and performance. One of the first to provide evidence of a performance boost from being task-involved was Vealey and Cambell (1989). Van Yperen and Duda (1999) found that when football players were task-oriented, an increase in skilled performance resulted (as perceived by the coach). In addition, the task-oriented players believed that soccer success depended on hard work. Similarly, Theeboom, De Knop, and Weiss (1995) investigated the effect of a mastery program on the development of motor skills of children and found that the task-involved group reported higher levels of enjoyment and reliably exhibited better motor skills than those who were ego-involved. The importance of significant others in the process of exerting effort cannot be overstated! White and colleagues (2005) reported a relationship between task orientation and the view that effort was the cause of success, when the athletes perceived their parents to believe that effort was the way to success.

On the other hand, the view that parents believed ability, external factors, and deceptive tactics were necessary to excel in sport, was associated with ego orientation. In a similar vein, Balaguer and colleagues (2002) reported interesting findings with elite team handball players. When the players perceived a stronger task-involving climate, the players also reported greater improvement and satisfaction with their performance and were also more positive to their coach.

However, the best evidence thus far that task-oriented athletes perform better than ego-oriented athletes has been presented by Sarrazin and colleagues (Sarrazin, Roberts, Cury, Biddle, & Famose, 2002) who investigated exerted effort and performance of adolescents involved in a climbing task. The results demonstrated that task-involved boys exerted more effort than ego-involved boys, and performed better (a success rate of 60% versus 42%); the degree of exerted effort was determined by an interaction of one's achievement goal, perceived ability and task difficulty. Ego-involved boys with high perceived ability and task-involved boys with low perceived ability exerted the most effort on the moderate and difficult courses; ego-involved boys with low perceived ability exerted the least effort on the moderate and very difficult courses. Finally, task-involved boys with high perceived ability exerted more effort when the task was perceived as more difficult.

In general, the research has shown that:

1. when task-involved, people exhibit (or report) greater effort than others (Cury, et al., 1996; Duda, 1988; Duda & Nicholls, 1992; Durand, Cury, Sarrazin, & Famose, 1996; Goudas et al., 1994; Sarrazin et al., 2002; Solmon, 1996; Tammen, Treasure, & Power, 1992); and
2. when ego-involved, people with low perceived ability exhibit reduced exerted effort as opposed to people with high perceived ability (e.g., Cury, Biddle, et al., 1997).

And there is developing evidence that being task-involved leads to better performance (e.g., Yoo, 2003). To enhance effort, one should focus on being as task-involved as possible: Task-involved people try harder! And, task-involved people perform better!

### Peer Relationships

Being task-oriented is associated with constructive peer relationships. Positive relationships between high task orientation and reported attraction to the team and perceived team integration have been reported (Chi & Lu, 1995; Duda, 2001). In contrast, being ego-oriented is associated with strong beliefs and perceptions that demonstrating superior ability to others leads to success, and that participants will enhance self importance and social status (Duda, 1989, Lochbaum & Roberts, 1993; Roberts & Ommundsen, 1996; Roberts et al., 1995; Roberts, Ommundsen, Sorensen, & Miller, in review; Smith, Balaguer, & Duda, 2006). It is argued that being ego-oriented gives rise to less sensitivity, empathy, cooperation towards fellow team members in the pursuit of individual achievement, and may facilitate intrateam rivalry, interpersonal conflict and the view that other players on the team are competitors to be conquered (Duda & Hall, 2001; Ommundsen et al., 2005; Roberts et al., 2007; Shields & Bredemeier, 1995; Smith, 2003; Smith et al., 2006). Consequently, mutual peer acceptance, interpersonal attraction as well as the quality of friendship may come to suffer (Chi & Lu, 1995).

In a recent investigation, Roberts et al. (in review) investigated goal-orientation profiles on perceptions of the motivational climate, peer relationships, and drop-out data. The sample consisted of a cross-sectional study of 1294 youths aged between 12–16 years of age (male $n$ = 787, female $n$ = 507) experienced youth sport participants. Four profiles emerged that are similar to previous research (Smith, Balaguer, & Duda, 2006). The profile groups were found to be different on all of the peer interaction variables, but not in drop-out rates. The overall trend was for participants who were higher in task orientation to have more positive peer relationships. They were lower in conflict, higher in companionship, peer acceptance, and lower in the perception of being bullied. In general, the findings suggest that better peer relationships are fostered with task-achievement goals. However, the study found that the motivational climate was associated with drop out. When the participants perceived that the climate created by the coach was mastery oriented, it was not related to dropping out, but when the climate was perceived as performance oriented, it was related to dropping out. The more the coach was seen as using ego involving criteria to assess success in the sport context, the greater the likelihood of the young participant dropping out!

### Moral Functioning and Cheating

Achievement goals have also been linked to moral cognitions and moral behavior in sport. A number of recent studies have identified fairly consistent relationships between task and ego orientations and sportspersonship, moral functioning, moral atmosphere, as well as endorsement of aggressive tactics among both youth and adult competitive athletes. In general, studies have shown that being high in ego orientation leads to lower sportspersonship, more self reported cheating, lower moral functioning (i.e., moral judgment, intention, and self-reported cheating behavior) and endorsement of aggression when compared to high task-oriented athletes (Lemyre, Roberts, Ommundsen, & Miller, 2001; Lemyre, Roberts, & Ommundsen, 2002; Kavussanu & Roberts, 2001; Kavussanu, Roberts, & Ntoumanis, 2002; Ryska, 2003).

In recent research, Lemyre and colleagues (2001, 2002) and Ryska (2003) have found that low ego/high task-oriented youth male soccer players consistently endorsed sportspersonship values of respect and concern for social conventions, rules, and officials, as well as their opponent. Similar to sportspersonship, moral functioning and aggression, as well as gender differences among these variables, have been highlighted in recent sport psychology research. Kavussanu (Kavussanu & Roberts, 2001; Kavussanu, et al., 2002) has consistently found ego orientation to positively predict lower moral functioning and males to be generally higher in ego orientation, lower in task orientation, and significantly lower in moral functioning as well as endorsing more aggression than female players. In a recent study, Sage and Kavussanu (2007) manipulated the motivational climate to investigate its influence on the moral behavior of participants. Both men and women college students played consecutive 10 minute games of table soccer. The highest levels of prosocial behaviors were players performing in a task-involving climate, and female participants demonstrated more prosocial behaviors than males. Additionally, players assigned to the ego-involving condition displayed more frequent antisocial behaviors.

In a study examining 325 young soccer players, Kavussanu (2007) found that task orientation was positively linked to prosocial behaviors while ego orientation was negatively linked. Consistent with previous findings (Duda et al., 1991; Kavussanu & Roberts, 2001; Lemyre et al., 2002), Kavussanu found that antisocial behaviors were best predicted by ego orientation. Kavussanu suggested that athletes focusing on self-referenced achievement may be better disposed to show empathy for others and to help others in a sport context. On the other hand, an ego orientation seems to predispose athletes to engage in unfair play and leads them to avoid positive moral behaviors that benefit other individuals.

Recent research has indicated that the coach-created motivational climate may also serve as a precursor to cheating among competitive youth sport participants. In a recent study, Kavussanu, Seal and Phillips (2006) observed prosocial and antisocial behaviors in young males playing soccer. The difference in age of the participants affected their moral behavior: older players generally demonstrated more frequent antisocial behaviors and more sporadic prosocial gestures than the younger players. The older players also perceived stronger performance climate cues and weaker mastery climate cues than the younger players. These findings suggest that as soccer players grow into adolescence, they engage in less prosocial behaviors and more antisocial behaviors. Miller and colleagues (Miller & Roberts, 2003; Miller, Roberts, & Ommundsen, 2004; 2005) found that a high ego-involving motivational climate was associated with low sportspersonship, low moral functioning, and the endorsement of aggression. Boys cheated more than girls, but within gender, ego-involved boys and girls cheated more than task-involved boys and girls. For boys in particular, being ego-involved meant that they were more likely to engage in cheating behavior, to engage in injurious acts, to be low in moral reasoning, and to perceive the moral atmosphere within the team to be supportive of cheating.

Kavussanu (2007) found that a perceived mastery climate was a positive predictor of prosocial behavior and a perceived performance climate was a positive predictor of antisocial behavior. When soccer players perceived that their coach emphasized personal progress, cooperative learning, and high effort to develop and master skills, they were more likely to help others. However, when players perceived that their coach favored some players at the expense of others and rewarded only the best players, they were less likely to help others. These findings suggest that emphasizing mastery cues in the sport context is critical to promote prosocial behaviors in sport.

Competitive sport often places individuals in conflicting situations that emphasize winning over sportspersonship and fair play. It would be wrong, however, to attribute this to the competitive nature of sport. The results above suggest that it is *not* the competitive context being the issue. Rather, it may be the salience of ego involvement in the athletic environment that induces differential concern for moral behavior, cheating, rules, respect for officials, prosocial, and fair play conventions among young players. If men and women are to develop sportspersonship behaviors with sound moral reasoning and, to prevent cheating, coaches should reinforce task-involving achievement criteria in the competitive environment.

### Burnout

Dedicated and high-performing athletes preparing for competition often reveal a resilient determination that helps them to persevere through the most demanding workouts and survive harsh training regimens. Unfortunately for some of these athletes, this dedicated achievement striving fails to produce desired outcomes and the perceived setbacks lead to frustration as well as physiological and/or psychological exhaustion. Consequently, the desire to achieve, that many believe to be the hallmark of elite athlete development (e.g., Gould, Dieffenbach, & Moffett, 2002; Hardy, Jones, & Gould, 1996) may become psychologically dysfunctional and contribute to maladaptive training responses (Gould, 1996; Hall, 2005; Hall, Cawthra & Kerr, 1997; Lemyre, Roberts, & Treasure, 2006). Recent research (Lemyre et al., 2006; Lemyre, Hall & Roberts, 2008; Roberts & Stray-Gundersen, 2007) from a motivational perspective has begun to systematically examine the factors that give rise to this pattern of cognition, affect, and behavior. Freudenberger (1980) described burnout as a syndrome that includes both physical and emotional exhaustion. These symptoms are believed to occur concurrently with patterns of behavior that are strongly achievement oriented (Hall & Kerr, 1997). Athletes experiencing burnout tend to show a strong commitment to the pursuit of goals and set high standards for themselves (Lemyre et al., 2008). Despite personal investment and great persistence, they often experience depression, depersonalization, disillusionment, and dissatisfaction as their goals are continually unmet. Hall and colleagues (Hall, Kerr, & Mathews, 1998) suggest a strong relationship existing between an athlete's perfectionism, achievement goals, and aptitudes to perform. It is when an athlete continually perceives his/her ability and effort to be inadequate to meet his/her achievement goals that the maladaptive nature of his/her achievement orientation becomes apparent. The athlete may drop out in order to maintain any real sense of self-worth. However, rigid adherence to intense achievement striving is believed to lead to athlete burnout when the athlete experiences enduring bouts of physical exhaustion combined with chronic negative affect and cognitions (Lemyre et al., 2008).

In the past, it has been suggested (Cohn, 1990) that athletes at risk of burning out were likely to participate in too much training and competition, lacked enjoyment while practicing their sport, and experienced too much self- or other-induced pressure. Investigating young elite tennis players, Gould and colleagues (Gould, 1996; Gould, Tuffey, Udry, & Loehr, 1996; Gould, Udry, Tuffey, & Loehr, 1996) found that burned-out athletes believed they had less input into their own training, were acting passively with no real sense of intention during training and games, and were more withdrawn. As burned-out players did not differ from non-burned-out athletes in terms of the number of hours they trained, Gould and colleagues posited that the crucial factors leading to burnout were psychological (motivational) rather than physical in nature, where athletes experiencing burnout may be the product of "motivation gone awry." This claim was investigated by Lemyre, Treasure, and Roberts (2006) in a longitudinal study that investigated variation in motivation and affect in elite swimmers over the course of a competitive season. Lemyre and colleagues (2006) found that athletes with negative motivational trends (motivation becoming less self-determined over the season) scored significantly higher on all three dimensions of burnout than athletes with positive motivational trends. A shift in motivational focus over time may be an important precursor of athlete burnout and is consistent with past research (Gould, 1996; Gould, Tuffey, Udry, & Loehr, 1996; Gould, Udry, Tuffey, & Loehr, 1996; Gould, Udry, Tuffey, & Loehr, 1997; Hall et al., 1997). These findings offer insight into the possible motivational dynamics that may put an athlete at risk for burnout. It is well established that ego goals and an emphasis on performance criteria evoke less self-determined forms of motivational regulation (Duda & Hall, 2001; Hewitt & Flett, 1991; Lemyre et al., 2008).

Independent of the source of motivation, it has generally been assumed that as long as athletes remain confident in their current ability, their patterns of achievement-related cognition, affect, and behavior appear to be adaptive (Dweck, 1986; Hall et al., 1997). However, when athletes become preoccupied with achievement-related challenges such as persistent goal failure, or goal blockage brought about by injury or overtraining, the inherently maladaptive nature of certain motivational parameters may appear. When athletes exhibit a motivational profile that encourages a focus on the demonstration of competence and self-validation, it may be inappropriate to label the resulting motivation as adaptive, even though it may result in athletic success. This motivational profile restricts adaptive achievement behavior to occasions when perceived ability is high. While the successful demonstration of ability may be sufficient to restore confidence after defeat, it is when difficulties persist and obstacles appear insurmountable that the debilitating nature of this profile becomes more pronounced. This means that a profile that encourages a focus on the demonstration of competence and self-validation may be a critical factor that predisposes talented athletes toward an increased risk for burnout because it engenders a sense of entrapment when self-worth is under threat (Hall, Cawthra, & Kerr, 1997; Lemyre et al., 2008; Raedeke, 1997). In a study investigating the psychological determinants of athlete burnout among elite winter sport athletes, Lemyre and colleagues (2008) examined the relationship between motivational disposition variables at the start of the season and signs of athlete burnout at season's end. Findings revealed that when the athlete was ego-involved, then that athlete was more at risk of developing symptoms of burnout than the more task-involved athlete. These findings suggest that the way individuals give meaning to achievement may combine with other social cognitive variables to play an important role in understanding the mechanisms that underpin the onset of burnout in elite athletes.

In another study, Lemyre, Roberts, and Stray-Gundersen (2007) investigated whether the quality of motivation at season's start in elite athletes and symptoms of overtraining can predict athlete burnout propensity. At the start of the season, 141 elite winter sport athletes responded to a motivation questionnaire and answered questions investigating overtraining symptoms and burnout at the end of the season. Findings indicated that self-determined motivation was negatively linked, and symptoms of overtraining were positively linked to dimensions of athlete burnout. Results suggest that the source of motivation for sport involvement in elite athletes at the beginning of the season and symptoms of overtraining are both independently linked to signs of burnout in elite athletes. These and other findings (e.g., Lemyre et al., 2006, 2007) support a motivational approach to study burnout propensity in elite athletes.

It has been suggested (e.g., Silva, 1990) that though psychological processes underpinning athlete burnout are important, the phenomenon occurs only when these psychological processes are combined with negative training adaptation. Sustained failure to adapt to training generates excessive fatigue. Training when the body's adaptivity is lost, leads to overtraining and increases vulnerability to athlete burnout (Kellmann, 2002). In an effort to better understand the psychological and physiological factors leading to burnout in elite athletes, Lemyre, Roberts, Treasure, Stray-Gundersen, and Matt (2004) investigated the relationship between psychological variables and hormonal variation. Initial findings suggest that failure to perceive a mastery-oriented motivational climate on the team was an important predictor of athlete burnout susceptibility.

Treasure and Roberts (1995) have suggested that favoring mastery-achievement striving in highly-competitive contexts such as elite sport was likely to be more successful than trying to eradicate performance oriented cues from the sport context. Therefore, a successful strategy should emphasise mastery oriented cues and support a motivational climate based on personal growth and self-referenced criteria of success. When Lemyre and colleagues (2004) looked at the contribution of both psychological and physiological variables to predict athlete-burnout susceptibility, they found that variation in basal cortisol during the course of the competitive season accounted for 15% of the variance in athlete burnout, while the psychological variables of perfectionism (20%), perceived mastery climate (12%), and subjective performance satisfaction (18%) explained a total of 50% of the total variance (67%) in athlete burnout at the end of the season. The findings of the study support the importance of subjective appraisals of performance as a potential determinant of athlete burnout vulnerability (e.g., Hall et al., 1997; Lemyre et al., 2006; Hall, 2006).

*Summary*

The literature reviewed above supports meaningful relationships between personal goals of achievement and perceptions of the motivational climate on cognitive and affective beliefs about involvement in physical activity, and we have shown that outcomes such as exerted effort, performance, moral behavior and cheating, and burnout are affected by whether one is task- or ego-involved. Research from an achievement-goal perspective in sport and physical education has demonstrated that goal orientations and perceptions of the motivational climate are relevant to the ongoing stream of achievement behavior, cognition, and affect. Given the body of empirical work that has documented the adaptive motivation and well-being responses of students who perceive mastery or task-involving climates, physical education teacher and sport coach education programs would seemingly benefit from integrating educational information pertaining to the creation of mastery climates into their curricula.

*Enhancing Motivation*

Researchers interested in the sport and physical education experience need to develop strategies and guidelines and explore ways in which coaches, parents, and other significant social agents can engage in the creation of a mastery or task-involving motivational climate. It is interesting, however, that a paucity of intervention research has been conducted to assess the viability of the teacher and coach education programs designed to enhance motivation from an achievement goal perspective (e.g., Digelidis et al., 2003; Lloyd & Fox, 1992; Solmon, 1996; Treasure & Roberts, 2001). In comparing two different approaches to teaching an aerobics/fitness class on exercise motivation and enjoyment of adolescent females, Lloyd and Fox found that participants in the mastery condition reported higher motivation to continue participating in aerobics and more enjoyment than those who participated in the performance condition. Consistent with these findings, Solmon found that seventh- and eighth-grade students who participated in the mastery condition demonstrated a willingness to persist in a difficult juggling task than those in the performance condition. In addition, students in the performance condition were more likely to attribute success during the intervention to normative ability than those in the mastery condition.

Similar to the intervention designed by Solmon (1996), Treasure and Roberts (2001) drew on strategies suggested by Ames (1992) to promote either a mastery or performance climate. The strategies were then organized into the interdependent structures that Epstein (1989) has argued define the achievement context, namely task, authority, recognition, grouping, evaluation, and time structures better known by the acronym TARGET. Responses of female and male young adolescent physical education students suggest that a teacher can influence the salience of a mastery or performance climate and, in so doing, affect a child's motivation for physical education. Digelidis and colleagues (2003) did an intervention designed to facilitate task-involvement in PE with junior high school pupils. Compared with a control group, the students in the intervention group demonstrated more positive attitudes towards exercise and healthy eating. The intervention group also reported lower ego and higher task orientation scores.

Clearly the results from the intervention studies have been promising, and the endorsement of a mastery environment is recommended. Although the results of the studies conducted by Digelidis and colleagues (2003), Solmon (1996), and Treasure and Roberts (2001) indicate that adopting and adapting classroom-based intervention programs in the context of physical education may be effective, it is important to recognize that there may be significant differences between the achievement contexts. In assessing and implementing interventions to enhance the quality of motivation in youth sport, therefore, researchers need to be sensitive to potential differences between the achievement contexts (Nicholls, 1992).

The few intervention studies that have been conducted clearly show that a mastery climate has positive behavioral, cognitive, and affective outcomes. All of the studies conducted to date, however, have been short-term and limited in what they assess. Randomized, controlled studies over time are needed to truly assess the causal role of the motivational climate on motivational outcomes.

## CONCLUSIONS

As reported by Roberts and colleagues (2007), we may draw two important conclusions from the above. The first one is that ego-involving goals (however they have been defined and/or conceptualized) are more likely to lead to maladaptive achievement behavior, especially when participants perceive their competence to be low, are concerned with failure, or are invested in protecting self-worth. When the above is the case, the evidence is quite clear: motivation ebbs, task investment is low, persistence is low, performance suffers, satisfaction and enjoyment are lower, peer relationships suffer, participants are more likely to cheat, burnout is more likely, participants are more likely to drop out, and participants feel more negatively about themselves and the achievement context. However, this does not mean that ego-involving goals are always negative; in some situations for some people they are positive. When one has an ego (or performance) goal with a high perception of competence (e.g., Pensgaard & Roberts, 2002), then such goals are facilitative of achievement and function as motivating constructs. (It must be admitted here that we did not review the research emanating from the Hierarchical Model of achievement goals [e.g., Elliot, 1997]. It has been argued elsewhere [Kaplan & Maehr, 2007; Roberts et al., 2007] that the hierarchical model may not be an extension of AGT as argued by Elliot and colleagues [e.g., 1997]. Therefore we did not include the work relating to approach and avoid valences.) But even then, performance (ego) goals are more "fragile," and can lead to maladaptive achievement striving as context information is processed (Dweck & Leggett, 1988).

Second, the research is unequivocal that task-involving (mastery) goals are adaptive. When task-involved, or participants perceive mastery involving criteria in the context, then motivation is optimized, participants are invested in the task, persist longer, performance is higher, satisfaction and enjoyment are higher, peer relationships are facilitated, cheating is less likely to occur, burnout is less likely, and participants feel more positively about themselves and the task. Being task-involved has been consistently associated with desirable cognitive and affective responses. The research is now clear that if we wish to optimize motivation in physical activity and foster positive outcomes, we ought to promote task involvement. We can do that through enhancing socialization experiences so that the individual has a task-goal orientation and is naturally task-involved, or we structure the physical activity context to be more task-involving as suggested by Ames. The evidence has led many sport psychologists to conclude that task involvement better enables learners to manage motivation in the sport experience, especially children and young adolescents. Consequently, sport psychologists, much like their educational colleagues, have urged those involved in pedagogy to promote task involvement as well as develop mastery-oriented environments in order to facilitate effective motivational patterns for all participants, even if the individuals are high in ego orientation (e.g., Brunel, 2000; Duda, 1993; Hall & Kerr, 1997; Pensgaard & Roberts, 2002; Roberts, 2001; Roberts et al., 1997, 2007; Smith et al., 2007; Theeboom, et al., 1996; Treasure & Roberts, 1995, 2001; Yoo, 2003).

It may well be that always fostering task-involving criteria may not satisfy all individuals in the sport experience, especially elite athletes (Hardy, 1997). It may well be that athletes at all levels of competition would benefit from being *both* task- and ego-involved. Being both task- and ego-involved is conceptually coherent with achievement goal theory, and may be valuable in the learning process because it provides multiple sources of competence information to the athlete. While encouraging individuals to be task-involved in achievement tasks has been demonstrated to optimize motivation, even with elite athletes, we need not be blind to the fact that some athletes do favor and are motivated by ego-involving criteria. The task for the investigator and the practitioner is to determine when task- or ego-involving criteria of success and failure are motivational for a particular athlete.

As our final conclusion, it may be stated that achievement goal research is an area with rich research traditions, both new and old. Where are we going in the future may be a pertinent question to ask after more than 25 years. Perhaps it is the time to begin to seriously attempt to integrate some key constructs and untangle the motivation puzzle as some have attempted (e.g., Kaplan & Maehr, 2002). Are achievement goals the manifestation of needs, values, the valence of outcomes, and/or cognitive schemas driving how one sees one's world and responds to the environmental cues extant with achievement striving? What gives meaning to achievement striving? Within sport and physical activity, as well as the academic context, we need to address these questions and expand our conceptual understanding of motivational processes and achievement behaviors so that we can intervene effectively to enhance motivation and make the achievement context enjoyable and satisfying for all.

## REFERENCES

Abrahamsen, F. E., Roberts, G. C., & Pensgaard, A. M. (2006). An examination of the factorial structure of the Norwegian version of the sport anxiety scale. Scandinavian *Journal of Medicine & Science in Sports, 16,* 358–363.

Abrahamsen, F. E., Roberts, G. C., Pensgaard, A. M., & Ronglan, L. T. (2008). Perceived ability and social support as mediators of achievement motivation and performance anxiety. *Scandinavian Journal of Medicine & Science in Sports, 18,* 810–821.

Abrahamsen, F. A., Roberts, G. C., & Pensgaard, A. M. (2008). Achievement goals and gender effects on multidimensional anxiety in national elite sport. *Psychology of Sport and Exercise, 9,* 449–464.

Ames, C. (1992). Achievement goals, motivational climate, and motivational processes. In G. C. Roberts (Ed.), *Motivation in Sport and Exercise*. (pp. 161–176): Champaign, IL: Human Kinetics.

Balaguer, I., Duda, J. L., Atienza, F. L., & Mayo, C. (2002). Situational and dispositional goals as predictors of perceptions of individual and team improvement, satisfaction and coach ratings among elite female handball teams. *Psychology of Sport and Exercise, 3,* 293–308.

Boixadós, M., Cruz, J., Torregrosa, M., & Valiente, L. (2004). Relationships among motivational climate, satisfaction, perceived ability, and fair play attitudes in young soccer players. *Journal of Applied Sport Psychology, 16,* 301–317.

Boyd, M. P. (1990). *The effects of participation orientation and success-failure on post-competitive affect in young adults*. Unpublished dissertation, University of Southern California, Los Angeles, CA.

Brunel, P. (2000). Achievement motivation: Toward interactive effects of dispositional and situational variables on motivation and social cognition. *Habilitation à diriger les recherches,* Université of Limoges, France.

Carr, S. (2006). An examination of multiple goals in children's physical education: Motivational effects of goal profiles and the role of perceived climate in multiple goal development. *Journal of Sport Sciences, 24*(3), 281–297.

Cohn, P. J. (1990). An exploratory study on sources of stress and athlete burnout in youth golf. *The Sport Psychologist,* 4, 95–106.

Cury, F., Biddle, S., Famose, J. P., Goudas, M., Sarrazin, P., & Durand, M. (1996). Personal and situational factors influencing intrinsic interest of adolescent girls in physical education: A structural equation modeling analysis. *Educational Psychology, 16*(3), 305–314.

Cury, F., Biddle, S., Sarrazin, P., & Famose, J. P. (1997). Achievement goals and perceived ability predict investment in learning a sport task. *British Journal of Educational Psychology, 67*(3), 293–309.

Cury, F. & Sarrazin, P. (1998). Achievement motivation and learning behaviors in a sport task. *Journal of Sport and Exercise Behavior, 20,* S11.

Cury, F., Sarrazin, & Famose (1997). Achievement goals, perceived ability and active search for information. In *European Yearbook of Sport Psychology* (Vol. 1, pp. 167–183). Sank Augustin.

Digelidis, N., Papaioannou, A., Laparidis, K., & Christodoulidis, T. (2003). A one-year intervention in 7th grade physical education classes aiming to change motivational climate and attitudes towards exercise. *Psychology of Sport and Exercise, 4,* 195–210.

Duda, J. L. (1988). The relationship between goal perspectives, persistence and behavioral intensity among male and female recreational sport participants. *Leisure Sciences, 10*(2), 95–106.

Duda, J. L. (1989). Relationship between task and ego orientation and the perceived purpose of sport among high school athletes. *Journal of Sport & Exercise Psychology, 11*(3), 318–335.

Duda, J. L. (1992). Motivation in sport settings: A goal perspective approach. In G.C. Roberts (Ed.), *Motivation in Sport and Exercise.* (pp. 57–91): Human Kinetics Books, Champaign, IL, US.

Duda, J. L. (2001). Achievement goal research in sport: Pushing the boundaries and clarifying some misunderstandings. In G. C. Roberts (Ed.). *Advances in motivation in sport and exercise* (pp 129–182). Human Kinetics, Champaign, IL.

Duda, J. L., Chi, L., Newton, M. L., Walling, M. D., & Catley, D. (1995). Task and ego orientation and intrinsic motivation in sport. *International Journal of Sport Psychology, 26*(1), 40–63.

Duda, J. L., Fox, K. R., Biddle, S. J., & Armstrong, N. (1992). Children's achievement goals and beliefs about success in sport. *British Journal of Educational Psychology, 62*(3), 313–323.

Duda, J. L., & Hall, H. (2001). Achievement goal theory in sport: Recent extensions and future directions. In R. N. Singer, H. A. Hausenblas, & C. M. Janelle (Eds.), *Handbook of sport psychology* (2$^{nd}$ Ed., pp. 417–443). New York: Wiley.

Duda, J. L., & Nicholls, J. G. (1992). Dimensions of achievement motivation in schoolwork and sport. *Journal of Educational Psychology, 84*(3), 290–299.

Duda, J. L., & White, S. A. (1992). Goal orientations and beliefs about the causes of sport success among elite skiers. *Sport Psychologist, 6*(4), 334–343.

Duda, J. L., Olson, L., & Templin, T. (1991). The relationship of task and ego orientation to sportsmanship attitudes and the perceived legitimacy of injurious acts. *Research Quarterly for Exercise and Sport, 62,* 79–87.

Duda, J. L., & Whitehead, J. (1998). Measurement of goal perspectives in the physical domain. In J. L. Duda (Ed.), *Advances in sport and exercise psychology measurement* (pp. 21–48). Morgantown, WV: Fitness Information Technology.

Durand, M., Cury, F., Sarrazin, P., & Famose, J-.P. (1996). Le Questionnaire du Succès en Sport: Validation Française du "Perception of Success Questionnaire." *International Journal of Sport Psychology, 27,* 251–268.

Dweck, C. S. (1986). Motivational processes affecting learning. *American Psychologist, 41,* 1040–1048.

Dweck, C., S., & Leggett, E., L. (1988). A Social-Cognitive Approach to Motivation and Personality. *Psychological Review, 95*(2), 256–273.

Eccles, J. S. & Harold, (1991). Gender differences in sport involvement: Applying the Eccles expectancy-value model. *Journal of Applied Sport Psychology, 3,* 7–35.

Elliot, A. J. (1997). Integrating the "classic" and "contemporary" approaches to achievement motivation: A hierarchical model of approach and avoidance achievement motivation. In M. Maehr & P. Pintrich (Eds.), *Advances in Motivation and Achievement* (Vol. 10, pp. 143–179). Greenwich, CT: JAI Press.

Elliott, E. S., & Dweck, C. S. (1988). Goals: An approach to motivation and achievement. *Journal of Personality & Social Psychology, 54,* 5–12.

Epstein, J. (1989). Family structures and student motivation: A developmental perspective. In C. Ames & R. Ames (Eds.), *Research on motivation in education* (Vol. 3, pp. 259–295). New York: Academic Press.

Freudenberger, H. J. (1980). *Burnout: The high cost of high achievement.* Garden City, NY: Anchor Press.

Gano-Overway, L. A. & Ewing, M. E. (2004). A longitudinal perspective of the relationship between perceived motivational climate, goal orientations, and strategy use. *Research Quarterly for Exercise and Sport, 75,* 315–325.

Goudas, M., Biddle, S. J. H., Fox, K. R., & Underwood, M. (1995). It ain't what you do, it's the way that you do it! Teaching style affects children's motivation in track and field lessons. *Sport Psychologist, 9,* 254–264.

Gould, D. (1996). Personal motivation gone awry: Burnout in competitive athletes. *Quest, 48,* 275–289.

Gould, D. R., Dieffenbach, K., & Moffett, A. (2002). Psychological characteristics and their development in Olympic champions. *Journal of Applied Sport Psychology, 14,* 172–204.

Gould, D., Udry, E., Tuffey, S., & Loehr, J. (1996). Burnout in competitive junior tennis players: I. A quantitative psychological assessment. *The Sport Psychologist, 10,* 322–340.

Gould, D., Tuffey, S., Udry, E., & Loehr, J. (1996). Burnout in competitive junior tennis players: II. Qualitative analysis. *The Sport Psychologist, 10,* 341–366.

Gould, D., Tuffey, S., Udry, E., & Loehr, J. (1997). Burnout in competitive junior tennis players: III. Individual differences in the burnout experience. *The Sport Psychologist, 11,* 257–276.

Goudas, M., Biddle, S., & Fox, K. (1994). Perceived locus of causality, goal orientations, and perceived competence in school physical education classes. *British Journal of Educational Psychology, 64*(3), 453–463.

Guivernau, M., & Duda, J. L. (1995). Psychometric properties of a Spanish version of the Task and Ego Orientation in Sport Questionnaire (TEOSQ) and beliefs about the causes of success inventory. *Revista de Psicologia del Deporte, 5,* 31–51.

Hagger, M. S., ASci, F. H., Lindwall, M., Hein, V., Mulazimoglu-Balli, O., Tarrant, M., Pastor Ruiz, Y., & Sell, V. (2007). Cross-cultural validity and measurement invariance of the social physique anxiety scale in five European nations. *Scandinavian Journal of Medicine Science in Sports, 17,* 703–719.

Hall, H.K. (2005). Perfectionism: A hallmark quality of world class performers, or a psychological impediment to athletic development? In D. Hackfort & G. Tenenbaum (Eds.) *Perspectives in Sport and Exercise Psychology: Essential processes for attaining peak performance, 1,* 179–211. Oxford UK: Meyer & Meyer Publishers.

Hall, H. K., Cawthraw, I. W., & Kerr, A. W. (1997). Motivation antecedents of precompetitive anxiety in youth sport. *The Sport Psychology, 11*(1), 24–42.

Hall, H. K., & Kerr, A. W. (1997). Motivational antecedents of precompetitive anxiety in youth sport. *Sport Psychologist, 11*(1), 24–42.

Hall, H. K., Kerr, A. W., & Matthews, J. (1998). Precompetitive anxiety in sport: The contribution of achievement goals and perfectionism. *Journal of Sport & Exercise Psychology, 20,* 194–217.

Hardy, L. (1997). The Coleman Roberts Griffith address: Three myths about applied consultancy work. *Journal of Applied Sport Psychology, 9,* 277–294.

Hein, V., & Hagger, M. S. (2007). Global self-esteem, goal achievement orientations, and self-determined behavioural regulations in a physical education setting. *Journal of Sports Sciences, 25*(2), 149–159.

Hewitt, P. L., & Flett, G. L. (1991). Perfectionism in the self and social context: Conceptualization, assessment and association with psychopathology. *Journal of Personality and Social Psychology, 60,* 456–470.

Hom, H. L., Duda, J. L., & Miller, A. (1993). Correlates of goal orientations among young athletes. *Pediatric Exercise Science, 5*(2), 168–176.

Jackson, S. & Roberts G. C. (1992). Positive performance states of athletes: Toward a conceptual understanding of peak performance. *The Sport Psychologist. 6,* 156–171.

Kaplan, A. & Maehr, M. (2002). Adolescents' achievement goals: Situating motivation in socio-cultural contexts. In T. Urdan & F. Pajears (Eds.), *Adolescence and education: Vol. 2, Academic motivation of adolescents* (pp. 125–167). Greenwich, CT: Information Age.

Kaplan, A., & Maehr, M. L. (2007). The contributions and prospects of goal orientation theory. *Educational Psychology Review.*

Kavussanu, M. (2007). Motivational predictors of prosocial and antisocial behavior in football. *Journal of Sports Sciences, 24*(6), 575–588.

Kavussanu, M., & Roberts, G. C. (2001). Moral functioning in sport: An achievement goal perspective. *Journal of Sport and Exercise Psychology, 23,* 37–54.

Kavussanu, M., Seal, A. R., & Phillips, D. R. (2006). Observed prosocial and antisocial behaviors in male soccer teams: Age differences across adolescence and the role of motivational variables. *Journal of Applied Sport Psychology, 18,* 326–344.

Kavussanu, M., & Roberts, G. C. (1996). Motivation in physical activity contexts: The relationship of perceived motivational climate to intrinsic motivation and self-efficacy. *Journal of Sport & Exercise Psychology, 18*(3), 264–280.

Kavussanu, M., Roberts, G. C., & Ntoumanis, N. (2002). Contextual influences on moral functioning of college basketball players. *The Sport Psychologist. 16,* 347–367.

Kellmann, M. (2002). Psychological assessment of underrecovery. In M. Kellmann (Ed.), *Enhancing recovery: Preventing underperformance in athletes* (pp. 37–55). Champaign, IL: Human Kinetics.

Kristiansen, E., Roberts, G. C., & Abrahamsen, F. E. (2006). Achievement involvement and stress coping in elite sport. *Scandinavian Journal of Medicine & Science in Sports,* in press.

Lemyre, P.-N., Hall, H. K. & Roberts, G .C. (2008). A Social Cognitive Approach to Burnout in Elite Athletes. *Scandinavian Journal of Medicine and Science in Sports, 18,* 221–234.

Lemyre,P.-N., Ommundsen,Y. & Roberts,C. C. (2000). Moral functioning in sport: The role of dispositional goals and perceived ability. *International Journal of Psychology, 35*(3–4), 23.

Lemyre, P.-N., Roberts, G. C., & Ommundsen, Y. (2002). Achievement goal orientations, perceived ability and sportspersonship in youth soccer. *Journal of Applied Sport Psychology, 14*, 120–136.

Lemyre, P.-N., Roberts, G. C., & Stray-Gundersen, J. (2007). Motivation, overtraining and burnout: Can self-determined motivation predict overtraining and burnout in elite athletes. *European Journal of Sport Sciences, 7*, 115–132.

Lemyre, P.-N., Roberts, G. C., Treasure, D. C., Stray-Gundersen, J., & Matt, K. (2004). Psychological and physiological determinants of overtraining and burnout in elite athletes. *Journal of Sport and Exercise Psychology, Supplement*, 144–145.

Lemyre, P.-N., Treasure, D. C., & Roberts, G. C. (2006). Influence of variability in motivation and affect on elite athlete burnout susceptibility. *Journal of Sport & Exercise Psychology, 28*, 32–48.

Lemyre, P.-N., Hall, H. K. & Roberts, G. C.(2008). A social cognitive approach to burnout in elite athletes. *Scandinavian Journal of Medicine and Science in Sports, 18*, 221–234.

Lloyd, J., & Fox, K. (1992). Achievement goals and motivation to exercise in adolescent girls: A preliminary intervention study. *British Journal of Physical Education Research Supplement, 11*, 12–16.

Lochbaum, M. R., & Roberts, G. C. (1993). Goal orientations and perceptions of the sport experience. *Journal of Sport & Exercise Psychology, 15*(2), 160–171.

Locke, E. A., & Latham, G. P. (1985). The application of goal setting to sports. *Journal of Sport Psychology, 7*, 205–222.

Maehr, M. L., & Braskamp, L. A. (1986). *The motivation factor: A theory of personal investment.* Lexington, MA: Lexington Books/D. C. Heath and Company.

Maehr, M. L., & Nicholls, J. G. (1980). Culture and achievement motivation: A second look. In N. Warren (Ed.), *Studies in Cross-cultural Psychology* (Vol. 2, pp. 221–267). New York: Academic Press.

Marsh, H. (1994). Sport motivation orientations: Beware of jingle-jangle fallacies. *Journal of Sport and exercise Psychology, 16*, 365–380.

Marsh, H. W., Papaioannou, A., Martin, A. J., & Theodorakis, Y. (2006). Motivational constructs in greek physical education classes: Factor structure, gender and age effects in a nationally representative longitudinal sample. *International Journal of Sport and Exercise Psychology, 4*, 121–148.

Miller, B. & Roberts, G. C. (2003). The effect of motivational climate on determinants of cheating among competitive Norwegian youth football players. In E. Müller, H. Schwameder, G. Zallinger & V. Fastenbauer (Eds.), *Proceedings of the 8th Annual Congress of the European College of Sport Science.* (pp 311–312). Salzburg, Austria: University of Salzburg.

Miller, B. W., Roberts, G. C. & Ommundsen, Y. (2004) Effect of motivational climate on sportspersonship among young male and female football players. *Scandinavian Journal of Medicine and Science in Sports. 14*, 193–202.

Miller, B. W., Roberts, G. C., & Ommundsen, Y. (2005). The relationship of perceived motivational climate to moral functioning, moral atmosphere perceptions, and the legitimacy of intentionally injurious acts among competitive youth football players. *Psychology of Sport & Exercise, 6,* 461–477.

Newton, M., & Duda, J. L. (1993). The relationship of task and ego orientation to performance-cognitive content, affect, and attributions in bowling. *Journal of Sport Behavior, 16*(4), 209–220.

Nicholls, J. G. (1984). Achievement motivation: Conceptions of ability, subjective experience, task choice, and performance. *Psychological Review, 91,* 328–346.

Nicholls, J. G. (1989). *The competitive ethos and democratic education.* Cambridge, MA: Harvard University Press.

Nicholls, J. G., & Miller, A. T. (1983). The differentiation of the concepts of difficulty and ability. *Child Development, 54*(4), 951–959.

Nicholls, J. G., & Miller, A. T. (1984a). Reasoning about the ability of self and others: A developmental study. *Child Development, 55*(6), 1990–1999.

Nicholls, J. G., & Miller, A. T. (1984b). Development and its discontents: The differentiation of the concept of ability. In J. G. Nicholls (Ed.), *Advances in motivation and achievement (Vol.3) The development of achievement motivation* (pp. 185–218). Greenwich, CT: JAI Press.

Nicholls, J., Patashnik, M. & Nolen S. (1985) Adolescent theories of education. *Journal of Educational Psychology, 77,* 683–692.

Newton, M., & Duda, J. L. (1993). The relationship of task and ego orientation to performance-cognitive content, affect, and attributions in bowling. *Journal of Sport Behavior, 16*(4), 209–220.

Ntoumanis, N. & Biddle, S.J.H. (1999). Affect and achievement goals in physical activity: A meta analysis. *Scandinavian Journal of Medicine and Science in Sports. 9,* 333–343.

Ommundsen, Y. & Pedersen, B. H. (1999). The role of achievement goal orientations and perceived ability upon somatic and cognitive indices of sport competition trait anxiety. *Scandinavian Journal of Medicine & Science in Sports, 9,* 333–343.

Ommundsen, Y., Roberts, G. C., Lemyre, N. & Miller, B. (2005). Peer relationships in adolescent competitive soccer. Associations to perceived motivation climate, achievement goals and perfectionism. *Journal of Sport Sciences, 23,* 977–989.

Papaioannou, A. & Kouli, O. (1999). The effect of task structure, perceived motivational climate and goal orientations on students' task involvement and anxiety. *Journal of Applied Sport Psychology, 11,* 51–71.

Papaioannou, A., & McDonald, A. I. (1993). Goal perspectives and purposes of physical education as perceived by Greek adolescents. *Physical Education Review, 16,* 41–48.

Pensgaard, A-M. & Roberts, G. C. (2002). Elite athletes' experiences of the motivational climate: The coach matters. *Scandinavian Journal of Medicine and Science in Sport, 12,* 54–60.

Pensgaard, A-M. & Roberts, G. C. (2003). Achievement goal orientations and the use of coping strategies among winter Olympians. *Psychology of Sport and Exercise, 4,* 101–116.

Rascle, O., Coulomb, G., & Pfister, R. (1998). Aggression and goal orientations in handball: Influence of institutional sport context. *Perceptual & Motor Skills, 86* (3, Pt 2), 1347–1360.

Raedeke T. D. (1997). Is athlete burnout more than just stress? A sport commitment perspective. *Journal of Sport and Exercise Psychology, 19*, 396–417.

Reinboth, M. & Duda, J. L. (2004). The motivational climate, perceived ability, and athletes' psychological and physical well-being. *The Sport Psychologist, 18*, 237–251.

Reinboth, M. & Duda, J. L. (2006). Perceived motivational climate, need satisfaction and indices of well-being in team sports: A longitudinal perspective. *Psychology of Sport and Exercise, 7*, 269–286.

Roberts, G. C. (1984). Achievement motivation in children's sport. In J. Nicholls (Ed.), *The Development of Achievement Motivation* (pp. 251–281). Greenwich, CT: JAI Press.

Roberts, G. C. (1986). The perception of stress: A potential source and its development. In M. R.Weiss & D. Gould (Eds.), *Sport for Children and Youths* (pp. 119–126). Champaign, IL: Human Kinetics Publishers, Inc.

Roberts, G. C. (1992). Motivation in sport and exercise: Conceptual constraints and convergence. In G. C. Roberts (Ed.). *Motivation in sport and exercise* (pp. 3–30 ), Champaign, IL: Human Kinetics.

Roberts, G. C. (2001). Understanding the dynamics of motivation in physical activity: The influence of achievement goals on motivational processes. In G. C. Roberts (Ed.), *Advances in motivation in Exercise and Sport.* (pp. 1–50). Champaign, IL: Human Kinetics.

Roberts, G. C. & Balague, G. (1989, August*). The development of a social cognitive scale of motivation.* Paper presented at the Seventh World Congress of Sport Psychology, Singapore.

Roberts, G. C., & Treasure, D. C. (1992). Children in sport. *Sport Science Review, 1,* 46–64.

Roberts, G. C., Hall, H. K., Jackson, S. A., Kimiecik, J. C., & Tonymon, P. (1995). Implicit theories of achievement and the sport experience: Goal perspectives and achievement strategies. *Perceptual and Motor Skills. 33*, 219–224.

Roberts, G. C., & Ommundsen, Y. (1996). Effect of goal orientations on achievement beliefs, cognitions, and strategies in team sport. *Scandinavian Journal of Medicine and Science in Sport, 6 ,* 46–56.

Roberts, G. C., Treasure, D. C., & Balague, G. (1998). Achievement goals in sport: The development and validation of the perception of success questionnaire. *Journal of Sport Sciences, 16*, 337–247.

Roberts, G. C., Treasure, D. C., & Kavussanu, M. (1997). Motivation in physical activity contexts: An achievement goal perspective. In P. Pintrich & M. Maehr (Eds.), *Advances in Motivation and Achievement* (Vol. 10, pp. 413–447). Stamford, CT: JAI Press.

Roberts, G. C., Treasure, D. C., & Kavussanu, M. (1996). Orthogonality of achievement goals and its relationship to beliefs about success and satisfaction in sport. *Sport Psychologist, 10*(4), 398–408.

Roberts, G. C., Ommundsen, Y., Sorensen, M, & Miller, B. (under review). Effect of achievement goals on peer interaction and persistence in youth sport.

Roberts, G. C., Treasure, D. C., & Conroy, D. E. (2007). Understanding the dynamics of motivation in sport and physical activity: An achievement goal interpretation. In G. Tenenbaum & R. Eklund (Eds), *Handbook of research in sport psychology* (pp 3–30). Boston: Wiley.

Ryska, Todd A. (2003). Sportsmanship in youth athletes: The role of competitiveness, motivational orientation, and perceived purposes of sport. *The Journal of Psychology, 137,* 273–293.

Sage, L., & Kavussanu, M. (2007). The effects of goal involvement on moral behavior in an experimentally manipulated competitive setting. *Journal of Sport and Exercise Psychology, 29,* 190–207.

Sakamoto, B., & Parsons, C. (1993, November 25). Libertyville coach quits after motivational skit backfires. *The Chicago Tribune,* Sports, p. 1.

Sarrazin, P., Roberts, G. C., Cury, F., Biddle, S., & Famose, J-P. (2002). Exerted effort and performance in climbing among boys: The influence of achievement goals, perceived ability, and task difficulty. *Research Quarterly for Exercise and Sport, 73,* 425–436.

Seifriz, J., Duda, J. L., Chi, L. (1992). The relationship of perceived motivational climate to intrinsic motivation and beliefs about success in basketball. *Journal of Sport and Exercise Psychology, 14,* 375–391.

Sherman, E. (1992, September 15). Sherrill unable to steer clear of controversy. *The Chicago Tribune,* Sports, p. 3.

Smith, R. E. (1989). Athletic Stress and Burnout: Conceptual Models and Intervention Strategies. In D. Hackfort & C. D. Spielberger (Eds.), *Anxiety in Sports* (1st Ed., pp. 183–201). New York: Hemisphere Publishing Corporation.

Smith, R. E., Smoll, F. L., & Barnett, N. P. (1995). Reduction of children's sport performance anxiety trough social support and stress-reduction training for coaches. *Journal of Applied Developmental Psychology, 16,* 125–142.

Smith, R. E., Smoll, F. L., & Cumming, S. P. (2007). Effects of a motivational climate intervention for coaches on young athletes' sport performance anxiety. *Journal of Sport & Exercise Psychology, 29,* 39–59.

Spray, C. M., Wang, J. C. K., Biddle, S. J. H., Chatzisarantis, N. L. D., & Warburton, V. E. (2006). An experimental test of self-theories of ability in youth sport. *Psychology of Sport and Exercise, 7,* 255–267.

Solmon, M.A. (1996). Impact of motivational climate on students' behaviors and perceptions in a physical education setting. *Journal of Educational Psychology, 88,* 731–738.

Silva, J. M. (1990). An analysis of the training stress syndrome in competitive athletics. *The Journal of Applied Sport Psychology, 2,* 5–20.

Tammen, V., Treasure, D., & Power, K. T. (1992). The relationship between competitive and mastery achievement goals and dimensions of intrinsic motivation. *Journal of Sport Sciences, 10,* 630.

Theeboom, M., De Knop, P., & Weiss, M. R. (1995). Motivational climate, psychological responses, and motor skill development in children's sport: A field-based intervention study. *Journal of Sport and Exercise Psychology, 17,* 294–311.

Thorkildsen, T. (1988). Theories of education among academically precocious adolescents. *Contemporary Educational Psychology, 13,* 323–330.

Treasure, D. C., & Roberts, G. C. (1994a). Cognitive and affective concomitants of task and ego goal orientations during the middle school years. *Journal of Sport & Exercise Psychology, 16*(1), 15–28.

Treasure, D. C., & Roberts, G. C. (1994b). Perception of Success Questionnaire: Preliminary validation in an adolescent population. *Perceptual & Motor Skills, 79* (1, Pt 2, Spec Issue) 607–610.

Treasure, D. C., & Roberts, G. C. (1995). Applications of achievement goal theory to physical education: Implications for enhancing motivation. *Quest, 47,* 475–489.

Treasure, D. C., & Roberts, G. C. (2001). Students' perceptions of the motivational climate, achievement beliefs and satisfaction in physical education. *Research Quarterly for Exercise and Sport, 72,* 165–175.

Van Yperen, N. W. & Duda, J. L. (1999). Goal orientations, beliefs about success, and performance improvement among young elite Dutch soccer players. *Scandinavian Journal of Medicine and Science in Sports, 9,* 358–264.

Vealey, R. S., & Campbell, J. L. (1988). Achievement goals of adolescent figure skaters: Impact on self-confidence, anxiety and performance. *Journal of Adolescent Research, 3*(2), 227–243.

Vlachopoulos, S., & Biddle, S. (1997). Modeling the relation of goal orientations to achievement-related affect in physical education: Does perceived ability matter? *Journal of Sport and Exercise Psychology, 19,* 169–187.

Vlachopoulos, S. & Biddle, S. (1996). Achievement goal orientations and intrinsic motivation in a track and field event in school physical education. *European Physical Education Review, 2,* 158–164.

Walling, M. D., Duda, J. L., & Chi, L. (1993). The perceived motivational climate in sport questionnaire: Construct and predictive validity. *Journal of Sport and Exercise Psychology, 15,* 172–183.

W Walling, M. D., & Duda, J. L. (1995). Goals and their associations with beliefs about success in and perceptions of the purposes of physical education. *Journal of Teaching in Physical Education, 14*(2), 140–156.

White, S. A., & Duda, J. L. (1993). Dimensions of goals and beliefs among adolescent athletes with physical disabilities. *Adapted Physical Activity Quarterly, 10*(2), 125–136.

White, S. A., Duda, J. L., & Keller, M. R. (1998). The relationship between goal orientation and perceived purposes of sport among youth sport participants. *Journal of Sport Behavior, 21*(4), 474–483.

White, S. A., Kavussanu, M., Tank, K. M., & Wingate, J. M. (2005). Perceived parental beliefs about the causes of success in sport: relationship to athletes' achievement goals and personal beliefs. *Scandinavian Journal of Medicine & Science in Sports, 14,* 57.

White, S. A., & Zellner, S. R. (1996). The relationship between goal orientation, beliefs about the causes of sport success, and trait anxiety among high school, intercollegiate, and recreational sport participants. *Sport Psychologist, 10*(1), 58–72.

Yoo, J. (2003). Motivational Climate and Perceived Competence in Anxiety and Tennis Performance. *Perceptual and Motor Skills, 96,* 403–413.

## CHAPTER 4

# MEANING-MAKING AND MOTIVATION

## A Dynamic Model

**Avi Kaplan, Hanoch Flum, and Keren Kemelman**

### INTRODUCTION

One of the main contributions of Martin Maehr to the field of achievement motivation has been the emphasis on the role of *meaning* in people's action. Up until the 1970s, the dominant psychological concept in achievement motivation theory and research was the Achievement Needs—the affective personality attributes that are supposedly established early in life, and which predispose individuals to respond positively or aversively to achievement cues in the environment (McClelland, 1961). Maehr (1974) was one of the early and main proponents of alternative perspectives that emphasize the situational nature of motivation. He argued that variability in people's investment of time, talent, and energy can be explained not only, or even primarily, by stable personality differences in affective motivational resources, but by the situated socio-cognitive *meaning* that people construct for the achievement situation. While this meaning involves personal dispositions, it also integrates the characteristics of the particular context and situation:

*Culture, Self, and Motivation: Essays in Honor of Martin L. Maehr,* pages 69–110
Copyright © 2009 by Information Age Publishing
All rights of reproduction in any form reserved.

Meaning is the critical determinant of motivation. Whether or not persons will invest themselves in a particular activity depends on what the activity means to them. Persons, it may be assumed, characteristically bring a certain package of meanings with them into a situation, which determines their behavior in the particular situation at hand. There are also features of any given situation that affect the meanings that may arise there for the person. It is these meanings that determine personal investment (Maehr, 1984, p. 123).

This emphasis on meaning was shared by other researchers whose collaborative efforts in the 1970s and 1980s, led to the emergence of the new perspective on achievement motivation which came to be known as achievement goal theory (Ames, 1992; Dweck & Leggett, 1988; Maehr, 1984; Nicholls, 1984). Arguably, achievement goal theory became the dominant perspective on achievement motivation in the past decade or so (Elliot, 2005). A large body of literature describes the various meanings that students adopt in achievement settings and the correlates of these meanings (for recent reviews see Elliot, 2005; Kaplan & Maehr, 2007; Meece, Anderman, & Anderman, 2006). Different researchers also provide their perspectives on the factors and processes that underlie these meanings. However, very few studies, if any, have attempted to investigate in-depth the process by which factors and processes integrate in the meaning-making process itself (Kaplan & Maehr, 2002; Maehr, 1984). This is the purpose of the current study. We begin by reviewing the tenets of achievement goal theory. We then describe Maehr's proposal for a meaning-making process that results with a situated meaning for achievement that involves a purpose for engagement—the achievement goal orientation. We follow by describing a study that set to investigate this meaning-making process among college students taking a course that was designed to emphasize mastery goals—engagement with the purpose of meaningful learning. We end by considering the implications of the findings to future research and practice.

## Achievement Goal Theory

Achievement goal theory is based on the premise that the meaning that people construct for an achievement situation guides their purpose for action in that situation. Unlike specific goals, objectives, or aims that people may set and pursue in achievement situations (i.e., *what* people try to achieve, such as "get a high grade on a test" or "do well on a personal project"), the theory emphasizes the broader, commonly implicit, underlying reasons behind adopting these objectives (i.e., *why* people try to achieve these objectives) (Anderman & Maehr, 1994). These underlying reasons, or purposes, were labeled "goal orientations." Goal orientations were defined as a broad mental frame, or a "cognitive program" (Elliott & Dweck, 1988):

an integrated pattern of beliefs, attributions, and affect that produces the intentions of behavior…and that is represented by different ways of approaching, engaging in, and responding to achievement-type activities (Ames, 1992,
p. 261)

Achievement goal theory proposes that, whereas meanings and their
resultant goal orientations may be idiosyncratic, there are several dimensions or categories of purposes that meaningfully distinguish between
more and less adaptive engagement in achievement tasks. Most attention
was given to two types of goal orientations: an orientation towards *developing competence*, variously labeled "mastery goals," "task goals," or "learning goals;" and an orientation towards *demonstrating competence*, variously
labeled "performance goals," "ego goals," or "ability goals." When students
adopt a mastery goals orientation, they perceive the achievement situation as an opportunity to learn and develop. They define success in the
situation as learning and understanding something new, they believe that
investment of effort leads to better understanding and learning, they consider themselves able to engage in effectively and learn, and they consider
difficulty a challenge to be mastered (Ames, 1992). When students adopt
a performance goals orientation, they perceive the achievement situation
as an evaluation of their ability, and that this evaluation has implications
for their self-worth. Most commonly, such evaluation of ability has a social component—it is public and involves recognition by others. Often,
evaluation of ability is based on normative criteria and involves social comparison with others. Hence, success in performance goals orientation is
often understood relative to others, and high ability is manifested when
performance is superior to that of others and is achieved with little effort
(Nicholls, 1984).

Research over the past couple of decades suggests quite strongly that
when students construct a mastery goal orientation in an achievement situation (i.e., adopt a purpose of learning, mastering skills or new knowledge,
and improving) the quality of their engagement is high (Ames, 1992; Kaplan, Middleton, Urdan, & Midgley, 2002; Pintrich, 2000; Urdan, 1997).
In contrast, when students construct a performance goal orientation (i.e.,
adopt a purpose of demonstrating smartness, outsmarting others, or succeeding with little effort), the quality of their engagement is not so high,
particularly when they are concerned about demonstrating low ability
(Ames, 1992; Elliot, 1999; Pintrich, 2000). Other categories of purpose
have been mentioned, but received less attention in research so far. These
include purposes of action that concern the extrinsic utility of engagement
(e.g., getting prizes, privileges, or access to desired activities), the social relationships that may be involved (e.g., wanting to associate or be associated
with certain people, to get approval, to behave responsibly), or the minimi-
zation of effort (e.g., wanting to get by with little investment or to con the

system) (Dowson & McInerney, 2001; Maehr, 1984; Nicholls, 1989; Urdan & Maehr, 1995; for a review see Kaplan & Maehr, 2007).

## Components of Meaning and Engagement: Purposes, Orientations, Reasons and Aims

In a critique of the achievement goal literature, Elliot (1999; Elliot & Thrash, 2001) noted that the definition of the achievement goal construct has been unclear. He suggested that achievement goal theorists and researchers seem to employ one of two general definitions for this construct: *purpose* and *orientation*. Elliot argued that there are problems with both of these definitions. He pointed out that the term "purpose" has more than one conceptual meaning. It can be used to refer to the *underlying reason* for engagement (e.g., development of competence, demonstrating superiority) as well as to the *objective* of engagement (e.g., learning a specific skill or doing better than others on a particular test or in a particular course). Elliot noted that the current use of the term "purpose" by researchers does not distinguish between the concepts of reason and aim, which makes it difficult to identify the core of the explanatory power of the construct (i.e., the reason, the aim, or their combination). Elliot also argued that defining the achievement goals construct as an "orientation"—that is, as an omnibus construct that integrates many other motivational constructs such as beliefs, attributions, and emotions (cf. Ames, 1992)—is problematic as it collapses the conceptual distinctions among these variables, and interferes with the ability to clearly conceptualize the relations of such omnibus concepts with the energization and direction of behavior.

Elliot (2005) argued that for conceptual clarity, achievement goals are best defined as aims or objectives: "a cognitive representation of a competence-based possibility that an individual seeks to attain" (Elliot & Thrash, 2001, p. 144). He contrasted these content-type goals with their underlying reasons, which are "more general, affect-laden dispositions that serve an energizational function in motivation by instigating or activating desires, concerns, and behavioral inclinations, as well as goal adoption" (p. 143). Elliot argued that each aim can be defined by its standard for success in a task (e.g., absolute, normative, self-referential) and by its valence (i.e., approach or avoidance). This led to defining six types of achievement aims or goals (as distinct from orientations) that are distinguished along the standard and valence dimensions. In the past decade or so, research using this definition has investigated four such achievement goals: mastery-approach, mastery-avoidance, performance-approach, and performance-avoidance (Elliot, 1999). Similar to research using the broader definitions, findings from research employing the narrow definition found strong support for the adaptive qualities of setting and pursuing mastery-approach goals—that is, pursuing the objectives of learning and mastering the task. This research also supported quite strongly the maladaptive characteristics associated with setting performance-avoidance goals—consciously attempting to avoid appearing unable or stupid. Findings concerning performance-approach goals—setting and pursuing the objective of surpassing others in achievement and appearing smart—generally point to positive outcomes such as high grades and positive affect, although these goals have been also associated with less positive outcomes such as surface learning strategies, disruptive behavior, and unwillingness to cooperate with peers. Research on mastery-avoidance goals—attempting not to forget what was learned or not miss opportunities to learn—is more scarce, with some findings more in line with those found for mastery-approach goals and others more in line with those found for performance-avoidance goals (Elliot, 1999, 2005; Pintrich, 2000, 2003).

However, Elliot and his colleagues also argue that achievement goals that are conceptualized as objectives or aims lack explanatory power on their own—one also needs to take account of the *reasons* behind the goals (Elliot, 1999, 2005; Elliot & Thrash, 2001). The reasons that can give rise to different goal setting and pursuit can be those that originally have been incorporated in the definition of achievement goal orientations, including development of competence that is oriented towards self-growth, and demonstration of competence that is oriented towards validation or self-worth. It is these reasons—elicited either by intrapsychic processes or by environmental triggers—that energize and guide the behavior. In turn, the aims are the psychological constructs that provide the more specific means for pursuing the reasons in particular contexts and situations. Thus, whereas Elliot and his colleagues distinguish between reasons and aims, they also contend that "in the process of regulating behavior in a given achievement setting, the reason and goal constructs essentially become intertwined" in a "dynamic integration" that they labeled "a goal complex" (Elliot, 2005; Elliot & Thrash, 2001, p. 148; Thrash & Elliot, 2001). These goal complexes are context-specific, and combine personal and contextual characteristics that elicit the reason for action and the goal of action. Hence,

> numerous goal complexes are possible in any given achievement setting, and each goal complex is likely to have a somewhat distinct predictive profile, even those possessing the same goal component. (p. 148)

Thus, similar to earlier definitions of achievement goal orientations, Elliot and his colleagues (Elliot, 2005; see also Sideridis & Mouratidis, 2007; Urdan & Mestas, 2006) see the explanatory power of achievement goal theory in the broader contextual processes that give rise to a dynamic meaning that integrates reasons, aims, and engagement. Unlike earlier definitions, Elliot's work contributed to specification of components involved in these integrated constructs. Still, what is missing from the literature is an understanding of the processes by which such contextual constructions are created, or in other words, the processes of *meaning-making*.

## Meaning-Making and Achievement Goal Orientations

Achievement goal theorists share the emphasis on the meaning of action in the achievement situation as the proximal construct explaining quality of engagement. However, in their individual research projects, each theorist emphasized different factors and processes as contributing to this meaning (Pintrich & Schunk, 2002). Some researchers emphasized the role of personality dispositions such as Need for Achievement and Fear of Failure (Elliot, 1997) or of personal theories of intelligence (Dweck, 1999; Molden & Dweck, 2000) as underlying the meaning that individuals construe for action in achievement situations. Other researchers emphasized the features of contexts as sending messages to students that elicit meanings of different types (Ames, 1992) and have pointed to certain educational practices as highlighting different purposes for engagement (e.g., Ames, 1992; Kaplan & Maehr, 1999; Maehr & Midgley, 1996; Meece, 1991). And other researchers pointed to situational characteristics (Nicholls, 1992), and to cultural processes (Maehr & Nicholls, 1980) as the important factors in the construction of these meanings.

Empirical research that employed different methods also supported the role of various processes in the eventual achievement goals or achievement goal orientation that participants adopted. Correlational research found that measures of certain dispositions are associated with endorsement of certain achievement goals (e.g., Elliot & Church, 1997); experimental research supports the role of environmental emphases in eliciting certain achievement goals more so than others (e.g., Barron & Harackiewicz, 2001; Elliott & Dweck, 1988; Elliot & Harackiewicz, 1996); and a few naturalistic studies supported the association between instructional practices and students' reports of their achievement goals (e.g., Elliot, McGregor, & Gable, 1999; Meece, 1991; Patrick et al., 2001; Turner et al., 2002).

Maehr's (1984; Kaplan & Maehr, 2002) model of achievement goal orientations is one among a few which attempt to depict the way the various environmental and personal factors integrate into the purpose of engagement (for others see DeShon & Gillespie, 2005; Elliot & Church, 1997). Maehr (1984) suggested that students' achievement goal orientations are constructed through the dynamic meaning-making process that integrates three processes: the perceived purpose of the situation, self-processes that are activated in the situation, and the action possibilities that are perceived as relevant in the situation. Maehr (1984) argued that cultural meanings as well as contextual and situational characteristics elicit constructions regarding the purpose of engagement in the situation. These messages integrate with salient identity processes and with self-processes that are triggered by the context and situation. And these highlight to the student the possible goals and actions that he or she could pursue in that situation (for an elaborated model see Kaplan & Maehr, 2002)

Whereas Maehr proposed his model during the 1980s, few studies attempted to investigate empirically how this meaning-making process actually takes place. This line of research is important in order to facilitate theoretical models of achievement motivation in context. It is even more important for informing interventions that aim at promoting the construction of certain meanings of achievement contexts and situations over others.

## The Present Study

The present study set out to investigate the ways by which students construct the meaning of an academic setting, their experiences in it, and the purpose of action in that setting. The perspective that guided the present study relies on the premise that the construction of the meaning of experiences is a fundamental human activity that guides cognition, emotion, and behavioral intentions (Kegan, 1982; Maehr, 1984; Weiner, 1986). Moreover, we assume that meaning of situations is to a large extent constructed by people through the stories that they tell themselves and others (Bering, 2003; Bruner, 1986, 1990; Sarbin, 1986; Shotter, 1997). These stories or narratives, while personal, are embedded in the cultural processes prevalent in the setting (Bruner, 1990), and arise from interpersonal interactions that take place in that setting (McCaslin & Good, 1996; Newman, Griffin, & Cole, 1989; Wertsch, 1991). The stories thus integrate socio-cultural, contextual, as well as personal characteristics and have the potential of highlighting salient issues and processes that are involved in the construction of meaning and purpose for action in a particular context (cf. Malpas, 2002). Utilizing a *contextualized* narrative approach—i.e., eliciting stories from different informants regarding a specific shared context—allowed us to employ students' own words and perspectives in order to capture the idiosyncrasies, complexity, and intricacies, as well as the potential commonalities in the interpretations of the same context by different individuals. Hence, the overall purpose of the present study was to explore the personal and contextual contents, and the cognitive and emotional strategies, that are involved in students' construction of meaning and purpose of engagement in a particular academic setting.

## METHOD

*Participants*

Participants were nine (3 men and 6 women, ages between 19 and 23) Jewish first year college students, majoring in Education[1], who studied in a mandatory Introduction to Educational Psychology course at the Department of Education in an Israeli University. Students were selected based on their responses to scales assessing Need for Achievement and Fear of Failure (Jackson, 1974), on which they had either a combination of high score on the former and low score on the latter, or the reverse. This was done in order to increase variability in personal approaches to achievement settings. Interviewers and researchers were blind to students' scores.

*The Context*

Introduction to Educational Psychology is a year-long mandatory course at the Department of Education that was designed to strongly emphasize mastery goals. The course includes several tasks that scaffold students' academic skills, culminating with a group project-based inquiry. Students are provided with the opportunity to resubmit their papers after receiving feedback. Whereas there are exams in the course, students are provided the opportunity to take a second term. Moreover, students are provided choice among questions within the exam and the questions in the exam are open-ended and are geared towards assessing deep understanding of naturalistic events. Students are allowed to use any material (e.g., text-book, notes) when taking the exam, as the explicit stated purpose of the exam is not memorization but application of the material that was learned in class to analysis of new situations. Throughout the course, the instructor and TAs provide intensive support to the students; explicitly emphasize the purpose of learning and understanding; and encourage dialogue concerning the purpose of activities and assignments.

*Procedure*

All students in the course were administered surveys at the beginning of the year that assessed their achievement needs. During the second semester, the students who were selected on the basis of their scores were

---

[1] Unlike the college system in the USA, Israeli students have to specify their major in their application to the university. Studying towards the major involves a program of study, with required courses already during the freshman year.

approached and invited to participate in a study about the experiences of students at the department of education. All the students were willing to participate. Students were interviewed in the middle of the second semester. Interviews were conducted individually by two research assistants who were trained for this task. Interviews took place at the university in a quiet room. Interviewers attempted to create a comfortable climate for the interview, and in fact, almost all the students commented that the experience was interesting and stimulating to them and that they learned things about themselves during the interview. The research assistants reported that they themselves were interested and enjoyed the interview experience. The research assistant explained the purpose of the interview to the participant, promised confidentiality, and asked for permission to record the interview. All interviews were recorded and later transcribed while removing identifying details.

A week before the interviews, teaching assistants in the course administered an activity in the course's discussion groups with instructions that primed either mastery goals or performance goals (an adaptation of Elliot & Harackiewicz, 1996 experimental manipulations). This was meant to create a focal situation, with known instructor intended motivational emphasis, about which students' meanings can be investigated. The instructions emphasizing mastery goals were:

> Following the feedback that we collected from students about the course, we designed our meeting today in order to promote students' deep understanding of the material. Our goal today is to focus on the parts of the material in which students felt they wanted to improve and to learn more deeply. At the end of the meeting, I'll administer an assignment that is similar to the one we give on the test. The goal of the assignment is to give you feedback on the things that you mastered and the things that you can still improve on.

The instructions emphasizing performance goals were:

> Following the feedback that we collected from students about the course, we designed our meeting today in order to see which students succeed and which ones have difficulties. Our goal today is to focus on students' abilities in the material. At the end of the meeting, I will administer an assignment that is similar to the one we give on the test. The goal of the assignment is to assess students' ability and to give you feedback regarding where you are relative to other students in the discussion group.

The assignment included a work-sheet with an assignment similar to the ones administered in the test. The assignment included a short vignette describing an educational event. Students had to answer two short questions that required the application of the theories learned in the semester (motivational theories) in order to understand the event. At the end of the assignment, students were asked to respond to a survey with scales assessing their perceived motivational emphasis in the assignment and their achievement goals orientations towards the assignment[2]. Students selected for interviews were divided between the two emphases. All interviews were conducted during the week after the focal activity.

### The Interview

The general approach guiding the interview was of narrative research (Josselson & Lieblich, 1993). However, the approach was adapted to suit the purpose of the present study. In general, the approach aims to elicit the interviewee's own story of his or her experiences. The interviewer engages in minimal intervention beyond indicating active listening, and encouraging the interviewee to elaborate on his or her story while using the interviewee's own terms and phrases. Probing questions asked participants to elaborate on an issue or event they mentioned and to provide concrete examples such as an actual occurrence they experienced for more general statements that they made (Rosenthal, 1993).

The study was presented to students as focusing on "the experiences of students' majoring in education." Initially, students were asked: "Please tell me about your experiences studying at the university this year." When, in the course of the interview, students mentioned the Department of Education, they were asked "Please tell me more about your experiences at the Department of Education." Similarly, when students mentioned the course Introduction to Educational Psychology, they were asked "Please tell me more about the course Introduction to Educational Psychology." This repeated when the interviewee mentioned the Discussion Groups, and at a convenient point in the interview, students were asked: "Please tell me about the last discussion group meeting you had with your TA." This question aimed at eliciting a description of the focal activity.

### Analysis

In general, the analysis followed the phenomenological approach, which views the whole interview as the ultimate unit-of-analysis (Ratner, 2002). The analysis aimed at identifying themes in the interview, as well as more specific components in each theme, that would then be integrated to create a more holistic description of the underlying framework organizing the narrative in the interview. However, in light of the nested nature of the set-

---

[2] Scales were adopted from the Patterns of Adaptive Learning Survey (Midgley et al., 2000). The data from these surveys were not used in the current study.

ting about which data was generated, the analysis also attended to different units-of-context in the interview: the university, the department, the course, and specific situations in the course.

The process of analysis followed several steps:

1.  Each interview was read through for the researcher to become familiar with the overall structure and nature of the student's narrative.

2.  The interview was read again, and divided into meaning-units, defined as segments of the narrative that concern a specific issue or event.

3.  In each meaning-unit, there was an attempt to identify a central anchor for meaning-making (e.g., instructor, peers, assignments) as well as to typify the meaning and the resultant purpose for action. Identification of purpose followed the definitions of goal orientations mentioned in the literature (e.g., mastery, performance, social, extrinsic, work-avoidance), but left open the possibility of identifying new, yet unmentioned purposes. Following Ames (1992) and Maehr (1984), identification of meaning and purpose involved specifying perceptions, beliefs, emotions, and behaviors.

4.  In each meaning-unit, there was an attempt to identify the cognitive and emotional strategies (i.e., explanations, justifications) that the participant used in order to arrive at the meaning and purpose that were constructed.

5.  Finally, there was an attempt to integrate themes and meanings into a general description that characterizes the narrative in terms of the personal, contextual, and situational contents and processes that were involved in meaning-making.

Interviews were analyzed by two of the authors. Each interview was analyzed independently by the two researchers and then analyses were compared. In case of disagreement, a final decision was made following discussion.

## RESULTS

The findings from the analysis of the nine interviews supported Maehr's (1984; Kaplan & Maehr, 2002) integrative meaning-making model. The findings pointed very clearly to the role and dynamic integration of cultural, developmental, personal, contextual, and situational factors in the meaning-making of action at the different units-of-analysis of the educational context, and to the manifestation of these factors in participants' perceived purpose of contexts and situations, identity issues and self-processes, and perceived action possibilities. However, as will be demonstrated later, the salience of different factors varied in different situations and for different participants. This finding indicated that in any particular shared setting, different students may construct different meanings that are based, primarily, on different tangible and psychological processes (cf. Pintrich, 2003).

We present and discuss the findings in several parts. First, we present the case-analysis of two interviews, each demonstrating in a different manner the more general theoretical processes identified in all of the interviews. Second, we summarize and discuss the general findings from the analysis of all of the interviews and their theoretical implications. This summary and discussion is presented along four main themes that emerged from the interviews as central in the integrative process of meaning-making of academic engagement: self and identity, contextual characteristics, situational characteristics, and meaning-making strategies. We conclude by noting the implications of these findings to motivational theory, research, and practice.

## CASE STUDIES

The following section presents two case studies out of the nine cases that were analyzed. The purpose is to provide a concrete demonstration of the processes that were identified among all of the participants. The two cases were selected as they represent these general processes while highlighting the individual differences and idiosyncrasies that combine to result with the meaning of engagement in learning.

*Mor*

Mor is a 21-year-old woman, studying for a double major in Education and Hebrew Literature. The Department of Education was her primary interest and her first choice.

### Choosing to Study Education

At the beginning of the interview, Mor described her choice to study education as a natural continuation of previous experiences and choices. For her, learning and "*doing*" education is a "*way of life.*" During her adolescence in a small agricultural community in the south of Israel, Mor was a counselor in a youth movement, an experience that was very influential to her self-definition. Later, during her military service[3], Mor was an infantry

---

3 In Israel, all Jewish citizens are required to enlist in mandatory military service, which they commonly do following high-school. The mandatory service is three years for men and two years for women.

trainer and instructor. She spoke about educating others with much appreciation expressing high personal relevance and using terms that suggested that she was intrinsically motivated towards the domain:

> I know that it is..simply..I love it. You feel satisfaction. There's nothing like... also to teach people, like as an army trainer I instructed in material so it's simply a pleasure, like...I really love it...to learn, to enrich, you learn like so much things through others.

So, when the time came to choose her major at the university, education was the obvious choice—"There was nothing else that interested me..."—indicating a strong identity commitment (Bosma, 1992).

However, along the interview, Mor admitted that she engaged in deliberations and explorations concerning this choice (cf. Grotevant, 1987; Super, Savickas, & Super, 1996). She also mentioned possible alternatives such as Behavioral Sciences (Psychology), which were of great interest to her but that she did not pursue. Indeed, the interview revealed a significant personal process that was very influential in affecting Mor's self-concept in relation to the domain of education and the humanities more generally—a relation that involved some strife and a sense of inferiority.

Mor grew up as one of three sisters and three older bothers. One of these sisters, Zohar, became a central reference point for Mor's self-definition and self-concept. This was apparent in Mor's description of her family life, her personality attributes, and her future professional planning. According to Mor, Zohar is an ambitious individual, and an excellent student with a talent for the math subjects. Mor constructed her own attributes in comparison: as oriented towards the humanities, and always as second best. According to Mor, she and Zohar are "opposites." Mor contended that her sister is successful because she has ambitions. In comparison, Mor stated that she prefers to take on things she knows she can cope with and are not too stressful: "Somehow it is set in me...if it is too difficult then I don't do it..." Mor depicted Zohar in idealistic terms and described herself in comparison as inferior: "I look at her and I say to myself 'I wish I could'...but I give up;" "I have a bad attitude...I don't push myself."

These expressions suggest the possibility of Fear of Failure (Atkinson, 1957) and of a helpless pattern of coping (Dweck & Leggett, 1988). Indeed, Mor construed her attributes as very stable and as resulting from her parents' differential treatment of their daughters. According to Mor, their parents expected Zohar to be accomplished and therefore she developed ambitions. In comparison, the parents did not expect or pushed Mor to succeed, and therefore she is not achievement oriented. All this was happening in "a family of academics. If you don't go to the university it says that you are not smart and not successful." Thus, Mor reported that she chose to major in Education because she perceived the major in Behavioral Sciences to be too difficult. She construed making the "second best" choice of Education over Behavioral Sciences as a part of a pattern related to her experiences growing up with Zohar: "We were always the three that would get the medals...and, Zohar would get the gold, and I the silver, but, and again it didn't bother me, but I guess I got used to being second place..."

Mor's focus on her sister Zohar as the reference for her own self-concept is striking in light of the practical absence of her other siblings in her narrative. Her brothers—all successful academics—were mentioned in one sentence only, and her younger sister—the third in the trio, the one who supposedly gets the bronze medal—was mentioned only in passing, without a name. The fact that this sister was not a reference point and did not play any meaningful role in the narrative is particularly important because, as Mor reported in response to an explicit question by the interviewer, this sister was also studying at the university, and she was majoring in...education! Thus, Mor was clearly highly selective in the reference points she employed for constructing her self-concept, and was guided by long-term developmental identifications and social comparisons that seemed to manifest in a predisposition to upward comparisons, Fear of Failure, and helpless coping.

Both Fear of Failure and helpless coping have been associated in achievement goal theory with the adoption of performance goals (Dweck & Leggett, 1988; Elliot & Church, 1997). And, as is described later on, Mor indeed reported on the need to cope with a sense of threat to her self-worth and with avoidant thoughts and emotions, particularly in evaluative situations. However, this was not Mor's primary motivational orientation in education. While Mor considered Education as only second best to Behavioral Sciences, it was not a bad choice. In fact, through the reflective and deliberative process that she went through in choosing her major (cf. Berzonsky, 1992), Mor managed to integrate her interest in psychology and her choice of education: while she did not aim at an M.A. in School Psychology, because that too was perceived to be "aiming too high" (and she did not want to become a teacher, because that would be "aiming too low"), she was considering the M.A. degree and profession of School Counseling, to which she perceived she had good chances to be admitted: "...from the beginning I choose for myself a challenge that I know I'll succeed in." This exploratory process (Flum & Kaplan, 2006), which highlights the way by which self-processes and context integrate to affect perceived action possibilities (Maehr, 1984), seems to have led Mor to develop a rather strong identification with and commitment to the domains of education and School Counseling. This identification manifested in the adoption of a mastery goal orientation and mastery aims in the domain of educational psychology—an orientation that provided Mor with resources for coping with threatening situations, as will be elaborated on later.

*The Department of Education*

While the analysis of the interview suggested that the domain of education was very meaningful to Mor's identity; interestingly, the Department of Education was not. In describing her experiences in the Department, Mor referred to individuals rather than to the collective entity of the department. Her response to a direct question about her experiences with the "students who study education," was that "each one in the department has their own friends." Mor did not perceive that grouping among the students was a significant issue; and overall, the analysis suggested that the individuals were more meaningful to her than the social identity of the department.

This lack of interest in the level of the department may seem peculiar considering that the department is the entity that would grant Mor her major. However, despite that fact, and in congruence with her disinterest in the students of the department as a group, Mor stated that she was also not concerned with her grades at the departmental level: "I'm not really concerned about my grades…even if I will not be an honors student…there isn't any dream that will be shattered." Clearly, this may be a defensive statement. It may also be an indication of a focus on meaningful learning rather than on grades—or a combination of the two. An insight may be gained from a comparison of this nonchalant attitude towards grades at the department level with the keen interest in grades in the domain in which Mor had clear vested stakes: educational psychology.

*Introduction to Educational Psychology*

According to Mor, her experiences in the course Introduction to Educational Psychology were very positive. This, she suggested, was due to her interest in the domain and to the characteristics of the course:

> Educational psychology is really fascinating. I very, very much enjoy the lessons with [the instructor], he teaches in an excellent way and the material is also very relevant, it's very…it touches on things that are interesting to you, that you want to know, about child development, how you understand, what you should teach in a way that..or talk to people so that they understand you, match their schemas and all that stuff, it's things that…and now the motivation…

Mor elaborated on her experiences and provided detailed and complex descriptions of her views on the course that spanned the course's contents, the instruction methods, the teaching staff, and the methods of evaluation. While she stated that she was familiar with much of the material taught in the course, she also emphasized the added value she got in the course— tools for applying the material for understanding herself, others, and the educational "field": "…these are things that in general you know, but you didn't have the tools to use them. Certain terms, to understand them and now it's all like coming together. I don't feel like my eyes were opened, but things that I had are now much clearer." Such statements seem to be clear indication for the mastery goal orientation that Mor adopted towards learning in the course. Her description of the instruction method in the course suggests that she found it interesting, diverse, and as matched to the students' interests and level of knowledge. She greatly esteemed the teaching staff for applying in the course the educational approach and theories that were taught. She emphasized the willingness of the teaching staff to listen to students' comments and to improve the course accordingly. She also noted her perception that the teaching staff was "cohesive"—that there were good relations among the instructor and TAs—and that this gave the students a good feeling. In addition, Mor highlighted the young age of the TAs as a factor that contributed to the positive interaction with the students. In her view, this characteristic of the TAs positively affected the way the material was taught since the TAs could understand the way the students related to the material. And especially, Mor pointed to the instructor's mastery of the material as a factor that contributed to her sense of security and competence.

These characteristics of the course and their contribution to students' positive experiences and interest in the content emerged in one way or another in all of the interviews. Their appearance supports the important role of the academic context in the construction of meaning and its resultant motivation. They also support the theoretical relations among instructional methods that emphasize mastery goals orientation and students' personal mastery goals orientation (Ames, 1992; Kaplan et al., 2002). Interestingly, in addition they point to the inseparable nature of an environmental mastery goals structure and the social relations among the teachers and the students (cf. Patrick, 2004; Patrick et al., 2007).

For Mor, these contextual course characteristics integrated well with her identity commitments and her personal dispositions that oriented her towards developing competencies in educational psychology. Hence, it could be argued that for Mor, the mastery goals orientation in educational psychology is the result of a fit between her identity commitments and the contextual emphasis on mastery goals. However, a deeper analysis of the theme of the course and the factors that contributed to Mor's positive experiences reveal an additional layer: the course characteristics provided a fit not only to her identity commitments but also to other dispositional characteristics that were unrelated to her orientation towards the material. For example, in her general self-description, Mor noted that she needs a guiding hand, and someone who would believe in her and encourage her to make progress: "perhaps if there was someone by me that...was...like guiding then maybe I would have made it..." The instructional structure of the course, which included very close guidance and tasks that increase in level of difficulty while building on previously developed skills, seemed to have been exactly what Mor needed:

Ehhh, I didn't care and..I don't know, I just need this encouragement...because I didn't have someone to guide me in how to improve, so I got lost. That is, I didn't know how and I didn't prepare to sit and work very, very hard and to summarize and summarize and at the end to reach the same outcome, ehhh.. so, the fact that they gave us these assignments, it really encouraged me.

In addition, Mor indicated that she found it hard to keep her concentration in very big courses where she feels a threat to her sense of ability relative to others in the group. Therefore, she was very pleased to belong to a smaller discussion group, to engage in cooperative learning activities, and to receive personal feedback in addition to a grade—course characteristics that matched her personal needs, reduced her anxieties, and allowed her to pursue her mastery aims.

In summary, the analysis suggested that the course Introduction to Educational Psychology involved contents that related to domains in Mor's identity, and hence provided a venue for pursuing these commitments. The course's characteristics supported Mor's mastery goal orientation with practices that encouraged the development of competence. Importantly, the course also allowed contexts that reduced personal anxieties and situations that might have triggered other personal dispositions that would have interfered with Mor's mastery goals orientation, thus allowing her the safe context within which to focus on learning. However, these other personality dispositions were not always dormant. The interview indicated that they indeed were triggered and had to be reckoned with in specific situations in the course.

### *Specific Situations in the Course Introduction to Educational Psychology*

The analysis of meaning units in Mor's interview that concerned specific situations provided insight into the interplay of dispositional, contextual, and situational characteristics in meaning-making. One such situation involved coping with a very low grade on the first assignment that Mor submitted in the course. The situation of receiving a low grade was very difficult for Mor as it triggered her Fear of Failure and manifested in thoughts representative of performance-avoidance goals. Mor described this experience as "humiliating," "frustrating," leading to a "drop in motivation," and as "a moment of almost breaking down" which is "like a slap on the face that makes you doubt yourself." On the one hand, Mor acknowledged that she had experiences to rely on to assert her ability. On the other hand, she admitted that she was very much bothered by the thought that her TA will think that she was "worthless." Her words in describing this event depicted a conception of ability as stable and as inversely related to effort—a conception characteristic of a performance goals orientation (Nicholls, 1984). Her attempt to negotiate this situated experience involved referring back to Zohar, her sister and reference for self-concept:

> Zohar tells me all the time that if I decide to do something, I'll succeed, and… maybe this is why I… like I am reluctant to say that if I want something and I don't succeed then it's like something is wrong with me, so, like, Ok, I didn't succeed because I didn't put effort, like…because, let's say with this paper, or this test, it was very difficult because you say, wow, I invested so much and you don't succeed so…I'm not built for these things. Zohar, say, will fall and get up and succeed again. I'll just give up and that's it. It's a matter of personality I guess.

Thus, the specific negative feedback in the evaluative situation overrode Mor's general mastery goals orientation to trigger a meaning of performance-avoidance goals orientation. This was despite the fact that Mor and the other students in the course received the opportunity to correct the paper based on the TAs' feedback and resubmit it. Indeed, it was less the grade itself that was her concern than the TA's perceptions of her ability and her "worthiness." This incongruence between her general perception of her engagement and her success in the course and the specific experience of failure initiated a process of causal explanation, coping, and exploration of the meaning of this experience and of her engagement:

> …and we invested, we sat a lot, put a lot of thought into the idea.. maybe the phrasing, I don't know what happened, but somehow we didn't write an introduction, and it's true, you should lower the grade, but to give a person like 46, it's simply like saying 'stupid…';…there really were things we needed to correct, it's legitimate, but to give a grade like this… and we sat and corrected and we got 80, but also the feeling she gave us that she doesn't…we did have things to rely on that we're not stupid, someone else would have given up and say, OK…but, ehh..maybe because it is her…I never got a grade like this, it was a grade I didn't even know how to cope with. But, that's it. It didn't break us completely, we're still here (laughing).

The meaning of this situated experience reflected on Mor's more general meaning of engagement in the course and led to explicit deliberations and exploration that involved an interplay between her identity commitments, personality dispositions, and the contextual characteristics of the course. This was clearly manifested in a later decision that Mor had to make in relation to her TA. In the transition between semesters, due to possible changes in students' schedules, the students have the opportunity to switch discussion groups and, hence, TAs. In her interview, Mor described a dilemma concerning switching to a different TA—a dilemma she deliberated with her friends who attended the same discussion group and who collaborated with her on assignments. Mor reported that she and her friends perceived the TA as a great instructor, who cares a lot about the quality of the students' learning, but also as a harsh grader. This perception was constructed through comparisons with other TAs: "…others [students] get good grades and we took someone who is very strict, and there are TAs who are less strict and more strict, and we fell on the more strict…" The conversation among the friends that Mor described, depicts a clear conflict and negotiation between different achievement goals or aims—mastery goals and extrinsic goals—in which arguments were made for both sides. This conversation demonstrates an explicit socially-shared exploration and negotiation of the meaning of engagement in the course. For Mor, this dilemma was clearly tied to her identity:

> I really had a conflict. On the one hand I say that the grade is important but because I study education, it is really important to me to study here, I come here really to learn the material and improve and understand, so, she [the TA] is stricter and my grades are harmed but I learn more, really. I mean, if she wouldn't have commented on it, then I wouldn't have known.

The end result of this negotiation was that while her friends switched to a different TA for the second semester, Mor chose to stay with her TA from the first semester. This seems to be an indication of the interplay of different personal and contextual processes that led to a situational difference between Mor and her friends' engagement priorities—a situational meaning-making that has consequences for the broader meaning of engagement in the course. For Mor, the decision seems to have stemmed from prioritizing her development and learning under this TA over that of the grade—a dominance of mastery goals orientation. Of course, it may also be that Mor's social relations with the TA played a role in her decision—a type of social goal. More generally, what is depicted is an exploratory process in which identity and self-processes, the perceived purposes of engagement in the context, and the action possibilities in the situation were negotiated and integrated to result with meaning, orientation, and commitment to action.

### The Focal Activity

Mor's focal activity included a mastery goals manipulation. Not surprisingly, Mor, who remembered very well the TA's instructions, interpreted the assignment along her general perception of the course as emphasizing mastery goals: a way for the teaching staff to evaluate themselves and improve the course.

### Summary

The analysis of Mor's interview highlighted a process of meaning-making that relies heavily on identity issues and personal dispositions that seemed to have developed primarily in the family context, and which involved multiple dispositional goal orientations: a general tendency towards performance goals, particularly performance-avoidance goals, with a strong orientation towards mastery goals orientation in the domains of education and psychology. This dispositional foundation integrated with the mastery goal structure in the course Introduction to Educational Psychology and with a fit between specific contextual and dispositional characteristics to result with the construction of a meaning of the course as a context for developing competencies and professional aspirations that correspond to central identity and self-concept domains. In addition, however, it was apparent how specific situations in the course that highlighted the risk of demonstrating low ability triggered this chronic dispositional tendency. Importantly, the conflict between the performance-avoidance goal orientation in the specific situation and the general mastery goal orientation in the course elicited explicit attempts at resolution and decision-making. These attempts involved intrapersonal dialogue as well as interpersonal exploration with friends. Mor's mastery goal orientation seemed to have provided her with cognitive and emotional resources that she employed in overcoming her performance-avoidance tendencies, and in negotiating action possibilities that allowed her to continue and pursue learning in the course.

### Yevgeny

Yevgeny is a 23-year-old man who immigrated to Israel as a child from Russia with his family. At the time of the interview, Yevgeny was a freshman at the university studying towards a double major in Hebrew Language and Education.

#### Choosing to Study Education

For Yevgeny, majoring in Education was a default choice. His main focus at the university was the domain of Hebrew language, for which Yevgeny had very high motivation. But, Israeli freshmen who study humanities or social sciences have to choose a second major:

> …that is, you need to have 120 credits, right? And you need to find another department. I wasn't enthusiastic about History. Bible studies, somehow I didn't dare to go. So, what was left was the Department of Education. I could have done Literature but it's very difficult, a lot to read, I wouldn't have stood the pressure. So, the last option that was left was Education, so OK…For me, Education simply helps to finish my B.A.

This disdain for the domain of education is strongly contrasted with Yevgeny's high identification with the Hebrew language studies, and with his commitment to pursue a career in that domain as…a teacher!

Similar to Mor, Yevgeny's choice of a major involved deliberations of action possibilities that were framed by self and identity issues. However, unlike Mor's criteria for evaluating action possibilities, which were mainly her perceived outcome expectancies in different domains and her Fear of Failure, Yevgeny's criteria were mainly the utility of the domain to a future career and the stereotypic expectations from his ethnic group—immigrants from Russia. Thus, for example, majoring in Bible Studies was not a real option for Yevgeny:

> ...my ambition was always to take something that would be useful...and I said 'Bible', since as long as this is a Jewish country, the subject of Bible will not disappear. But, it was like 'Bible and Russian?' How would that work out? Something limits you...It's customary that Russians don't go to study Bible, it's not for them, so I didn't go.

Interestingly, despite the fact that the domain of Hebrew language is hardly an expected domain for immigrants, other self-processes intervened to affect Yevgeny's choice of this domain as his major—primarily, his perceived ability and identification with the domain:

> ...there are social norms. Even still the Department of Hebrew Language, they say, is a bit strange [for a Russian]. They say 'a Russian goes to be a Hebrew teacher and teach Israelis?' But the minute you show enthusiasm and great desire, then you can go all the way, and I always knew well the Hebrew language grammar.

Yevgeny's commitment and motivation for learning and teaching the Hebrew language was established through a lengthy process of exploration that involved his high perceived ability in the domain—boosted by his high grades in the Hebrew language matriculation exam—and experiences in teaching in a Hebrew language school for new immigrant children (Ulpan). Importantly, his decision to pursue a major in Hebrew language and a career as a Hebrew teacher was influenced by encouragement and support from his high-school teacher who convinced him to take a position as an instructor in Ulpan, and by his successful teaching experiences at the Ulpan:

> My homeroom teacher recognized my advantage in conducting a dialogue in the group and my ability to explain...and somehow she suggested that I do this [teaching in Ulpan]...and of course [my decision to pursue this as a career] didn't happen after the first year, maybe the second year, when I saw the success. And really, the last year in the Ulpan—always I remember the experiences, the jokes, this atmosphere...there's simply nothing, nothing...—and in addition, the principal tells me, "listen, take half the course-load at the university and continue to teach here...

Yevgeny reported explicitly on the exploratory processed he engaged in, which primarily revolved around career goals, and which led to his commitment to teaching:

> ...actually, I had worries until the last minute: wow, where am I going? Who? What? Maybe continue to a military career...but the minute I entered teaching, I closed all the doors and said 'this is the only thing I'm going for.'"

Yevgeny's commitment was clearly deep: "I sometimes dream dreams that I teach."

Yevgeny's identity formation processes figured into his decision to pursue a career as a Hebrew language teacher even further when he imagined his contribution to society through helping the absorption of new immigrants to Israel. In his narrative, Yevgeny highlighted an initiative he took while teaching in the Ulpan to conduct activities with the parents of the immigrant children that would facilitate their familiarity with the Hebrew language and the Israeli culture. Yevgeny's description of his role as a Hebrew language teacher was clearly value-laden and ideological:

> ...So after the second activity I continued to teach and tried to instill in them things beyond the language rules, let's say a bit of the culture if possible...It was really fun. We used to laugh about experiences in Russia, food, weather... they were showing me pictures of Russia, but all the time I encouraged them, telling them that there is no other country. This is the country of the Jews... So, a bit of Zionism.

Yevgeny's description of his engagement in learning and teaching the Hebrew language clearly indicates his meaningful engagement and mastery goals orientation for the domain: "I just got really into it, I got really excited and I invested tons..." But, the interview clearly pointed to additional important motivations that guided Yevgeny's meaning-making of his engagement at the university. Yevgeny was very aware of the need to secure an economic future, an orientation that was likely also related to his immigrant background: "Because you need something that you can use...of course, you want to take care of your good future, a good salary, good work conditions." Hence, his choice of domains of study at the university was also evaluated along extrinsic considerations – "what it will give me." Thus, for example, his choice to pursue a career as a Hebrew language teacher followed exploration of teachers' work benefits: "I checked the issue of salary. You can make a living; and what's important for me in this country and in my future – whoever works in a governmental job is secure and has all the conditions. What's important is tenure." This utilitarian perspective, which was integrated well with Yevgeny's ideology and perceived ability in the domain of Hebrew language, also guided him to construe the domain of education as a default and as an easy way to complete his B.A.

### The Department of Education

Throughout the interview, Yevgeny's meaning-making of his experiences and engagement in the Department of Education was based on comparisons with the Department of Hebrew Language:

> I study at the Department of Hebrew Language out of intrinsic motivation, to know the material in-depth. In contrast, if you ask me how I study at the Department of Education—it's extrinsic. It's really important to me to get more than 85 for admission to MA. But is it really really, like what's called internalizing the material all through? then no."

Surprisingly, Yevgeny perceived the domain of education as theoretical and impractical and therefore as irrelevant to his professional plans for a teaching career. Hence, studying education only served the extrinsic goals of completing the BA with high enough grades to be admitted to MA programs. Going over the courses that he was taking at the Department of Education, Yevgeny made this irrelevance and his ultimate motivation quite clear: "You can do arm-chair philosophy for years and years, but it gives you nothing. Statistics? I don't like math that much. English? 85...not that I don't have my ambitions. My ambitions are extrinsic, grades, I want to see the 9 and not the 8." This orientation to grades also manifested in Yevgeny's motivation towards his studies of Hebrew language. But, again, the domains were compared in the process of fine-tuning the purpose in courses at the Department of Education. This was apparent, for example, when Yevgeny considered the meaning of possibly getting a low grade in Education courses: "...but inside, it won't hurt me like it would if I get it in the Department of Hebrew language...the Department of Hebrew language it's like...like, if it was philosophy, I told you, I get 85 and I say 'thank God'."

Yevgeny entered his studies at the Department of Education expecting, and finding at least initially, experiences that were irrelevant to his identity and to his professional goals. However, this orientation changed slightly, as was apparent when he moved to talk about the course Introduction to Educational Psychology.

### Introduction to Educational Psychology: The Interplay of Context and Specific Situations

Yevgeny's experiences and meaning-making of his engagement in the course Introduction to Educational Psychology went through a certain transformation along the few months he has been taking the course. Similar to his approach towards the other courses in the Department of Education, Yevgeny started the course Introduction to Educational Psychology with the goal of getting high grades, but with no interest and no perceived relevance to his professional goals. However, several experiences in specific situations seemed to have triggered self- and identity-processes that changed the meaning of engagement in the course for Yevgeny.

One domain that seemed to have affected Yevgeny's meaning of engagement in the course was experiences of high achievement. These experiences boosted Yevgeny's extrinsic motivation and even triggered self-worth contingencies that seemed to have led to performance goals:

> ...that is, I got the highest grade, so now I sometimes think that if I get less than 90 than my standard is going to go down. So now I need a 95. Once you're hooked, that's it. They call it primacy halo effect. Once you are perceived in a certain way, you need to keep it up, you go back to the expectations, what others expect of you.

It was clear also that these meanings of high achievement experiences to Yevgeny's self-worth were not independent of his ethnic identity:

> ...and then when I get to the long line of those who failed, with their 30s and 40s, and then suddenly this student, joking or out of jealousy, one can't know, is like 'look who got 90 and it wasn't enough for him.' And then I hear from the other side one going 'how did this Russian get more than us.' I guess he just wasn't thinking. It's not important.

The high grades that Yevgeny got raised the stakes of achieving in this course for him. It was not only the extrinsic utilitarian motivation anymore; rather, now it was also self-worth contingencies on intrapersonal, interpersonal, and intergroup comparative grade standards (Crocker & Wolfe, 2001; Kaplan, 2004; Nicholls, 1990)—arguably, a performance goals orientation and various forms of performance-approach and avoidance aims.

A second domain of experiences that seemed to have changed Yevgeny's meaning for engagement in the course were based on unexpected experiences of self-relevance in the course's assignments. This sense of relevance appeared to be triggered by an insight that Yevgeny had that he was experiencing unintentional meaningful learning and growth: "...psychology, it gives you a bit. In the assignments, I noticed, it expands your views and raises your, ahhh...you suddenly jump up a level, you go up in your thinking, still, you go through this process—how do you say maturity or maturity[4]? You grow-up, your views." These learning experiences may seem to be characterized by a mastery goal orientation. However, rather than being oriented towards deep and complex learning of the material itself, they may be more accurately described as oriented towards using the material to explore and learn about oneself and the kind of person one wants to be—an "exploratory" orientation (Flum & Kaplan, 2006):

> And I remember, [the instructor] spoke about the motivation of demonstrating your ability relative to others and how it shows. And then, one of the characteristics, I remember, when a person wants to demonstrate his own high ability, he may even try to harm the success of others, because he wants to be first, and it's important to him that others don't get to his level. And then suddenly, I started to think, why is it important to me to be first? Wait a minute, did it really happen to me that it was important that others get less than me? If I want to be the first, is it also important to me that others are less than me? And then I think, it relates to philosophy, it's not moral..."

Yevgeny's employment of the material in the course for exploring the self (Flum & Kaplan, 2006) did not stop at self-knowledge; it also concerned his teaching behavior:

> ...and many recommendations, and what [the instructor] teaches I apply in my PERACH.[5] Like self-efficacy, to show him [the tutee] that he is sometimes smarter than I am, like 'I don't know, you tell me.' Exchanging roles, and you

---

[4] Two different pronunciations.

[5] A scholarship program in Israeli universities in which college students tutor an elementary or a secondary-school student.

see him smiling, like 'what is this student asking me?'…psychology does help with application, and let's say that when I study psychology there are certain things, ahhh, not that when I taught I made mistakes, but it could be that I would change a few things, maybe behavior…

Thus, in a gradual process that seemed to have started unintentionally, the course characteristics, and specific situations in the course, integrated with Yevgeny's self and identity processes to modify his initial construction of meaning and extrinsic purpose of engagement in the course towards a meaning that combined the contingency of his self-worth on high achievement in the course with an orientation towards expanding views and perspectives and employing the material for exploring self-knowledge and action—even in teaching!

And yet, despite this change in meaning, emerging relevance, and more meaningful purposes for engagement, Yevgeny still construed the course as embedded in the Department of Education, as distinct from the Department of Hebrew Language, as not so relevant to his future professional goals, and, therefore, as requiring less investment:

> I told you, and I hope that [the lecturer] doesn't hear me, that I loath philosophy. Statistics, let's say so so. And really, psychology is an interesting domain, but not for going too deep. I don't see myself as if I'm going to study psychology. It's interesting; opens your views, something like, let's say a bit of your perspective changes, and quite a lot of implications. And what [the lecturer] teachers I apply in my PERACH, so yes, it makes a contribution. I won't say that the Department of Education is only a burden and that it isn't worth anything, but only from a certain perspective. My main goal is still to be a Hebrew language teacher.

### The Discussion Group and the Focal Activity

In describing his experiences in the discussion group, Yevgeny again expressed his exploratory orientation—his engagement with the material for self-understanding:

> …and every time you bump into something in the material, you start projecting it on yourself..you simply relate the theory to yours' and others' behavior and you actually relate it to your life.

This also came up when Yevgeny was asked about "the last meeting of the discussion group"—the focal activity. Yevgeny did not recall the TA's instructions. Instead, Yevgeny focused on the surveys that were administered as part of the manipulation-check. The motivational items in these surveys seemed to have triggered in Yevgeny an exploratory process about his own motivation in the course:

> She gave us surveys, and I always remember this question, there is a range of one to five, how important is it to you that others don't think that you are stupid. And I'm always there in the middle, I marked three, because it is im-

portant, but not...because if I put five then I show that what's important to me is to be perceived as good and that's it, no intrinsic motivation; the main thing is that they know that I'm smart. On the other hand, I can't completely ignore the others' eye. How will they say what they think about you? So I always pay attention to this question, and it can repeat itself like three times.

Similar to Mor, this exploratory, self-reflective, internal debate is part of the meaning-making process that was triggered by the situated activity, but seemed to have corresponded with a larger exploratory process that was triggered by the assignments and the content in the course as a whole. It is through these exploratory processes, which involve the integration of identity contents, self-processes, contextual characteristics and the situated activity, that Yevgeny examined the meaning of his engagement in the activity, in the course as a whole, and in academics more broadly. In the current situation, the deliberations highlighted an apparent conflict of values that Yevgeny struggled with: the worthiness of intrinsic versus extrinsic types of motivation. It is such explicit explorations that hold the potential for the transformation of meaning and purpose of engagement in learning activities (Flum & Kaplan, 2006; Kaplan & Maehr, 2002; Nicholls, 1989).

### Summary

The analysis of Yevgeny's interview highlights a meaning-making process that integrates identity issues, self-processes, contextual characteristics and situations. The analysis suggests quite clearly that Yevgeny's ethnic identification as an immigrant from Russia, the socio-cultural stereotypes about this group, the intergroup relations with the Israeli-born students, and other related self-issues such as his strong extrinsic orientation and the contingency of his self-worth on high achievement play a framing role in the meaning he constructed for engagement in different academic domains. It was also clear that contextual characteristics and situational experiences integrated with these identity processes to guide perceptions of action possibilities that defined Yevgeny's purpose for engagement. However, as important are the findings that context and situations can have the power to modify initial, strongly held, meaning and purpose of engagement. In a way that parallels Mor's experience, Yevgeny's experience also highlights that contexts and situations whose characteristics match identity issues and dispositional characteristic seem to boost that type of dispositional motivation. For Yevgeny this manifested in two quite different ways. First, his dispositions to extrinsic and performance goals orientations were matched by course characteristics that involved grades and allowed social comparison among students. It is noteworthy that it was extrinsic-oriented Yevgeny who meaningfully attended to these course characteristics whereas mastery-oriented

Mor did not. Second, the course assignments afforded the opportunity and triggered and encouraged Yevgeny to engage in exploration of the self. This exploration seems to be somewhat different from the classic definition of mastery goals, which focuses on mastering the material. In comparison, Yevgeny's focus was on employing the material to explore the self (Flum & Kaplan, 2006). Again, similar to Mor, it is in situations of incongruence or a sense of personal or moral dilemma that the exploratory process is triggered. Clearly, for Yevgeny this constituted a different purpose of engagement in the course than his initial extrinsic orientation and goals.

## SUMMARY OF FINDINGS

*Self-Processes of University Students: The Developmental "Bedrock"
of Identity Formation*

The analysis of the interviews suggested that among all of the participants, the meaning-making process of action in the academic context was framed by the developmental task of identity formation and career development (Erikson, 1968). Throughout the interviews, all participants reported engaging in reflection on the development of who they are, who they want to be, and how studying at the university, the department, and the course, was related to these processes (cf. Kroger, 1992; Marcia, 1980). Among all of the participants, the choice of studying at the Department of Education involved some type of exploration: deliberations, consideration of alternatives, and reflection on the personal values and attributes that were perceived to be a fit or a mismatch with perceptions of a career in education (cf. Super et al., 1996). For some of the participants, the choice of studying education actualized commitments that were made in prior years, whereas for others it was a temporary commitment that followed an on-going exploration of potential careers. Importantly, the manifestations of identity formation and career development processes incorporated cultural values, norms, and beliefs (Côté & Levine, 1988). In the examples above, this could be clearly noted in the role that Yevgeny's conception of his ethnicity and its stereotypes and Mor's notions of careers in psychology, counseling, and teaching played in their exploration of careers and domains of study. Societal and group's notions of the status of particular careers in education and beliefs about their value to society and to the self were manifested in the narratives of all of the participants.

However, in line with the identity formation and career development literature, while all participants were concerned with identity and career development, each participant approached these domains with a different orientation or identity style (cf. Berzonsky, 1992), and was preoccupied with different identity issues. This could be clearly noticed in the differences between the ways Mor and Yevgeny approached the domains of education and of educational psychology. Individual differences in identity orientation and issues could be traced in the narratives to earlier experiences in the family, with friends, at school, and in other settings (e.g., military service). For some participants, such experiences also involved immigration, sickness, and failure. These different personal "baggage" (Maehr, 1984) manifested in different frames of engagement in studying education, educational psychology, and even in specific tasks in the course—frames that included different perceptions, emotions, and motivation. For example, as part of their identity and career exploration, some of the participants (such as Mor) saw education as a primary domain in their future career, while others viewed it as secondary or as almost irrelevant (like Yevgeny). Some approached their studies in the Department of Education and the course Introduction to Educational Psychology with a primary commitment to acquire applicable knowledge and skills (Mor and, to some degree, Yevgeny), while others viewed their engagement in these academic contexts more along purposes such as broadening horizons and learning about oneself. Moreover, different initial commitments that few of the participants already made to specific careers in education (e.g., teacher, counselor, psychologist) provided different frames for the meaning of engagement in the course and even in specific academic tasks within the course (e.g., the perceived value of theory-focused versus application-focused course assignments).

Thus, an important conclusion is that self-processes that are based in students' developmental stage (Erikson, 1959), as well as their identity-formation style (cf. Berzonsky, 1992), identity commitments (cf. Bosma, 1992), and self-worth contingencies (cf. Crocker & Wolfe, 2001) are likely to provide important foundations or frames for their meaning-making of purpose and value of engagement in a certain academic context, domain, and task. Current theory and research in motivation has paid too little attention to developmental perspectives such as self- and identity-development (e.g., Erikson, 1968; Kegan, 1982), and to their potential contribution to understanding students' motivation (Flum & Kaplan, 2006; Kaplan & Flum, 2009; Wigfield & Wagner, 2005).

### Contextual Characteristics

Whereas self and identity processes and issues were central in the meanings that participants constructed for their academic experiences and engagement, to a large extent these self and identity processes were inseparable from characteristics of the context. Contextual characteristics appeared

in all of the narratives and were integrated in the meaning-making processes in various manners. For example, all participants attended to the *general*
subject domains that characterized the different units-of-analysis: academic
learning in general at the university level, the domain of education at the
department level, and the domain of educational psychology at the course
level. Additionally, participants attended to *particular* contextual characteristics at the different units-of-analysis. These included formal procedures
(e.g., admission) and the reputation of the particular university; the character, status, and the culture of learning in the department; the content,
social climate, motivational emphases, and instructional practices in the
course; and the motivational emphases, instructional practices, and group
dynamics in the discussion group.

It is noteworthy that all of the participants made phenomenological
distinctions between the various units-of-analysis of the academic context
(i.e., university, department, course, discussion group). Overall, participants perceived smaller units-of-analysis (e.g., course) as embedded within
larger units-of-analysis (e.g., department). However, the participants also
constructed the motivational emphases and the meaning of action within a
more specific unit as distinct from the meaning of action in broader units.
In fact, rather than being perceived as a simple nested structure, the hierar-
chy of units-of-analysis commonly provided a framework for comparison between perceived motivational emphases in different levels (e.g., comparing
emphases at the department in comparison to the university, at a course in
comparison to the department, and at a discussion group in comparison to
the course), and of different sub-contexts within the same unit-of-analysis
(e.g., comparing different departments at the university, different courses
at the department, and different discussion groups at the course). These
distinctions appeared in Yevgeny's comparison between the Departments
of Hebrew Language and Education, in his comparisons of courses within
the Department of Education, and in both Mor's and Yevgeny's distinct approach towards the Department of Education vis-à-vis the course Introduction to Educational Psychology.

Similar to the finding regarding identity processes, whereas contextual
characteristics were prevalent in the meanings of all of the participants,
here, too, there were individual differences in the way these contextual
characteristics were employed in the meaning-making process, which led to
the construction of different meanings and purposes for engagement. For
example, participants differed in how salient were different units-of-analysis
to them, with some distinctions between units-of-analysis being almost irrelevant in some narratives (e.g., Mor's lack of attention to the Departmental
unit-of-analysis). This suggested that distinctions between contextual units-
of-analysis were not just a result of the interview protocol or method of
analysis. More importantly, the specific content that constituted the con-

textual contribution to the meaning-making process, and the way by which the "known" contextual characteristics (e.g., course assignments and the specific manipulated discussion group meeting) were integrated into the comprehensive meaning of action in different units-of-analysis, were also unique for each participant. The analysis suggested that different participants paid attention to different aspects of the context, expressed different values and experienced different emotions in relation to these contextual aspects, and reported different types of engagement in these contexts. Thus, for example, whereas some participants paid particular attention to the way the instructor taught the course, other participants paid more attention to the peer group, and yet others highlighted the material and the content of the assignments. For Mor, for example, the instructional scaffolds and the TAs' support were of primary importance in her meaning-making whereas for Yevgeny, it was the material and the way the instructor relayed it. These different foci of attention resulted with different meanings, emotional experiences, and adopted purposes of engagement. Moreover, even when participants attended to the same contextual aspect (e.g., the instructor), its interpretation was framed by different personal dispositions. For example, all participants considered the very supportive educational environment in the course to be a positive instructional feature that facilitated adaptive engagement, competence, and interest. Whereas some participants perceived it as categorically highly nurturing of learning and engagement, other participants noted that it also undermined students' autonomy and suggested that it indicated that the staff treated students as immature and as unable to cope with the challenging material.

In summary, it is clear that strong contextual characteristics, such as explicit and consistent messages by the instructor, were influential in students' experiences and were integrated into the meanings that they constructed for their engagement. However, the context has many components and is multi-faceted, and not all of these figured into the meanings of each and every individual. The particular contextual elements and the manner by which they integrated into students' meanings depended on personal self and identity processes. Hence, the analysis indicated that personal self and identity processes and contextual characteristics were blended and could not have been separated in the attempt to identify the antecedents to the content and form of the meanings that students constructed.

### Situational Characteristics

Contexts are experienced through specific situations. General motivational emphases, consistent instructional practices, and overall social climate exist as aggregates of their manifestation in particular events. But these aggregates are made of different types of situations, and students clearly distinguish between engagement purposes in different situations. A course context is constructed from situations such as lectures, discussions, assignments, exams, peer-interactions, and personal encounters with the instructor. Each of these situations has its unique characteristics, those normative to the culture and to the broader units-of-analysis, as well as those of the specific context and situation. These situational characteristics are integrated with the personal and with the broader, more abstract, contextual characteristics, in the meaning and purpose of engagement in each situation.

For example, the characteristics of exam situations in the course involve cultural and normative aspects of exams as evaluative situations that focus on the demonstration of ability and knowledge. These characteristics also involve contextual aspects that emphasize exams as requiring demonstration of high-level cognitive processes such as analysis and application of knowledge over mere memorization of information. An additional influential contextual characteristic of exams in the course is the opportunity to take the exam again. These characteristics are integrated with personal characteristics such as perceived competence, proneness to test-anxiety, and task-value of the exam (e.g., instrumental value of the grade), and with more situated personal characteristics such as mood, fatigue, and self-efficacy for the test, to result with the construction of meaning and purpose of engagement in a particular exam.

Again, the integration of multiple processes into the phenomenological meaning of a situation resulted with individual differences among the participants in meaning and purpose of engagement in the "same" academic situations. However, it was clear that certain situations were more influential than others in affecting meaning and purpose of engagement—in the situation itself as well as in its implication to the meaning of broader units-of-analysis, particularly the course. Some of these influential situations were idiosyncratic and their significance to the student was a result of personal characteristics (e.g., a lecture that concerned content that relates to a meaningful experience in the student's life, as was the case for Yevgeny). Other types of situations were important for all participants, albeit in different ways. Not surprisingly, evaluative situations (e.g., exams, papers) were prominent in all of the interviews and were influential in the meaning and purpose of engagement in the course. Interestingly, it was not uncommon for evaluative situations to be construed by the participants as incongruent with the overall emphasis of the course, and their significance seemed to be, in part, a result of this perceived incongruence. This was the case for both Mor and Yevgeny, albeit in different ways. For Yevgeny, the incongruence was between his general perception of the course as irrelevant and his high achievement on the exam. For Mor, the incongruence was between her general perception of the course as promoting meaningful learning and her low grade. Indeed, an experience of incongruence between a situation and a previously held meaning was a common characteristic of influential situations (Weiner, 1986). Such situations activated intense personal processes that overshadowed prior meanings and contextual characteristics in their effect on the meaning and purpose of engagement in the situation, and potentially on the meaning of broader units-of-analysis, most particularly the course. Often, these incongruent situational experiences triggered an exploratory process, and the employment of cognitive and emotional strategies, which were aimed at resolving the incongruence, establishing a personal purpose of engagement, and taking actions accordingly—processes that were apparent in both the narratives of Mor and Yevgeny. It is in the descriptions of these events that the meaning-making process manifested most explicitly and clearly.

The difference between "influential" and "less-influential" types of situations was particularly apparent in comparing the participants' narrative of evaluative situations in the course with their attention to the study's "focal" evaluative situation: the manipulation of performance goals in the discussion groups. In comparison to the central role that personally-constructed incongruent evaluative situations had in participants' narratives, the "manufactured" incongruent emphasis in the discussion group was not acknowledged at all. In fact, even participants who recalled the TA's instructions in the performance-oriented discussion group did not perceive it as a performance-goal emphasis, but rather re-interpreted it as an aspect of the general concern of the teaching staff for students' development and learning. Thus, it seems that when a contextual emphasis is strong, and the meaning of a context is relatively coherent, "weak" events are likely to be interpreted along the lines of this meaning, even if nominally they represent an incongruent meaning (cf. Kaplan & Gadasi, 2003; Patrick et al., 2001; Urdan et al., 1999).

In summary, the analysis points to the influential role of certain situational characteristics in the construction of meaning and purpose of engagement in the situation, and in affecting the meaning of engagement in the course. The situations that are particularly influential are those that are highly relevant and meaningful to students. The relevance can stem from the normative importance of the situation (e.g., an exam), from a perceived important incongruence between the situation and a more general meaning or perception (e.g., low grade on a paper that is incongruent with high perceived competence), or from a connection between an aspect in the situation and an aspect of the student's self or identity (e.g., a topic in the lecture that relates to the student's life). Specific relevant situations elicit explicit and conscious cognitive and emotional strategies that reveal some of the ways by which participants attempt to integrate their experiences in the achievement situation into the broader meanings of the context and themselves in the context. It is to these meaning-making strategies that we turn next.

### Meaning-Making Strategies

Along the narratives, but particularly around particular situations and events that involved ambiguity, incongruent expectations and experiences, dilemmas, or personally important content, participants reported on employing cognitive-emotional strategies in their attempt to construct the meaning of situations and contexts and of the self-in-context.

By far, the most common strategy that was employed was *comparison relative to a reference point*: comparing the experience or the self to a certain reference along criteria meaningful to the student. This strategy was employed in almost every aspect in students' experiences and in all units-of-analysis. For example, participants compared themselves to others, themselves to who they perceived themselves to be in the past, studying at the university to studying in high-school, studying at the university to serving in the military, studying at the Department of Education to studying at other departments, studying at the course Introduction to Educational Psychology to studying at other courses at the department and in other departments, studying with one TA to studying with other TAs, etc. Whereas the "reference point" strategy was prevalent in all of the interviews, here too there were individual differences. Some of the differences were in the particular reference points chosen, which stemmed from the participants' different personal background (e.g., Mor's continuous comparison of herself to her sister; Yevgeny's continuous comparison of the domains of education and Hebrew language). However, other differences in choice of reference point and in the criteria for comparison were related to participants' self- and identity-related issues. For example, in comparing the course Introduction to Educational Psychology to other courses, some participants chose to compare the instructor's affect and disposition to those of other instructors; some compared the level of interest in the material in the course to that in other courses; and others compared the social relations in the peer-group in the course to that in other academic peer-groups. The differential attention of participants to such issues—all valid aspects of the same educational context—seemed to have been based in the participants' different sensitivities that were related to different identity issues and self-processes that the participants was pre-occupied with, including the commitment to education and educational psychology as a career, identification with authority figures, and concern with social belonging.

Other significant strategies that participants described involved a conscious and explicit exploration of the meaning of incongruent or ambiguous experiences and situations. For example, several participants, including Yevgeny and Mor, described an *internal dialogue* that they engaged in, in which they reflected on their own attributes in relation to the academic context, debated the meaning of an event, and sought a course of action. Another prevalent meaning-exploration strategy among the participants was *dialogue with significant others*, such as a parent, a sibling, a partner, or a friend. Participants reported on dialogues that concerned seeking support, learning from the significant other's own experiences and decisions in similar situations, figuring out the significant other's expectations, and receiving the significant other's perspective on the event. This was clear, for example, in Mor's interaction with her peers around the decision whether to switch a TA. Participants also engaged in *information-seeking strategies*, such as searching for evaluation criteria in syllabi, finding out from older students about the nature of a course, and even looking at the campus map in order to disperse a sense of physical displacement. Some other cognitive-emotional strategies that students employed for constructing meaning from events included making *causal attributions* that aimed at protecting the self and *projecting their experience* on that of others in the course, as in generalizing their personal negative affect to peers in order to legitimize their experience and protect the self.

*Summary*

The analysis of the interviews pointed to a general process of meaning-making of academic contexts that integrated personal dispositions, contextual characteristics, and situational characteristics. The developmental task of identity formation and career development was an overarching frame for these college students' meaning-making of their experiences in the different units-of-analysis of the academic context. Yet, participants differed in their approach to coping with these developmental tasks, and in their commitments to values and careers in education, and these differences were related to different experiences and meanings of engagement in academic learning at the Department of Education and the course Introduction to Educational Psychology. However, contextual characteristics, particularly those in the course, constituted powerful content that integrated with participants' identity processes and issues to affect the meaning that was constructed. Finally, when situations were meaningful to the participant, their characteristics also became salient and were integrated with the identity and the context to result with a situated meaning of engagement. Importantly, situations that were phenomenologically meaningful and had a significant effect on the meaning of experience and of engagement often involved a sense of personally relevant difference to students—ambiguity, uncertainty, or difference from what was expected (cf. Weiner, 1986). When a situation was powerful and involved such a relevant difference, and particularly when the difference was in relation to the general emphasis of the course, the situation's characteristics overrode those of the course in affecting the situated meaning of the task. However, participants also engaged in self-reflection and in dialogue with others about such situations in an attempt to create a coherent meaning that would incorporate the characteristics of the course with the discrepant experience in the specific situation. It is in these attempts in construction of coherence out of ambiguity or dissonant experiences that the meaning-making process of the purpose of contexts and of personal engagement manifested very clearly. Finally, the analysis pointed to various emotional-cognitive strategies that participants employed in this process of meaning-making. *Comparison with a reference point* and *exploratory strategies* were found to provide the most prominent means by which meanings of self, context, situation, and engagement were constructed.

## CONCLUSION

Both of the cases presented, and the seven that were not presented, demonstrate the complex dynamic integration of self and identity issues and processes, contextual characteristics, and features of specific situations in the construction of meaning of engagement in academic tasks. This abstract dynamic process manifested in all of the participants' meaning-making of their experiences and their purposes for engagement. It involved a dynamic reciprocity of influence among different units-of-analysis in affecting the meaning of experience and purpose of engagement, at times demonstrating a top-down influence from broader self or contextual processes to the meaning of specific situations; and at other times, a bottom-up influence, from specific situations to the meaning of contexts and also to the self. While describing an abstract process that was similar among all of the participants, the process also highlighted the unique characteristics of each participant—both in the personal dispositions that the individuals brought with them to the context and situations (cf. Maehr, 1984) and in the way certain features of the contexts and the situations were preferred over others to be integrated into the purpose-forming interpretative process.

The analysis pointed very clearly to the individual's identity and self processes as framing the meaning-making process. Importantly, however, these identity and self-processes were not independent of the larger sociocultural processes within which they developed. As significant were the findings that highlight the power of the context in the dynamic meaning-making process. Among all of the participants, and regardless of the centrality of the domains of education and of educational psychology to their identity, the characteristics of the context—and more specifically, the course characteristics that were employed in order to emphasize mastery goals—were clearly influential in the meaning construction process, guiding the participants' meaning of engagement towards more meaningful learning of the content. This finding provides a general support to the recommendations in the literature concerning practices that facilitate mastery goals (Ames, 1992; Maehr & Midgley, 1991; Kaplan & Maehr, 1999). The findings suggest that such practices may indeed promote more adaptive purposes for engagement among quite different students. However, the findings also suggest that the nature of these adaptive purposes may be somewhat different among the different participants. This conclusion highlights the conceptual diversity of adaptive engagement purposes, pointing to mastery goals (and performance goals) as "generic" orientations (Silva & Nicholls, 1993) that may be insufficient for describing the contextual purposes that students adopt towards learning. The findings clearly pointed to the importance of considering self-processes and contextual characteristics as inseparable in students' meaning of engagement. Finally, the findings also provided insight into the cognitive and emotional strategies that students employ in order to construct the meaning of contexts and situations. The major strategy of *comparison relative to a reference* may provide an important direction for future research as it has potential for interventions that may help students modify their meanings and adopt more adaptive purposes for engagement. The finding that experiences of incongruence or discrepancy between expected and experienced events elicit exploration and negotiation of new meanings also provides insight into possible methods for facilitating re-construction of meanings of engagement (Kaplan & Flum, 2006).

The current study provides an initial demonstration of the processes that are involved in the meaning-making processes of purposes for engagement. Its strengths are in the depth of insight into the rich contents and processes operating among different individuals. Its limitations are in the breadth of experiences examined—all students were Jewish, late-adolescents or emerging adults (Arnett, 2000), studying in their first year at an Israeli university. Research is required in order to generalize the abstract meaning-making processes to other individuals and groups, of various ages and backgrounds. Moreover, the meaning-making processes were investigated in a very particular setting: a course concerned with psychological processes, which are more readily applied to self-knowledge and hence to perceptions of self-relevance. This course was also unique in that it was structured to emphasize mastery goals. It may be that in other subject-domains, and in courses that are structured to emphasize other achievement goal structures, other processes may be triggered or become salient in the meaning-making process. It would be important to investigate these processes, perhaps in particular, in educational environments that send only vague or ambivalent messages, or alternatively, very strict messages about achievement goal structures, where the dynamics of meaning-making may assume a different character.

Despite all of the above, the findings of the current study represent a legitimate and important part of the repertoire of meaning-making processes in academic settings. It is noteworthy that these findings highlight the benefits of educational practices that emphasize mastery goals in contributing to constructions of more adaptive meanings and motivation among students—one of Marty Maehr's main contributions to the educational psychology literature (Kaplan & Maehr, 2002; Maehr & Midgley, 1996). The findings also highlight the important role of identity-formation in students' meaning of academic engagement. This finding calls for future theory development and research into the potential employment of exploration of self and identity through academic assignments and material for promoting the learning of the material as well as the facilitation of adaptive developmental processes (Flum & Kaplan, 2006; Wigfield & Wagner, 2005).

## REFERENCES

Ames, C. (1992). Classrooms: Goals, structures, and student motivation. *Journal of Educational Psychology, 84*, 261–271.

Anderman, E. M., & Maehr, M. L. (1994). Motivation and schooling in the middle grades, *Review of Educational Research, 64*, 287–309.

Arnett, J. J. (2000). Emerging adulthood: A theory of development from the late teens through the twenties. *American Psychologist, 55*, 469–480.

Atkinson, J. W. (1957). Motivational determinants of risk-taking behavior. *Psychological Review, 64*, 359–372.

Barron, K. E., & Harackiewicz, J. M. (2001). Achievement goals and optimal motivation: Testing multiple goal models. *Journal of Personality and Social Psychology, 80*, 706–722.

Bering, J. M. (2003). Towards a cognitive theory of existential meaning. *New Ideas in Psychology, 21*, 101–120.

Berzonsky, M. D. (1992). A process perspective on identity and stress management. In G. R. Adams, T. P. Gullotta, & R. Montemayor (Eds.), *Adolescent identity formation* (pp. 193–215). Newbury Park, CA: Sage.

Bosma, H. A. (1992). Identity in adolescence: Managing commitments. In G. R. Adams, T. P. Gullotta, & R. Montemayor (Eds.) *Adolescent identity formation* (pp. 91–121). Newbury Park, CA: Sage.

Bruner, J. (1986). *Actual minds, possible worlds*. Cambridge, MA: Harvard University Press.

Bruner, J. (1990). *Acts of meaning*. Cambridge, MA: Harvard University Press.

Côté, J. E., & Levine, C. (1988). A critical examination of ego identity status paradigm. *Developmental Review, 8*, 147–188.

Crocker, J., & Wolfe, C. T. (2001). Contingencies of self-worth. *Psychological Review, 108*, 593–623.

DeShon, R. P., & Gillespie, J. Z. (2005). A motivated action theory account of goal orientation. *Journal of Applied Psychology, 90*, 1096–1127.

Dowson, M., & McInerney, D. M. (2001). Psychological parameters of students' social and work avoidance goals: A qualitative investigation. *Journal of Educational Psychology, 93*, 35–42.

Dweck, C. S. (1999). *Self-theories: Their role I motivation, personality, and development.* Philadelphia, PA: Psychology Press.

Dweck, C. S., & Leggett, E. L. (1988). A social-cognitive approach to motivation and personality. *Psychological Review, 95*, 256–273.

Elliot, A. J. (1997). Integrating the 'classic' and 'contemporary' approaches to achievement motivation: A hierarchical model of approach and avoidance achievement motivation. In M. L. Maehr & P. R. Pintrich (Eds.), *Advances in motivation and achievement* (Vol. 10, pp. 143–179). Greenwich, CT : JAI Press Inc.

Elliot, A. J. (1999). Approach and avoidance motivation and achievement goals. *Educational Psychologist, 34*, 169–189.

Elliot, A. J. (2005). A conceptual history of the achievement goal construct. In A. J. Elliot & C. S. Dweck (Eds.), Handbook of competence and motivation (pp. 52– 72). New York: Guildford.

Elliot, A. J., (2008, April). *Why are you doing this? The reasons behind performance approach goals may alter achievement outcomes.* Paper presented at the annual meeting of the American Educational Research Association, New York.

Elliot, A. J., & Church, M. A. (1997). A hierarchical model of approach and avoidance achievement motivation. *Journal of Personality and Social Psychology, 72*, 218–232.

Elliot, A. J., & Harackiewicz, J. M. (1996). Approach and avoidance achievement goals and intrinsic motivation: A mediational analysis. *Journal of Personality and Social Psychology, 70*, 461–475.

Elliot, A., McGregor, H., & Gable, S. (1999). Achievement goals, study strategies, and exam performance: A mediational analysis. *Journal of Educational Psychology, 91*, 549–563.

Elliot, A. J., & Moller, A. (2003). Performance-approach goals: Good or bad forms of regulation? *International Journal of Educational Research, 39*, 339–356.

Elliot, A. J., & Thrash, T. M. (2001). Achievement goals and the hierarchical model of achievement motivation. *Educational Psychology Review, 13*, 139–156.

Elliott, E. S., & Dweck, C. S. (1988). Goals: An approach to motivation and achievement. *Journal of Personality and Social Psychology, 54*, 5–12.

Erikson, E. H. (1959). Identity and the life cycle. *Psychological Issues, 1* (Monograph No. 1). New York: International Universities Press.

Erikson, E. H. (1968). *Identity: Youth and crisis.* New York: Norton.

Flum, H., & Kaplan, A. (2006). Exploratory orientation as an educational goal. *Educational Psychologist, 41*, 99–110.

Grotevant, H. D., (1987). Toward a process model of identity formation. Journal of Adolescent Research, 2, 203–222.

Jackson, D. N. (1974). *Manual for the personality research form.* Goshen, NY: Research Psychology Press.

Josselson, R. L. & Lieblich, A. (Eds.) (1993). *The narrative study of lives* (Vol. 1). Newbury Park, CA; Sage.

Kaplan, A. (2004). Achievement goals and intergroup relations. In P. R. Pintrich & M. L. Maehr (Eds.), *Advances in research on motivation and achievement: Vol. 13: Motivating Students, Improving Schools: The Legacy of Carol Midgley* (pp. 97–136). United Kingdom: Elsevier.

Kaplan, A., & Flum, H. (2006, July). Facilitating an exploratory orientation in school. Paper presented at the 4th International Biennial SELF Research Conference, Ann Arbor, MI.

Kaplan, A., & Flum, H. (Guest Eds.) (2009, in press). Motivation and identity: Special issue. *Educational Psychologist.*

Kaplan, A., & Flum, H. (2009). *Academic motivational orientations and identity formation styles.* Manuscript submitted for publication.

Kaplan, A., & Gadasi, A. (2003, April). *Perceived emphasis on mastery and performance goals of teacher behavior: Culture, context and individual differences.* Paper presented at the annual meeting of the American Educational Research Association, Chicago, IL.

Kaplan, A., & Maehr, M. L. (1999). Enhancing the motivation of African American students: An achievement goal theory perspective. *Journal of Negro Education, 68,* 23–35.

Kaplan, A., & Maehr, M. L. (2002). Adolescents' achievement goals: Situating motivation in socio-cultural contexts. In F. Pajaers & T. Urdan (Eds.), *Adolescence and education: Vol. 2, Academic motivation of adolescents* (pp. 125–167). Greenwich, CT: Information Age.

Kaplan, A., & Maehr, M. L. (2007). The contribution and prospects of goal orientation theory. *Educational Psychology Review, 19,* 141–187.

Kaplan, A., & Middleton, M. J. (2002). Should childhood be a journey or a race?: A response to Harackiewicz et al., (2002). *Journal of Educational Psychology, 94,* 646–648.

Kaplan, A., Middleton, M. J., Urdan, T., & Midgley, C. (2002). Achievement goals and goal structures. In C. Midgley (Ed.) *Goals, goal structures and patterns of adaptive learning* (pp. 21– 53). Mahwah, NJ: Erlbaum.

Kegan, R. (1982). *The evolving self: Problem and process in human development.* Cambridge, MA: Harvard University Press.

Kroger, J. (1992). Intrapsychic dimensions of identity during late adolescence. In G. R. Adams, T. P. Gullotta, & R. Montemayor (Eds.) *Adolescent identity formation* (pp. 123–143). Newbury Park, CA: Sage.

Maehr, M. L. (1974). Culture and achievement motivation. *American Psychologist, 29,* 887–896.

Maehr, M. L. (1984). Meaning and motivation: Toward a theory of personal investment. In C. Ames & R. Ames (Eds.), *Research on motivation in education* (Vol. 1, pp. 115–144). New York: Academic Press.

Maehr, M. L., & Midgley, C. (1991). Enhancing student motivation: A schoolwide approach. *Educational Psychologist, 26,* 399–427.

Maehr, M. L., & Nicholls, J. G. (1980). Culture and achievement motivation: A second look. In N. Warren, (Ed.), *Studies on cross-cultural psychology,* (Vol. 2, pp. 221–267). New York: Academic Press.

Maehr, M. L., & Midgley, C. (1996). *Transforming school cultures.* Boulder, CO: Westview Press.

Malpas, J. (2002). The weave of meaning: Holism and contextuality. *Language & Communication, 22,* 403–419.

Marcia, J. E. (1980). Identity in adolescence. In J. Adelson (Ed.), *Handbook of adolescent psychology* (pp. 159–187). New York: John Wiley.

McCaslin, M., & Good, T. L. (1996). The informal curriculum. In D. C. Berliner & R. C. Calfee (Eds.), *Handbook of educational psychology* (pp. 622–670). New York: Simon & Schuster Macmillan.

McClelland, D. C. (1961). *The achieving society.* New York: Free Press.

Meece, J. L. (1991). The classroom context and students' motivational goals. In M. L. Maehr & P. R. Pintrich (Eds.), *Advances in motivation and achievement* (Vol. 7, pp. 261–285). Greenwich, CT: JAI Press Inc.

Meece, J. L., Anderman, E. M., & Anderman, L. H. (2006). Classroom goal structure, student motivation and academic achievement. *Annual Review of Psychology, 57,* 487–503.

Midgley, C., Maehr, M. L., Hruda, L. Z., Anderman, E, Anderman, L., Freeman, K. E., Gheen, M., Kaplan, A., Kumar, R., Middleton, M. J., Nelson, J., Roeser, R., & Urdan, T. (2000). *Patterns of adaptive learning survey (PALS).* University of Michigan.

Molden, D., & Dweck, C. S. (2000). Meaning and motivation. In C. Sansone & J. M. Harackiewicz (Eds.), *Intrinsic and extrinsic motivation: The search for optimal motivation and performance* (pp. 131–159). San Diego, CA: Academic Press.

Newman, D., Griffin, P., & Cole, M. (1989). *The construction zone: Working for cognitive change in school.* New York, New York: Cambridge University Press.

Nicholls, J. G. (1984). Achievement motivation: Conceptions of ability, subjective experience, task choice, and performance. *Psychological Review, 91,* 328–346.

Nicholls, J. G. (1989). *The competitive ethos and democratic education.* Cambridge, MA: Harvard University Press.

Nicholls, J. G. (1990). What is ability and why are we mindful of it? A developmental perspective. In R. Sternberg & J. Kolligian (Eds.), *Competence considered.* (pp. 11–40). New Haven, CT: Yale University Press.

Nicholls, J. G. (1992). Students as educational theorists. In D. Schunk & J. Meece (Eds.), *Student perceptions in the classroom* (Ch.12, pp. 267–286). Hillsdale, NJ: Lawrence Erlbaum.

Patrick, H. (2004). Re-examining classroom mastery goal structure. In P. R. Pintrich & M. L. Maehr (Eds.), *Advances in research on motivation and achievement: Vol. 13: Motivating Students, Improving Schools: The Legacy of Carol Midgley* (pp. 233–263). United Kingdom: Elsevier.

Patrick, H., Anderman, L. H., Ryan, A. M., Edelin, K. C., & Midgley, C. (2001). Teachers' communication of goal orientations in four fifth-grade classrooms. *The Elementary School Journal, 102,* 35–58.

Patrick, H., Ryan, A., & Kaplan, A. (2007). Early adolescents' perceptions of the classroom social environment, motivational beliefs, and engagement. *Journal of Educational Psychology, 99*, 83–98.

Pintrich, P. R. (2000). The role of goal orientation in self-regulated learning. In M. Boedaerts, P. Pintrich, & M. Zeidner (Eds.), *Handbook of self-regulation: Theory, research and applications.* San Diego, CA: Academic Press.

Pintrich, P. R. (2003). A motivational science perspective on the role of student motivation in learning and teaching contexts. *Journal of Educational Psychology, 95*, 667– 686.

Pintrich, P. R., & Schunk, D. (2002). *Motivation in education: theory, research, and applications* (2nd Ed.). Upper Saddle River, NJ: Prentice-Hall.

Ratner, C. (2002). *Cultural psychology: Theory and method.* New York: Kluwer.

Rosenthal, G. (1993). Reconstruction of life stories: Principles of selection in generating stories for narrative biographical interviews. In R. L. Josselson & A. Lieblich (Eds.), *The Narrative Study of Lives* (Vol. 1, pp. 59–91). Newbury Park, CA; Sage.

Sarbin, T. R. (1986). The narrative as a root metaphor for psychology. In T. R. Sarbin (Ed.), *Narrative psychology: The storied nature of human conduct* (pp. 3–21). New York, NY: Praeger.

Shotter, J. (1997). The social construction of our inner selves. *Journal of Constructivist Psychology, 10*, 7–24.

Sideridis, G., & Mouratidis, A. (2007, April). *What is really "behind" students' goal orientations? A content analysis in physical education.* Paper presented at the annual meeting of the American Educational Research Association, Chicago.

Silva, T., & Nicholls, J. G. (1993). College students as writing theorists: Goals and beliefs about the causes of success. *Contemporary Educational Psychology, 18*, 281–293.

Super, D. E., Savickas, M. L., & Super, C. M. (1996). The life-span, life-space approach to careers. In D. Brown & L. Brooks (Eds.), *Career choice and development* (3rd Ed., pp. 121–178). San Francisco, CA: Jossey-Bass.

Thrash, T. M., & Elliot, A. J. (2001). Delimiting and integrating achievement motive and goal constructs. In A. Efklides, J. Kuhl, & R. M. Sorrentino (Eds.), *Trends and prospects in motivational research* (pp. 1–19). The Netherlands: Kluwer.

Turner, J. C., Midgley, C., Meyer, D. K., Gheen, M., Anderman, E., Kang, Y., & Patrick, H. (2002). The classroom environment and students' reports of avoidance behaviors in mathematics: A multimethod study. *Journal of Educational Psychology, 94*, 88–106.

Urdan, T. (1997). Achievement goal theory: Past results, future directions. In M. L. Maehr & P. R. Pintrich (Eds.), *Advances in motivation and achievement* (Vol. 10, pp. 99–141). Greenwich, CT: JAI Press.

Urdan, T. C., Kneisel, L., & Mason, V. (1999). The effect of particular instructional practices on student motivation: An exploration of teachers' and students' perceptions. In T. Urdan (Ed.), *Advances in motivation and achievement*, Vol. 11 (pp. 123– 158). Stamford, CT: JAI.

Urdan, T. C., & Maehr, M. L. (1995). Beyond a two-goal theory of motivation and achievement: A case for social goals. *Review of Educational Research, 65*, 213–243.

Urdan, T. C., & Mestas (2006). The goals behind performance goals. *Journal of Educational Psychology, 98,* 354–365.

Weiner, B. (1986). *An attributional theory of motivation and emotion.* New York: Springer-Verlag.

Wertsch, J. V. (1991). *Voices of the mind: A sociocultural approach to mediated action.* Cambridge, MA: Harvard University Press.

Wigfield, A., & Wagner, A. L. (2005). Competence, motivation and identity development during adolescence. In A. J. Elliot & C. S. Dweck (Eds.), *Handbook of competence and motivation* (pp. 222–239). New York: Guilford.

CHAPTER 5

# ACHIEVEMENT GOALS IN THE CONTEXT OF THE HIERARCHICAL MODEL OF APPROACH-AVOIDANCE ACHIEVEMENT MOTIVATION

**Ron Friedman, Arlen C. Moller, James W. Fryer, Ista Zahn, Wilbert Law, Ryan D. Acuff, Daniela Niesta, Kou Murayama, Angelika M. Meier, Beate Jelstad, and Andrew J. Elliot**

## INTRODUCTION

The distinction between approach and avoidance motivation has a long intellectual history, dating back to the writings of the ancient Greeks (Elliot & Thrash, 2002). This distinction also has a broad intellectual history, having been utilized within a number of major theoretical traditions. It has been shown to have conceptual and empirical utility within a diverse range of psychological literatures, including developmental psychology, educational psychology, industrial-organizational psychology, social-personality psychology, and sport psychology.

*Culture, Self, and Motivation: Essays in Honor of Martin L. Maehr*, pages 111–133
Copyright © 2009 by Information Age Publishing

In this chapter, we begin by defining the approach-avoidance distinction, and providing a brief historical overview that documents its deep philosophical and psychological heritage. We then proceed to examine empirical work on this distinction, highlighting research in the domain of achievement motivation. Finally, we consider the antecedents and consequences of approach and avoidance achievement motivation domain in depicting our hierarchical model of approach-avoidance achievement motivation. This chapter is authored by the members of the fall 2006 approach-avoidance motivation research group at the University of Rochester, and is meant to pay tribute to the rich and generative scholarly contributions of Dr. Marty Maehr. Dr. Maehr's work on achievement goals has greatly influenced our own work on this construct; given that achievement goals are at the centerpiece of the hierarchical model, it is plain to see that Dr. Maehr's ideas exert a deep influence on the research emerging from our laboratory.

## Defining the Approach-Avoidance Distinction

Approach motivation may be defined as the energization of behavior by, or the direction of behavior *toward* positive stimuli (objects, events, or possibilities). Avoidance motivation, on the other hand, may be defined as the energization of behavior by, or the direction of behavior *away from* negative stimuli (objects, events, or possibilities). Five aspects of this definition are considered further in the following.

First, being a motivational distinction, approach-avoidance encompasses both the energization and direction of behavior. The term *energization* refers to the initial instigation or "spring to action" (James, 1890/1950, vol. 2, p. 555) that orients the organism in a general way (Elliot, 1997). Worth noting is that this use of energization does not imply that an organism is passive until instigated to action. Indeed, on the contrary, we view organisms as perpetually active, with instigation representing a shift from one form of orienting to another (Atkinson & Birch, 1970). The term *direction* refers to the guiding or channeling of behavior in a precise way.

Second, inherent in the approach-avoidance distinction is the concept of physical or psychological movement. Positively evaluated stimuli are inherently associated with an approach orientation to bring or keep the stimuli close to the organism (literally or figuratively). Negatively evaluated stimuli are inherently associated with an avoidance orientation to push or keep the stimuli away from the organism (literally or figuratively). Although positively and negatively evaluated stimuli produce a physiological and somatic preparedness for physical movement toward and away from the stimuli, respectively (Arnold, 1960; Corwin, 1921), this preparedness may or may not manifest itself in overt behavior, per se.

Third, both movement toward and movement away from a stimulus can each take one of two distinguishable forms. "Movement toward" can represent either getting something positive that is currently absent, or it can represent keeping something positive that is currently present (functionally, continuing toward). Likewise, "movement away" can represent keeping away from something negative that is currently absent (functionally, continuing away from) or it can represent getting away from something negative that is currently present. That is, the initial presence/absence of a stimulus may be crossed with its valence to discern two different types of approach and avoidance motivation (Elliot & Friedman, 2006; for a conceptual parallel, see Herzberg, 1966). Thus, approach motivation not only encompasses promoting new positive situations, but also maintaining and sustaining existing positive situations. Similarly, avoidance motivation not only encompasses preventing new negative situations, but also escaping from and rectifying existing negative situations.

Fourth, approach-avoidance is thought to encompass situation-specific terms used to denote positive and negative valence, respectively. "Positive" and "negative" are presumed to take on somewhat different meanings in different contexts, including beneficial/harmful, liked/disliked, and desirable/undesirable. Research indicates that these dimensions are conceptually and empirically comparable to a high degree, although there does exist some empirical work suggesting that in certain instances they may be separable (Berridge, 1999). At present, given their substantial comparability, it appears best to construe beneficial/harmful, liked/disliked, and desirable/undesirable as functionally equivalent dimensions that may be subsumed under the positive/negative rubric. Nevertheless, it is possible that future research will establish a need to distinguish among these dimensions in defining the approach-avoidance distinction.

Fifth, the term "stimuli" may represent either concrete, observable objects/events/possibilities, or abstract, internally-generated representations of objects/events/possibilities. Furthermore, "stimuli" is meant to connote an essentially limitless array of focal endpoints, specific to the individual.

Now that the intricacies of the approach-avoidance distinction have been elucidated, we proceed to historical considerations that have contributed to psychologists' present understanding of the term.

### History of the Approach-Avoidance Distinction

The approach-avoidance distinction is not new in analyses of motivation and behavior. To the contrary, this distinction may be considered one of the oldest ideas in the history of psychological thinking about organisms. What *is* new is the depth and sophistication with which the approach-avoidance distinction is being used to explain and predict motivated behavior.

Scholars have made use of the approach-avoidance distinction for over two thousand years. It first appeared in the writing of the ancient Greek philosopher Democritus (460-370 B.C.E.) who articulated an ethical hedonism in which the immediate pursuit of pleasure and avoidance of pain were prescribed as the guide for human action (see also the writing of Socrates's pupil Aristippus [435-356 B.C.E] and Epicurus [342-270 B.C.E]). The eighteenth century British philosopher Jeremy Bentham was the first to postulate a psychological hedonism that moved beyond a prescription of how we ought to behave to a description of how we actually do behave. This principle is directly stated in what is one of Bentham's most commonly-quoted propositions:

> Nature has placed mankind under the governance of two sovereign masters, pain and pleasure. It is for them alone to point out what we ought to do, as well as to determine what we shall do (Bentham, 1779/1879, p. 1).

Within the field of scientific psychology, the approach-avoidance distinction was utilized from the beginning. For example, William James (1890), in his classic *Principles of Psychology* (Vol. 2), considered pleasure and pain to be "springs of action," noting that pleasure is a "tremendous reinforcer" of behavior and pain a "tremendous inhibitor" of behavior (pp. 549-559). Likewise, Freud (1915) construed the procurement of pleasure and the avoidance of pain (i.e., unpleasure) as the basic motivational impetus underlying psychodynamic activity. Indeed, many other prominent contributors to psychological theory from the time of James and Freud through the 1960s also made central use of the approach-avoidance distinction (see Elliot, 1999; Elliot & Covington, 2001; for reviews).

In the 1970s through the 1980s, cognitive and social-cognitive theorists drew a sharp distinction between cognition and motivation, and sought alternative, non-affective explanations for motivational accounts of behavior. In this context, the approach-avoidance distinction was still utilized in theorizing to some degree, but in a much more limited way than in years past. It was with the acknowledgement in the 1990s that cognition and motivation are deeply intertwined, and need not be viewed as conceptual competitors, that motivational considerations in general, and the approach-avoidance distinction specifically, returned to prominence.

This return to prominence is noteworthy, because use of the approach-avoidance distinction in the contemporary scene would appear to differ from prior use in two important ways. First, until recently, the approach-avoidance distinction had been widely utilized and applied without taking a step back to explicitly define and articulate the nature of approach and avoidance motivation per se. Thus, philosophers, theorists, and researchers over the years have proffered approach- and avoidance-relevant ideas and constructs, and have even debated the sufficiency of hedonism as an explanatory principle, but have rarely taken a step back to clearly explicate the conceptual space represented by approach and avoidance motivation. Recent work has directly attended to this definitional issue (see Elliot & Covington, 2001; Elliot & Mapes, 2005).

Second, until recently, the approach-avoidance distinction has been applied to isolated situations and constructs without broader consideration of how this distinction might be applied as a general organizer of motivation and action. In essence, the approach-avoidance distinction has moved from the ground to the figure, such that this distinction is now being considered as fundamental and basic in many motivational analyses (see Buck, 1999; Cacioppo & Berntsen, 1994; Carver & Scheier, 1998; Elliot & Church, 1997; Higgins, 1997).

## Approach and Avoidance Goals

Numerous psychological constructs have been used over the years to explain and predict people's behavior within specific situations. In particular, goal-related concepts have been present throughout the history of psychological thought (Austin & Vancouver, 1996; Elliot & Fryer, 2008).

Aristotle (384-322 B.C.) is often regarded as the first truly psychological thinker, and his writings make clear reference to the directional nature of behavior. For Aristotle, behavior is always purposeful, and imagined end-states are viewed as having an important influence on human action. Aristotle used the work of a sculptor creating a statue to illustrate this notion of purpose and directedness. Standing before a block of marble, the sculptor has an idea of what is wanted at the end of the sculpting process. It is this imagined end-state that is thought to determine the way that the marble is chiseled as the sculptor produces the statue.

Goals remained on the periphery of the psychological literature throughout the latter part of the 19th and (very) beginning of the 20th century. When goal-relevant constructs did appear, the term "end" was typically utilized, or, on occasion, "aim" or "object." With the rise of behaviorism in the second decade of the 20th century, however, mentalistic processes, including goal-relevant concepts, began to be seen as outside the purview of a scientific psychology. During this time a shift occurred in which psychology sought to limit itself to observable behavior. Internal mental events such as goals were considered unobservable, and therefore, unscientific.

With time, however, psychologists questioned this viewpoint. Edward Tolman was among the first to do so, observing that behavior "reeks of purpose and of cognition" (Tolman, 1932, p. 12). As a behaviorist, Tolman sought to account for the seemingly goal-seeking nature of behavior while continuing to rely on observable behavior. In doing so, he defined "goal-object" as the object or situation toward which or away from which the organism moved. Tolman's contributions are important in that they helped retain a central place for the goal construct in psychology, and demonstrated that the goal construct is not incompatible with behaviorism. A contemporary of Tolman, Kurt Lewin, developed an elaborate, dynamic analysis of behavior that was unabashedly mentalistic and goal-based. Lewin (e.g., 1935) attempted to construct an extensive theoretical account of behavior by focusing on the goals toward or away from which behavior was directed. That is, Lewin conceptualized goals as the positively or negatively "valenced" activities or objects that attract or repel the person, respectively.

By the 1930s, the goal construct had come into its own in the psychological literature. The word goal was commonplace, and was used as a scientific term to describe or explain psychological phenomena. Today, the term goal is defined as a cognitive representation of a future object that the organism is committed to approach or avoid (Elliot & Fryer, in press). Goals are viewed as important in the self-regulation process because they serve to focus people's attention, providing precise guidance toward concrete aims. In doing so, goals facilitate specific behavioral patterns.

In general, goals can be categorized as either approach-focused or avoidance-focused. Approach goals involve the pursuit or maintenance of a positively valenced object. In contrast, avoidance goals involve distancing or staying away from a negatively valenced object. Both approach and avoidance "movement" may entail either physical activity (e.g., "Exercise three times a week.") or psychological activity (e.g., "Be more empathic.").

Worth noting is the difference between approach/avoidance goals and approach/avoidance motivation. Goal-directed behavior is characterized by a cognitive representation of a positive or negative end-state. Motivated behavior per se, may or may not be goal-directed. For example, even simple animals such as amoeba appear motivated to approach desirable stimuli and avoid undesirable stimuli, but it is unlikely that cognitive representations are involved; more sophisticated animals (including humans) may commonly engage in goal-directed behavior. Goals may be relatively concrete and specific (e.g., "get an A on an upcoming quiz") or more abstract and general (e.g., "be a successful person"), and they may be hierarchically arranged, (e.g., one may set a goal of earning high grades in order to further the goal of being a successful person).

While some situations strongly pull for approach or avoidance goals, others are more ambiguous. For example, when confronted with a hungry bear in the woods, most people would presumably focus on the goal of not being devoured, regardless of individual differences. In more ambiguous situations, however, where a person's physical well-being is not in immediate danger, people vary in their goal selection. It is in these situations that motives, temperaments, and other personality factors play a role in determining the type of goal adopted.

## Achievement Goals

The achievement goal approach to achievement motivation emerged in the late 1970s and early 1980s, and the work of Marty Maehr played a foundational role in this emergence. Maehr (1983; 1984; Maehr & Nicholls, 1980) contended that the quantitative focus in the dominant achievement motive approach to achievement motivation was too drive/affect-based, too dispositionally-focused, and too undifferentiated to adequately account for achievement behavior. He proposed the need to attend to a more cognitively-based, situationally-focused, and differentiated achievement goal construct. Maehr and Nicholls' 1980 article outlining the need for an achievement goal approach to achievement motivation stands as a seminal, groundbreaking contribution to the achievement motivation literature. Two close colleagues of Maehr's at the University of Illinois in the late 1970s and early 1980s, Carol Dweck and John Nicholls, developed specific achievement goal conceptualizations, and given the ensuing popularity of these models, we will overview them in the following.

Dweck distinguished between two types of achievement goals: *performance goals*, in which the purpose of behavior is to demonstrate one's competence (or avoid demonstrating one's incompetence), and *learning goals*, in which the purpose of behavior is to develop one's competence and task mastery. Much of Dweck's work on the performance-learning distinction arose from her research focused on helplessness behavior exhibited by grade-school children within achievement settings. In a series of studies, Dweck and her colleagues (Diener & Dweck, 1978; 1980; Dweck, 1975; Dweck & Reppucci, 1973) demonstrated that children of equal ability respond differently to failure on achievement tasks. Some children display an adaptive, "mastery" response pattern, characterized by attributing failure to insufficient effort, continued positive affect and expectancies, sustained or enhanced persistence and performance, and pursuit of subsequent challenge. Other children display a maladaptive, "helpless" response pattern, characterized by attributing failure to insufficient ability, the onset of negative affect and expectancies, decrements in persistence and performance, and avoidance of subsequent challenge.

Dweck (Dweck, 1986; Dweck & Elliott, 1983) sought to explain why children of equal ability display such divergent responses to failure. In doing so, she embraced the achievement goal construct as the key explanatory variable. Children were posited to adopt different goals in achievement settings and these goals were presumed to lead to differential task construals and differential patterns of affect, cognition, and behavior. Performance goals were presumed to lead to the "helpless" response pattern upon failure, because failure directly implies a lack of normative ability. Learning goals, on the other hand, were posited to lead to the "mastery" response pattern, because failure could simply be construed as helpful information in the process of developing competence or mastering a task.

Furthermore, achievement goals were posited to interact with confidence in one's ability in predicting achievement-relevant affect, cognition, and behavior. Performance goals were thought to lead to the "mastery" response pattern when accompanied by high confidence in ability, but were thought to lead to the "helpless" pattern when accompanied by low confidence in ability. Learning goals were viewed as leading to the "mastery" pattern regardless of level of confidence in ability.

Nicholls offered an achievement goal conceptualization similar to that of Dweck. In his model, he distinguished between task involvement and ego involvement. *Task involvement* referred to seeking ability in the undifferentiated sense (i.e., seeking to develop skills by learning or mastering tasks), and *ego involvement* referred to seeking ability in the differentiated sense (i.e., seeking to demonstrate that one has capacity by outperforming others, especially with less effort expenditure). Research on the task-ego involvement distinction emerged from research on the development of conceptions of ability in children. According to Nicholls (Nicholls, 1976; 1978; 1980), children do not initially distinguish between ability and effort. From this perspective, high ability is essentially equated with learning and improvement through effort; the more effort expended, the more learning and improvement (and, therefore, ability) implied. By around the age of twelve, however, children acquire a differentiated conception of ability in which they distinguish between ability and effort, and construe ability as a fixed capacity. From this perspective, effort must be "controlled for" when making ability inferences; high ability is inferred when one outperforms others while expending equal effort or performs the same as others while expending less effort.

Researchers sought to integrate findings on the development of conceptions of ability with existing theories of adolescent and adult achievement motivation. In doing so, they posited that the purpose of achievement behavior is either to demonstrate or develop high ability. For adolescents and adults, ability may be construed in both undifferentiated and differentiated fashion, such that two different types of goals—task involvement and ego involvement—may be identified on this basis.

These two types of goals were presumed to lead to different patterns of achievement-relevant processes and outcomes. Task involvement was portrayed as an intrinsically motivated state that leads to positive achievement-relevant affect, cognition, and behavior, whereas ego involvement was portrayed as a self-conscious, evaluative motivational state that leads to a negative pattern of affect, cognition, and behavior. These goal states were posited to interact with perceived ability in predicting some processes and outcomes (e.g., task choice). Ego involvement was viewed as leading to positive consequences (e.g., selecting moderately challenging tasks) when accompanied by high perceived ability, but was viewed as leading to negative consequences (e.g., selecting very easy or very difficult tasks) when accompanied by low perceived ability. Task involvement was viewed as leading to positive consequences across levels of perceived ability.

In the mid to late 1980s, empirical work emerged that supported these ideas (e.g., Ames & Archer, 1988; Butler, 1988; Duda, 1988; Elliott & Dweck, 1988; Jagacinski & Nicholls, 1987; Koestner, Zuckerman, & Koestner, 1987; Meece, Blumenfeld, & Hoyle, 1988; Nicholls, Patashnick, & Nolen, 1985; Nolen, 1988; Sansone, Sachau, & Weir, 1989; Stipek & Kowalski, 1989; Thorkildsen, 1989). This research documented the utility of the fledgling achievement goal approach to achievement motivation.

In an influential set of articles, Ames and Archer (1987, 1988) laid out the rationale for an integrative achievement goal approach that brought together not only the conceptualizations of Dweck and Nicholls, but also those of Ames (1984), Covington (1984), Maehr (1983), and Ryan (1982). Ames and Archer (1987, 1988) argued that the conceptual accounts proposed by the aforementioned theorists were similar enough to justify terminological convergence in the form of a mastery/performance goal dichotomy. This integrative move brought cohesion to the extant literature on achievement goals, and helped to solidify the importance of the achievement goal construct.

In the early 1990s, research on achievement goals began to proliferate. There were undoubtedly many reasons for this influx of empirical attention: the achievement goal construct was intuitively appealing, the achievement goal construct fit nicely with the widespread interest in cognitively-based constructs, achievement goal ideas clearly had straightforward applied value, achievement goals were relatively easy to measure and manipulate, and Ames and Archer's (1987, 1988) integration helped generate new research ideas. By this time, empirical research on achievement goals was being generated by theorists in a broad range of disciplines including developmental psychology (see work by Butler, Stipek), educational psychology (see work by Ames, Maehr, Meece, Nicholls, Pintrich), sport psychology (see work by Duda, Roberts), and social-personality psychology (see work by Dweck, Harackiewicz).

As the achievement goal approach emerged as the predominant account of achievement behavior, the approach-avoidance distinction was initially overlooked. All researchers either followed the lead of Dweck in not attending to separable approach and avoidance forms of performance goals

(Butler, 1992; Skaalvik, Valans, & Sletta, 1994) or they followed the lead of Nicholls in explicitly characterizing both mastery and performance goals as approach forms of motivation (Ames, 1992; Meece & Holt, 1993).

### The Trichotomous Achievement Goal Framework

On the basis of the long-documented utility of the approach-avoidance distinction, Elliot posited that the dichotomous (mastery-performance) achievement goal framework be revised to form a trichotomous framework (Elliot, 1994; Elliot & Harackiewicz, 1996). More specifically, Elliot separated the conventional performance goal into conceptually independent approach and avoidance goals, and introduced three distinct achievement goals: a *mastery goal* focused on the development of competence or the attainment of task mastery, a *performance-approach goal* focused on the attainment of normative competence, and a *performance-avoidance goal* focused on the avoidance of normative incompetence. Mastery and performance-approach goals were characterized as approach goals because they focused on potential positive outcomes (improvement/mastery and normative competence, respectively), whereas performance-avoidance goals were characterized as avoidance goals because they focused on a potential negative outcome (normative incompetence).

The focus on positive possibilities in both mastery and performance-approach goal regulation was posited to lead to a similar set of positive processes and outcomes. However, some differences in the predictive profile of these two forms of approach motivation were also predicted, given their differential evaluative standards. Specifically, the external, evaluative focus inherent in performance-approach goals was thought to limit the extent to which they, relative to mastery goals, produced positive phenomenological processes and outcomes. However, this same characteristic of performance-approach goals was thought to make them better facilitators of performance attainment than mastery goals, particularly in situations where such attainment depends on externally imposed criteria rather than inherently interesting aspects of the task itself (Elliot, 1994; Elliot & Harackiewicz, 1996; Elliot & Moller, 2003). The focus on negative possibilities in performance-avoidance goals was posited to lead to a broad range of negative processes and outcomes.

Rather than view perceived competence as a moderator of achievement goal effects, Elliot posited it to be an antecedent of achievement goal adoption (Elliot, 1994; Elliot & Church, 1997). High perceived competence was posited to orient individuals to the possibility of success and to facilitate the adoption of approach goals, both mastery and performance-approach, whereas low perceived competence was posited to orient individuals to the possibility of failure and to facilitate the adoption of performance-avoidance goals. Thus, competence expectancies were presumed to exert their effects on processes and outcomes indirectly through their influence on achievement goal adoption, rather than directly in interaction with achievement goals.

Importantly, the influence of perceived competence on achievement goal adoption was thought to only be of moderate magnitude. Many other factors besides perceived competence were viewed as contributing to achievement goal adoption, including achievement motives, implicit theories of ability, and characteristics of the achievement task or evaluative setting (Elliot, 1994, 1997). This is a critical point, because several theorists in the 1970s and 1980s had portrayed high-low perceptions of competence as functionally isomorphic with approach-avoidance motivational tendencies (Kukla, 1972; Meyer, 1987). Indeed, it is likely that this portrait of approach-avoidance motivation as reducible to perceived competence was a major reason that approach-avoidance constructs laid fallow during the 1970s and 1980s. That is, perceived competence constructs were quite popular as explanatory constructs during this time, and approach-avoidance motivation was presumed to be redundant with such constructs. In contrast, Elliot portrayed achievement goals as emerging from competence perceptions (as well as other influences), thereby affecting processes and outcomes independent of perceived competence.

By the early 2000s, over 60 studies from 12 different countries had appeared in print, the vast majority of which were published in educational, industrial-organizational, and social-personality psychology journals. This research clearly documented and illustrated the importance of separating performance-approach and performance-avoidance goals, and placed the majority of the deleterious consequences of performance-based goals on performance-avoidance goals. Mastery goals were shown to have widespread positive effects, whereas performance-approach goals were shown to have a primarily positive, but truncated set of positive consequences.

## *The 2 X 2 Achievement Goal Framework*

The trichotomous achievement goal framework incorporated the distinction between approach and avoidance motivation within performance goals, but left mastery goals intact. In subsequent work, Elliot (1999) proposed a 2 x 2 achievement goal framework that incorporated the approach-avoidance distinction within mastery goals as well as performance goals.

Previous work on mastery goals had yielded a rather clear pattern of findings that indicated that these goals led to a host of positive processes and outcomes. However, Elliot (1999) argued that these results were due to the fact that the manipulations and measures used in this research focused uniformly on positive possibilities. That is, in contrast to the extant research on performance goals, in which approach and avoidance motivation were often mixed indiscriminately, in the extant research on mastery goals, avoidance motivation was simply omitted altogether. As such, whereas the trichotomous framework separated omnibus performance goals into conceptually independent performance-approach and performance-avoidance goals, the 2 x 2 framework added mastery-avoidance goals as the conceptually independent complement to the mastery-approach goals that were already in place.

Mastery-avoidance goals were described as a focus on avoiding self-referential or task-referential incompetence. Whereas mastery-approach goals entail striving to develop one's skills and abilities, advance one's learning, understand material, or master a task, mastery-avoidance goals entail striving to avoid losing one's skills and abilities (or having their development stagnate), forgetting what one has learned, misunderstanding material, or leaving a task incomplete. These goals were characterized as mastery goals because of their focus on development and task mastery; they were characterized as avoidance goals because of their focus on a potential negative outcome (self- or task-referential incompetence).

Predictions for mastery-avoidance goals were proffered tentatively, given the fact that the mastery component of the goal was usually viewed as facilitating positive processes and outcomes, whereas the avoidance component of the goal was usually viewed as producing negative processes and outcomes. Nothing was known about the precise way in which these two components would integrate and function together in self-regulation, so specific hypotheses were viewed as difficult to generate a priori. In general, mastery-avoidance goals were expected to produce less optimal consequences than those for mastery-approach goals, but less deleterious consequences than those for performance-avoidance goals (Elliot, 1999; Elliot & McGregor, 2001). Perceived competence was not expected to moderate the influence of mastery-avoidance goals on processes and outcomes. Rather, perceived competence was viewed as an antecedent of mastery-avoidance goals such that low perceptions of competence were thought to orient individuals to the possibility of task- or self-referential incompetence and, therefore, to prompt the adoption of mastery-avoidance goals.

Overall, mastery-avoidance goals were presumed to be less prevalent than mastery-approach, performance-approach, and performance-avoidance goals, at least in the achievement contexts typically studied in the achievement goal literature. However, mastery-avoidance goals were viewed as quite common in some instances and for some types of individuals. For example, these goals were thought to be quite common among the elderly. Physical and mental skills and abilities gradually diminish during the aging process, and it is likely that many who experience this diminution adopt a variant of the goal "avoid losing my skills and abilities." Athletes, students, or employees who have sought to maximize their skills and abilities may at some point feel that they have fully exploited their potential ("reached their peak"), and shift to a focus on "not doing worse than I have done in the past." Perfectionists may be particularly likely to adopt goals such as "avoid making any mistakes" or "not lose a single point." Mastery-avoidance goals may also be common among those who think that they have a bad memory, and consequently focus on "not forgetting what I have learned" (Elliot, 1999; Elliot & Thrash, 2001). Thus, mastery-avoidance goals were construed as important forms of regulation in some instances, and attending to these goals was viewed as necessary in the interest of more fully accounting for the diverse nature of achievement strivings in real world situations.

In addition to fully incorporating the approach-avoidance distinction into the achievement goal construct, the 2 x 2 framework sought to explicitly establish competence as the conceptual core of the achievement goal construct. Competence has always been considered an important part of the achievement goal construct, however other motivational concepts (e.g., self-presentation, self-assessment, impression management) have also been included in conceptualizing and operationalizing achievement goals. In the 2 x 2 framework, "achievement" was explicitly portrayed in terms of competence, and the achievement goal construct was explicitly grounded in competence alone. Other motivational concerns and foci were thought to commonly become associated with competence-based goals, but these other concerns and foci were portrayed as antecedents or consequences of competence-based goal adoption, rather than as part of the goal per se (Elliot & Thrash, 2001; Thrash & Elliot, 2001).

Work on the 2 x 2 framework commenced with the development of a four-goal measure, followed by factor analytic data supporting the separability of the four goals (Elliot & McGregor, 2001). It was also shown that each of the four goals had a distinct nomological network (Elliot & McGregor, 2001). Subsequent experimental and field work provided additional support for the viability of the 2 x 2 framework in general, and the mastery-avoidance goal variable specifically (Conroy, 2004; Conroy & Elliot, 2004; Conroy, Elliot, & Hofer, 2003; Cury, Elliot, Da Fonseca, & Moller, 2006; Elliot & Reis, 2003; Finny, Pieper, & Barron, 2004; Karabenick, 2003, 2004; Malka & Covington, 2005; Van Yperen, 2003; see Moller & Elliot, 2006). The available data seemed to indicate that mastery-avoidance goals have antecedents and consequences that are much more similar to performance-avoidance goals than to mastery-approach goals.

An empirical pattern that began to be acknowledged in the 1990s, but became particularly salient as evidence from the 2 x 2, trichotomous, and dichotomous frameworks accumulated, was that mastery-approach goals often did not positively predict performance attainment, whereas performance-approach goals did so on a rather consistent basis (see Harackiewicz, Barron, & Elliot, 1998). This and other positive findings for performance-approach goals elicited an ongoing, engaging dialogue on the costs and benefits of these goals, and, importantly, on implications for application (see Elliot & Moller, 2003; Harackiewicz, Barron, Pintrich, Elliot, & Thrash, 2002; Kaplan & Middleton, 2002; Midgley, Kaplan, & Midgley, 2001; Moller & Elliot, 2006).

*Hierarchical Model of Approach-Avoidance Achievement Motivation*

As work on achievement goals continued to grow, it became clear that a more complete picture of achievement motivation, beyond that of goals alone, was needed. Such a picture must account for both the *energization* of behavior and the *direction* of behavior (Elliot, 1997). One theoretical conceptualization that attends to both the energization and direction aspects of motivation is the hierarchical model of approach-avoidance motivation (Elliot & Thrash, 2001). According to the hierarchical model of approach-avoidance *achievement* motivation, achievement goals are viewed as concrete, situation-specific variables that explain the specific aim or direction of people's competence pursuits. Higher-order variables are needed to explain why people orient toward different definitions and valences of competence in the first place, and why they adopt particular types of achievement goals.

At the core of the hierarchical model, goals are viewed as cognitive manifestations of higher-order motivational propensities and concerns generated by such constructs as temperaments and motives. That is, temperaments and motives produce inclinations that orient the individual to pursue certain valenced possibilities. The rudimentary sense of direction provided by this orienting is usually insufficient to regulate behavior effectively in that no specific standard or guideline for behavior is provided. Accordingly, goals are often adopted to focus the individual on specific end-states that can address the higher-order inclination or desire/fear that has been activated. Temperaments and motives (and other person-based variables) can and sometimes do lead directly to behavior, but such regulation often appears rigid and/or unfocused (Elliot, McGregor, & Thrash, 2002). In contrast, goals provide precise direction that can lead to more effective and efficient regulation.

Thus, temperaments/motives and goals commonly operate in concert in the motivational process, with temperaments/motives energizing and orienting the individual, and goals channeling this energy toward specific aims. In this way, temperaments and motives may be considered distal, indirect predictors of overt behavior, and goals may be considered more proximal, direct predictors of action. These constructs serve complementary and indispensable roles in explaining motivated behavior; temperaments and motives explain the *why* of behavior, whereas goals explain the *how* of behavior.

A central assumption of the hierarchical model is that goals and their underlying sources or reasons (Elliot & Thrash, 2001) such as temperaments and motives must be defined and conceptualized as separate entities. However, goals and their underlying reasons are posited to operate in conjunction during the actual process of goal regulation. The underlying impetus for goal pursuit is not simply left behind once a goal has been adopted, but instead, this impetus remains connected to the goal, and continues to impact affect, cognition, and behavior throughout the process of goal pursuit (see Lewin's [1926, 1935] discussion of the need-goal relation for a similar analysis). This dynamic intertwining of goal and underlying source is construed as a third construct in and of itself in the hierarchical model, and is termed "goal complex."(Elliot & Thrash, 2001; Thrash & Elliot, 2001; see Murray's [1938, p. 110] "need integrate" construct for an example of a similar, compound construct).

A goal complex is a context-specific regulatory construct that is formed when a goal is adopted, and is represented in memory until the goal is achieved or the reason for adopting the goal is abandoned, altered, or successfully addressed through another route. This mental representation is presumed to include information regarding both the goal and the underlying reason that the goal is being pursued. In many instances, the reason underlying goal adoption is not consciously accessible and, therefore, cannot be articulated by the individual. When the reason underlying goal adoption is accessible, the goal complex may be characterized in the form: "[goal] *in order to* [underlying reason]." For example, if an individual with a strong fear of failure adopts a performance-avoidance goal in a classroom setting, the goal complex may take on the form of "Avoid doing poorly relative to others in this class *in order to* avoid the shame of failure." It is the unique compendium of goal and underlying reason within a goal complex that is posited as the best predictor of affect, cognition, and behavior in a given situation.

Temperaments and motives are not the only higher-order constructs that prompt goal adoption. Many other higher-order intrapsychic constructs are also involved in the goal adoption process (e.g., self-conceptions, perceptions of competence, implicit theories, attachment schemas, internalized values and norms, etc.). We selected temperaments and motives for illustrative purposes herein, because these constructs are most directly and centrally involved in the energization function of motivation, and are thus perhaps most important to incorporate into a motivational analysis of behavior. Other intrapsychic constructs may indirectly implicate energization (e.g., attachment schemas are likely embedded, in part, in need for affiliation and fear of rejection) or may influence goal adoption independently of energization processes (e.g., perceptions of competence may exert an entirely cognitive influence by providing information on what the individual expects to be able to accomplish given his or her skills and abilities). Furthermore, goals may be induced by situational affordances, impedances, and prompts (e.g., the direct assignment of a goal by a supervisor), although the influence of external factors in such instances is likely mediated by temperamental inclinations, motive-based desires/fears, and other intrapsychic processes.

The definitional and conceptual separation of goals from their underlying sources such as temperaments and motives necessitates a narrowing and restricting of the goal construct. At first glance, it may appear as if this constraining of the goal construct would limit its applicability, or minimize its explanatory power in analyses of motivation. On the contrary, however, we contend that greater precision regarding the goal construct actually enhances its significance and utility, and affords a more thorough and complete account of motivation. Perhaps the most important benefit of our restricted conception of goals is that it clearly points to the need for integrating the goal construct with other higher-order motivational constructs. If, indeed, goals are limited to accounting for the directionality of behavior, it becomes clear that additional variables are needed to explain energization, or why individuals adopt and pursue specific goals. When goals are linked to their underlying sources within a hierarchical model, we submit that the resulting goal complexes yield a great deal of insight into the motivational process.

According to the hierarchical model of approach-avoidance achievement motivation, the same achievement goal has different effects on affect, cognition, and behavior depending on the reason underlying goal pursuit. For example, a person with the goal of outperforming others in a class may seek to do so out of a dispositional desire for achievement (i.e., a strong need for achievement), or may seek to do so out of a dispositional desire to avoid failure (i.e., a strong fear of failure). The former goal complex will likely prompt more appetitive, open, and flexible responding in the classroom than the latter. Likewise, upper level constructs such as temperaments and motives are thought to have different effects on affect, cognition, and behavior depending on the goals through which these temperamental inclinations and motive dispositions are channeled. For example, a strong fear of failure may prompt the adoption of a performance-avoidance goal focused on not doing poorly relative to others or it may prompt the adoption of a performance-approach goals focused on doing well relative to others. In this case, the latter goal complex is likely to promote more positive processes and outcomes than the former.

The complexity of motivation comes into even bolder relief when one is reminded that the aforementioned examples represent isolated, simplified illustrations. A single goal can emerge from multiple sources. A single source such as a temperament or motive can prompt the adoption of multiple goals to serve it. Furthermore, once a goal is adopted, it is commonly pursued using a variety of different levels and types of subgoals (e.g., strategies, plans, implementation intentions). Clearly, from a hierarchical standpoint, motivation is an intricate and involved process. As such, nomothetic analyses can be informative with regard to understanding basic and relatively isolated motivational principles, but it is important to bear in mind that such work does not fully capture the fuller idiographic reality of daily striving (Allport, 1937; Murray, 1938).

The hierarchical model also highlights the flexibility of human regulation. Although the behavior of lower animals is governed largely by subcortical mechanisms (see Schneirla, 1959), human behavior is more flexible in that aspects of motivation beyond deeply engrained dispositional propensities or tendencies may be involved in producing action (Elliot & Thrash, 2002; Lang, 1995). One prominent role of the self is the executive function, which involves the monitoring and regulating of basic response predispositions (Baumeister & Vohs, 2003). Through self-regulation, human motivation may involve either the support and realization of initial approach or avoidance inclinations, or the overriding and/or rechannelling of such basic tendencies. Of course, one prominent form of self-regulation is goal adoption and pursuit.

Accordingly, neither biology nor socialization are destiny in human functioning; self-regulation allows hierarchical combinations of approach and avoidance that help the individual to mature and grow in optimal fashion. An individual with a strong avoidance temperament need not incessantly focus on negative possibilities across achievement situations, but can, via self-regulation, learn to override their avoidance-based propensities to proactively seek positive achievement outcomes. Although this type of overriding of basic tendencies may initially be difficult and entail a large expenditure of attentional and ego-based resources (Elliot, Sheldon, & Church, 1997), over time and repetition such regulation may become more natural, efficient, and perhaps even automatic (Logan, 1988; Muraven, Baumeister, & Tice, 1999).

## CLOSING STATEMENT

As this chapter has illustrated, the approach-avoidance distinction affords considerable conceptual and empirical utility in motivational analyses of behavior. This distinction may be applied to nearly any psychological construct, lending distinct insights that would not otherwise be attained. That organisms are motivated in multifarious ways to approach the positive and avoid the negative may be construed as something of a psychological law. As valuable as the approach-avoidance distinction is, however, human behavior simply cannot be reduced to a single psychological attribute. Indeed, as we have outlined, other psychological distinctions are needed to understand motivated behavior more completely. In the achievement domain, one such distinction is the mastery-performance distinction that has been and continues to be the cornerstone of the achievement goal approach to achievement motivation.

## REFERENCES

Allport, G. W. (1937). *Personality: A psychological interpretation.* New York: Holt.

Ames, C. (1984). Achievement attributions and self-instructions in competitive and individualistic goal structures. *Journal of Educational Psychology, 76,* 478–487.

Ames, C. (1992). Classrooms: Goals, structures, and student motivation. *Journal of Educational Psychology, 84,* 261–271.

Ames, C., & Archer, J. (1987). Mothers' belief about the role of ability and effort in school learning. *Journal of Educational Psychology, 79,* 409–414.

Ames, C., & Archer, J. (1988). Achievement goals in the classroom: Students' learning strategies and motivation processes. *Journal of Educational Psychology, 80,* 260– 267.

Arnold, M. (1960). *Emotion and personality.* New York: Columbia University Press.

Atkinson, J. W., & Birch, D. (1970). *The dynamics of action.* New York: Wiley.

Austin, J. T., & Vancouver, J. B. (1996). Goal constructs in psychology: Structure, process, and content. *Psychological Bulletin, 120,* 338–375.

Baumeister, R. F., Vohs, K. D. (2003). Willpower, choice, and self-control. In G. Loewenstein, D. Read, & R. Baumeister (Eds.), *Time and decision: Economic and psychological perspectives on intertemporal choice* (pp. 201–216). New York: Russell Sage Foundation.

Bentham, J. (1779/1879). *Introduction to the principles of morals and legislation.* Oxford: Clarendon Press.

Berridge, K. (1999). Pleasure, pain, desire, and dread: Hidden core processes of emotion. In D. Kahneman, E. Diener, & N. Schwarz (Eds.), *Wellbeing: The foundations of hedonic psychology* (pp. 525–557). New York: Russell Sage Foundation.

Buck, R. (1999). The biology of affects: A typology. *Psychological Review, 106,* 301–336.

Butler, R. (1988). Task-involving and ego-involving properties of evaluation: Effects of different feedback conditions on motivational perceptions, interest, and performance. *Journal of Educational Psychology, 79,* 474–482.

Butler, R. (1992). What young people want to know when: Effects of mastery and ability goals on interest in different kinds of social comparisons. *Journal of Personality and Social Psychology, 62,* 934–943.

Cacioppo, J., & Bernston, G. (1994). Relationship between attitudes and evaluative space: A critical review with emphasis on the separability of positive and negative substrates. *Psychological Bulletin, 115,* 401–422.

Carver, C., & Scheier, M. (1998). *On the self-regulation of behavior.* New York: Cambridge University Press.

Corwin, G. (1921). Minor studies from the psychological laboratory of Cornell University. *American Journal of Psychology, 32,* 563–570.

Conroy, D. E. (2004). The unique psychological meanings of multidimensional fears of failing. *Journal of Sport and Exercise Psychology, 26,* 484–491

Conroy, D. E., & Elliot, A. J. (2004). Fear of failure and achievement goals in sport: Addressing the issue of the chicken and the egg. *Anxiety, Stress, and Coping, 17,* 271–285.

Conroy, D. E., Elliot, A. J., & Hofer, S. M. (2003). A 2 x 2 achievement goals questionnaire for sport. *Journal of Sport and Exercise Psychology, 25,* 456–476.

Covington, M. V. (1984). Strategic thinking and the fear of failure. In J. Segal, S. Chipman, & R. Glaser (Eds.), *Thinking and learning skills: Relating instruction to basic research* (pp. 389–416). NJ: Erlbaum.

Cury, F., Elliot, A. J., Da Fonseca, D., & Moller, A. C. (2006). The social-cognitive model of achievement motivation and the 2 x 2 achievement goal framework. *Journal of Personality and Social Psychology, 90,* 666–679.

Diener, C. I. & Dweck, C. S. (1978). An analysis of learned helplessness: Continuous changes in performance, strategy, and achievement cognitions following failure. *Journal of Personality and Social Psychology, 36,* 451–462.

Diener, C. I. & Dweck, C. S. (1980). An analysis of learned helplessness: The processing of success. *Journal of Personality and Social Psychology, 39,* 940–952.

Duda, J. L. (1988). The relationship between goal perspectives, persistence and behavioral intensity among male and female recreational sport participants. *Leisure Studies, 10,* 95–106.

Dweck, C. S. (1975). The role of expectations and attributions in the alleviation of learned helplessness. *Journal of Personality and Social Psychology, 31, 674–685.*

Dweck, C. S. (1986). Motivational processes affecting learning. *American Psychologist, 41,* 1040–1048.

Dweck, C. S., & Elliott, E. S. (1983). Achievement motivation. In E. M. Heatherington (Ed.), *Handbook of child psychology: Socialization, personality, and social development* (Vol. 4, pp. 643–691). New York: Wiley.

Dweck, C. S., & Reppucci, D. (1973). Learned helplessness and reinforcement responsibility in children. *Journal of Personality and Social Psychology, 25,* 109–116.

Elliot, A. J. (1994). Approach and avoidance achievement goals: An intrinsic motivation analysis. Unpublished doctoral dissertation. University of Wisconsin-Madison.

Elliot, A. J. (1997). Integrating «classic» and «contemporary» approaches to achievement motivation: A hierarchical model of approach and avoidance achievement motivation. In P. Pintrich & M. Maehr (Eds.), *Advances in motivation and achievement* (Vol. 10, pp. 143–179). Greenwich, CT: JAI Press.

Elliot, A. J. (1999). Approach and avoidance motivation and achievement goals. *Educational Psychologist, 34,* 169–189.

Elliot, A. J., & Church, M. A. (1997). A hierarchical model of approach and avoidance achievement motivation. *Journal of Personality and Social Psychology, 72,* 218–232.

Elliot, A. J., & Covington, M. V. (2001). Approach and avoidance motivation. *Educational Psychology Review, 13,* 73–92.

Elliot, A. J., & Friedman, R. (2006). Approach and avoidance personal goals. In B. Little, K. Salmela-Aro, & S. Phillips (Eds.), *Personal project pursuit: Goals, action, and human flourishing* (pp. 97–116). Hillsdale, NJ: Lawrence Erlbaum Associates.

Elliot, A. J. & Fryer, J. (2008). The goal construct in psychology. In J. Shah and W. Gardner (Eds.), *Handbook of motivational science* (pp. 235–250). New York: Guilford Press.

Elliot, A. J., & Harackiewicz, J. M. (1996). Approach and avoidance achievement goals and intrinsic motivation: A meditational analysis. *Journal of Personality and Social Psychology, 70,* 461–475.

Elliot, A. J., & Mapes, R. R. (2005). Approach-avoidance motivation and self-concept evaluation. In A. Tesser, J. Wood, & D. Stapel (Eds.), *On building, defending, and regulating the self: A psychological perspective* (pp. 171–196). Washington, DC: Psychological Press.

Elliot, A. J., & McGregor, H. A. (2001). A 2 x 2 achievement goal framework. *Journal of Personality and Social Psychology, 80,* 501–519.

Elliot, A. J., McGregor, H. A., & Thrash, T. M. (2002). The need for competence. In E. Deci & R. Ryan (Eds.), *Handbook of Self-determination Research* (pp. 361–387). Rochester, NY: University of Rochester Press.

Elliot, A. J., & Reis, H. T. (2003). Attachment and exploration in adulthood. *Journal of Personality and Social Psychology, 85,* 317–331.

Elliot, A. J., Sheldon, K., & Church, M. (1997). Avoidance personal goals and subjective well-being. *Personality and Social Psychology Bulletin, 23,* 915–927.

Elliot, A. J., & Thrash, T. M. (2001). Achievement goals and the hierarchical model of achievement motivation. *Educational Psychology Review, 12,* 139–156.

Elliot, A. J., & Thrash, T. M. (2002). Approach-avoidance motivation in personality: Approach and avoidance temperaments and goals. *Journal of Personality and Social Psychology, 82,* 804–818.

Elliott, E. S., & Dweck, C. S. (1988). Goals: An approach to motivation and achievement. *Journal of Personality and Social Psychology, 54,* 5–12.

Elliot, A. J., & Moller, A. (2003). Performance-approach goals: Good or bad forms of regulation? *International Journal of Educational Research, 39,* 339–356.

Finney, S. J., Pieper, S. L., & Barren, K. E. (2004). Examining the psychometric properties of the achievement goal questionnaire in a general academic context. *Educational and Psychological Measurement, 64,* 365–382.

Freud, S. (1915). Repression. In the standard edition of *Complete psychological works of Sigmund Freud*, Vol. XIV. London: Hogarth, 1957.

Harackiewicz, J. M., Barron, K. E., & Elliot, A. J. (1998). Rethinking achievement goals: When are they adaptive for college students and why? *Educational Psychologist, 33,* 121.

Harackiewicz, J. M., Barron, K. E., Pintrich, P. R., Elliot, A. J., & Thrash, T. M. (2002). Revision of achievement goal theory: Necessary and illuminating. *Journal of Educational Psychology, 94,* 638–645.

Herzberg, F. (1966). *Work and the nature of man.* Cleveland, OH: Ward

Higgins, E. T. (1997). Beyond pleasure and pain. *American Psychologist, 52,* 1280–1300.

Jagacinski, C. M., & Nicholls, J. G. (1987). Competence and affect in task involvement and ego involvement: The impact of social comparison information. *Journal of Educational Psychology, 79,* 107–114.

James, W. (1890). *The principles of psychology.* New York: Henry Holt & Co.

Kaplan, A., & Middleton, M. J. (2002). Should childhood be a journey of a race? Response to Harackiewicz et al. (2002). *Journal of Educational Psychology, 94,* 646–648.

Karabenick, S. A. (2003). Seeking help in large college classes: A person-centered approach. *Contemporary Educational Psychology, 28,* 37–58.

Karabenick, S. A. (2004). Perceived achievement goal structure and college student help seeking. *Journal of Educational Psychology, 96,* 569–581.

Koesnter, R., Zuckerman, M., & Koestner, J. (1987). Praise, involvement, and intrinsic motivation. *Journal of Personality and Social Psychology, 53,* 383–390.

Kukla, A. (1972). Attributional determinants of achievement-related behavior. *Journal of Personality and Social Psychology, 21,* 166–174.

Lang, P. J. (1995). The emotion probe: Studies of motivation and attention. *American Psychologist, 50,* 372–385.

Lewin, K. (1926). Vorsatz, Wille und Bedürfnis [Intention, will, and need]. *Psychologische Forschung, 7,* 330–385.

Lewin, K. (1935). *A dynamic theory of personality.* New York: McGraw-Hill.

Logan, G. (1988). Toward and instance theory of automatization. *Psychological Review, 95,* 492–527.

Maehr, M. L. (1983). On doing well in science: Why Johnny no longer excels, why Sarah never did. In S. G. Paris, G. M. Olson, & H. W. Stevenson (Eds.), *Learning & Motivation in the classroom,* Hillsdale, NJ: LEA.

Maehr, M. L. (1984). Meaning and motivation. In R. Ames & C. Ames (Eds.), *Research on motivation in education: Student motivation* (Vol. 1, pp. 115–144). New York: Academic Press.

Maehr, M. L., & Nicholls, J. (1980). Culture and achievement motivation: A second look. In N. Warren (Ed.), *Studies in cross-cultural psychology* (Vol. 2, 221–267). New York: Academic Press.

Malka, A., & Covington, M. V. (2005). Perceiving school performance as instrumental to future goal attainment: Effects on graded performance. *Contemporary Educational Psychology, 30,* 60–80.

Meece, J. L., Blumenfeld, P. C., & Hoyle, R. H. (1988). Students' goal orientations and cognitive engagement in classroom activities. *Journal of Educational Psychology, 80,* 514–523.

Meece, J. L., & Holt, K. (1993). A pattern analysis of students' achievement goals. *Journal of Educational Psychology, 85,* 582–590.

Meyer, W. (1987). Perceived ability and achievement-related behavior. In F. Halisch & J. Kuhl (Eds.), *Motivation, intention, and volition* (pp. 73–86). New York: Springer- Verlag.

Midgley, C., Kaplan, A., & Middleton, M. (2001). Performance-approach goals: Good for what, for whom, under what circumstances, and at what cost? *Journal of Educational Psychology, 93,* 77–86.

Moller, A. C., & Elliot, A. J. (2006). The 2 x 2 Achievement Goal Framework: An Overview of Empirical Research. In A.V. Mittel (Ed), *Focus on educational psychology* (pp. 307–326). New York: Nova Science Publishers.

Muraven, M., Baumeister, R. F., & Tice, D. M. (1999). Longitudinal improvement of self- regulation through practice: Building self-control through repeated exercise. *Journal of Social Psychology, 139,* 446–457.

Murray, H. A. (1938). *Explorations in personality.* New York: Oxford University Press.

Nicholls, J. G. (1976). Effort is virtuous, but it's better to have ability: Evaluative responses to perceptions of effort and ability. *Journal of Personality and Social Psychology, 31,* 306–315.

Nicholls, J. G. (1978). The development of concepts of effort and ability, perception of own attainment, and the understanding that difficult tasks require more ability. *Child Development, 49,* 800–814.

Nicholls, J. G. (1980). The development of the concept of difficulty. *Merrill-Palmer Quarterly, 26,* 271–281.

Nicholls, J. G., Patashnick, M., & Nolen, S. (1985). Adolescents' theories of education. *Journal of Educational Psychology, 77,* 683–692.

Nolen, S. B. (1988). Reasons for studying: Motivational orientations and study strategies. *Cognition and Instruction, 5,* 269–287.

Ryan, R. M. (1982). Control and information in the interpersonal sphere: An extension of cognitive evaluation theory. *Journal of Personality and Social Psychology, 43,* 450–461.

Sansone, C., Sachau, D. A., & Weir, C. (1989). Effects of instruction on intrinsic interest: The importance of context. *Journal of Personality and Social Psychology, 57,* 819–829.

Schneirla, T. (1959). An evolutionary and developmental theory of biphasic processes underlying approach and withdrawal. In *Nebraska Symposium on Motivation* (pp. 1–42). Lincoln, NE: University of Nebraska Press.

Skaalvik, E. M., Valans, H., & Sletta, O. (1994). Task involvement and ego involvement: Relations with academic achievement, academic self-concept, and self-esteem. *Scandanavian Journal of Educational Research, 38,* 231–243.

Stipek, D. J., & Kowalski, P. S. (1989). Learned helplessness in task-orienting versus performance-orienting test conditions. *Journal of Educational Psychology, 81,* 384–391.

Tolman, E. (1932). *Purposive behavior in animals and men.* New York: The Century.

Thrash, T. M., & Elliot, A. J. (2001). Delimiting and integrating achievement motive and goal constructs. In A. Efklides, J. Kuhl, & R. Sorrentino (Eds.), *Trends and prospects in motivational research* (p. 119). The Netherlands: Kluwer Academic Publishers.

Thorkildsen, T. A. (1989). Pluralism in children's reasoning about social justice. *Child Development, 60,* 965–972.

Van Yperen, N. W. (2003). Task Interest and Actual Performance: The Moderating Effects of Assigned and Adopted Purpose Goals. *Journal of Personality and Social Psychology, 85,* 1006–1015.

CHAPTER 6

# MARTY MAEHR'S CONTRIBUTIONS TO RESEARCH IN PASTEUR'S QUADRANT

## The Mathematics and Science Partnership—Motivation Assessment Program

**Stuart A. Karabenick, Bridget V. Dever, Juliane Blazevski, AnneMarie M. Conley, Jeanne M. Friedel, Melissa C. Gilbert, and Lauren E. Musu**

One of Marty Maehr's most important collaborators, Paul Pintrich, frequently invoked Pasteur's Quadrant (Stokes, 1997) to characterize the contribution of motivation science to teaching and learning (e.g., Pintrich,

Research in this chapter is based on work supported by the National Science Foundation under Grant No. 0335369. Any opinions, findings, and conclusions or recommendations expressed in this material are ours and do not necessarily reflect the views of the National Science Foundation.

**135**

2003). Pasteur's quadrant refers to use-inspired basic research, the purpose of which is both to understand fundamental principles (e.g., of microbiology) and solve practical problems (e.g., prevent spoilage of milk). Marty's creative contributions, which include the *Theory of Personal Investment* (Maehr & Braskamp, 1986), *continuing motivation* (Maehr, 1976) and *achievement goals* (Maehr, 1984), fall within that rubric. These contributions have provided educational researchers theoretical lenses through which to understand the personal and situational determinants of student learning and performance and serve as guides for how to create motivationally adaptive learning contexts. The dual objective of science and application was expressed most clearly in an ambitious program conducted with Carol Midgley to transform school cultures (Maehr & Midgley, 1996). This chapter describes yet another embodiment of Marty's commitment to motivation in education on a national scale—the Mathematics and Science Partnership-Motivation Assessment Program (MSP-MAP). This program engaged in basic research to improve the assessment of motivation while providing assistance to school-based interventions designed to increase student learning and performance in the areas of mathematics and science. The program's dual goals of research and program evaluation situated it squarely within Pasteur's quadrant (Karabenick, 2005).

## THE MATHEMATICS AND SCIENCE PARTNERSHIP PROGRAM: AN OVERVIEW

A salutary feature of the No Child Left Behind (NCLB, 2002) legislation is that of providing federal funding for the Mathematics and Science Partnership program (MSP; mspnet.org). Directed by the US Department of Education (ED) and the National Science Foundation (NSF), the MSP program is dedicated to improving math and science education at levels K-12 by fostering partnerships among school districts, state education agencies, and colleges and universities. In addition to Math and Science Partnerships (MSPs), the NSF program funded a series of Research, Evaluation, and Technical Assistance (RETA) projects to support the MSPs. NSF's mandate included conducting research to more completely understand the processes of math and science teaching and learning, and providing technical expertise for a more rigorous evaluation of MSP interventions. RETA activities varied considerably within these broad objectives, from the development of more reliable and efficient instruments to assess teachers' mathematical content knowledge to conducting workshops on evaluation.

*The Importance of Motivation to the MSP Mission*

MSP-MAP responded to the fact that, whereas many MSP projects acknowledged the importance of motivation in the teaching and learning process, few had specific plans to address motivational issues as part of their interventions, thus implying that MSPs assumed that more adaptive student motivation would follow from the introduction of reform math and science teaching practices. Furthermore, there was little evidence that MSPs devoted sufficient attention to the assessment of student motivation. Given the voluminous evidence for the impact of motivation on student learning (e.g., Perry, Turner, & Meyer, 2006; Schunk, Pintrich, & Meece, 2007), and student learning in mathematics and science in particular (e.g., Bell & Linn, 2002; Grouws, 1992; Koller, Baumert, & Schnabel, 2001; McLeod & Adams, 1989; Pintrich, Marx, & Boyle, 1993; Schoenfeld, 1985, 1989), this was a serious omission.

By enabling MSPs to better understand motivation-related beliefs and strategies, MSP-MAP contributed important information for both formative and summative evaluation about how their programs and interventions affect students. Such information, it was theorized, could also contribute to teachers' professional development by providing them with insight into how their approaches to teaching math and science influenced student motivation-related beliefs and use of self-regulated learning strategies. Having appropriate reliable and valid tools available to assess these motivation-related processes and outcomes was considered necessary for the success of such a program. Stated more emphatically, in the absence of such tools, MSPs might overlook important ways their projects may have affected students, especially since changes in motivation, beliefs, and learning strategies may often precede changes in student achievement.

Most generally, motivation-related outcomes include student goals for mathematics and science, student confidence in their capabilities to do mathematical and scientific work, as well as interest, utility, and value for mathematics and science. They also encompass various strategies for approaching (or avoiding) mathematical and scientific work, student beliefs about the nature of mathematics and science, including epistemology, and student beliefs about the nature of teaching and learning in these disciplines. As noted in many national curriculum projects and standards in mathematics and science (e.g., Kilpatrick, Swafford, & Findell, 2001; National Council of Teachers of Mathematics, 1989; Project 2061-American Association for the Advancement of Science, 1993), motivation-related outcomes are important goals for mathematics and science instruction.

## THE MATHEMATICS AND SCIENCE PARTNERSHIP–
## MOTIVATION ASSESSMENT PROGRAM

Initiated by Paul Pintrich and Stuart Karabenick, in collaboration with Marty Maehr, MSP-MAP's initial project goals were:

- To develop and make available reliable, valid, and practical tools to assess student motivational beliefs, strategies for self-regulated learning, beliefs about the epistemology of the disciplines of math and science, and beliefs about teaching and learning that can be used by mathematics and science classroom teachers, and by MSPs, to evaluate the effectiveness of their interventions;
- To increase teachers' and MSPs' knowledge about the role of these beliefs and strategies as either mediators or moderators of instruction and how they are related to student achievement in mathematics and science, in a manner that informs the design and evaluation of interventions; and
- To assist teachers and MSPs by providing information about how students' motivational beliefs and strategies, and their linkages to student achievement, generalize or may differ as a function of gender, age, race, ethnicity, and SES.

The research team at the University of Michigan brought their experience with K-12 students, teachers, and administrators to bear on developing supportive collaborations with several MSPs. Because that experience included interventions designed to facilitate motivation and achievement (e.g., promoting mastery-oriented learning contexts; Maehr & Midgley, 1996; Midgley, 2002), MSP-MAP was well positioned to assist MSP projects that involved similar interventions in a manner that was by design intended to be a highly reciprocal and collaborative process.

The resources that MSP-MAP provided included measures of student motivation and strategies for self-regulated learning that are widely used. Most prominently, colleagues of the MSP-MAP program had developed the Patterns of Adaptive Learning Survey (PALS; Midgley, Kaplan, Middleton, Maehr, Urdan, Hicks-Anderman, Anderman, & Roeser, 1998; Midgley et al., 2000), which focuses on student motivation, goals, and strategies for learning in academic subjects. PALS had been used in numerous studies and was the self-report instrument used most often to measure student motivation and goals. Pintrich and his colleagues had also developed the Motivated Strategies for Learning Questionnaire (MSLQ; Pintrich & De-Groot, 1990; Pintrich, Smith, Garcia, & McKeachie, 1993; Wolters, Pintrich, & Karabenick, 2003), which provides reliable and valid measures of student motivation and self-regulated learning for secondary and college students.

Importantly, both the MSLQ and PALS were designed to be subject matter or discipline-specific, which meant they are useful tools for the study of mathematics and science classrooms.

## CONTRIBUTIONS TO EDUCATIONAL PRACTICE

*MSP-MAP Collaborations with MSPs*

Although MSP-MAP could potentially interact with the over 50 MSPs through the connections provided by the MSP network, two collaborations in particular afforded exceptional opportunities to demonstrate how motivational research and educational practice can inform one another toward the goal of educational improvement. These two partnerships were Transforming East Alabama Mathematics (TEAM-Math), based at Auburn University and Tuskegee University, and Teachers Assisting Students to Excel in Learning Mathematics (TASEL-M) centered at California State University–Fullerton. Although the partnerships were similar in their general goals and objectives, collaborations with MSP-MAP were structured to improve their motivation-related evaluation instruments and designed to accommodate their specific needs and student demographics.

### Process

Collaborations between MSP-MAP and MSPs were mutually supportive and beneficial: MSP-MAP provided expertise regarding motivation, evaluation, and research design; in turn, MSPs granted access to large and diverse populations of students and teachers. MSP-MAP began the collaboration by examining MSP goals, objectives, measures, and evaluation designs, which included explicit logic models, then suggested ways to substitute and/or augment evaluation instruments and procedures with accompanying rationale. Several exchanges were frequently required to resolve issues and arrive at accommodations, including informal memos of understanding. Throughout multiple waves of data collection the process was repeated, with increasing levels of understanding and mutuality.

### TEAM-Math

Situated in East Alabama, TEAM-Math had assumed the ambitious task of improving mathematics learning and instruction at the elementary, middle, and high school levels. Set in one of the poorest sections of the US, a large proportion of the student population came from low SES families, nearly half African American. Their intervention featured standards-based reform instruction, which emphasizes more constructivist and interactive methods for changing the way mathematics is taught, including the use of collaborative learning rather than traditional direct instruction and drill and practice. TEAM-Math evaluation of students and teachers involved cross-sectional and longitudinal studies to determine how instruction, learning, and beliefs about mathematics changed over time as a function of their intervention.

Although increased math achievement was the critical outcome, early discussions indicated that project personnel fully understood the importance of student *and* teacher motivation to reach that goal. Early in the collaborative process, MSP-MAP had both transformed TEAM-Math's views of motivation and added more comprehensive motivation assessment (e.g., scales from PALS) to their program evaluations. The assessment of classroom goals, teacher expectations, student efficacy, personal goals, interest, and perceived utility value of math provided TEAM-Math with more detailed knowledge of motivational processes and outcomes. In addition, TEAM-Math profited through increased knowledge of how motivation contributes to students' experiences and outcomes in mathematics, and MSP-MAP by a more thorough understanding of mathematics instruction and the challenges that teachers confront in general, and in low SES and diverse populations in particular.

### TASEL-M

A similar evolution occurred in the collaboration with TASEL-M, a partnership focused on improving the mathematics learning and performance of middle and high schools in Southern California. The population consisted primarily of Latino/a students (and a smaller proportion of Vietnamese), from working class families, many of whom had recently immigrated to the US and were English language learners. Initial interactions with TASEL-M teachers, teacher leaders, and other educational personnel indicated that stakeholders intuitively knew that "motivation mattered," and were interested in knowing more about how, why, and what they could do to provide a more motivationally supportive context for instruction. Over the course of three academic years (seven waves of data collection), MSP-MAP worked closely with the TASEL-M team to collect quantitative self-report data from as many as 13,000 students and 200 teachers at each time point. Students were assessed regarding their goals, values, and efficacy for mathematics, as well as their perceptions of the math classroom, in order to gain a better understanding of how the process of motivation unfolds in the classroom to influence student motivation and learning. Teachers were asked about their approaches to instruction and efficacy for various aspects of teaching. Parent involvement was also studied: students reported the extent of parental support for learning, and teachers were asked about their beliefs and experiences with parental involvement.

## MSP-MAP Professional Development

As the collaborations evolved, in addition to its technical advisory role, MSP-MAP became increasingly integrated into MSP interventions, primarily professional development (PD) that had three objectives:

1. explain contemporary motivation theory and applications to education;
2. provide extensive feedback regarding analyses based on data obtained from the MSP's student and teacher populations; and
3. discuss with teachers the implications of the results for classroom practice.

To meet the objectives of disseminating current directions in motivational research and tying research to instructional practice, we used a modified version of Ames' (1990) TARGET framework. The framework delineates aspects of classroom instruction that can influence student motivation: features of learning Tasks, the degree of student Autonomy, types of Reward and Recognition, Grouping, Evaluation, and Time. To these were added Teacher Expectations and the Social environment of the classroom (i.e., TARGETTS). Motivationally adaptive consequences are considered more likely when students are:

a. presented a variety of interesting and challenging tasks,
b. given autonomy (e.g., choices) regarding activities in which to engage,
c. recognized and rewarded appropriately for effort and improvement,
d. engaged in collaborative learning with their peers,
e. evaluated privately and self-referentially,
f. allowed to self-schedule their tasks,
g. supported by clear teacher expectations for student success and
h. educated in a socially supportive classroom environment.

MSP-MAP PD curricula were adapted to each MSP project's goals, objectives and PD context. In addition to giving a general overview of motivational concepts as they apply to classroom instructional practice (e.g., efficacy, value, and achievement goals), and developmental (cross-sectional) trends, including variability in students' perceptions of mathematics classroom contexts (e.g., teacher support, achievement goal structure), MSP-MAP engaged teachers in practical discussions of how instruction can be more supportive of adaptive student motivation. Especially important, however, was the presentation of detailed and comprehensive data obtained from the respective student and teacher populations. For example, TASEL-M PD sessions featured profiles of student motivation at the beginning and end of the school year. Data were summarized both at the school and teacher levels. Teachers received confidential summaries of each of their classes (over 2000 classes in all). These reports formed the basis for data-driven discussions, including in some instances recommended changes in teacher practices. Feedback from TASEL-M personnel strongly suggested that such locally-obtained information contributed considerably to teachers' understanding of the motivational constructs. Reflecting Marty's general approach to working with the schools, discussions were also held on specific motivation-related topics that emerged during the workshop. These included his commitment to mitigate the detrimental effects of ego-performance achievement goals and to stress the benefits of a mastery-focused context.

Although similar in many respects, TEAM-Math professional development sessions required adjustments given the audience, which consisted of "teacher leaders" who were intermediaries with additional project-related responsibilities such as communicating new ideas and frameworks to the teachers at their schools. As with TASEL-M, the TARGETTS framework was presented and promoted as an important lesson analysis and planning tool, aligned with specific instructional practices that TEAM-Math was attempting to promote. Thus, the workshop presented a framework in close alignment with content that TEAM-Math teacher leaders were familiar with and already implementing in their schools. PD sessions included presentations of data-based models of the relations among motivational and achievement variables based on locally-obtained student information. The models were able to show, for example, that TEAM-Math students who perceived more frequent use of reform practices by their teachers, and had teachers with higher expectations and standards (the main focus of TEAM-Math's teacher intervention) reported more adaptive levels of mastery goal endorsement, efficacy, and interest in math, as well as decreased math anxiety. The model also indicated these motivational effects predicted more time spent studying, higher expected math grades, and better performance on the state standardized test. Furthermore, students who reported that their teachers used more reform instructional practices were students whose teachers were more involved in TEAM-Math and endorsed those practices. This project-specific information was an important part of keeping teachers involved in TEAM-Math activities by providing evidence of impact. It also provided additional evidence of the important role that student motivation plays in ongoing systemic change.

## ADVANCES IN MOTIVATION-RELATED RESEARCH

*Motivation-Related Assessment*

A primary goal of MSP-MAP was the improvement of existing motivation-related scales and those adapted and created by the program, especially instruments designed to assess students' perceptions of their teachers and classrooms, which was a major concern of the MSPs. Examples of scale development and other studies emerging from collaborative research between MSP-MAP and our partners on other MSP projects are described below. In addition to standard psychometrics, considerable resources were devoted to improving assessment through the rigorous application of cognitive interviewing (Karabenick, Woolley, Friedel, Ammon, Blazevski, Bonney, De Groot, Gilbert, Musu, Kempler, & Kelly, 2007). Analyses utilizing constructed scales, for example, revealed typical grade-level trends of student motivational characteristics as well as student perceptions of the classroom context.

In general, consistent with other research (Schunk et al., 2007), students in higher grades compared to those in lower grades reported lower levels of mathematics self-efficacy, interest in mathematics, perceived utility of mathematics, mastery goals, help-seeking behaviors, and positive affect related to mathematics. Interestingly, endorsement of performance goals showed a similar trend, indicating that students at higher grade levels were less likely to focus on their ability relative to others. Achievement in math was also related to higher levels of mastery-oriented achievement goals, efficacy and value of math and lower levels of performance goals—a more adaptive motivational profile for high-achieving students. Furthermore, students' perceptions of the classroom context were related to motivational characteristics. Specifically, the more that students perceived their classroom environment to emphasize mastery-oriented goals, the more they reported higher levels of efficacy, interest, and positive affect, and were more likely to believe that math is useful. The following sections describe results of specific studies that emerged from the MSP-MAP project and collaborations, which include cognitive validity, teacher efficacy, mathematical understanding, parent involvement and person-oriented approaches to motivation research.

*Cognitive Validity*

Recent advances in survey methodology involve obtaining data directly from members of targeted respondent populations (Ruiz-Prima, Schultz, Ki, & Shavelson, 2001; Thelk & Hoole, & Lottridge, 2005) to understand the cognitive processing that occurs when individuals respond to surveys (Tourangeau, Rips, & Rasinski, 2000) and to improve the validity of responses to survey questions (Forsyth & Lessler, 1991; Jabine, Straf, Tanur, & Tourangeau, 1984). In particular, the systematic use of cognitive pretesting (CP) involves assessing the validity of individual items rather than the performance of an entire scale based on psychometric analyses (e.g., Cronbach α, factor analysis, and convergence with criterion measures). Three critical cognitive information processing steps used to establish a cognitively valid response to an item are:

1.  interpretation of the item's meaning,
2.  recall of memories relevant to the item, and
3.  choosing an answer that accurately reflects those memories.

In brief interviews, respondents are asked, for example: What is this question trying to find out from you? Which answer would you choose as the right answer for you? Can you explain to me why you chose that answer? Responses are coded according to rigorously-specified criteria that determine whether items are responded to as researchers intend. Given acceptable inter-rater reliability, the proportions of respondents meeting those criteria can differentiate items that are performing well from those which may require modification.

For example, one set of items that MSP-MAP focused on was classroom-level mastery goal structure (PALS; Midgley et al., 1998; Midgley et al., 2000; Meece, Anderman, & Anderman, 2006). Although evidence supports the validity of PALS goal structure scales, issues remain regarding the basis of students' judgments (Patrick, 2004; Urdan, 2004; Urdan, Kniesel, & Mason, 1999). Two versions of an item from the scale were subjected to CP: "My teacher thinks it's okay to make mistakes as long as you are learning" and "In my science classroom it's okay to make mistakes as long as you are learning." Results clearly indicated that the "My teacher" frame elicited a higher proportion of acceptable responses. When administered the "In my science class" wording, students were either more likely to reflect on classroom contexts other than science, or on personal goals rather than the science classroom goal structure. For example:

*S:*   In my science class, it's okay to make mistakes as long as you are learning.
*I:*   What is that trying to find out?
*S:*   It's trying to find out, like, uh, if you learn from mistakes
*I:*   OK. What would you say?
*S:*   I'd say, 5.
*I:*   Why?

*S:*   Because, um, I have noticed, like, a lot of times, for, for example like, um, if you like, do uh, like if you're taking swimming class and you stroke your arms wrong, and then you do it, and then you do it how you're supposed to, and it comes out right, you learn from that mistake not to do that.

Presented with "My teacher," students were much more likely to focus on the teacher and less likely to consider their personal goals. For example:

S: My teacher thinks it's okay to make mistakes in science as long as you are learning.
I: What is that trying to find out?
S: It's trying to find out, like, once again, um, you learn from mistakes. And, uh, it's just this time, your opinion of your teacher.
I: Ok, what do you think about that?
S: 5.
I: A 5? Why do you think that?
S: Because, um, I think that because um, uh, my teacher, she um, she sometimes, like, uh, just today, um, my friend, she said, she said, 'carbon dioxoyde' instead of carbon dioxide, she said 'It's ok, keep trying, you're on the right track'.

This example illustrates the richness of elaboration captured by cognitive interviews and probing techniques. Obtaining such evidence represents a growing trend in educational research to employ qualitative techniques to improve the validity of self-report assessment within an overall quantitative research agenda (e.g., Desimone & Le Floch, 2004). Including information obtained using these techniques is consistent with the view that validity can include multiple sources of evidence that informs the interpretation or meaning of test scores (Messick, 1995).

### Teacher Efficacy for Motivation

Teacher efficacy for supporting student motivation refers to the extent to which teachers believe themselves capable of supporting their students' motivation to learn (e.g., supporting students' own efficacy beliefs, perceived value of material, and interest in the domain). As reviewed by Blazevski (2006), however, relatively little research had focused on teachers' personal efficacy to motivate their students, despite the likely influence of efficacy beliefs on student motivation and learning (Bandura, 2006). Accordingly, Blazevski developed and validated a survey instrument for that purpose and examined relations between teacher efficacy for supporting student motivation and students' motivational beliefs and achievement in math. Results of confirmatory factor analysis involving data generated from middle school and high school mathematics teachers fit a measurement model in which teacher efficacy for supporting student motivation was distinct from teacher efficacy in other domains (i.e., instruction and classroom management). Data also fit a structural equation model in which teacher efficacy for supporting student motivation was indirectly related to student achievement in math and was partially mediated by student perceptions of classroom goal structure and student efficacy beliefs. Hierarchical linear modeling also found that teacher efficacy for supporting student motivation was a significant predictor of between-teacher variance in their students' efficacy for and interest in math. Teaching experience was a significant negative predictor of teacher efficacy for supporting student motivation—those teaching longer believed themselves less efficacious.

### Motivation and Components of Mathematical Understanding and Performance

In a study by Gilbert (2007), a subsample of TASEL-M pre-algebra students ($n = 479$) were surveyed to examine motivation-related beliefs and given a performance assessment that focused on their procedural/conceptual understanding and adaptive reasoning for the topic of addition of unlike fractions. The performance assessment results revealed that many students had difficulty with both procedural/conceptual understanding and adaptive reasoning, and that understanding was a necessary but not sufficient condition for reasoning. Analyses relating motivational factors to performance suggested that, in addition to students' perceptions of value (including cost) and efficacy, their focus on learning and understanding (i.e., mastery-goal endorsement) was an important correlate of adaptive reasoning (Gilbert, 2008). The results also showed that students who scored high on measures of both interest and efficacy were not necessarily high-achieving; rather, their performance depended on the relative levels of other aspects of motivation, such as their perceptions of cost (i.e., effort and time required) and their math achievement goals (i.e., personal goal orientation). The findings indicated that using a more refined conception of mathematical competence together with measures of a differentiated set of motivational constructs can help in understanding the relationship between motivation and student learning in mathematics. This study thus provided a framework for research on motivation in mathematics education that could further the understanding of how aspects of motivation relate to mathematical proficiency and achievement.

### Perceived Classroom Context

#### Student Help Seeking

With its goal of increasing understanding, instrumental (also termed adaptive and autonomous) help seeking can be classified with other desirable strategies available to learners who determine that they require assistance to solve problems or reach other learning goals. In addition to relatively enduring characteristics that students bring to learning tasks, context plays an especially important role given the largely social-interactive process involved in seeking help (Karabenick, 2004; Newman, 2000; Urdan, Ryan, Anderman, & Gheen, 2002). Most directly, help seeking depends on students' beliefs about how receptive their teachers are to questions and other requests for assistance (Karabenick & Sharma, 1994; Le Mare & Sohbat, 2002; Newman & Goldin, 1990). Such teacher responses are not isolated events, however, but are components of an integrated set of practices that reflect the overall classroom climate and structure that influences student motivation, self-regulated learning, and performance (e.g., Ames, 1992). Accordingly, MSP-MAP examined whether help seeking was influenced by how students perceived several critical features of that context.

Students ($n = 14,000+$) in 487 classrooms participating in the TASEL-M initiative completed surveys that assessed help seeking and several dimensions of students' perceptions of the classroom context: mastery, performance approach and avoidance *classroom achievement goal structure* (PALS; Midgley et al., 2000) *teacher caring* (Feldlaufer, Midgley, & Eccles, 1988; Moos, 1980; Ryan & Patrick, 2001); *teacher respect and fairness* (Ryan & Patrick, 2001); *teacher support of questioning* (Nolen, 2003; Ryan & Patrick, 2001; Karabenick & Sharma, 1994); *teacher support for collaboration;* and *academic press*—the extent to which teachers encourage students to take on challenging work (PALS; Midgley et al., 2000; Blumenfeld, Middleton, Geier, & Marx, 2004). Psychometric analysis (EFA) supported four higher-order factors: mastery achievement goal structure; combined performance approach and avoid achievement goal structure, all of the teacher support scales, and academic press.

Results of hierarchical modeling indicated that the more that students, collectively, viewed their classes to be focused on learning and understanding, and the more they viewed their teachers as generally supportive:

a.   the more likely they were to seek needed help in the form of explanations from their teachers and other students in their classes, and

b.   the less threatened, avoidant, and likely to seek expedient help if they did.

By contrast, the more that classes were perceived as focused on competition, with heightened concerns about poor performance, the more likely students in those classes were to exhibit an avoidance help-seeking pattern. However, perceived performance goal structure did not predict help-seeking approach tendencies. There is also evidence that students in classes with higher levels of press for challenge and high quality work were more likely to exhibit an adaptive help-seeking approach pattern. However, press did not predict help-seeking avoidance. The results speak to the importance of examining these other dimensions of classroom context. At the same time, the factor analysis results suggest that students' perceptions of the classroom context may not be as nuanced as theory would suggest.

An implication of this work is that interventions to influence goals, support, and press can have salutary effects not only on help seeking but also on other adaptive and maladaptive strategies. Specifically, the avoidance of help seeking can be considered a proxy for other behaviors (e.g., self-handicapping, cheating, avoidance of challenge, procrastination) that comprise an avoidant pattern of responses to performance-focused teachers and classes (Urdan, et al., 2002). Those and other future studies can benefit from the improved understanding and assessment of classroom context provided here.

### Authoritative Teaching Style

Baumrind (1991) characterized four parenting styles based upon levels of responsiveness and demandingness. The authoritative style is defined by high levels of both of these characteristics, whereas authoritarian parents are high in demandingness and low in responsiveness, permissive parents exhibit high levels of responsiveness within a context of low demandingness, and neglectful parents are neither responsive nor demanding. Research has indicated that parents who are high in both responsiveness and demandingness rear children with better behavioral outcomes than parents who exhibit high levels of only one or neither of these parenting qualities, generally speaking (e.g. Steinberg, Lamborn, Dornbusch, & Darling, 1992). However, among Asian American and African American populations, authoritarian parenting has been linked to favorable outcomes, suggesting racial/ethnic differences in what constitutes the best parenting style (Steinberg, Dornbusch, & Brown, 1992).

Research concerning teachers and schools has begun to explore whether responsiveness, often termed teacher caring or support, and demandingness, often termed teacher control or academic press, are predictive of better motivational and achievement outcomes among children and adolescents (e.g. Ryan & Patrick, 2001; Wentzel, 1997, 1998, 2002). However, this research has largely ignored race and ethnicity as potential moderators of the effects of teaching style on motivation. Ammon and Conley (2006) considered the effectiveness of teacher support and academic press through the lens of risk and protection theory among an ethnically diverse, socioeconomically disadvantaged population.

Participants were 3,885 middle and high school students in 198 math classrooms (from the TASEL-M collaboration). Latino, Vietnamese, and Caucasian students were included in this sample. In order to consider interactions between student-level characteristics and classroom-level teaching style variables, hierarchical linear modeling (HLM) was used. The student-level model indicated that as grade level increased, interest in mathematics decreased. Females reported less interest in mathematics as compared to their male peers. Latino and White students displayed similar levels of interest in math, but Vietnamese students reported higher levels of interest than either of these groups. The classroom-level model indicated that, on average across ethnic groups, academic press predicted student interest in math, whereas teacher caring did not.

Finally, Ammon and Conley (2006) considered the effects of interactions between student-level race/ethnicity and classroom-level teaching style on student interest. Latino and White students were most interested in mathematics in an authoritative context, although academic press seemed to be more important than teacher caring. However, Vietnamese students were most interested when the context was more authoritarian in nature. This research suggests, much like the parenting literature, that one teaching style is not necessarily the best for all. Rather, a fit between the context and the students' cultural expectations and beliefs regarding teacher and students roles may be the most important in predicting motivational outcomes.

*Parent Involvement*

Research regarding students' perceptions of family involvement behaviors and the beliefs and values they convey to students is a relatively new area of research (Friedel, Cortina, Turner, & Midgley, 2007; Hoover-Dempsey & Sandler, 2005; Karabenick & Friedel, 2007). Friedel and Karabenick (2008) extended research at the intersection of family involvement and achievement motivation by examining students' perceptions of family involvement at home and at school in the domain of mathematics, and their perceptions of the beliefs, goals, and values that families emphasize. They addressed two general research questions. The first is whether students distinguish between different types of family-involvement activities, or construe family involvement more generally as degrees or levels of involvement across domains. Specifically, they asked students ($n = 1,700$ in middle and high school) about ways their families monitored their school-related work, the different types of assistance families provided, students' judgments of their families' capacities to provide assistance, and the extent of family-teacher communication and school-based involvement. Students were also asked to judge the emphases their parents and families placed on mastery and performance achievement goals, the value parents and families placed on students' academic performance, and the confidence families had in students' mathematical abilities.

Items were developed to assess students' perceptions of family involvement and motivation-related beliefs and values based on current theories of achievement motivation, including expectancy-value theory (Wigfield & Eccles, 2000) and goal orientation theory (Ames, 1992; Kaplan & Maehr, 2002, 2007; Midgley et al., 2000) as well as family involvement research (Hoover-Dempsey & Sandler, 2005; Sheldon & Epstein, 2007; Walker et al., 2004). Application of standard psychometric analyses resulted in the following student perception scales: family emphasis on mastery and performance (approach and avoidance combined), value of mathematics (usefulness, importance, interest, cost) and confidence in student ability. Students in middle and high school were able to differentiate between different types of family involvement, including perceived family capacity to provide help, home-based monitoring and assistance, and family-teacher communication (school-based involvement).

Results indicated that perceptions of family capacity to provide help and family monitoring and assistance positively predicted students' perceptions of family mastery and performance goal emphases, valuing of math, and family confidence in students' abilities. Perceptions of school-based involvement negatively predicted perceptions of mastery goal emphasis, valuing of math, and confidence in student ability, but positively predicted family performance goal emphasis. These findings highlight the importance of understanding students' perceptions of family involvement behaviors, and the role of such behaviors in shaping students' perceptions of family beliefs and values related to their engagement in math. The differences between home- and school-based involvement are particularly noteworthy and suggest further studies to provide evidence of causal influence.

### Person-Oriented Approach to the Study of Motivation

Conley (2007) used a person-centered approach to examine mastery and performance achievement goals, task values, and competence beliefs among 1,870 middle school students. In person-centered analyses, as opposed to variable-centered analysis, the individual is the focal unit. Cluster analysis revealed seven patterns of motivation, which were related to differences in negative and positive affect as well as later achievement in math. This research, focused on various combinations or clusters of motivation-related variables within and among students, was related to conversations we had with MSPs about motivation as intricate, complex patterns of many variables rather than one unitary concept that is either present or absent.

In one adaptive pattern, students reported moderate interest in math and a sole focus on mastery goals, supporting a traditional perspective on how goals operate. In another, students focused on both performance approach and mastery goals, suggesting that different goal orientations may predict equally positive outcomes for different students. Across all clusters, cost value was important in distinguishing among adaptive patterns, suggesting that perceptions of the time and effort required to learn math play an important role in motivation. Conley's (2007) research provided evidence that a sole focus on goals or values only may give an incomplete picture of motivation, and that complex interactions are often hidden within traditional models of motivational variables. These findings help educators by making it evident that motivation is not "one size fits all;" rather, different goals and different values can combine in multiple ways, yet predict similarly adaptive achievement and affective outcomes.

## SUMMARY

The origin, collaborations, evolution, and research emanating from MSP-MAP embody much of Marty Maehr's contribution to motivation in education. His work fits squarely in Pasteur's Quadrant, which combines both an understanding of the fundamental processes of motivation and the application of those principles to the improvement of classrooms and schools (e.g. Maehr & Midgley, 1996). The research briefly described here exemplifies just a few of the many directions that follow from that perspective. These include issues of motivation assessment and construct validity (e.g., the PALS), motivation and mathematical understanding, parent involvement, achievement goals, perceived classroom context, and the intricacies of within-student patterns of motivation. Collectively they project Marty's view that students thrive in learning contexts that focus on learning and understanding rather than competition and ability. In addition, his recent work has stressed the importance of viewing motivation as an instructional outcome and the reframing of motivation in terms of decision theory. The latter has included the role of possible options—that what students do in any situation is governed by the possible alternative courses of action they consider.

The collaborations formed under the Math-Science Partnership program provided the means to test theoretical predictions and the assessment of constructs as part of that effort. MSP-MAP participated in several interventions, with diverse populations of students and teachers in different regions of the US. In addition to sites for research, they afforded the opportunity to promote motivationally adaptive practices along the lines that Marty Maehr has long advocated. As described and emphasized earlier, in addition to generalizations based on considerable research and theoretical development, there is ample evidence to suggest that the presentation of data obtained from each student and teacher population was an important reason for the success of several professional development initiatives. Abstract concepts became reified as teachers and MSP personnel could, in the case of the TASEL-M collaboration, examine motivational profiles of their students at the beginning and end of the school year, and therefore the changes that occurred in the interim. In several instances the changes could be attributed to the MSP's interventions, which accordingly resulted in a more comprehensive program evaluation and potentially more accurate evidence-based curricular decisions.

The MSP-MAP program is but one aspect of a broader effort to create and improve learning and instruction in US and other nations' classrooms and schools by increasing knowledge of adaptive motivation principles and practices in the classroom (Perry, et al., 2006), schools (Maehr & Midgley, 1996), and in public policy (Ryan & Brown, 2005). It is axiomatic that all instruction has motivational consequences, either directly or indirectly by influencing subsequent motivation to learn. Educators at every level often take for granted such influences but would profit from a greater understanding of the implications of their instructional practices. Attending to Marty Maehr's research over the years would be an excellent way to reach that goal.

## REFERENCES

Ames, C. (1992). Classrooms: Goals, structures, and student motivation. *Journal of Educational Psychology, 84,* 261–271.

Ames, C. A. (1990). Motivation: What teachers need to know. *Teachers College Record, 91*(3), 409–421.

Ammon, B. V., & Conley, A. M. (2006). *Interest among at-risk student populations: The roles of teacher caring and press.* Paper presented at the annual meeting of the American Educational Research Association, San Francisco, CA.

Bandura, A. (2006). Adolescent development from an agentic perspective. In F. Pajares & T. Urdan (Series Eds.), *Self-efficacy beliefs of adolescents: A volume in adolescence and education* (pp. 1–44). Greenwich, CT: Information Age Publishing.

Baumrind, D. (1991). Effective parenting during the early adolescent transition. In P. A. Cowan & M. Hetherington (Eds.), *Family Transitions* (pp. 111–164). Hillsdale, NJ: Erlbaum.

Bell, P., & Linn, M. (2002). Beliefs about science: How does science instruction contribute? In B. Hofer & P. R. Pintrich (Eds.), *Personal epistemology: The psychology of beliefs about knowledge and knowing* (pp. 321–346). Mahwah, NJ; Lawrence Erlbaum Associates

Blazevski, J. L. (2006). *Teachers' efficacy for supporting students' motivation.* Unpublished PhD Dissertation, University of Michigan.

Blumenfeld, P.C., Middleton, M., Geier, R., & Marx, R.W. (2004, April). *Connecting standards based instruction, motivation, and achievement in urban middle school sci-*

*ence classrooms*. Paper presented at the annual meeting of the American Educational Research Association, San Diego.

Conley, A. M. (2007). *Patterns and pathways: A person-oriented approach to understanding students' motivation to learn*. Unpublished PhD Dissertation, University of Michigan.

Desimone, L. M., & Le Floch, K. C. (2004). Are we asking the right questions? Using cognitive interviews to improve surveys in education research. *Educational Evaluation and Policy Analysis, 26*(1), 1–22.

Feldlaufer, H., Midgley, C., & Eccles, J. S. (1988). Student, teacher and observer perceptions of the classroom environment before and after the transition to junior high school. *Journal of Early Adolescence, 8*, 133–156.

Forsyth, B. H., & Lessler, J. T. (1991). Cognitive laboratory methods: A taxonomy. In P. P. Biemer, R. M. Groves, L. E. Lyberg, N. A. Mathiowietz, & S. Sudman (Eds.), *Measurement errors in surveys* (pp. 393–418). New York: Wiley & Sons.

Friedel, J., & Karabenick, S. (2008). *Students' perceptions of family involvement behaviors: Indicators of family achievement goal emphases, task values, and confidence beliefs in math*. Paper presented at the annual meeting of the American Education Research Association, New York, NY.

Friedel, J. M., Cortina, K. S., Turner, J. C., & Midgley, C. (2007). Achievement goals, efficacy beliefs and coping strategies in mathematics: The roles of perceived parent and teacher goal emphases. *Contemporary Educational Psychology, 32*(3), 434–458.

Gilbert, M. C. (2007). *Applying contemporary views of mathematical proficiency to the examination of the relationship of motivation and mathematics achievement*. Unpublished PhD Dissertation, University of Michigan.

Gilbert, M. C. (2008). *Applying contemporary views of mathematical proficiency to the motivation-achievement relationship*. Paper presented at the annual meeting of the American Educational Research Association, New York, NY.

Grouws, D. A. (1992). *Handbook of research on mathematics teaching and learning: A project of the National Council of Teachers of Mathematics*. New York, NY: Macmillan.

Hoover-Dempsey, K. V., & Sandler, H. M. (2005). *Final Performance Report for OERI Grant # R305T010673: The Social Context of Parental Involvement: A Path to Enhanced Achievement*. Presented to Project Monitor, Institute of Education Sciences, US Department of Education, March 22, 2005.

Jabine, T. B., Straf, M. L., Tanur, J. M., & Tourangeau, R. (1984). *Cognitive aspects of survey methodology: Building a bridge between disciplines*. Washington DC: National Academy Press.

Kaplan, A., & Maehr, M. L. (2002). Adolescents' achievement goals: Situating motivation in sociocultural contexts. In F. Pajares & T. Urdan (Eds.), *Academic motivation of adolescents* (pp. 125–167). Greenwich, CT: Information Age Publishing.

Kaplan, A., & Maehr, M. L. (2007). The contributions and prospects of goal orientation theory. *Educational Psychology Review, 19*, 141–184.

Karabenick, S. A. (2004). Perceived achievement goal structure and college student help seeking. *Journal of Educational Psychology, 96*, 569–581.

Karabenick, S. A. (2005, April). *Evidence-Based Motivation-Related Outcomes of Mathematics Improvement Interventions: Collaborative Adventures in Pasteur's Quadrant*.

Symposium presented at the annual meeting of the American Educational Research Association, Montreal.

Karabenick, S. A., & Friedel, J. M. (2007). *Perceived family support for learning, achievement goal emphases, and students' achievement goal orientations.* Paper presented at the 12th Biennial Conference of the European Association for Research on Learning and Instruction, Budapest, Hungary.

Karabenick, S. A., & Sharma, R. (1994). Perceived teacher support of student questioning in the college classroom: Its relation to student characteristics and role in the classroom questioning process. *Journal of Educational Psychology, 86,* 90–103.

Karabenick, S. A., Woolley, M. E., Friedel, J. M., Ammon, B. V., Blazevski, J., Bonney, C. R., De Groot, E., Gilbert, M. C., Musu, L., Kempler, T. M., & Kelly, K. L. (2007). Cognitive processing of self-report items in educational research: Do they think what we mean? *Educational Psychologist, 42,* 139–151.

Kilpatrick, J., Swafford, J. O., & Findell, B. (Eds.). (2001). *Adding it up: Helping children learn mathematics.* Washington, DC: National Academy Press.

Koller, O., Baumert, J., & Schnabel, K. (2001). Does interest matter? The relationship between academic interest and achievement in mathematics. *Journal for Research in Mathematics Education, 32*(5), 448–470.

Le Mare, L., & Sohbat, E. (2002). Canadian students' perceptions of teacher characteristics that support or inhibit help seeking. *Elementary School Journal, 102*(3), 239–253.

Maehr, M. L. (1976). Continuing motivation: An analysis of a seldom considered educational outcome. *Review of Educational Research, 46*(3), 443–462.

Maehr, M. L. (1984). Meaning and motivation: Toward a theory of personal investment. In C. Ames & R. Ames (Eds.), *Research on motivation in education* (Vol. 1, pp. 115–144). New York: Academic Press.

Maehr, M. L., & Braskamp, L. A. (1986). *The Motivation Factor: A Theory of Personal Investment.* Lexington, MA: D. C. Heath & Co.

Maehr, M. L., & Midgley, C. (1996). *Transforming School Cultures.* Boulder, CO: Westview Press.

McLeod, D. B., & Adams, V. M. (1989). *Affect and mathematical problem solving: A new perspective.* New York, NY: Springer-Verlag Publishing.

Meece, J. L., Anderman, E. M., & Anderman, L. H. (2006). Classroom goal structure, student motivation, and academic achievement. *Annual Review of Psychology, 57,* 487–503.

Messick, S. (1995). Validity of psychological assessment: Validation of inferences from persons' responses and performance as scientific inquiry into scoring meaning. *American Psychologist, 9,* 741–749.

Midgley, C. (Ed.). (2002). *Goals, goal structures, and patterns of adaptive learning.* Mahwah, NJ: Erlbaum.

Midgley, C., Kaplan, A., Middleton, M., Urdan, T., Maehr. M. L., Hicks, L., Anderman, E., & Roeser, R. W. (1998). Development and validation of scales assessing students' achievement goal orientation. *Contemporary Educational Psychology, 23,* 113–131.

Midgley, C., Maehr, M. L., Hruda, L. Z., Anderman, E., Anderman, L., Freeman, K. E., Gheen, M., Kaplan, A., Kumar, R., Middleton, M. J., Nelson, J., Roeser,

R., & Urdan, T. (2000). *Patterns of Adaptive Learning Survey (PALS) manual.* Ann Arbor: University of Michigan. See also: http://www.umich.edu/~pals/manuals.html

Moos, R. H. (1980). Evaluating classroom learning environments. *Studies in Educational Evaluation, 6,* 239–252.

National Council of Teachers of Mathematics (1989). *Curriculum and evaluation standards for school mathematics.* Reston, VA: Author

NCLB: No Child Left Behind Act of 2001, Pub. L. No. 107–110. (2002).

Newman, R. S. (2000). Social influences on the development of children's adaptive help seeking: The role of parents, teachers, and peers. *Developmental Review, 20*(3), 350–404.

Newman, R. S., & Goldin, L. (1990). Children's reluctance to seek help with school-work. *Journal of Educational Psychology, 82,* 92–100.

Nolen, S. B. (2003). Learning environment, motivation and achievement in high school science. *Journal of Research in Science Teaching, 40,* 347–368.

Patrick, H. (2004). Re-examining classroom mastery goal structure. In P. R. Pintrich & M. L. Maehr (Eds.), *Advances in motivation. Volume 13: Motivating students, improving schools: The legacy of Carol Midgley* (pp. 233–263). Amsterdam, The Netherlands: Elsevier JAI Press.

Perry, N. E., Turner, J. C., & Meyer, D. K. (2006). Classrooms as contexts for motivating learning. In P. A. Alexander & P. H. Winne (Eds.), *Handbook of Educational Psychology (2ⁿᵈ Edition),* Washington, DC: American Psychological Association.

Perry, N., Turner, J. C., & Meyer, D.K. (2006). Student Engagement in the classroom. In P. Alexander & P. Winne (Eds.), *Handbook of educational psychology* (pp. 327–348). Mahwah, NJ: Erlbaum.

Pintrich, P. R., & DeGroot, E. V. (1990). Motivational and self-regulated learning components of classroom academic performance. *Journal of Educational Psychology, 82,* 33–40.

Pintrich, P. R. (2003). A motivational science perspective on the role of student motivation in learning contexts. *Journal of Educational Psychology, 95*(4), 667–686.

Pintrich, P. R., Marx, R. W., & Boyle, R. A. (1993). Beyond cold conceptual change: The role of motivational beliefs and classroom contextual factors in the process of conceptual change. *Review of Educational Research, 63,* 167–199.

Pintrich, P. R., Smith, D. A., Garcia, T., & McKeachie, W. J. (1993). Reliability and predictive validity of the Motivated Strategies for Learning Questionnaire (MSLQ). *Educational and Psychological Measurement, 53,* 801–813.

Project 2061-American Association for the Advancement of Science. (1993). *Benchmarks for science literacy.* New York: Oxford University Press.

Ruiz-Prima, M. A., Schultz, S. E., Ki, M., & Shavelson, R. (2001). On the validity of cognitive interpretations of scores from alternative concept-mapping techniques. *Educational Assessment, 7*(2), 99–141.

Ryan, A. M., & Patrick, H. (2001). The Classroom social environment and changes in adolescents' motivation and engagement during middle school. *American Educational Research Journal, 38,* 437–460.

Ryan, R. M., & Brown, K. W. (2005). Legislating competence: The motivational impact of high stakes testing as an educational reform. In C. Dweck & A. E. Elliot (Eds.), *Handbook of competence* and motivation (pp. 354–374). New York: Guilford Press.

Schoenfeld, A. H. (1985). Making sense of 'out loud' problem-solving protocols. *Journal of Mathematical Behavior, 4*(2), 171–191.

Schoenfeld, A. H. (1989). Explorations of students' mathematical beliefs and behavior. *Journal for Research in Mathematics Education, 20*(4), 338–355.

Schunk, D. H., Pintrich, P. R., & Meece, J. L. (2007). *Motivation in education: Theory, research, and applications* (3rd Ed.). Upper Saddle River, New Jersey: Prentice-Hall.

Sheldon, S. B., & Epstein, J. L. (2007). *Student survey on family and community involvement in the elementary and middle grades.* Baltimore: Center on School, Family, and Community Partnerships, Johns Hopkins University.

Steinberg, L., Dornbusch, S. M., & Brown, B. B. (1992). Ethnic differences in adolescent achievement: An ecological perspective. *American Psychologist, 47*(6), 723–729.

Steinberg, L., Lamborn, S. D., Dornbusch, S. M., & Darling, N. (1992). Impact of parenting practices on adolescent achievement: Authoritative parenting, school involvement, and encouragement to succeed. *Child Development, 61,* 508–523.

Stokes, D. (1997). *Pasteur's quadrant: Basic science and technological innovation.* Washington, DC: Brookings Institution Press.

Thelk, A. D., Hoole, E. R., & Lottridge, S. M. (2005). *What are you thinking? Postsecondary student think-alouds of scientific and quantitative reasoning items.* Unpublished manuscript, James Madison University. Retrieved July 29, 2005 from http://www.jmu.edu/assessment/gradpapers.shtml

Tourangeau, R., Rips, L. J., & Rasinski, K. (2000). *The psychology of survey response.* Cambridge, UK: Cambridge University Press.

Urdan, T. (2004). Using multiple methods to assess students' perceptions of classroom goal structures. *European Psychologist, 9*(4), 222–231.

Urdan, T. C., Kneisel, L., & Mason, V. (1999). Interpreting messages about motivation in the classroom. In T. C. Urdan (Ed.), *Advances in motivation and achievement: The role of context* (Vol. 11, pp. 123–158). Stamford, CT: JAI Press.

Urdan, T., Ryan, A. M., Anderman, E., & Gheen, M. H. (2002). Goals, goal structures, and avoidance behaviors. In C. Midgley (Ed.), *Goals, goal structures, and patterns of adaptive learning* (pp. 55–83), Mahwah, NJ: Erlbaum.

Walker, J. M. T., Hoover-Dempsey, K. V., Whetsel, D. R., & Green, C. L. (2004). *Parental involvement in homework: A review of current research and its implications for teachers, after school program staff, and parent leaders.* Cambridge, MA: Harvard Family Research Project.

Wentzel, K. R. (1997). Student motivation in middle school: The role of perceived pedagogical caring. *Journal of Educational Psychology, 89*(3), 411–419.

Wentzel, K. R. (1998). Social relationships and motivation in middle school: The role of parents, teachers, and peers. *Journal of Educational Psychology, 90,* 202–209.

Wentzel, K. R. (2002). Are effective teachers like good parents? Teaching styles and student adjustment in early adolescence. *Child Development, 73,* 287–301.

Wigfield, A., & Eccles, J. S. (2000). Expectancy-value theory of achievement motivation. *Contemporary Educational Psychology, 25,* 68–81.

Wolters, C., Pintrich, P. R., & Karabenick, S. A. (2003). Measuring academic self-regulated learning. In K. A. Moore & L. Lippman (Eds.), *Conceptualizing and measuring indicators of positive development: What do children need to flourish?* (pp. 251–270), New York: Kluwer Academic/Plenum Press.

# PART II

CULTURE AND MOTIVATION

CHAPTER 7

# SCHOOL CULTURE MATTERS FOR TEACHERS' AND STUDENTS' ACHIEVEMENT GOALS

**Lennia Matos, Willy Lens, and Maarten Vansteenkiste**

## INTRODUCTION

Traditionally, schools were considered a place where knowledge was transferred to students by teachers. In a world where information is growing in a fast and irrepressible way in all aspects of human life, education is of tremendous importance, more than ever before in history (Maehr & Midgley, 1996). However, it is impossible to teach all the knowledge and skills needed in the future. Therefore, a very important purpose of education should be to turn students into life-long learners (Maehr & Midgley, 1996). The task of developing ways to engage students in learning throughout their lives has to do not only with students' learning skills but also with their will or motivation to do so. In this sense, motivation in the school system is central because a successful educational system requires motivated students. But motivated students require motivated teachers (Maehr, 2001). Teachers are therefore a key element in the educational process. It is their responsibility to create adequate learning environments and to motivate students to learn, so that they become life-long learners.

Achievement goal theory is widely used to understand and explain why students engage in academic settings (Patrick et al., 2001; Pintrich, Conley, & Kempler, 2003) and it also has great applicability in studying teachers' pedagogical goals and approaches to instruction (Roeser, Marachi, & Gehlbach, 2002). Surprisingly, research on teachers' motivation has received much less attention than students' motivation, in spite of the interdependencies between the two of them (Maehr, 2001; Roeser et al., 2002).

Within achievement goal theory, achievement goals refer to the purposes or reasons for engaging in achievement behavior (Linnenbrink & Pintrich, 2000). Three types of achievement goals have been distinguished (Elliot & Harackiewicz, 1996): mastery goals, performance-approach, and performance-avoidance goals. When students pursue mastery goals they are concerned with increasing and enhancing their competence, with understanding and mastering a material, with learning something, gaining knowledge, or with developing a new skill (Covington, 2000; Dweck, 1986; Heyman, & Dweck, 1992; Zimmerman, 1994). These students define competence based on a self-referenced or task-based standard, so they evaluate their progress with respect to how well they did in the past or according to the task itself (Elliot & McGregor, 2001).

With a performance-approach goal, a person tries to look competent when comparing with others and tries to be the best or better than someone else in the classroom. With a performance-avoidance goal, a person tries to avoid bad judgments and will protect him or herself from being the worst of the classroom or from looking dumb compared to others (Harackiewicz, Barron, Tauer, Carter, & Elliot, 2000; Elliot & Church, 1997; Elliot & Harackiewicz, 1996; Middleton & Midgley, 1997). Students holding performance goals use an interpersonal or normative standard to define competence, as they evaluate their competence by comparing themselves to others.

Achievement goal theory has not only been used in the study of students' personal achievement goals, but also in the examination of goal structures. Goal structures refer to the type of achievement goal that is salient in a specific context according to the instructional practices (teachers' achievement goals) and policies within a classroom or school (Anderman, Patrick, Hruda, & Linnenbrink, 2002; Wolters, 2004). Therefore, schools will be characterized by a different school culture (Maehr & Midgley, 1996), depending on the type of achievement goals that are stressed within the school. Empirical evidence suggests that school culture influences students' motivation (Maehr & Buck, 1992) and affects teachers' conceptions of good teaching, their instructional practices, and their expectations for their students. Moreover, the goal structures prevailing in the school have not only been associated with students' motivation, but also with other outcomes such as students' learning and academic achievement (Ames, 1992; Ames & Archer, 1988).

The aim of the current research was to study the relationship between students' perceptions of the school culture, the classroom goal structure (i.e., students' perceptions of teachers' achievement goals), and students' own achievement goals. We studied the school culture and also the teachers as part of the students' learning context, as both are likely to be important in shaping students' achievement goals. Even though achievement goal theory has been used to study both contexts (at school and classroom levels), there is a lack of studies that consider both goal structures simultaneously, that is, in terms of the classroom context as created by the teachers' instructional practices and the school culture. We consider both aspects (school culture and classroom context) as being very important to understand students' motivation. We therefore measured the perceived school culture, the perceived achievement goals as held by the teachers and expressed in their instructional practices and students' own motivation and we examined the interrelationships between these three constructs. We first elaborate on the concept of school culture before turning towards teachers' and students' achievement goals in a second and third section.

## School Culture

Deal and Peterson (1990, in Stolp, 1994) defined school culture as "deep patterns of values, beliefs, and traditions that have been formed over the course of [the school's] history." Heckman (1993, in Stolp, 1994) stated that the school culture lies in "the commonly held beliefs of teachers, students, and principals." When Maehr (2000) refers to the

> character of schools and learning contexts [he refers] especially, though not exclusively to how leaders, staff, and students perceive the purpose of schooling –and how they enact those perceptions, not only in word, but also in deed (p. 6).

These shared beliefs shape people's purposes and the way they act (Maehr & Midgley, 1996; Stolp, 1994). Maehr and Fyans (1989) stated that

> Groups ... arrive at certain shared understandings regarding how, when, and where activities are to occur... In particular, thoughts and perceptions about what is worth striving for, are a critical feature of any culture (p. 218).

The school environment is a very important context for the students because it affects the definition of education that the teachers will hold and that students are likely to develop (Wolters, 2004). Talking about school culture involves seeing schools as a functioning system, in which different groups that play an important role at school will relate and interact with one another in a particular way. The term culture "emphasizes shared living and being that is derived from or related to beliefs and values and most especially purposes" (Maehr & Midgley, 1996, p. 14).

All schools develop their own purposes and emphasize different aspects of what is "schooling" about, and every school has its own distinctive culture. One way to characterize school culture is to consider the type of goals they favor (Maehr & Midgley, 1996). Rosenholtz (1989) found that schools where people have shared goals, beliefs, and values (i.e., high "consensus" schools) considered teaching activities, and children's needs and interests of primary importance helping new teachers to share the same vision they have. According to Maehr, Midgley and collaborators, schools can be described as having a culture that emphasizes the pursuit and attainment of mastery or performance goals and these goals help students adopt their own purposes and goals for learning and education. As Maehr and Midgley (1996) affirmed, "schools differ one from the other in the way they work as well as on the 'effects' they have on the lives of children" (p. 55). School culture will affect the direction, intensity, and quality of students' motivation and learning.

The students' perception of a mastery-oriented school culture was associated with students' mastery goals. When they perceived their schools as performance-oriented, students were more likely to adopt performance goals (Roeser, Midgley, & Urdan, 1996). Other variables such as family and peers play also an important role in explaining students' motivation and learning, but Maehr, Midgley, and collaborators found that school culture explained more of the variance in motivation and learning than either of the two other contextual predictors.

Maehr and Fyans (1989) were concerned with the moderating role of the socio-economic background of students in the relationship between school culture and student motivation. Their findings can be summarized as follows: school culture has a stronger impact on the motivation of students from lower, compared to higher, socio-economic backgrounds. This suggests that school culture might be more important for students coming from disadvantaged situations (Maehr & Midgley, 1996).

*Teachers' Achievement goals*

Different groups of researchers in achievement goal theory have studied students' motivation more extensively than teachers' motivation. Research on teachers' achievement goals is less common, but nevertheless very important to understand students' motivation (Roeser et al., 2002).

Although there is a lack of research on teachers' goals related to instruction, some studies have found that teachers' instructional practices can explain many of the effects of schooling on student outcomes (Roeser, Marachi, & Gehlbach, 2002). For instance, it has been found that in schools in which principals reported making use of more performance practices or policies (e.g., with competition among teachers), teachers reported being more performance-oriented. In middle schools in which principals reported making use of more learning practices or policies (e.g., more improvement opportunities for teachers), there were more teachers reporting making use of more mastery goal approaches (see Roeser, Marachi, & Gehlbach, 2002).

Midgley, Anderman, and Hicks (1995) showed that, in general, secondary school teachers and students perceived their school culture as more performance-focused and less mastery-focused than elementary teachers and students did. Similarly, Marachi and colleagues (2001 in Roeser, Marachi, & Gehlbach, 2002) reported that middle and high school teachers made more use of performance-approach instructional practices when compared with teachers from elementary schools, and that teachers made less use of mastery goals-oriented approaches in secondary schools than in elementary schools. Roeser, Marachi, and Gehlbach (2002) reported that teachers' instructional practices are "associated with students' perceptions of the goal structure in their classrooms as well as consequential psychological and behavioral outcomes" (p. 209).

Talbert and McLaughlin (1996) stated that even inside the same school, teachers' classrooms differ in many ways (e.g., how teachers present the lessons, in an active or passive way, etc.). It is also important to underline that students (and teachers) can develop different achievement goals in different situations (Pintrich, 2000). Being a major component of students' learning environments, teachers play an important role in determining the achievement goals of their students.

Teachers' instructional practices are very important because "good teaching includes teaching students how to learn, how to remember, how to think, and how to motivate themselves" (Weinstein & Mayer, 1986; p. 315). Classroom structures influence students' way of viewing the nature and purposes of learning (Ames, 1992). Therefore, we consider the teacher as an important actor in creating a special classroom environment. Mastery and performance goals can be elicited by different instructional demands and can influence the salience of a particular goal (Ames, 1992).

Teachers' achievement goals influence their teaching practice and, hence, also the mastery or performance achievement goals of their students. Teachers perceived as highly mastery-oriented referred to learning as an active process, and this was reflected in their practice. These teachers asked for students' involvement, emphasized effort and gaining understanding, and they promoted student interaction. They were concerned about and gave social and affective support for students' learning and progress (Patrick et al., 2001). Some of the teacher practices used by high mastery-oriented teachers include giving students new and challenging tasks, explaining the reasons why particular tasks are important, so that they become meaningful for students, giving process instead of outcome oriented feedback, providing the opportunity to redo one's work if needed, and giving different options of tasks so that students can choose from a variety of tasks (Kaplan et al., 2002; Roeser, et al., 2002). Teachers with low mastery-oriented classrooms did not make use of these practices and considered it, in contrast, very important to get answers without mistakes.

Teachers with a high-performance focus stressed formal evaluations and grades (Patrick et al., 2001) and emphasized the importance of ability and doing better than one's classmates. Examples of teacher practices used by such teachers include forming groups on the basis of ability, exposing only the "best" work, giving rewards and privileges for the best achievements, thereby creating competition among students, giving feedback in front of other students, and restricting choice (Roeser et al. 2002). Based on Maehr and Midgley (1996), Maehr (2000), Pintrich and Schunk (2002), and Ames (1992), teacher practices can be related to, among others, the type of tasks they offer, how they evaluate students and what kind of feedback they give.

Variety and diversity of tasks can foster more interest in learning and a mastery achievement goal in students. It is important to emphasize meaningful reasons and personal relevance for engaging in an activity and the activity should be challenging and interesting. The fun of learning should be emphasized.

Another aspect to consider is evaluation. The way in which students are evaluated is an important factor in students' motivation (Struyf, Vandenberghe, & Lens, 2001). Evaluation is defined as "processes and means by which what is done is appraised" (Maehr, 2000). Evaluation is an essential part of the educational process but the critical point is what is assessed, how it is done, and how the findings are reported to the students. The answers to these questions give students the frame of what the purpose and the meaning of schooling is in their school.

Different types of evaluation can foster different achievement goals. Evaluations of only the final product or outcome which always emphasize correctness and absence of errors stress performance achievement goals. When a teacher communicates the results of evaluations and tests in public (e.g., in front of other students), he or she favors social comparison and this promotes performance achievement goals (announce highest and lowest grades, rankings, ability grouping). When students experience social comparison their perception of ability is affected, especially when they are focused on outperforming others or being the winners. A focus on social comparison standards does not foster deep information processing which needs more expenditure of effort (Graham & Golan, 1991). Grolnick and Ryan (1987) found that when evaluation is perceived by students as controlling rather than as informational, adaptive metacognitive processes are diminished.

Maehr and Midgley (1996) further affirmed that an emphasis on objective tests and curve graded results augments test anxiety or fear of failure.

If evaluation is seen as outcome oriented (i.e., focused on losers and winners), then it fosters performance goals. When evaluation is, in contrast, seen as informative about students' progress, it can promote mastery goals. Evaluation and academic achievement are considered more important when students progress from one school level to another, being stronger in high school than in elementary school.

Types of feedback given by teachers to students play an important role. If a teacher considers mistakes as part of the learning process and emphasizes effort, he or she will foster mastery goals. If the evaluation criteria allow evaluation of individual progress and development instead of normative comparisons, students will be more mastery oriented than performance oriented (Ames, 1992). The use of rewards, incentives, and praise are also related to students' motivation. Rewards are good if they are given as informational feedback about students' progress (Deci & Ryan, 1985). It is important that all students have opportunities to receive positive feedback in order to foster the intrinsic motivation to learn.

### Students' Achievement goals

Students' achievement goals have been associated with several beneficial and more maladaptive outcomes. Research has consistently demonstrated that students' mastery goals were related to adaptive outcomes such as the use of deep-level learning strategies (e.g., Ames & Archer, 1988; Pintrich & De Groot, 1990) and more cognitive engagement (e.g., Pintrich & Schrauben, 1992), and in some cases even better academic achievement (Vansteenkiste, Simons, Lens, Soenens, Matos, & Lacante, 2004). On the other hand, negative effects (i.e., lower grades, self-handicapping) were associated with espousing performance-avoidance goals (e.g., Midgley & Urdan, 2001). Regarding performance-approach goals, evidence is not as conclusive as in the case of mastery goals. These achievement goals have been positively related or unrelated with different outcomes such as the use of learning strategies and academic achievement (e.g., Matos, 2005; Matos, Lens, & Vansteenkiste, 2007; Wolters, Yu, & Pintrich, 1996).

### The Present Research

The main aim of this study was to examine the direct effects of school culture on two outcomes, that is, students' perceptions of teachers' achievement goals and students' personal achievement goals. We hypothesized that mastery and performance school culture would positively predict students' own mastery and performance-approach goals, respectively, as well as students' perceptions of teachers' mastery and performance-approach goals, respectively. Furthermore, we expected that the predicted direct effect of mastery and performance school culture on students' mastery and performance-approach goals would be at least partially explained (i.e., mediated) by students' perceptions of teachers' mastery and performance-approach goals, respectively. In other words, if students perceive the school culture to be mastery-oriented, they will hold more mastery-oriented goals themselves and this would, at least partially, be due to the fact that they would perceive their own teachers as holding more mastery goals. A similar set of predictions was made for a performance school culture. In short, we expect that students' perceptions of teachers' achievement-goals will to a great extent account for the effect of school culture on students' achievement goals. These hypotheses were studied in a Latin-American culture that has received little prior attention within achievement goal theory, that is, Peru.

## METHOD

*Participants and Procedure*

Participants in this study were 1505 high school students from three public schools ($N$ = 945; male = 474; female = 470; 1 student did not report his/her gender) and six private schools ($N$ = 560; male = 313, female = 247) in Lima (Peru). In this sample, 538 students were from eighth grade (336 from public schools and 202 from private schools), 565 from ninth grade (320 from public schools and 245 from private schools) and 402 from tenth grade (289 from public schools and 113 from private schools) and the mean age of the total sample was 14.55 years ($SD$ = 1.20).

Contacts with the schools were established by sending letters to their principals. All questionnaires were applied during the last quarter of the academic year. The questionnaires were administered during regular class hours for Spanish language course. The instructions were read aloud and stated that the questionnaire was not a test with good or bad answers but that the main interest was to know students' personal opinion about some aspects of schooling (Midgley et al, 1998). There was an example item to teach students how to answer each item using a Likert-scale. Students could ask questions anytime they wanted. In each classroom there was always somebody present who was familiar with the research. Students were explicitly told that they were free to collaborate or not.

*Measures*

To evaluate students' perceptions of school culture, students' perceptions of teachers' achievement goals (their instructional practices), and students' achievement goals, the Patterns of Adaptive Learning Survey (PALS—1997 and 2000) was used (Anderman & Midgley, 2002; Midgley et al., 1997, 1998, 2000). The PALS is a self-report instrument with a Likert-type scale that goes from 1 (*not at all true*) to 5 (*very true*). The PALS was translated from English into Spanish. An expert in English (Spanish speaking) was asked to do the back-translation from Spanish into English as suggested by Hambleton (1994).

### School Culture

Perceived mastery school culture measures the extent to which students perceive their school as stressing that the purpose of engaging in academic activities is to develop competence and gain understanding (e.g., "In this school the importance of trying hard is really stressed to students."). Perceived performance school culture refers to the students' perceptions that, at the school level, the goal of engaging in academic activities is to demonstrate competence and to outperform others (e.g., "In this school, students are encouraged to compete with each other academically.").

### Perception of Teachers' Goals

This questionnaire assesses the students' perceptions of the goals that the teacher stresses during the class. Three types of perceptions of teachers' goals were evaluated. Teachers 'mastery achievement goals refer to students' perceptions that the teacher is stressing to engage in academic activities to gain competence and understanding (e.g., "In this class, my teacher thinks mistakes are okay as long as we are learning."). Teachers' performance-approach goals measure students' perceptions that their teacher stresses to engage in academic activities to demonstrate superiority when compared to others (e.g., "In this class, my teacher lets us know which students get the highest scores on a test."). Teachers' performance-avoidance achievement goals assess students' perceptions that the teacher stresses to engage in academic activities to avoid demonstration of incompetence (e.g., "In this class, my teacher says that showing others that we are not bad at class work should be our goal").

### Students' Achievement Goals

Students' achievement goals refer to purposes or reasons to engage in academic achievement behaviors. The scale measures beliefs about purposes, competence, success, ability, effort, errors, and standards. Three types of students' achievement goals were assessed. Mastery goals measure the students' purpose of developing competence and skills, gaining knowledge, and understanding. The focus is on the task itself (e.g., "In this class, it's important to me that I improve my skills this year."). Performance-approach achievement goals assess the students' purpose of comparing favorably to others, to demonstrate their competence and superiority, and to outperform others (e.g., "In this class, one of my goals is to show others that I'm good at my class work."). Performance–avoidance achievement goals refer to the students' purpose of avoiding negative judgments about their competence and avoiding demonstration of incompetence (e.g., "One of my goals in class is to avoid looking like I have trouble doing the work.").

## RESULTS

*Preliminary Analyses*

As preliminary analyses, Confirmatory Factor Analyses (CFA) were performed to study the construct validity of our instruments and the internal consistency of our measures was examined using Cronbach's Alpha. Finally, we performed correlation analyses among the research variables. Zero-order correlations were performed to explore the associations between the study variables.

The construct validity of our instruments was investigated through Confirmatory Factor Analyses using LISREL 8.50 (Jöreskog & Sörbom, 2001). The following indices are presented: Chi-square ($\chi^2$), the root mean square error of approximation (RMSEA) for which values lower than 0.05 represent a good fit (Raykov & Marcoulides, 2000) and values lower than 0.08 represent a reasonable good fit (Byrne, 1998), and the standardized root mean square residual (SRMR) which should be lower than 0.08 for an excellent fit. The use of these indices (i.e. RMSEA and SRMR) is suggested by Hu and Bentler (1999). As a rule of thumb, they indicate that together RMSEA values closer to 0.06 and SRMR values closer to 0.08 show an excellent fit (Hu & Bentler, 1999). Regarding the item loadings, the ones equal to or higher than 0.35 were maintained.

With regard to students' perceptions of school culture, we expected that a model with two factors (i.e., mastery and performance school culture) would have a good fit. The fit of this model was indeed adequate: $\chi^2$ (34, $N$ = 1378) = 264.99, $p < .001;$ RMSEA = 0.070; SRMR = 0.053. Item loadings varied between 0.50 and 0.69. The results presented here are from the second model we tested. Three items needed to be deleted due to low factor loadings. Cronbach's alpha was .70 and .62 for mastery and performance school culture, respectively.

Concerning students' perceptions of teachers' goals we expected a three-factor model[1] to yield an adequate fit (teachers' mastery, performance-approach, and performance-avoidance goals). Fit indices of the three-factor model indicated an adequate fit: $\chi^2$ (62, $N$ = 1366) = 416.65, $p < .001;$ RMSEA = 0.065; SRMR = 0.059. All loadings were 0.54 or higher. Cronbach's alpha coefficients were .78, .64, and .60 for perceptions of teachers' mastery, performance-approach, and performance-avoidance goals, respectively.

We tested a model in which the same three different types of achievement goals were expected for the students themselves (i.e., mastery goals, performance-approach and performance-avoidance goals). The model obtained an excellent fit $\chi^2$ (186, $N$ = 1290) = 981.02, $p < .001$; RMSEA = 0.058; SRMR = 0.051. All loadings were 0.36 or higher. Cronbach's alpha coefficients were .81, .84, and .72 for students' mastery, performance-approach, and performance-avoidance achievement goals, respectively (Matos, Lens & Vansteenkiste, 2007).

## Correlations

As we can see in Table 1, there were positive and significant correlations among all the research variables. Mastery school culture and performance school culture were positively correlated, suggesting that schools can be perceived as placing emphasis on both mastery and performance goals at the same time. Further, as can be expected, mastery school culture and perceptions of teachers' mastery goals were positively correlated and this association was stronger than the correlation between mastery school culture and perceptions of teachers' performance-approach goals and perceptions of teachers' performance-avoidance goals. Performance school culture was positively correlated with students' perceptions of teachers' performance-approach and performance-avoidance goals and these associations were stronger than the correlation between performance school culture and perceptions of teachers as being mastery-oriented.

Next, mastery school culture positively correlated with all three types of students' achievement goals. Also in this case, the association with mastery goals was stronger than the association with either performance-approach or performance-avoidance goals. Performance school culture was positively correlated with the three types of students' achievement goals: performance-approach goals, performance-avoidance goals, and mastery goals. The three correlations are almost equal.

Although perceptions of teachers' achievement goals were positively correlated with the three types of students' achievement goals, the correlation between perceptions of teachers' mastery goals and students' mastery goals was much higher than the correlation with students' performance-approach and with their performance-avoidance goals. Moreover, the correlations between perceptions of teachers' performance-approach goals and students' performance-approach and performance-avoidance goals were much higher than the correlation between teachers' performance-approach goals and students' mastery goals. This was also the case for perceptions of teachers' performance-avoidance goals which correlated higher with students' performance-avoidance goals and approach-goals than with students' mastery goals.

**TABLE 1. CORRELATIONS BETWEEN THE RESEARCH VARIABLES**

| Area | Mean | SD | 1 | 2 | 3 | 4 | 5 | 6 | 7 |
|---|---|---|---|---|---|---|---|---|---|
| School culture | | | | | | | | | |
| 1.Mastery | 3.87 | 0.68 | | | | | | | |
| 2.Performance | 3.53 | 0.79 | .42*** | | | | | | |
| Perception of Teachers' Goals | | | | | | | | | |
| 3. Mastery | 3.92 | 0.83 | .49*** | .22*** | | | | | |
| 4. Performance-Approach | 2.98 | 0.9 | .13*** | .31*** | .06* | | | | |
| 5. Performance-Avoidance | 3.03 | 0.86 | .23*** | .31*** | .20*** | .42*** | | | |
| Students' Achievement Goals | | | | | | | | | |
| 6. Mastery | 4.28 | 0.57 | .46*** | .31*** | .51*** | .09** | .21*** | | |
| 7. Performance-Approach | 3.46 | 0.77 | .26*** | .34*** | .24*** | .34*** | .49*** | .41*** | |
| 8. Performance-Avoidance | 3.16 | 0.79 | .16*** | .32*** | .09** | .36*** | .50*** | .27*** | .67*** |

*** $p < 0.001$ level, ** $p < .01$ level, * $p < .05$ level $N= 1332\text{-}1433$

There were positive and significant correlations between the three measures of students' goal orientations. Mastery goals correlated higher with performance-approach than with performance-avoidance goals. Finally, performance-approach and performance-avoidance goals were highly intercorrelated.

*Primary Analysis*

To confirm our research hypotheses, a theoretically-driven model was evaluated using Structural Equation Modeling (SEM; Bollen, 1989). In establishing our research model, we first considered that achievement goal theory stresses the importance of school culture in shaping students' goals for learning and education and also teachers' achievement goals and instructional practices. The role of teachers is important in shaping students' achievement goals. A direct effect from mastery school culture to students' mastery achievement goals was tested as well as the effect of perceptions of teachers' mastery goals as a mediator of this relation. The same relations were tested for performance school culture and teachers' and students' performance-approach goals. However, we could not test the direct effect of school culture as being performance-avoidance oriented on teachers' and students' performance avoidance goals because the way in which performance school culture was measured referred to performance-approach goals only (and not to performance-avoidance goals). This path was not included because we wanted to evaluate a theoretically consistent and more parsimonious model.

In order to start the Structural Equation Modeling, a measurement model was first evaluated. To adequately represent latent variables, item parcels were created by obtaining the mean from several randomly selected items (Landis, Beal, & Tesluk, 2000; Hoyle, 1995). Parcels were created for school culture, perceptions of teachers´ achievement goals and students´ achievement goals. The estimated model for Spanish Classes yielded an excellent fit, $\chi^2$ (221) = 522.39 (RMSEA = 0.049; SRMR = 0.040). The parcels obtained strong loadings ($\lambda > 0.48$) with its correspondent latent factor[2].

Then we proceeded by testing our hypothesized integrated model. Results from the SEM showed that the theoretically-driven model obtained a good fit. Fit indices were $\chi^2$ ($df = 254$) = 733.45; RMSEA = 0.058; SRMR = 0.062; the model is depicted in Figure 1. As can be noticed, a mastery-oriented school culture had an effect on students' mastery goals ($\beta = .38$, $p < .001$). This direct effect was partially mediated by students' perceptions of teachers' mastery goals, because mastery school culture predicted students' mastery goals both directly and indirectly (through perceptions of teachers' mastery goals)[3]. Such partial mediation was not observed in the case of performance school culture. Performance school culture had a direct effect on performance-approach goals (β =.80) and it also predicted teachers' performance-approach goals (β =.64), but the latter did not predict students' performance approach goals (β = −.07, n.s.). Perceptions of teachers' performance-avoidance goals positively predicted students' performance-avoidance goals (β =.80). See Figure 1.

*Discussion*

In the present research, achievement goal theory was used to understand the relationship between school culture, students' perceptions of teachers' achievement goals and students' achievement goals. This theory stresses the importance of school culture in shaping students' and teachers' achievement goals.

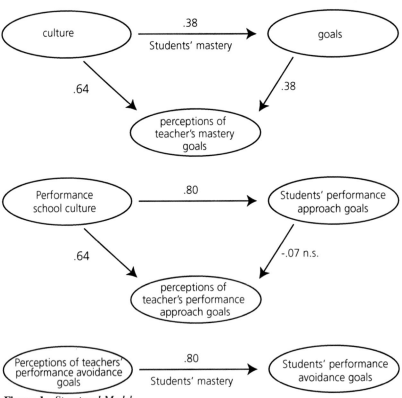

**Figure 1.** *Structural Model.*
*Note:* Non significant paths are in italics.

Previous research showed the importance of school culture in shaping students' motivation and educational outcomes (e.g., Maehr & Midgley, 1996). However, less research tested the importance of classroom goal structures in different educational outcomes. Wolters (2004) addresses the gap in this area. Although the importance of teachers as agents in shaping students' motivation is well recognized, it is not much studied yet. In the present research, we tried to address this gap and we tried to expand the knowledge regarding the relation between students' perceptions of their learning environments such as the school and the classroom contexts and their personal achievement goals.

We asked for the students' personal achievement goals as well as their perceptions of the achievement goals stressed in their schools and in their classrooms. We measured the students' perceptions of their teachers' achievement goals. Ames (1992) stressed the importance of considering how students perceive their learning contexts, because at the end, it could be that students' perceptions of the environment will shape their own motivation and behavior. However, there is still the need to do more research on what is really happening in the classroom and at the school level (Kaplan & Maehr, 2002; Kaplan et al., 2002).

We expected that the effects of mastery and performance school cultures on, respectively, students' mastery and performance-approach goals would be partially mediated by students' perceptions of respectively teachers' mastery and performance-approach goals. This was the case for students' mastery goals in which the effect of mastery school culture was partially mediated by students' perceptions of teachers' mastery goals. However, this was not the case for students' performance-approach goals in which the effect of performance school culture was not mediated by perceptions of teachers' performance-approach goals. Therefore, students' perceptions of teachers' achievement goals partially accounted for the effects of school culture on students' mastery goals but not for performance-approach goals.

As it has been shown in the structural equation modeling (SEM) results, mastery and performance school culture had a strong effect on students' mastery and performance approach achievement goals respectively and this might be related to the fact that students have been exposed to the same school culture for an average of 6 years. However, the partial mediation effects showed that teachers still significantly contribute in the case of students' mastery achievement goals. It is however not clear why students' perceptions of teachers goals affect students' mastery goals but not students' performance-approach goals. Two elements might help to explain the current findings.

One possible explanation for this might be that if teachers promote a performance approach environment in the classroom (i.e., showing the best works to the classroom, congratulating the students with the highest grades in front of everybody, etc.) there are only few students that are able to attain the promoted achievement goals considering that only very few can be the best students in the classroom. So only a minority of the students adopt the achievement goal promoted by the teacher. On the other hand, if teachers foster a mastery classroom environment (i.e., emphasizing the importance of learning and skill development, encouraging students to comprehend the material, making students trying hard, etc.), all students in a classroom are able to attain these promoted achievement goals, considering that all students can always make an improvement if they compare their development with their own standards and not with normative standards as in the case of performance-approach goals.

Rather than focusing on the lack of effect of students' perceptions of teachers' performance-approach goals on students' performance-approach goals, it might also be the case that the performance school culture is so strong and dominating that (perceptions of) teachers' performance-approach goals yield little unique additional effects. Thus, the performance school culture overrules the observed positive relationship between teachers' and students' performance-approach goals at the correlational level.

We also found that teachers' performance-avoidance goals as perceived by students, were related to students' performance-avoidance goals. However, as previously said, we did not test the effect of performance school culture on perceptions of teachers' performance-avoidance goals because the way in which performance school culture was measured was related to performance-approach goals only. However, research has been successful in developing ways to identify performance-avoidance goals at the classroom level (Midgley et al., 2000); nevertheless, there is still the need to conduct research regarding the possibility of developing scales to measure performance-avoidance goals at the school level.

It is important to consider the practical implications of the present research at the classroom and school levels. Does school culture matter for teachers' and students' achievement goals? The answer is "yes it does." More interestingly, a mastery-oriented school culture had an effect on students' personal mastery goals and this effect was partially mediated by perceptions of teachers' mastery goals. However these relationships among variables were not found for a performance-oriented school culture. While it had a direct effect on students' personal performance-approach goals and also on students' perceptions of teachers' performance-approach goals, the effect on students' performance-approach goals was not mediated by students' perception of teachers' performance-approach goals. Students' perceptions of teachers' performance-avoidance goals was positively related to students' personal performance-avoidance goals.

The importance of a mastery-oriented school culture and the role of teachers are emphasized in students' personal mastery goals. Besides the effect of school culture on students' mastery goals, teachers perceived as fostering mastery goals had an effect on students' mastery achievement goals (and therefore with other educational outcomes fostered by mastery goals). Teachers can still have a role in promoting these goals which is very important as an agent of change at the classroom and at the school level in order to improve the learning process. This is of vital importance when elaborating and planning intervention programs.

## Limitations

We need to remember that our study was limited due to its correlational nature. We observed some specific variables in a school setting and we were interested in examining and identifying significant and meaningful associations among these variables. Therefore we cannot draw any conclusions about cause and effect relationships (Meece, Herman, & McCombs, 2003). In our reasoning, we assumed that the effects go primarily from schools to teachers and students and from teachers to students but the causality can work, of course, in both ways. Therefore longitudinal studies can shed light on the directionality of the currently observed effects (e.g., Kaplan & Midgley, 1999).

## ENDNOTES

We tested a two-factor model for school culture because it evaluated mastery and performance approach oriented school cultures and not performance-avoidance goals. Regarding, perceptions of teachers' goals, we could test a three-factor model because these measures were available in the literature (PALS 2000).

Models presented here were part of a larger project that included more outcome variables. We only present here the results for the first part of these models and that are relevant for this topic (Matos, 2005).

Previous regression analyses tested showed that the direct effect of mastery school culture on students´ mastery goals was $\beta = .31$ ($p < .001$) and when perceptions of teachers' mastery goals were included into the analyses, the effect on students´ mastery goals dropped ($\beta = .17$, $p < .001$).

## REFERENCES

Ames, C. (1992). Classrooms: Goals, structures, and student motivation. *Journal of Educational Psychology, 84*, 261–271.

Ames, C., & Archer, J. (1988). Achievement goals in the classroom: Students' learning strategies and motivation processes. *Journal of Educational Psychology, 80,* 260–267.

Anderman, E. M., & Midgley, C. (2002). Methods for studying goals, goal structures, and patterns of adaptive learning. In C. Midgley (Ed.), *Goals, goal structures, and patterns of adaptive learning* (pp. 1–20). Mahwah, NJ: Erlbaum.

Anderman, L. H., Patrick, H., Hruda, L. Z., & Linnenbrink, E. A. (2002). Observing classroom goal structures to clarify and expand goal theory. In C. Midgley (Ed.), *Goals, goal structures, and patterns of adaptive learning* (pp. 243–278). New Jersey: Erlbaum.

Bollen, K. A. (1989). A new incremental fit index for general structural equation models. *Sociological Research and Methods, 16,* 492–503.

Byrne, B. M. (1998). *Structural equation modeling with Lisrel, Prelis and Simplis: Basic concepts, applications and programming.* Mahwah, NJ: Erlbaum.

Covington, M. V. (2000). Goal theory, motivation and school achievement: An integrative review. *Annual Review of Psychology, 51,* 171–200.

Deci, E. L., & Ryan, R. M. (1985). *Intrinsic motivation and self-determination in human behavior.* New York: Plenum.

Dweck, C. S. (1986). Motivational processes affecting learning. *American Psychologist, 41,* 1040–1048.

Elliot, A. J., & Church, M A. (1997). A hierarchical model of approach and avoidance achievement motivation. *Journal of Personality and Social Psychology, 72,* 218–232.

Elliot, A. J., & Harackiewicz, J. M. (1996). Approach and avoidance achievement goals and intrinsic motivation: A mediational analysis. *Journal of Personality and Social Psychology, 70,* 461–475.

Elliot, A. J., & McGregor, H. A. (2001). A 2 x 2 Achievement goal framework. *Journal of Personality and Social Psychology, 80,* 501–519.

Graham, S., & Golan, S. (1991). Motivational influences on cognition: Task involvement, ego involvement, and depth of information processing. *Journal of Educational Psychology, 83,* 187–194.

Grolnick, W. S., & Ryan, R. M. (1987). Autonomy in children's learning: An experimental and individual difference investigation. *Journal of Personality and Social Psychology, 52,* 890–898.

Hambleton, R. K. (1994). Guidelines for adapting educational and psychological tests: A progress report. *European Journal of Psychological Assessment, 10,* 229–244.

Harackiewicz, J. M., Barron, K. E., Tauer, J. M., Carter, S. M., & Elliot, A. J. (2000). Short-term and long-term consequences of achievement goals predicting interest and performance over time. *Journal of Educational Psychology, 92,* 316–330.

Heyman, G. D., & Dweck, C. S. (1992). Achievement goals and intrinsic motivation: Their relation and their role in adaptive motivation. *Motivation and Emotion, 16,* 231–247.

Hoyle, R. H. (1995). The structural equation modeling approach: Basic concepts and fundamental issues. In R. H. Hoyle (Ed.), *Structural equation modeling: Concepts, issues and applications* (pp. 1–15). London: Sage.

Hu, L., & Bentler, P. M. (1999). Cutoff criteria for fit indexes in covariance structure analysis: Conventional criteria versus new alternatives. *Structural Equation Modeling, 6*, 1–55.

Jöreskog, K., & Sörbom, D. (2001). *Lisrel 8: Structural equation modeling with the Simplis command language.* Hillsdale, NJ: Erlbaum.

Kaplan, A., & Maehr, M. L. (2002). Adolescents' achievement goals. In F. Pajares, & T. Urdan. *Academic motivation of adolescents* (pp. 125–167), Greenwich, CT: Information Age.

Kaplan, A., Middleton, M. J., Urdan, T., & Midgley, C. (2002). Achievement goals and goal structures. In C. Midgley (Ed.), *Goals, goal structures, and patterns of adaptive learning* (pp. 21–53). Hillsdale, NJ. Erlbaum.

Kaplan, A., & Midgley, C. (1999). The relationship between perceptions of the classroom goal structure and early adolescents' affect in school: The mediating role of coping strategies. *Learning and Individual Differences, 11*, 187–212.

Landis, R. S., Beal, D. J., & Tesluk, P. E. (2000). A comparison of approaches to forming composite measures in structural equation models. *Organizational Research Methods, 3*, 186–207.

Linnenbrink, E., & Pintrich, P. R. (2000). Multiple pathways to learning and achievement: The role of goal orientation in fostering adaptive motivation, affect, and cognition. In C. Sansone & J. M. Harackiewicz (Eds.), *Intrinsic and extrinsic motivation: The search for optimal motivation and performance* (pp. 195–227). New York: Academic Press.

Maehr, M. L. (2000). *Transforming school cultures to enhance student motivation and learning.* Paper for a talk to teachers and principals in Leuven, Belgium (May).

Maehr, M. L. (2001).Studiemotivatie en leren bevorderen door de schoolcultuur te veranderen [Enhancing student motivation and learning by changing the school culture]. *Informatie Vernieuwing Onderwijs [Information Educational Innovation], 84*, 36–52.

Maehr, M. L., & Buck, R. (1992). Transforming school culture. In M. Sashkin & H. J. Walberg (Eds.), *Educational leadership and school culture* (pp. 40–57). Berkeley: McCutchan.

Maehr, M. & Fyans, L., (1989) School culture, motivation and achievement. In C. Ames & M. Maehr (Eds.), *Advances in Motivation and Achievement* (Vol. 6). Greenwich, CT: JAI Press.

Maehr, M. L., & Midgley, C. (1996). *Transforming school cultures.* Boulder: Westview Press.

Matos, L. (2005). *School culture, teachers' and students' achievement goals as communicating vessels. A study in Peruvian Secondary schools.* Unpublished doctoral dissertation. University of Leuven, Belgium. http://hdl.handle.net/1979/149

Matos, L., Lens, W., & Vansteenkiste, M. (2007). Achievement goals, learning strategies and language achievement among Peruvian high school students. *Psychologica Belgica, 47*, 51–70.

Meece, J. L., Herman, P., & McCombs, B. L. (2003). Relations of learner centered teaching practices to adolescents' achievement goals. *International Journal of Educational Research, 39*, 457–476.

Middleton, M., & Midgley, C. (1997). Avoiding the demonstration of lack of ability: An underexplored aspect of goal theory. *Journal of Educational Psychology, 89,* 710–718.

Midgley, C., Anderman, E., & Hicks, L. (1995). Differences between elementary and middle school teachers and students: A goal theory approach. *Journal of Early Adolescence, 15,* 90–113.

Midgley, C., Kaplan, A., Middleton, M., Maehr, M. L., Urdan, T., Anderman, L. H., Anderman, E., & Roeser, R. (1998). The development and validation of the scales assessing students' achievement goal orientations. *Contemporary Educational Psychology, 23,* 113–131.

Midgley, C., Maehr, M. L., Hicks, L., Roeser, R., Urdan, T., Anderman, E., et al. (1997). *Manual for the patterns of adaptive learning survey (PALS).* Ann Arbor, MI University of Michigan.

Midgley, C., Maehr, M. L., Hruda, L. Z., Anderman, E., Anderman, L., Freeman, K. E., et al. (2000). *Manual for the patterns of adaptive learning scales (PALS).* Ann Arbor, MI: University of Michigan.

Midgley, C., & Urdan, T. (2001). Academic self-handicapping and achievement goals: A further examination. *Contemporary Educational Psychology, 26,* 61–75.

Patrick, H., Anderman, L. H., Ryan, A. M., Edelin, K. C., & Midgley, C. (2001). Teachers' communication of goal orientations in four fifth-grade classrooms. *The Elementary School Journal, 102,* 35–58.

Pintrich, P. R. (2000). Multiple goals, multiple pathways: The role of goal orientation in learning and achievement. *Journal of Educational Psychology, 92,* 544–555.

Pintrich, P. R., Conley, A. M., & Kempler, T. M. (2003). Current issues in achievement goal theory and research. *International Journal of Educational Research, 39,* 319–337.

Pintrich, P. R., & De Groot, E. V. (1990). Motivational and self-regulated learning components of classroom academic performance. *Journal of Educational Psychology, 82,* 33–40.

Pintrich, P. R., & Schrauben, B. (1992). Students' motivational beliefs and their cognitive engagement in classroom academic tasks. In D. H. Schunk & J. L. Meece (Eds.), *Student perceptions in the classrooms* (pp. 149–183). Hillsdale, NJ: Erlbaum.

Pintrich, P. R., & Schunk, D. H. (2002). *Motivation in education: Theory, research and application* (2nd Ed.). Upper Saddle River, NJ: Prentice Hall.

Raykov, T., & Marcoulides, G. A. (2000). *A first course in Structural Equation Modeling.* Hillsdale NJ: Erlbaum.

Roeser, R. W., Marachi, R., & Gehlbach, H. (2002) A goal theory perspective on teachers' professional identities and the contexts of teaching. In C. Midgley (Ed.), *Goals, goal structures, and patterns of adaptive learning* (pp. 205–241). Hillsdale, NJ: Erlbaum.

Roeser, R. W., Midgley, C., & Urdan, T. C. (1996). Perceptions of the school psychological environment and early adolescents' psychological and behavioral functioning in school: The mediating role of goals and belonging. *Journal of Educational Psychology, 3,* 408–422.

Rosenholtz, S. J. (1989). *Teachers' workplace. The social organization of schools.* New York: Longman.

Stolp, S. (1994). Leadership for school culture. *ERIC digest, (91),* ED 370198.

Struyf, E., Vandenberghe, R., & Lens, W. (2001). The evaluation practice of teachers as a learning opportunity for students. *Studies in Educational Evaluation, 27,* 215–238.

Talbert, J. E., & McLaughlin, M. W. (1996). Teacher professionalism in local school contexts. In F. Goodson & A. Hargreaves (Eds.), *Teachers' professional lives* (pp. 127–153). London: Farber Press.

Vansteenkiste , M., Simons, J., Lens, W., Soenens, B., Matos, L., & Lacante, M. (2004). Less is sometimes more: Goal-content matters. *Journal of Educational Psychology, 96,* 755–764.

Weinstein, C. E., & Mayer, R. E. (1986). The teaching of learning strategies. In M. Wittrock, *Handbook of research on teaching* (pp. 315–327). New York: MacMillan.

Wolters, C. A. (2004). Advancing achievement goal theory: Using goal structures and goal orientations to predict students' motivation, cognition, and achievement. *Journal of Educational Psychology, 96,* 236–250.

Wolters C. A., Yu, S. L., & Pintrich, P. R. (1996). The relation between goal orientation and students' motivational beliefs and self-regulated learning. *Learning and Individual Differences, 8,* 211–238

Zimmerman, B. J. (1994). Dimensions of academic self-regulation: A conceptual framework for education. In D. Schunk & B. Zimmerman (Eds.), *Self-regulation of learning and performance* (pp. 3–21). Hillsdale, NJ: Erlbaum.

# CHAPTER 8

# A MODEL OF CULTURE AND ACHIEVEMENT BEHAVIOR

## Farideh Salili

This chapter presents a series of systematic research designed to explore cultural, situational, and contextual influences on student achievement behavior as well as the applicability of Western theories of achievement motivation to other cultures. The results of these studies showed that achievement motivation is a complex construct that is influenced by many interacting factors and cannot be explained by the traditional theories. These factors influence achievement behavior at many levels. At the classroom and school levels, we provided evidence that teacher evaluative behavior affected intrinsic/continuing motivation and causal attributions for achievement. At the societal level the findings showed that development of achievement judgment is different in different cultures studied. Several cross-cultural studies using different approaches provided evidence that while dimensions of achievement is the same for the cultures studied, achievement may mean different things in different cultures and people of all cultures can have many different achievement goals at the same time. These goals and dimensions fall into two broad categories: individualistic and affiliative goals and three dimensions: outcome of achievement, instrumental activities, and causal attribution for achievement respectively. The two categories of achievement are related to each other in different ways for different cultures. Different types of achievement goals produce different outcome, require different activities and are attributed to different causes. Based on these results we proposed a model

*Culture, Self, and Motivation: Essays in Honor of Martin L. Maehr*, pages 183–212
Copyright © 2009 by Information Age Publishing
**183**

of achievement behavior that can apply to both socially-oriented and individualistically-oriented cultures. The model takes into account both affiliative and individualistic achievement goals, and the three dimensions of achievement. Further interesting evidence supporting these findings were provided through the semantic differential (SD) study.

## INTRODUCTION

At the start of my PhD studies (in 1972) at the University of Illinois, I was fortunate to be appointed as a Research Assistant to two great scholars. The first was Martin L. Maehr, my PhD Advisor in the Department of Educational Psychology whose work on culture and achievement motivation influenced and inspired me in my own research in this area. The second was Charles E. Osgood who was well-known among other things for his work on measurement of affective meaning (Osgood, May, & Miron, 1975) and the Semantic Differential (SD) Scales, a cross-cultural instrument for measuring affective meaning. Working with Osgood provided me with an opportunity to explore cross-cultural universals and differences in affective and connotative meanings. It also familiarized me with a useful cross-cultural tool that I used in some of my studies on culture and student motivation.

Martin Maehr introduced me to the field of achievement motivation and taught me to look critically at the applicability of various theories of motivation to other cultures. I recall long discussions in our weekly graduate seminars where he shared his new ideas on culture and achievement motivation. We learned that achievement motivation is a complex construct influenced by many interacting factors. Maehr's ideas on which the theories of personal and work investments are based were being discussed and developed long before their publication in the book *The Motivation Factor: A Theory of Personal Investment* (Maehr & Braskemp, 1986). Interestingly, participants in these seminars were from different cultures with different perspectives on achievement motivation. This chapter which summarizes some of my own research on culture and student motivation is dedicated to my teacher and mentor Professor Martin Maehr, who has always guided me in my academic career. The first section discusses the initial but important work on culture and motivation. We conducted these studies to explored applicability of Western theories of achievement motivation to other cultures as well as examining situational and contextual influences on achievement behavior. These pioneering studies provided a foundation for our later work and were conducted during my PhD studies under the supervision of Professor Martin Maehr. The focus of the second section is mainly on Chinese students and they explored learning and motivational characteristics of the Chinese students.

*Socio-Cultural, Situational, and Contextual Influences on Achievement Behavior*

In early 1970s McClelland et al.'s personality theory of achievement motivation (McClelland, Atkinson, Lowell, & Clark, 1953), the Thematic Apperception Test (TAT) used to measure achievement motivation, and their cross-cultural studies were prominent in discussions during my PhD studies. McClelland's theories and research findings claimed a link between the level of achievement motivation in nations and their economic development, and even the rise and fall of nations. McClelland and his colleagues defined achievement motivation as an individual need or drive to compete and strive to succeed against a standard of excellence in task situations where the outcome was evaluated in terms of success and failure (McClelland et al., 1953). According to McClelland and his colleagues achievement motivation was a personality disposition learned early in life through child rearming practices that emphasized mastery, competitiveness, independence, taking initiative, persistence, and seeking challenging tasks. These parenting practices were found more in predominantly protestant countries where people followed protestant work ethics. McClelland's theories and definition of achievement motivation was criticized for being ethnocentric, biased towards individualistic competitive notion of achievement and ignoring socio-cultural, situational and contextual influences on achievement (Maehr, 1978), thus prompting research on the validity of McClelland's theories and research findings. Many scholars explored alternative ways of looking at achievement motivation (e.g., DeVos, 1973; Maehr & Braskemp 1986). Prominent among them is Martin Maehr whose research and theorizing have made enormous contribution to our understanding of the complexities of achievement motivation construct and behavior.

The University of Illinois campus at Urbana Champaign provided us with access to students with different backgrounds and different cultures. Most of the overseas students appeared to be highly motivated and diligent. The library was one of the places where different levels of diligence in studying could be observed. As evening went by most Western students left the library and by 7 or 8 pm the overwhelming majority of students were from Asia and particularly East Asia. If McClelland's theory was applicable to other cultures, then Asian students should score high on TAT. These students were assumed to be highly motivated to achieve by virtue of engaging in higher education at the University of Illinois. Our initial attempt to test this hypothesis was a failure. To explore cultural differences in achievement motivation, we administered the TAT to groups of graduate Asian and American students. The results showed many of the limitations of the TAT. The picture cues did not elicit as many responses from our Asian students compared with the American students. While their presence at the University of Illinois and their performance suggested that all group of students were highly achievement motivated, the stories produced by the Asian students were often devoid of achievement theme. Many stories were summarized in one sentence and could not be scored. Thus while this study taught us about the problems of measurement equivalence in cross-cultural research, the results were inconclusive and could not be taken seriously. In our more recent cross-cultural study we developed and used a modified version of the TAT in order to address the problem of measurement equivalence (see Salili, 1996).

The situational and contextual variables that influence achievement behavior were being investigated by several researchers. An interesting article by Meahr and Stalling (1972) reported detrimental effects of external evaluation (i.e., grading) on continuing motivation. Similarly Lepper, Green and Nisbett (1973) found that young preschool children in extrinsic reward condition spent significantly less time on an intrinsically interesting task than those in the same condition despite not being rewarded. These studies suggested that immediate classroom conditions such as external reward or even grading students may have detrimental effect on intrinsic motivation. We tested the validity of this hypothesis in a different and contrasting cultural context, namely in Iranian schools. Iranian families and society are hierarchically structured and authoritarian. Parents are overly protective of their children. They allow them less freedom of action and "children are under watchful eyes of their parents who evaluate, reward and punish their children at their own discretion" (Salili, Maehr, Sorenson & Fyans, Jr. 1976, p. 87). Similar pattern is found in schools where teachers command authority and heavy emphasis is placed on external evaluation of students' performance, that is, "external school evaluation is more integrated with extra school experiences" (Salili et al., 1976, p. 87). It was thus hypothesized that children in Iran might react differently to evaluation compared with US children. Participants were 10–12 year-old primary school students. They were randomly assigned to three evaluative conditions and administered an anagram language test (word puzzle). At the end of the test they were given an answer sheet to score their own performance. One group of children were told their scores will be given to their teacher and counted in their final examination (teacher evaluation). A second group of students were told that the purpose of the test was to see how students performed compared to their classmates (peer comparison). The experimenter then collected the score sheets and called out the names with their marks and commented how well they did compared to their classmates. The third group was told that their scores would not be known to anyone but themselves (self-knowledge of results). Once the anagram test was over the students were told that, in order to fill up the rest of the class time they could choose either to read an interesting story provided for them or practice on similar word games. The subjects' choice was used as the first index of continuing motivation. The amount of time spent on these anagrams was a second index. After the class the experimenter left a box and told students they could obtain more copies of these word puzzles if they wished by writing a note to the experimenter to request it and place it in the box. Whether or not they wrote the note was used as the third index of continuing motivation. Two other indices of continuing motivation were student's performance on the task and the time they engaged in doing the word puzzle.

Subjects' immediate perception of causes of success and failure was also assessed immediately after the performance. They were asked whether their performance was due to their ability, hard work/effort, task difficulty, or luck and, given similar task in future, how did they expect to perform. In addition, other data including demographic information, their achievement aspiration and achievement motivation-related measures were also collected (the results related to these variables will not be reported here, the readers should refer to Salili, Maehr, Sorensen, and Fyans, Jr. [1976] for more detail). The results confirmed the US study showing that, while evaluation condition had no significant effect on the actual level of performance, it had a major impact on continuing/intrinsic motivation. Contrary to expectations, the results with regard to self-knowledge and teacher evaluation were also similar to those of the US findings. Students in self-knowledge condition scored significantly higher on continuing motivation than did students in teacher evaluation condition. This showed that "extrinsic reinforcement, even as it is inherent in normal grading practices, can be detrimental to continuing motivation" (Salili et al., 1976, p. 99). However, peer comparison (also an external evaluation) produced approximately the same results to that of self-knowledge condition. We speculated that developmental factors may have been responsible for this finding. As proposed by Veroff (1969), at that age peer comparison may have an important impact on motivation. Peer effect on student motivation has not received enough attention from researchers in the field of motivation, considering its important influence on school children particularly the adolescents. Some recent studies have shown that children may engage in self-handicapping activities in order to be accepted by their peers (see Salili, Chiu, & Lai, 2001).

An interesting finding of this study was that students who attributed their results to internal factors scored significantly higher on continuing motivation. In sum, the findings of this research provided further support that situational and contextual factors are important determinants of achievement motivation.

The findings of several studies conducted in different cultures also shed more doubt on McClelland et al's. individualistic Western conception of achievement. Evidence from these often-cited studies showed that there were considerable variations in antecedent of achievement (e.g., DeVos,

1973; Galimore, Boggs, & Jordan, 1974, Ramirez & Price-Williams, 1976; Gallimore, 1981). These studies showed that need for affiliation rather than need for achievement predicted achievement outcome in socially-oriented cultures.

Since different cultures appeared to have different values and meanings for achievement, would this be reflected in their achievement judgment? To answer this question we (Salili, Maehr, & Gilmore, 1976) replicated Weiner and Peter's (1973) study of development of moral and achievement judgment, among Iranian students. Weiner's cognitive conceptualization of achievement motivation assumed that a universal pattern of cognitive development underlies both moral and achievement cognitions, affecting performance in these two areas. That is, both achievement and moral judgments undergo similar patterns of developmental changes. Based on Piaget's cognitive developmental theory of moral judgment, Weiner hypothesized that because of their limited cognitive abilities young children can only focus on concrete and external outcome of an event when making achievement or moral judgments. Young children ignored the intention of the person involved in a moral event or the amount of effort that a person expended in an achievement task, and in their moral and achievement judgment they only focused on the outcome of the event. As children developed cognitively, the emphasis shifted from outcome to intent and effort in moral and achievement judgments, respectively. Their increased cognitive capacities would allow them to consider not only the intent/effort, but also the ability and other complex aspects of the situation. Thus, older children would place more importance on intent/effort. Weiner and Peter's conceptualization of development of achievement judgment was supported in their study, with one exception. Intent and effort became more important until the age of 12, but for older children there was a reversal tendency for achievement judgment—the outcome once again became the major determinant of achievement evaluation. Weiner and Peter speculated that while cognitive development establish certain pattern of development, cultural factors can alter that pattern. American culture and society being production-oriented, success without a positive outcome is not considered acceptable.

If established cognitive development patterns can be modified by the culture of a society, we hypothesized that different patterns of development should be found among children growing up in a highly moralistic culture such as Iran. Hence one important purpose of our study was to see whether the regressive pattern of findings in Weiner et al.'s study was universal or culturally specific. Using the translation of the same scenarios (but with Iranian names for the actors) in which levels of ability, effort/intent, and difficulty of the task and outcome were systematically varied, participants were required to evaluate each scenario and assign a reward or punishment for the actors in the scenarios on 5-point rating scales. We found important differences in the developmental pattern of achievement and moral judgments between Iranian and American students. Contrary to Weiner et al's findings, effort/intent become increasingly more important determinants of achievement and moral judgments while outcome became less important and no reversal to outcome orientation was found in the case of achievement. We speculated that this is because Iranian culture is more solidly based on moralistic values and places great emphasis on effort/intent. Examples of this emphasis are found abundantly in school books and children's story books as well as in Persian poems and folklores taught to children and emphasized by parents and teachers. The role of ability in the judgment was also very interesting. While in the American study high ability was rewarded and low ability was punished in judgment of morality, in the Iranian study lack of ability was rewarded more than positive ability. This finding again showed the influence of Iranian culture which is based on a strong moral foundation. In contrast to US findings, in the case of achievement, high ability was highly rewarded in the judgment of the outcome.

To sum up, our study partially confirmed Weiner and Peter's findings. That is, while our results confirmed their findings with regard to moral judgment, in the case of achievement judgment, there was no reversal to outcome orientation for older children.

McClelland's motivation explanations emphasized the importance of values that cultures placed on achievement and the meanings that different cultures attach to success or failure. However, only those behaviors that fit his definition were considered achievement motivated. Our study showed that cultural values influence achievement judgments, reinforcing the idea that achievement may mean different things to people of different cultures. Other studies argued that the meanings people attach to achievement influence achievement behavior (cf., Ewing, 1981; Fieze, Maehr, & Nichol, 1980; Malpass, 1977). Meanings are, however subjective and difficult to measure. Maehr and Nichols (1980) argued that "individuals tend to behave so as to maximize the experience of success and minimize the experience of failure—as they define these experiences and identify the domains that gave rise to them" (cited in Fyans, Salili, Maehr, & Desai, 1983, p.1000). Thus personal definition of success and failure is important in understanding cross-cultural differences in achievement motivation (Duda, 1981). Our next study was designed to explore this issue and focused on cross-cultural variations and universals in the meaning of achievement.

We had learned from our previous study with the TAT that assessing meaning of achievement cross-culturally required an assessment tool that is culturally equivalent. Semantic Differential scales (SD) developed systematically by Osgood and his collaborators (Osgood, Suci, & Tannenbaum, 1957) are claimed to be cross-culturally equivalent and a good instrument for measuring connotative (subjective) meanings of concepts. Osgood believed that SD technique would "circumvent the language barrier in measuring the affective or connotative aspects of language" or the "subjective culture" in different language cultures (Salili, 2002, p.6). To avoid language bias in cross-cultural research, Osgood believed that one should search for universals within the language and use them to develop an instrument which is not translation equivalents but can tap these universals. SD was developed based on this principle. To avoid translation bias and ethnocentrism, each language/culture group selected adjective qualifiers from their own language. In order to make the cross-cultural comparison possible standard methodology was used in these intra-cultural samplings. These studies revealed three dominant affective dimensions of language: Evluation (E) (e.g., good-bad), Potency (P) (e.g., strong-weak), and Activity (A) (e.g., active- passive). These dimensions formed a universal framework underlying affective or connotative aspect of language and can be used to compare affective meaning of concepts in different cultures. According to Osgood

> the semantic differential technique literally forces the metaphorical usage of scales since every concept must be rated against every scale. This means that in many concept/scale pairing, the judgments must be metaphorically determined (e.g., TORNADO must be judged fair or unfair, MOTHER must be judged hot or cold, and SPONGE must be judged honest or dishonest) with shared affect as the only guide (so the TORNADO is unfair, MOTHER may be hot, and SPONGE probably dishonest) (Osgood & Tsang, 1990, p. 16).

In SD studies participants are asked to rate concepts related to the topic of study on a set of 12 bipolar adjectives using 7-point scales defined by verbal opposites, each four scales representing one of the three dimensions of meaning (i.e., E., P., and A.) . The data then can be analyzed in different ways depending on the purpose of the study. Osgood reported that many studies over the years using SD have all shown the same three dimensions of meaning. This does not mean that concepts have similar meaning for all, but rather

> the semantic framework within which these affective judgments are made are constant....Indeed, it is only by virtue of this common frame of reference that differences between people for the same concept and between concepts for the same people can be specified (Osgood & Tsang, 1990, p. 306).

It is these features of SD that makes it a very useful tool for measuring affective meaning of achievement.

Cross-cultural semantic differential studies of Osgood thus provided us with a wealth of data from some 30 cultural and linguistic groups. Osgood and his collaborators had systematically assessed meanings of over 600 concepts from these cultural and linguistic groups. The data was collected from 16 year-old male high school students. Their findings has been summarized in the *Atlas of Affective Meanings* (see Osgood, May, & Miron 1975). Based on existing theories of motivation and characteristics of achievement motivated individuals, we selected some 100 achievement related concepts and conducted a secondary analysis to explore two basic and complimentary questions:

1.  Is it possible to identify a factor that is universal and relevant to all cultures?
2.  What variations exist in the meaning of achievement between cultures?

Maehr and Nicholls's (1980) at the time suggested that achievement meanings largely fall into three categories:

1.  the goals of achievement which is best reflected in one's definition of success (Maehr & Nicholls's, 1980),
2.  judgment of self which includes personal causation, self-esteem and competence (Harter & Connell, 1984), and
3.  instrumental behavior such as working hard towards achieving the goal.

Guided by this theory, the concepts were selected from the *Atlas of Affective Meaning* so as to represent these dimensions of achievement.

The results showed both universal and uniqueness in the subjective meaning of achievement. We found a cross-cultural factor loaded on items with masculine orientation such as father. This cross-cultural factor was associated with concepts that traditionally in the Western literature are related to achieving orientations such as work, worker, and freedom. "The notion of effort and energy in striving for achievement was recognized across 30 different cultures" (Fyans, Salili, Maehr, & Desai, 1983, p. 1005). The concept of knowledge was also important for all cultures showing the importance of knowledge and education to achievement. Knowledge which can also be considered as an internal attribution to ability and competence, also linked to achievement motivation, was apparently relevant to all cultures. This cross-cultural factor was also associated with courage, success, and power and was generalizable across cultures with a high generalizability coefficient (i.e., 77%). Various cultures were then compared on this factor. The highest scoring cultures on this factor were the United States (American English), Iran, Afghanistan (Pashtu), and West Germany. The lowest scoring groups were United States (Black English), Sweden, India (Mysore), Romania, and Poland. We followed these findings by exploring differences in the meaning of achievement between the high-scoring and low-scoring cultures on this factor. A small number of concepts were selected as criterion concepts and differential patterns of meaning associated with these concepts were calculated for the highest and lowest cultural groups. Guided by theories of motivation, the concepts of *success, reward, taking initiative, choice* and *competition* were selected as criterion concepts. Here the results concerning success and reward will be presented only (see Fyans, Salili, Maehr, & Desai, 1983 for more details). The results showed the high-scoring cultures tended to see success associated with *I myself, initiative, freedom, education, work,* and *masculinity.* The low-scoring cultures had different meanings of success. Success for them was associated with *femininity, charity, devotion, yesterday,* and *illiterate.* The high-scoring group associated reward with *future,* and *leader* while the low scoring culture associated the *reward* with *tradition* and *follower.* Taken together the results of this study showed a cross-culturally generalizable achievement motivation factor which concerns *freedom, taking initiative,* and *effort,* an achievement ethic that is universally recognized (Fyans, Salili, Sorenspn & Desai, 1983). However, it seems this achievement ethic is not equally relevant to different cultures. That is, the findings suggested that success may mean different thing to different people.

### Chinese Learning and Motivational Characteristics

Our more recent research on culture and learning motivation is a natural progression of the earlier studies and was designed to explore further cultural, situational, and contextual factors affecting Hong Kong Chinese students' achievement motivation as well as examining their learning and motivational characteristics. Extraordinary achievement of Chinese students compared to their American counterparts has been recognized by many educators and researchers in recent years (see Stevenson & Stigler, 1992). This superiority in academic achievement has often been attributed to socio-cultural factors (see, for example, Sue & Okazaki, 1990). In the following section I will provide a brief background to Chinese culture and context of education in Hong Kong as a framework for the studies that follow.

### Context of Learning in the Chinese Culture

Hong Kong was a British colony until the 1997 handover to China, and, since then, has been a special administrative region of China with great degree of autonomy. There are many different types of schools depending on their medium of instruction. These include: English expatriate schools (e.g., English Schools Foundation Schools), international schools (with different nationalities using different languages as the medium of instruction, e.g., American International School), English schools for Chinese, Chinese middle schools (using Chinese as the medium of instruction), and the Anglo-Chinese schools (with Chinese-language of instruction, in elementary school and English in the secondary schools). The majority of Chinese students attend the Anglo-Chinese schools. Even though Hong Kong is a cosmopolitan city and is becoming increasingly Westernized, many of the Chinese cultural values still persist (Hui, 1988). Thus, the school system until recently followed the British structure of education at the macro-level with Chinese characteristic at the micro-level. That is, within the school and classroom context teachers, administrators, and the students followed Chinese values and practices with regards to education.

There is a stark difference between the classroom climate of expatriate schools, which is characterized in the Western literature as open and child-oriented, and that of the Chinese schools, which is closed and teacher-oriented. In the Chinese classroom about 40 students are seated quietly facing the teacher who commands authority and respect. The style of teaching up to recently was predominantly didactic and lecture type with little interaction between teachers and students. Up until very recently, education system in Hong Kong was highly competitive and examination oriented. Students were not taught or evaluated for expressive or critical skills, but diligence in mastery of facts and Chinese learners have often been characterized as rote learners especially by expatriate teachers. In studies investigating the strategies that Chinese use in learning we found that memorization strategies were used significantly more than other strategies (Salili, Chiu, & Lai 2001; Salili & Tsui, 2004). We speculated that although cultural beliefs influenced the use of these strategies, having to learn complex high-school subjects in English, which is not their mother tongue, also promoted the use of memorization strategies (see Salili & Tsui, 2004). There is a debate as to what extent the observation that Chinese learners are rote learners is a valid interpretation of the strategy used. A study by Biggs (1992) showed that typically Chinese students first try to understand the subject matter before memorizing it. This stems from the Chinese cultural belief that in order to learn, one has to understand the material first and then practice it repeatedly until it is memorized. It is only when the material can be recalled that one can claim it is learned (see Lee, 1996). Thus, as Biggs suggested Chinese students may use a strategy that involves memorization with understanding. Based on these cultural beliefs, students were given extraordinary amounts of homework that occupied most of their out-of-school time. There are also constant competitive tests and examinations and the situation is described as "Exam hell" (see Wu, 1996). The standard of achievement is very high and geared towards the gifted and brightest students. Under pressure from their teachers and parents, students work very hard, but are seldom praised for their achievement. On the contrary, punishment is frequently administered for poor performance which is often attributed to laziness. Praise, if any, is administered publically for high ability, high effort, and a host of other virtues (see Salili & Hau, 1994; Salili, Hwang, & Choi, 1989, Wan & Salili, 1996). In a recent study comparing Hong Kong and Canadian students, we found that Hong Kong students spent significantly more time studying, they were more anxious, felt less competent, and received lower grades than their Canadian counterparts (Salili, Chiu, & Lai, 2001).

As a result of this harsh learning environment, many less-able students drop out of school after 9 years of compulsory education or enter less demanding vocational schools. Only the bright and capable students manage to graduate and enter local or overseas universities. It is well-known in Hong Kong that students who are not doing so well in local Chinese schools excel academically when placed in international or expatriate schools. Expatriate schools are not as demanding and are child-centered. The curriculum and standard of achievement in these schools are geared towards the average child with the possibilities for the intellectually-gifted children to take higher-level courses or attend enrichment programs.

Chinese children are also under pressure at home from parents to excel academically. Parents place great importance on their children's education and believe that education is important for developing one's character and providing opportunity for landing a good and prosperous career, social advancement, and mobility (Sue & Okazaki, 1990). It is a common sight in Hong Kong to see young children doing their homework in a corner of their family's shop under the watchful eyes and supervision of their parents, who attend to their customers at the same time. Many parents, who are financially able, hire tutors for their children or send their children to extra-curricular tutorial sessions after school. The emphasis on education is derived from an ancient Chinese practice of recruiting only individuals who excelled in public examinations as high-ranking Government officials. This traditional practice is probably responsible for examination-oriented learning context of many Asian cultures such as in Hong Kong (Chen, Stevenson, Hayward, & Burgess,1995). Parents have very high expectations and set a very high standard of achievement for their children (Chen & Stevenson, 1989; Salili, 1995). Chinese children who reported higher achievement expectation from their parents performed better than those who perceived low expectations (Salili, 1995).

Research in Hong Kong has shown that most parenting styles are authoritarian and controlling. From an early age parents establish strict rules of behavior for their children and enforce this through scolding, punishment, and criticism, believing that punishment is helpful and good for their development (Salili, 1995). Children are taught to respect and obey their parents and teachers, they are taught impulse control and persistence in academic work. Tseng and Hsu (1972) reported that Chinese parents tend to discourage independence and exploratory activities, because such activities carry the risk of injuries to the child. Although this study is old and modern parents try to bring up their children more independent, our observation shows that the majority still follow the old tradition. This parenting style is contrary to what is described by McClelland et al. (1953) as child rearing-processes that lead to achievement motivated individuals.

As our earlier studies suggested, we believe that Western theories of achievement may not apply to Eastern cultures. In the West, studies generally show a positive correlation between authoritative parenting styles and high academic achievement. Authoritarian parenting was reported to have adverse effect on children's self-esteem, sense of competence and achievement motivation (see Bee, 1998). Among the Chinese, however, it is found that children who are brought up by authoritarian parents performed better academically than their American counterparts (Stevenson & Lee, 1990). Our recent cross-cultural study comparing Hong Kong and Canadian students also found that social goals of pleasing peers, teachers, and especially pleasing parents were significantly higher for the Chinese students compared with their Canadian counterparts and there was a high correlation between academic achievement and pleasing parents and teachers. The findings of these studies suggest that Chinese parents and teachers can be strong motivators for their children.

### Model of Culture and Achievement Behavior

Research evidence cited above suggests that the model of achievement behavior in the West may not apply to the Chinese. Our next large-scale cross-cultural study was an attempt to explore this issue further more systematically. It was designed to answer the following questions:

1. What are the similarities and differences between Chinese students and British students in their conception of achievement?
2. What is the relationship between need for achievement and level of achievement among the Chinese?
3. Are Chinese who are socially oriented less motivated to achieve than their individualistic British counterparts?

Based on our previous studies and experiences with Chinese students we hypothesized that a model of achievement could apply to both Chinese and British which will be applicable to both individualistic and affiliatively oriented cultures. Based on our observation and previous findings, we also hypothesized that the affiliatively oriented Chinese would be more motivated to achieve and would score higher on academic achievement than their individualistically oriented British counterparts.

Three studies were conducted using the same students, the first two attempted to answer the first question and the second explored the last two questions. Participants were 692 British and 1260 Chinese high-school students aged 13–19.

In a span of two weeks, students were administered three different measures, namely, the Repertory Grid Technique (RG), the Semantic Differential Scales (SD), and the TAT. Various demographic data were also collected. Considerable amount of time was spent in developing and testing the RG and the TAT, so as to make sure the instruments were culturally equivalent.

### Meaning of Achievement: Repertory Grid Technique

The RG is based on the personal construct theory of George Kelly (1955). For more details about this instrument the reader should refer to Fransella & Banister (1977) and Salili (1994). Briefly, what each subject considered success within different life domains (i.e., elements) and their related characteristics (i.e., constructs) were elicited from him/her through individual interviews with 72 individuals who were representative of different groups under investigation. Following Kelly's procedure, triadic method was used to elicit the constructs. The most frequently used and the highest rating elements and their constructs were selected to form a group grid. The group grid was then administered to high school students of both cultures. Participants had to:

1.   rank order areas of success or failure according to their importance by rating them on a 7-point scale,
2.   rate each success situations on all constructs using a 7-point scale from +3 to –3.

Hence three sets of data were obtained: importance ratings of success areas, ratings of success areas on constructs and by transposing the grid, we also obtained ratings of constructs on success situation (see Salili, 1994)

Factor analyses of the importance ratings showed four common factors for all the subjects regardless of age, sex, and culture (see Table 1). These were:

1.   success in personal social life,
2.   success in academic work, career and acquiring wealth,
3.   success in extracurricular activities, and
4.   success in family social life.

**TABLE 1.   Importance Ratings of Success Situations Factors**

| Success Situation | Factor Loading |
|---|---|
| **Factor 1: Personal social life** | |
| Marriage /getting married | .64 |
| Love and romance | .57 |
| Achievement of children and spouse | .57 |
| Developing good personal characteristics | .51 |
| Percent of variance | 57.80 % |
| **Factor 2: Academic work, career, and wealth** | |
| School work/good results | .74 |
| Outstanding achievement (scientific/academic) | .71 |
| Career | .59 |
| Having wealth and possessions | .47 |
| Percent of variance | 15.10 % |
| **Factor 3: Extracurricular activities** | |
| Sports | .47 |
| Arts (all kind) | .45 |
| Community work. | .40 |
| Percent of variance | 10.16 % |
| **Factor 4: Family social life** | |
| Parenthood | .57 |
| Family relationship | .57 |
| Maintaining good health | .51 |
| Percent of variance | 7.1% |

Analyses of variance of the ratings of these four factors revealed significant culture, age and sex differences. For the British students factors 1 and 4 (both socially/affiliatively-oriented factors) were positively correlated but unrelated to factors 2 and 3 (individualistically-oriented factors). For the Chinese students all four factors were significantly correlated. As Table 2 shows, factor analysis of the importance ratings of success situations on constructs showed two common factors for all:

1.  success in personal, social and family life (affiliative success),
2.  success in academic, curricular, and extracurricular activities (individualistic achievement).

Correlation analyses showed that these two areas were highly correlated for the Chinese, but unrelated to each other for the British. Ratings of

**TABLE 2.  Success Situations Rated on
Constructs Factors**

| Success Situation | Factor Loading |
| --- | --- |
| **Factor 1: Affiliative Success** | |
| Family social relationship | .76 |
| Marriage /getting married | .76 |
| Love and romance | .74 |
| Parenthood | .70 |
| Personal social relationship | .69 |
| Achievement of children and spouse | .51 |
| Developing good personal characteristics | .29 |
| Percent of variance | 9.40 % |
| | |
| **Factor 2: Individualistic Success** | |
| Outstanding achievement | .80 |
| School work/good results | .80 |
| Career | .58 |
| Having wealth and possessions | .56 |
| Arts (all kind) | .57 |
| Percent of variance | 23.51 % |

constructs on success situations revealed three factors or dimensions of achievement:

1.  outcome or emotional state,
2.  causal attributions, and
3.  instrumental activities (see Table 3).

The results revealed interesting similarities as well as differences between the two groups. They showed that regardless of age, sex, or culture, what people consider achievement is not confined to competitive and business areas of life, but can be from any walk of life. Certain areas of achievement are more important than others (see Table 4). On top of the list are more general and abstract goals such as maintaining good health and control over one's life, followed by more concrete achievement goals like success in academic work and career. In the bottom of the list were the areas perceived as least important to the students, such as religious work. Two major categories of achievement were recognized by both groups regardless of culture, sex, and age. The content of these categories are roughly the same for both groups, but the importance attached to them and the relationship between the two areas were different between the two cultures. The two factors were highly correlated for the Chinese but unrelated for the British. The collectivisitic Chinese considered success in academic career,

**TABLE 3.  Construct Ratings on Success Situations**

| Construct Factors | Factor Loading |
|---|---|
| **Factor 1: Outcome/emotional State** | |
| Happy—sad | .83 |
| Rewarding—not rewarding | .79 |
| Pride—Feeling lost | .77 |
| A need—not a need | .73 |
| Honor—sense of failure | .73 |
| Challenging—not challenging | .67 |
| Useful—not useful | .60 |
| Long lasting—temporary | .54 |
| Percent of variance | 59.80 % |
| **Factor 2: Instrumental Activities** | |
| Interpersonal skill—Intellectual skill | .61 |
| Emotional need—Sense of achievement | .58 |
| Family—work | .57 |
| Human relationship—learning | .57 |
| Human relationship—experience | .55 |
| Ability—personality | - .41 |
| Work—affection | - .51 |
| Percent of variance | 24.79 % |
| **Factor 3: Causal Attribution** | |
| Ability—luck | .63 |
| Ability—God's will | .58 |
| Effort—luck | .57 |
| Self control—external control | .49 |
| Effort—personality | .48 |
| Ability—personality | . 43 |
| Work—affection | .36 |
| Percent of variance | 4.84 |

and wealth related to succeeding in family, personal, and social life but the British considered these two areas as unrelated. Their findings are in line with our observations and experiences living among the Chinese. There is a Chinese saying that at home you rely on your family and outside of home you rely on your friends. Success in individualistic areas requires successful social and family relations for the Chinese.

The model of culture and achievement behavior resulting from this study is presented in Figure 1. It shows that regardless of culture, age and sex, there are three dimensions of achievement that are recognized by all:

**TABLE 4.  Mean Ratings of Success Situation in the Order of Importance for British and Chinese Students**

| Success Situation | Mean |
| --- | --- |
| Health | 6.0 |
| Control over one's life | 5.8 |
| Personal Characteristics | 5.8 |
| Career | 5.8 |
| Family relationship | 5.7 |
| Success in school | 5.7 |
| Parenthood | 5.5 |
| Personal/social life | 5.4 |
| Outstanding achievement | 5.3 |
| Love and romance | 5.2 |
| Marriage | 4.7 |
| Wealth | 4.7 |
| Children and spouse | 4.6 |
| Community service | 4.5 |
| Arts (all kind) | 3.9 |
| Sports | 3.7 |
| Religious work | 3.0 |

1.  Outcome of achievement. An achievement act always results in an outcome which could be reward, feeling good or punishment,
2.  Instrumental activities required to succeed in the task, different achievement goals require different instrumental activities, for example in order to succeed academically one has to expend effort or have a good personality if the goal of achievement is to have good social relationships,
3.  Perception of self-and causes of success and failure (causal attributions).

Different goals elicit different causal cognition.

*Meaning of Achievement: Semantic Differential Study*

The SD technique was used in order to have additional data on the meaning and dimensions of achievement using a different cross-cultural measure. The initial SD study described above used data from the *Atlas of Affective Meaning* collected by Osgood and his collaborators from 16 years old high school boys in the 1960's. No data on girls and older students were available in the *Atlas*. We thought it would be interesting to see how males as well as female students of 1990s responded to the same achievement concepts. We also hoped that in the process we could validate our findings with the RG technique as well as collect additional information that would shed further light on the influence of culture on achievement behavior. The concepts selected included those used in our initial study (Fyans, Salili, Maehr, & Desai, 1983). The same theoretical framework and methodology as described above was also used in this study. "Differences in the meaning of achievement were measured by the affective structure of the achievement related concepts. This included dimension scores, conceptual organization of the concepts, and the inter-concept distances in semantic space" (not reported in this chapter) (Salili, 2002, p. 312).

Cluster analyses revealed several clusters portraying different aspects of achievement. Supporting the findings of RG study, in many of these clusters there are one or two identifiable achievement goals or situations, instrumental activities and personal characteristics perceived to be appropriate for reaching the goal.

As expected, success for the Chinese was clustered with *effort, devotion, top of the class, determination, knowledge,* and *lone.* This represents an individualistic type of achievement. In line with other findings it shows that Chinese students are generally highly motivated to succeed academically and spend a lot of time and effort studying (see Salili et al., 2001). The Chinese students also lead a more protected and restricted life at this stage and their concerns are mainly with academic achievement (see Table 5).

The British associated this concept with *freedom, good family relationship, scholarship, romance personal relationship, reward...*etc., typical characteristics of teenagers in the West. The teenagers in the expatriate schools are concerned not only with academic work, but also with personal relationship, particularly with the opposite sex, and this is openly observed in expatriate high schools. It is interesting to note that in our RG study (not reported in

**TABLE 5.  Cluster of Concepts Formed with Success**

| Chinese | British |
|---|---|
| Effort | Freedom |
| Success | Family relationship |
| Devotion | Scholarship |
| Top of class | Romance |
| Determination | Personal relationship |
| Knowledge | Success |
| Lone | Capable |
| | Cooperation |
| | Reward |
| | Charity |

**TABLE 6.  Cluster of Concepts Formed with _I Myself_**

| Chinese | British |
|---|---|
| Foresight | Family |
| Questioning things | Top of class |
| I myself | Progress |
| Performing arts | I myself |
| Play | Progressive |
| Taking initiatives | Taking initiative |
| | Alert |

this chapter), these students consider _romance_ as a success situation, while the Chinese considered "being a good daughter or son" a success situation. These findings show that while success in social and personal areas of life is important for both groups, the individual goals within this area may be different and influenced by their cultural values.

This does not mean that the British students are not concerned with academic achievement, but rather they consider success as being a well-rounded person rather than being only academically successful. This can be seen in the cluster of concepts associated with _I myself_, representing ideal-self. For the British this concept was clustered with _family, top of the class, progress, taking initiative, being alert_, and _having children_, a mixture of both individualistic and affiliative goals (see Table 6).

For the Chinese, on the other hand, _I myself_ was associated with _individuality questioning things, performing arts, play_, and _taking initiative_' suggesting that teenage Chinese would like to see themselves as being more individu-

**TABLE 7.  Clusters Formed with Self-efficacy**

| Chinese | British |
|---|---|
| Capable | Capable |
| Ability | Efficient |
| Freedom | Intelligent |
| Efficient | Being oneself |
| Intelligent | Independent |
| Courage | Responsible |
| Health | Wealth |
| Clear thinking | Purpose |
| Self-insight | Personal growth |
| Free will | Free will |
| Independent | Effort |
| Progressive | Individuality |
| Self-reliant | |
| Alert | |

alistic and having more fun. That is, they aspire to be what may be missing from their daily life.

An interesting cluster of concepts formed with concept *being capable* for both cultural groups included those representing characteristics of individualistically-oriented, achievement-motivated individuals with high self-efficacy as portrayed in the Western research literature (e.g., Bandura, 1997). As can be seen from Table 7 many concepts in this cluster overlapped for the two groups. The cluster formed for the Chinese included concepts of *being capable, ability, freedom, efficient, courage, clear thinking self-insight, free will, independent, progressive, self-reliant,* and *alert.* For the British this cluster included *being capable, efficient, intelligent, being oneself, independent, responsible, wealth, purpose, personal growth, effort,* and *individuality.* The cluster suggests that regardless of what achievement may mean to the two cultures, similar characteristics are attributed to highly-motivated individuals. The presence of the concept *health* for the Chinese and *wealth* for the British is, nevertheless, very interesting, and may represent the Chinese preoccupation with having good health (see Ho, Spinks, & Yeung, 1985) and the British with material wealth. In the Chinese culture a person's body is considered to belong to his/her parents and taking care of one's health is important so as not to inflict pain on them. In our RG study maintaining good health was a highly-rated achievement goal for both groups, but relatively more salient for the Chinese than for the British. On the other hand, Western culture emphasizes material possessions and wealth, this was also shown in the RG study. For example, concepts *career* and *wealth* were rated significantly higher by the British, while maintaining *good health* and *academic achievement* was rated significantly more important by the Chinese. The presence of concepts such as *being oneself* and *personal growth* for the British and *freedom,* for the Chinese in this cluster portrays differences in what is considered important achievement goals in the two cultures.

Both Chinese and British students associated failure with very negative concepts such as *pessimism* and *insecure.* However, the Chinese also associated this concept with *fatalism, compliance before authority, fear, stubborn, shame,* and *punishment.* We speculated that this is because failure in the Chinese culture has much more severe consequences by bringing shame to the entire family and is often severely punished. For the British *failure* was clustered with *being insecure, pessimistic, shame,* and *inhibiting* (see Table 8).

An interesting finding of this study concerns the concept of filial piety which was viewed very positively in all dimensions by the Chinese and clustered with, *being industrious, education, family relationship, marriage, scholarship, self-control, being responsible, respect, being sincere, cooperation,* and *friendship* (Table 9 ). These concepts are among highly-rated concepts on all three dimensions, all representing the characteristics of a filially-pious person in the Chinese culture that is highly valued. The British on the other hand,

**TABLE 8. Cluster of Concepts Formed with Failure**

| Chinese | British |
|---|---|
| Fatalism | Failure |
| Compliant before Authority | Insecure |
| Shame | Pessimistic |
| Fear | |
| Stubborn | |
| Punishment | |
| Failure | |
| Insecure | |
| Inhibited | |
| Pessimistic | |

viewed this concept somewhat negatively, and associated it with *accepting things as they are, conforming, conventional, cautious,* and *follower.* These are low-rated concepts on all three dimensions, indicating that filial piety for the British is not highly regarded or valued.

As in our initial study reported above, the concepts *masculinity, power, leader,* and *competition* were clustered together for both groups. Femininity, on the other hand was associated with *luck, easy-going,* and other affiliatively-related concepts for both groups. Both femininity and masculinity clusters reflected the stereotypical, traditional sex-role by male and female students suggesting that sex-role stereotyping still exists in modern times even among young students. There were, however, some differences between the two groups on the concept of *femininity:* For the Chinese it was clustered with *luck, social relationship, easy-going, sympathy, romance, having*

**TABLE 9  Cluster of concepts formed with Filial Piety**

| Chinese | British |
|---|---|
| Industrious | Accepting things as they are |
| Education | Conforming |
| Family relationship | Conventional |
| Filial piety | Cautious |
| Marriage | Filial piety |
| Scholarship | Follower |
| Self-control | |
| Responsible | |
| Respect | |
| Sincere | |
| Charity | |
| Cooperation | |
| Friendship | |

*children, community service, religious,* and *being stable,* showing that Chinese students considered femininity a nurturing role—a traditional female sex role. Femininity had similar meaning for the British, although for them other more progressive concepts were also included as well, such as *industrious, school, work,* and *scientific work,* which reflected the progress made by British females in the Western culture in being able to engage in work outside their traditional nurturing role.

Analysis of the ratings on the individual affective dimensions, namely *evaluation, potency,* and *activity* showed that, generally, the evaluation dimension was more salient for the Chinese than the British students, while the potency dimension was more salient for the British, and activity dimension was similarly salient for both groups. Cluster analyses on all participants pooled together revealed very similar findings. As expected, both groups were in agreement with regards to ratings of very negative achievement outcome concepts such as the concept of *failure.* There was also considerable agreement between the groups on the ratings of positive achievement outcome concepts, instrumental activities, and desirable goals of achievement. These concepts were rated highly positive on all dimensions by both groups. However, differences sometimes appeared in the ratings of these concepts in evaluation and potency dimensions (see Salili 2002, for more detail). For example, the cluster of *I myself-self* was rated significantly higher by the Chinese on evaluation dimension than for the British, reflecting the positive attitude that Chinese hold for this concept. However, *I myself* was rated significantly higher on potency dimension by the British suggesting that British considered themselves stronger and more important than the Chinese did. This cluster included personal social goals which were rated positively by both groups also in our previous study.

Taken all together, the results clearly show that there are similarities and differences between the two cultures in the meaning of achievement. As in the RG study, we found many similarities between the two groups in the dimensions of achievement. For example, the meanings attached to the outcome of achievement (i.e., success and failure), the role of self-efficacy, the individualistic, affiliative and androgynous achievement goals, and their characteristics represented by concepts that clustered together, and with instrumental activities associated with them, as well as the perception of sex role were all very similar.

Many clusters supported the Western-formulated aspects of achievement. The similarities were often based on shared experiences and feelings of humans in all cultures (e.g., the concepts of success and failure), and others based on shared cultural values (e.g., self-efficacy), expectations, and practices (e.g., meaning of femininity and masculinity). Differences in the clusters, on the other hand, reflected the unique cultural values and different learning experiences (e.g., meaning attached to filial piety and success).

Our study showed that the two groups generally agreed on dimensions of achievement, but sometimes differed in the type of goals they associated with each dimension, the characteristics or activities they considered important in achieving the goal/s as well as their consequences (for example, *success cluster,* see Table 5).

On the practical level, this study provided important clues for educators and counselors about students' affective meaning of achievement. In the case of Chinese students in particular, the composition of the cluster *success* reflects the culture of the school and the pressure that parents and teachers exert on students. Our findings concerning gender differences also revealed that we need to work harder so as to eliminate gender inequality for both cultures.

### Comparison between British and Chinese Students on the Level of Need for Achievement

The studies discussed above showed that achievement goals are not confined to entrepreneurial and business areas, that people can have many different goals of achievement. The findings in the RG study and to a certain extent in our SD study, also showed that, contrary to their individualistic British counterparts, Chinese achievement was affiliatively oriented. Previous studies also showed that Chinese students achieve higher in almost all subjects compared to their Western counterparts. They showed all the characteristics that are attributed to high achievement-motivated individuals. They work hard at academic tasks and spend a lot of time studying. They attribute their success and failure to internal and controllable variables of ability, effort, and study skills (Hau & Salili, 1990) and their achievement goals are both learning and performance goals oriented (Salili, Chui, & Lai, 2001). These characteristics are similar to those described by McClelland et al. (1953) of individualistic achievement motivated individuals . Our next study was therefore designed to compare the level of need for achievement (nAch) between individualistic British and affiliative Chinese.

Participants were 438 male and female British and Chinese students who participated in the above studies. An adapted version of the TAT (McClelland et al., 1953) was used. Rather than using pictures, sentence stems were used to elicit stories and efforts were made to make as culture and gender free as possible (see Salili, 1996 for details).

Analysis of variance showed significant main effect of culture and sex and interaction of culture and sex. As expected, the results revealed that Chinese students on the whole were significantly more achievement motivated than the British students. The results also showed that females of both cultures had significantly higher levels of nAch. than their male counterparts. Other studies have also reported higher levels of nAch. for females in neutral condition (see McClelland et al, 1953, Alport, 1974). This finding confirmed our hypothesis that in collectivistic cultures such as in Hong Kong, family and social relationship provide strong incentives for achievement.

## SUMMARY AND CONCLUSION

In this chapter I discussed a series of systematic research designed to explore cultural, situational, and contextual influences on student motivation and achievement. At the micro level our earlier studies showed how classroom context and teachers' evaluation practices can impact continuing/intrinsic motivation and, in turn, influence causal attributions for performance. Students who were free from teacher evaluation showed significantly higher levels of continuing motivation and attributed their performance more to the internal factors of ability and effort than did students who had been evaluated by the teacher. We also showed that developmental factors may influence the type of incentive that can promote intrinsic motivation. In our study among the Iranian 10–12 years old students, peer comparison was an important factor in promoting continuing motivation.

At the societal level our studies revealed how cultural beliefs and values influence the meaning people attached to achievement and the way they go about achieving their success goals. The studies were conducted among students of different cultures using different methodologies. The results provided evidence that culture has important influence on achievement behavior. We found that traditional Western Models of achievement do not apply to people from non-Western cultures. Our studies showed that there are both similarities and differences in the conception of achievement among different cultures. People can have many achievement goals at the same time. These goals fall into two broad categories of affiliative and individualistic areas. The two areas complemented each other for the collectivistic Chinese students, but were unrelated for the individualistic British students. Social orientation of the Chinese students does not necessarily mean that Chinese students do not strive to achieve in individualistic areas, but rather succeeding in affiliative goals provides strong incentive and is important for succeeding in the individualistic achievement areas. Indeed our research findings revealed that socially-oriented Chinese had significantly higher levels of nAch than the British students.

The content of achievement goal categories is similar for the cultures studied, but the importance attached to them and the way they are achieved may be different for different cultures. That is, the meaning associated with achievement was different for different cultures. The socially-oriented Chinese saw success in maintaining good family and social relationship important for achieving their individualistic goals such as succeeding in career or acquiring wealth, but for the British no relationship existed between affiliative goals and individualistic goals. Both SD and RG studies also revealed that dimensions of achievement is the same for participating cultures. The RG study showed that achievement involves an outcome (which could be positive or negative), causal attribution for achievement, and instrumental activities. Similarly, the SD study showed that cultures differentiated between dimensions of meaning, but different dimensions were more or less

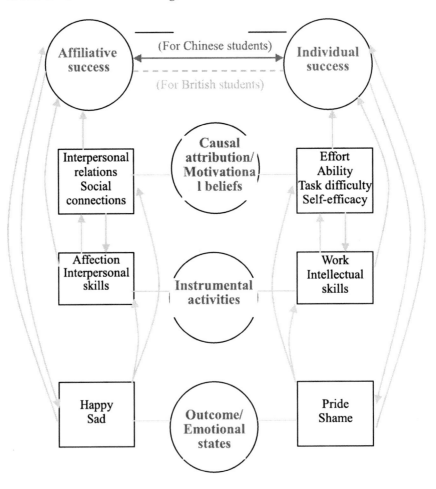

**FIGURE 1.  Model of Culture and Achievement Behavior**

salient for different cultures. Both cultures associated positive and highly rated concepts to *success* but the content of clusters formed were somewhat different.

Both cultures and sexes also related *masculinity* with *success* and highly positively rated concepts on all dimensions, but they differed slightly on the conception of femininity. *Femininity* was associated with traditional role of females for both cultural groups, but with more progressive concepts for the British. There were many overlaps in what were associated with achievement, but again the cultures differed in concepts related to instrumental activities and the relationship between the concepts. In conclusion, our studies on culture and achievement motivation began with trying to find out whether traditional Western model of achievement applied to different cultures. The results supported our contention that achievement motivation is a complex construct and influenced by many interacting socio-cultural, situational, contextual, and developmental factors. The traditional theory of achievement motivation cannot explain all these complexities of achievement behavior. In particular, it does not apply to achievement behavior of people of different cultures, especially the collectivistic cultures. Based on these findings we thus proposed a new model of achievement behavior that could explain achievement behavior of both individualistic and collectivistic cultures and flexible enough to include all types of achievement goals. This model was discussed above and is shown in Figure 1. More studies are needed to explore the validity of this model.

## REFERENCES

Alport, T. G. (1974). Achievement motivation in college women: A now-you-see-it-now-you-don't phenomenon. *American Psychologist, 29,* 194–203.

Bandura, A. (1997). *Self-efficacy: The exercise of control.* New York: Freeman.

Bee, H. (1986). **Life-span development.** US: Addison-Welsley Educational Publishers.

Biggs, J. B. (1992). *Learning and schooling in ethnic Chinese: An Asian solution to a Western problem.* Unpublished manuscript, University of Hong Kong.

Chen, C. Stevenson, H. W., Hayward, C., & Burgess, S. (1995). Culture and academic achievement. In M. L. Maehr & P. R. Pintrich (Eds.), *Advances in motivation and achievement* (pp. 73–118). Greenwich, CT: JAI

Chen, C., & Stevenson, H. W. (1989). Homework: A cross-cultural examination. *Child Development, 60,* 551–561.

DeVos, G. A. (1973). *Socialization for achievement: Essays on the cultural psychology of Japanese.* Berkley: University of California Press.

Duda, J. (1981). A cross-cultural analysis of achievement motivation in sports and the classroom. Unpublished doctoral dissertation, University of Illinois at Urbana Champaign, 1981.

Ewing, M. E. (1981). Achievement orientations and sports behavior of males and females, Unpublished doctoral dissertation, University of Illinois at Urbana Champaign, 1981.

Fransella, F., & Banister, D. (1977). *A manual for repertory grid technique*. London: Academic Press.

Frieze, Maehr, M. L., & Nicholls, J. G. (1980). Culture and achievement motivation: A second look. In N. Warren (Ed.), *Studies in cross-cultural psychology* (Vol. 3), New York: Academic Press.

Fyans L. J., Jr., Leslie J. Salili, F., Maehr, M. L., & Desai, K. A. (1983). A cross-cultural exploration into the meaning of achievement. *Journal of Personality and Social Psychology, 44*(5), 1000–1013.

Gallimore, R. (1981). Affiliation, Social context, industriousness, and achievement. In R. L. Munroe, R. H. Munroe, & B. Whiting (Eds.), *Handbook of cross-cultural human development*. New York: Garland.

Gallimore, R., Boggs, J. W., & Jordan, C. (1974). *Culture, behavior, and education: A study of Hawaiian-Americans*. Beverly Hills: Sage.

Harter, S., & Connell, J. P. (1984). A structural model of the relationships among children's academic achievement and their self-perceptions of competence, control, and motivational orientation in the cognitive domain. In J. Nicholls (Ed.), *The development of achievement motivation*. Greenwich, CT: JAI Press.

Hau, K. T., & Salili, F. (1990). Examination results attribution, expectancy, and achievement, goals among Chinese students in Hong Kong. *Educational Studies, 16*(1), 17–31

Ho, Y. F., Spinks, J. A., & Yeung, C. S-Y. (1985). *Chinese patterns of behavior: A sourcebook of psychological and psychiatric studies*. New York: Prager.

Hui, C. H. (1988). Measurement of Individualism-Collectivism. *Journal of Research in Personality, 22*, 17–36.

Kelly, G. (1955). *The psychology of personal constructs*. New York: W. W. Norton.

Lee, W. O. (1996). The cultural context for Chinese learners: conception of learning in Confucian tradition (pp. 25–43). In D.A. Watkins & J.B. Biggs, *The Chinese learner: Cultural, psychological, and contextual influences*. Hong Kong: CERC & ACER

Lepper, M. R., Green, D., & Nisbett, R. (1973). Undermining children's intrinsic interest with extrinsic reward: test of the "over justification" hypothesis. *Journal of Personality and Social Psychology, 28*, 129–137.

Maehr , M. L. & Braskemp, L. A. (1986). *Motivation factor: A theory of personal investment*. Lexington, MA: Lexington.

Maehr, M. L., & Nicholls, J. G. (1980). Culture and achievement motivation: A second look. In N. Warren (Ed.), *Studies in crosscultural psychology*, (Vol. 3). New York: Academic Press.

Maehr, M. L. (1978). Sociocultural origins of achievement motivation. In D. Bar-Tal, & I. Sax (Eds.), *Social psychology of education: theory and research*. New York: John Wiley & Sons.

Maehr, M. L., & Stalling, W. M. (1972). Freedom from external evaluation. *Child Development, 43*. 177–185.

Malpass, R. S. (1977). Theory and method in cross-cultural psychology. *American Psychologist, 32*, 1069–1079.

McClelland, D. C., Atkinson, J., Clark, R., & Lawell, E. (1953). *The achievement motive.* New York: Appleton-Century-Crofts.

Osgood, C. E., & Tsang, O. C. S. (1990). *Language, meaning, and culture: The selected papers of C.E. Osgood.* New York: Prager.

Osgood, C. E., May, W., & Miron, M. (1975). *Cross-cultural universals of affective meaning.* Urbana, IL: University of Illinois Press.

Osgood, C. E., Suci, G. J. & Tannenbaum, P. H. (1957). *The measurement of meaning.* Urbana: University of Illinois Press.

Ramirez, M., III, & Price Williams, D. L. (1976). Achievement motivation in children of three ethnic groups in the United States. *Journal of Cross-Cultural Psychology, 7,* 49–60.

Salili, F. (1994). Age, sex, and cultural differences in the meaning and dimensions of achievement. *Personality and Social Psychology Bulletin, 20*(6), 635–648.

Salili, F. (1995). Explaining Chinese students' motivation and achievement: A sociocultural analysis. In *Advances in motivation and achievement* (Vol. 9, pp. 73–118)

Salili, F. (1996). Achievement motivation: A cross-cultural comparison of British and Chinese students. *Educational Psychology: An International Journal of Experimental Educational Psychology, 16*(3), 271–279.

Salili, F. (2002). Cross-cultural differences in affective meaning of achievement: A semantic differential study. In D. M. McInerney & S. Van Etten (Eds.), *Sociocultural influences on motivation and learning (Vol. 2). Research in Sociocultural influences on motivation and learning* (pp. 297–329). Greenwich, CT: Information Age Publishing.

Salili, F. Chiu, C-Y., & Lai, S. (2001). The influence of culture and context on students' motivational orientation and performance. In F. Salili, C-Y. Chiu & Y-Y. Hong (Eds.), *Student motivation: The culture and context of learning* (pp. 221–245). New York: Kluwer Academic/Plenum Publishes.

Salili, F. Hwang, C. E., & Choi, N. F. (1989). Teachers' evaluative behavior: a cross-cultural study of the relationship between teachers' comments and perceived ability. *Journal of Cross-Cultural Psychology, 20,* 115–132.

Salili, F., & Hau, K. T. (1994). The effect of teachers' evaluative feedback on Chinese students' perception of ability: a cultural and situational analysis. *Educational Studies, 20*(2), 223–236.

Salili, F., & Tsui, A, B. M. (2004). The effects of medium of instruction on students' motivation and learning. In R. Hoosain & F. Salili (Eds.), *Language in multicultural education. Vol. 4, Research in multicultural education and international perspectives.* Greenwich, CT: Information Age Publishing.

Salili, F., Maehr, M. L., & Gilmore, G. (1976). Achievement and morality: A cross-cultural analysis of causal attribution and evaluation. *Journal of Personality and Social Psychology, 33,* 327–337.

Salili, F., Maehr, M. L., Sorenson. R. L., & Fyans, L. J., Jr. (1976). A further consideration of the effect of evaluation on motivation. *American Educational Research Journal, 13,* 85–102.

Stevenson, H. W., & Lee, S. (1990). *Context of achievement, Monographs of the Society for Research in Child Development,* Serial no. 221, Vol. 55, Nos. 1–2.

Stevenson, H. W., & Stigler J. W. (1992). *The learning gap: Why our schools are failing and what we can learn from Japanese and Chinese education.* New York: Summit Books.

Sue, S., & Okazaki, S. (1990). Asian-American educational achievement: A phenomenon in search of an explanation. *American Psychologist, 45*(8), 913–920.

Tseng, W. S., & Hsu, J. (1972). The Chinese attitude toward parental authority as expressed in Chinese children's stories. *Archives of General Psychiatry, 26,* 28–34.

Veroff, J. (1969). Social comparison and the development of achievement motivation. In C. P. Smith (Ed.), *Achievement-related motives in children.* New York: Russell-Sage.

Wan, F., & Salili, F. (1996). Perceived effectiveness of reward and punishment strategies by Hong Kong secondary school students. *Psychologia, 39,* 256–275.

Weiner, B., & Peler, N. (91730. A cognitive developmental analysis of achievement and moral judgements. *Developmental Psychology, 9,* 290–309.

Wu, D. Y. H. (1996). Chinese childhood socialization. In M. H. Bond (Ed.), *The handbook of Chinese psychology* (pp. 143–154). Hong Kong: Oxford University Press.

CHAPTER 9

# ACHIEVEMENT MOTIVATION IN CROSS-CULTURAL CONTEXT

## Application of Personal Investment Theory in Educational Settings

**Dennis M. McInerney and Gregory Arief D. Liem**

There have always been inherent difficulties in utilizing traditional models of achievement and motivation in cultures other than Western Societies, which often result in paradoxical research findings. Marty Maehr was a major figure in critically examining motivation models, theory, and research from a cross-cultural perspective. Through numerous publications and, in particular, his theorizing synthesized in the Personal Investment framework, Marty Maehr contributed significantly to developments of the cross-cultural study of motivation in school and work settings. This chapter explores some of the early models of achievement motivation that had inherent difficulties and then focuses on research and theory developed by Marty Maehr that has shaped the first author's approach to cross-cultural research in students' achievement motivation.

*Culture, Self, and Motivation: Essays in Honor of Martin L. Maehr*, pages 213–241
Copyright © 2009 by Information Age Publishing
All rights of reproduction in any form reserved.
**213**

## WESTERN PSYCHOLOGY: CROSS-CULTURALLY
## TRANSFERABLE, MODIFIABLE, OR INAPPLICABLE?

Cross-cultural research began as early as in the 1960s (Jahoda & Krewer, 1997). Typically, Western researchers, and their collaborators in non-Western countries, assess diverse cultural and social groups on a range of criteria related to various constructs such as intelligence, anxiety, self-esteem, and achievement motivation, most of which were conceptually derived from research with American or Western European samples. For example, Maehr and Salili utilized Murray's Thematic Apperception Test (TAT) to explore cultural differences in achievement motivation between East Asian international students and their American counterparts (see Salili, this volume). Most of the East Asian students were observed not only to be highly motivated and diligent but also to perform very well in their studies. Maehr and Salili hypothesized that if McClelland's theory was applicable to individuals from non-Western cultures, the high-achievement motivation of the East Asian students should therefore be reflected in their TAT scores. Instead of confirming their hypothesis, Maehr and Salili found that the East Asian students were less achievement oriented than the American students. This finding was paradoxical given the former's observed achievement behaviors and performance. They also concluded that the TAT pictures were not fully applicable to measure achievement motivation of non-Western groups.

Further, at a macro level, McClelland's (1961) original postulation suggesting a link between nations' levels of achievement motivation and their economic development was not fully supported. If East Asian people, like the Japanese reported in McClelland's (1961) study, were less achievement oriented than their American and European counterparts, how could the growth of many East Asian economies reach the levels on par, if not higher, than those of North American and European economies, leading to the so called East Asian's "economic miracle" (Hicks & Redding, 1983)? Clearly, McClelland and his associates' conclusion and interpretation did not hold up under scrutiny. Both Western (e.g., Spence, 1985) and Eastern (e.g., Yang, 1986) scholars are now in agreement in pointing out that McClelland's theory of achievement motivation implies a strong orientation toward the individual or the self, and thus not cross-culturally transferable to non-Western, more collectivistic societies. In other words, the concepts of achievement motivation in different cultures are not only different in quantity, but also in quality. That is, in cultures where the subordination of individual goals to collective ones, filial piety, family orientation, and other collectivist values are molded and emphasized, individuals may be more driven by socially-oriented achievement motivation like social approval, social responsibility, and conformity, rather than individual-oriented achievement motivation (Yu & Yang, 1994).

As illustrated above, adopting the so-called *pseudo-etic* (Triandis, 1972) or *imposed etic* (Berry, 1989) approach to research (i.e., applying constructs and methodologies originating from a particular culture to other cultures with different characteristics) generates perplexing and inconclusive findings. The impetus to reformulate research constructs and methodologies to make them cross-culturally more appropriate began in the late 1970s. The drive for this came from a growing realization of the differing nature of psychological processes in individuals from culturally non-Western backgrounds, as discussed by Pederson (1979) and Draguns (1979). Triandis (1980) was moved to say at that time that, "In the past fifteen years or so it has become very clear that one cannot take a psychological method and use it in another culture without drastic modification" (p. 7). It was in this context that Maehr (1974a) wrote a seminal little book with a big impact, *Sociocultural Origins of Achievement* and his very influential article "Culture and Achievement Motivation" in *American Psychologist* (Maehr, 1974b; see also Maehr & Nicholls, 1980).

### A Historical Foundation

Marty Maehr and his associates were well versed in motivation theory and methodology and were influenced in their thinking by the work of McClelland, Atkinson, and their associates (Atkinson, 1958; Atkinson & Feather, 1966; Atkinson & Raynor, 1974; McClelland, 1961; McClelland, Atkinson, Clark, & Lowell, 1953; McClelland, Baldwin, Bronfenbrenner, & Strodtbeck, 1958). The conception of Personal Investment (PI) theoretical perspective and its essential elements was rooted in Maehr's early cross-cultural study of achievement motivation (Fyans, Salili, Maehr, & Desai, 1983) which was underpinned by the dispositional-personality perspective of motivation to search for cross-cultural variability in achievement motivation. The research reported emerged out of the work on meaning systems and subjective culture conducted by Charles Osgood and his research group (cf. Osgood, Miron, & May, 1975). Indeed, it was specifically based on a massive amount of cross cultural data gathered with the "semantic differential" method developed and extensively employed by Osgood and his colleagues. A secondary analysis of these data was conducted to address two basic issues. The first issue was, whether one could identify a meaning system or a "factor" that reflected achievement motivation similarly across the varied cultural groupings contained in the Osgood et al. data set. Such a factor or meaning system was identified. Fyans et al. (1983) found support for a cross-cultural factor of achievement very similar to the concept of achievement developed by McClelland. The achievement motivation factor appeared to be relevant regardless of culture. The cross-cultural factor of achievement that was isolated was masculine in orientation, with the concepts of father and masculinity loading high on the factor. While this finding could be attributed to the samples that comprised adolescent males, it was also a reflection of widely-held values in the cultural groups involved (Fyans et al., 1983). Notably, the factor was associated with concepts that, at least in the United States, connoted an achievement orientation, such as worker, work, and freedom. The concept of knowledge and courage also figured strongly in this cross-cultural factor, and it was found that achievement was conceptually linked to pragmatic end products such as success and power. The authors suggested that an arguably valid cross-cultural standard of achievement meaning was determined, and cultures scoring high and low in this standard could be identified.

A second phase of the analysis examined the issue of how groups rated high or low on this cross-cultural factor compared on a series of criterial concepts related to this factor. In other words, the analysis set out to determine how the meaning of achievement was differentially constructed within the highest and lowest groups. To this end, a series of multiple regression analyses were used. Among the significant findings were that high-scoring cultures on the cross-cultural achievement factor tended to see success associated with self, initiative, freedom, education, work, and masculinity, while the low-scoring cultures associated success with femininity, devotion, and the past. There was an emphasis on *the future* in high-scoring cultures and an emphasis on *tradition* and *the past* in low-scoring cultures.

Low-scoring cultures tended to view education as a means of learning what is perpetuated through tradition and family, which implies the process of learning is to acquire and confirm old ways rather than to explore new knowledge or the unknown. In contrast, high-scoring cultures tended to see education as a means to progress, compete, and succeed. With regard to the criterial concept of self as cause, Fyans et al. found that, whereas in high-scoring cultures self seemed to be tied to achievement, in low-scoring cultures it was tied to family, cooperation, and love. Fyans et al. went on to say "... high-scoring cultures appear to stress achievement, and low-scoring cultures affiliation," a point quite in accord with McClelland's (1961) suggestion in *The Achieving Society* (p. 1008). These authors suggested that although a universal factor seemed to be identified, this factor did not seem to have equal relevance or salience for all cultural groups, and that striving for success was likely to take different forms in different cultures. While those who scored high on the identified factor appeared to view success in terms of demonstrating independent competence, it was found that those who scored low appeared to stress retaining social ties and enhancing interpersonal relationships as the means to success.

The findings of the Fyans et al. (1983) study were, then, interesting in a number of respects. The study was initially conducted to consider the cross-cultural variability of motivation. Importantly, however, the results reflected not only variability but also similarity in the construction of achievement and possibly achievement motivation across widely diverse cultural groups. A thorough examination of cross-cultural interpretations of the meaning of achievement indicated in these data suggested a near universal and widely shared view of achievement and possibly a substantially universal view of achievement motivation. However, instead of attributing this to one specific "need," the results in this study suggested that they may be best attributable to the individuals' three socio-cognitive systems:

1. belief in self,
2. some incentive or possibly purposive system, and
3. perhaps also what might be called "normative options" for choosing, acting, thinking, and feeling.

## PERSONAL INVESTMENT THEORY

Based upon the Fyans et al. (1983) study as well as Maehr and his colleagues' very comprehensive reviews of early models of motivation emerged a model that not only built upon the various dimensions that Maehr (1974b) and Maehr and Nicholls (1980) considered important in any explanation and analysis of motivation cross-culturally, but also essentially and effectively drew together salient features of the models and approaches of McClelland, Weiner, Duda, Osgood, Triandis, and De Charms (among many others who were working in the area at the time). Maehr (1984; see also Maehr & Braskamp, 1986) postulated a personal investment model of achievement motivation. The model addressed the apparent paradox between the low assessment of individuals from other cultural groups on achievement tests, on one hand, and their obvious achievement and motivation across a range of activities as illustrated by persistence, level of activity, high performance and continuing motivation in chosen areas of behavior, on the other.

Personal Investment (PI) theory, as its name implies, stressed that the study of motivation must begin and end with the study of behavior, specifying very carefully the behavior that gave rise to motivational inferences. PI theory is, therefore, concerned with how persons choose to invest their energy, talent, and time in particular activities. The theory is particularly relevant to investigations into how individuals of varying social and cultural backgrounds relate to differing achievement situations. This is because it does not assume that people from a given culture or group will invest effort in the same achievement situations or, if they do, for the same reasons, as those from other cultures and groups. Thus, PI theory conceptualizes achievement motivation in terms that recognize the possibility of diverse modes of achievement behaviour across cultures and groups.

PI theory also emphasizes the role played by social and cultural contexts in determining motivational patterns in performing achievement tasks. Moreover, it is phenomenologically based, and emphasizes the subjective meaning of situations in light of individuals' culturally determined belief systems (see Braskamp & Maehr, 1983; Maehr, 1984; Maehr & Braskamp, 1986; Maehr & McInerney, 2004). These systems include:

1. Beliefs about self, referring to the more or less organized collections of perceptions, beliefs, and feelings related to who one is. Sense of self is presumed to be composed of a number of components, such as sense of competence, reference groups, sense of autonomy and responsibility, and sense of mission; each of which contributes to the motivational orientation of the individual.

2. Perceived goals of behavior in a situation, referring to the motivational focus of activity, importantly what the person defines as "success" and "failure" in this situation. Among the performance or achievement goals postulated by PI theory are task, ego, social solidarity, and extrinsic rewards. Each of these is subdivided into two facets (see Table 1).

3. Perceived alternatives for pursuing goals, or the action possibilities, referring to the behavioral alternatives that a person perceives to be available and appropriate (in terms of sociocultural norms that exist for the individual) in a given situation.

The three major constructs used in PI theory are considered to be etic (that is universally present and relevant, and therefore potentially compa-

**TABLE 1. Classification of Achievement Goals, Facets, and Their Definitions According to Personal Investment Theory (adapted from Braskamp & Maehr, 1983)**

| Achievement Goal | Facet | Underlying Purpose |
|---|---|---|
| Task | Task involvement | Experiencing adventure/novelty |
| | Striving for excellence | Understanding something |
| Ego | Competitiveness | Doing better than others |
| | Power | Winning and having a higher social status than others |
| Social solidarity | Affiliation | Pleasing others |
| | Social concern | Making others happy |
| Extrinsic rewards | Recognition | Earning a prize |
| | Financial rewards | Making money |

rable across cultures) while allowing for the generation of emic (that is local, indigenous, or culture-specific) contents. Thus, according to Maehr (1984; Maehr & Braskamp, 1986), each of these three components may be influenced differentially by the design or structure of the task, the personal experience and access to information of the individual, and the sociocultural context in which the tasks, the situations, and the person are embedded. Maehr suggested, for example, that personal experience seems to have a major impact on one's sense of self, whereas information and the sociocultural context tend to be especially important in selecting behavioural options or achievement goals. According to the PI model, the contents of each of these meaning components are derived from the dual factors of situation and person, and in a complex of person x situation interactions as stated in the following paragraph:

> . . . persons not only perceive success and failure differently because they have different standards for their performance, but also because they make different judgements about the worth of the task. Cross cultural studies are one source for illustrating this point. Most practicing educators are aware that students place different values on school tasks quite apart from their ability to perform. That this may be the critical feature in explaining cross-cultural variation in achievement patterns has been recently illustrated in a series of cross-cultural studies. . . . Generally, it seems that individuals project different pictures of what they would like to be or become. They derive these pictures from personal experiences within their own culture . . . all have their own pictures of the nature of successful achievement. But the critical point is that, as events are interpreted as conforming to these pictures of achievement, they are associated with success. Simply a performance outcome or any information that is perceived as indicating that we are becoming what we want to become is readily defined as success. . . . Of course, events, outcomes, and information to the contrary eventuate in perception of failure (Maehr, 1984, p. 12).

The theory is essentially social-cognitive, as it assumes that the primary antecedents of choice, persistence, and variations in activity levels are the thoughts, perceptions, and beliefs that the person has which are embedded in beliefs about self and situation. As a model, PI theory alleviated some of the problems inherent in earlier motivation models. It conceptualized achievement motivation in wider terms than simply a personality related characteristic (i.e., need or trait), as initially hypothesized by Murray (1938) and subsequently by McClelland and his associates (1953, 1958), which was common in many early studies of motivation, and which led to the assumption that one could predict achievement behavior if one knew the individual's level of motivation. In these personality models, low achievement was explained in terms of motivational deficit, an explanation which ignored the situational determinants present in a culture and omitted the possibility of diverse modes of achievement behaviour across cultures.

PI theory predated goal theory but incorporated within its framework three elements that were to become increasingly the major focus of motivational research in educational settings, namely, mastery (task) goals, performance (ego) goals, and social goals. However, while much goal theory research over the last twenty years has concentrated on comparing and contrasting the effects on achievement-related processes and outcomes of mastery and performance goals (e.g., Ames, 1992; Dweck, 1986; Nicholls, 1989; see also Elliot, 2005 for a recent review) with a much more recent and somewhat belated attempt to broaden goals to include social goals (see e.g., Juvonen & Wentzel, 1996; Ryan & Shim, 2006; Urdan & Maehr, 1995; Wentzel, 2005), PI theory was not only a multiple goal oriented framework from its inception, but also included sense of self and action possibility dimensions that made it, potentially, a far richer and more sensitive source of information on the motivational determinants of achievement behaviour. Particularly this was the case in socioculturally diverse settings because, as a model, PI theory struck a better balance between the interaction of personality, situation, and motivational levels, while incorporating situational dimensions that had been found useful in analyzing levels of achievement motivation such as normative, locus of control, interpersonal, and task dimensions (Maehr, 1974b). Effectively PI theory is far more complex than goal theory, but life and motivated behaviors are complex and should not be reduced to simple dimensions.

## EXTENDING THE EMPIRICAL BASE-ENRICHING THE THEORY: PI IN EDUCATIONAL SETTINGS

Since its inception, various researchers have utilized PI model in a variety of settings and professions such as in exercise and sport (Duda, 1989; Granzin & Mason, 1999; Gray-Lee & Granzin, 1997), workforce (Maehr & Braskamp, 1986), personal development of college students (Braskamp, this issue), and health professionals (Perrot, Deloney, Hastings, Savell, & Savidge, 2001). Among these, research on personal investment in relation to individuals' exercise- and sport-related behaviours have been notably well developed, in particular in a series of research projects led by Joan L. Duda and her colleagues (e.g., Duda, 1989, Duda, Smart, & Tappe, 1989; Duda & Tappe, 1989; see also Duda & Hall, 2001). Duda et al. (1989), for instance, investigated the relationship between the three facets of subjective meaning— personal incentives, sense of self, and perceived behavioral options—and adherence behaviors in the athletic injury rehabilitation setting among injured intercollegiate athletes. Duda et al. found that athletes' attendance at their rehabilitative exercise sessions was well predicted by their perceived efficacy of the treatment, perceived social support for rehabilitation, self-motivation, and task involvement; completion of the exercise protocol during rehabilitation was accounted for by the athletes' perceived social support, perceived efficacy of treatment, self motivation, and locus of control; and intensity of the exercise during rehabilitation could be explained by the athletes' perceived physical ability, knowledge of treatment, self-motivation, and task involvement. These findings provided strong support to the application of PI theory as a motivational framework for adherence to athletic injury rehabilitation.

### Quantitative Psychometric Studies

Probably the largest program of research utilizing the PI framework has been conducted by McInerney and his associates, who have not only tested the full model in an educational setting utilizing the Inventory of School Motivation (ISM; McInerney, 1988; McInerney & Sinclair, 1991, 1992; see also Flowerday & Shaughnessy, 2005 for the development of the ISM) and the Facilitating Conditions Questionnaire (FCQ; McInerney, Dowson, & Yeung, 2005) but, in particular, extended the application of PI theory to a variety of cultural groups. The results and conclusions of these studies are multifaceted. First, and foremost, empirical evidence has been amassed to support the dimensions of the PI model across culturally diverse backgrounds (see McInerney, 1988, 1989a, 1989b, 1990, 1991a, 1991b, 1992, 1994, 1995, 2003; McInerney & Ali, 2006; McInerney & Sinclair, 1991, 1992; McInerney & Swisher, 1995; McInerney, Dowson, & Yeung, 2005 (FCQ); McInerney, Hinkley, Dowson, & Van Etten, 1998; McInerney, Marsh, & Yeung, 2003; McInerney, Roche, McInerney, & Marsh, 1997; McInerney, Yeung, & McInerney, 2001; Nelson, O'Mara, McInerney, & Dowson, 2006; Suliman & McInerney, 2006; Watkins, McInerney, & Boholst, 2003; Watkins, McInerney, & Lee, 2002; Watkins, McInerney, Akande, & Lee, 2003; Watkins, McInerney, Lee, Akande, & Regmi, 2002; Yeung & McInerney, 2005).

These studies essentially suggest that the range of goal orientations (task, performance, social, and extrinsic), sense of self values (sense of purpose for the future, self esteem, and self reliance) and facilitating conditions for action, appear broadly valid and reliable constructs across very diverse cultural groups. Further, scales of the ISM and the FCQ seem to have equivalent statistical validity and reliability across many diverse groups, reveal very few significant differences between groups, and predict in similar ways achievement outcomes across groups. For example, rather than the expected polarities between Anglo, European, Asian, Aboriginal, Middle Eastern, African, and Native American (Navajo) groups on key dimensions such as competition, affiliation, social concern, power, and extrinsic rewards, all groups are very similar in means and standard deviations across the range of scales analyzed across multiple studies. Even where there are significant differences these are a matter of degree rather than kind, of little practical significance, and often run counter to cultural stereotypes. Moreover, much of the data indicates that while all groups are relatively low on competitiveness and social power, Anglo groups are relatively lower than others such as Navajo Indians and Australian Aboriginals who are stereotypically presumed to be less competitive and social power seeking than Anglos (see, e.g., McInerney, 2003; McInerney et al., 1997). In summary, this bulk of research indicates that, by and large, diverse groups endorse the same educational goals and values as each other. More specifically, mastery goals, such as task and effort, are strongly endorsed irrespective of the groups, extrinsic rewards such as token and praise are moderately endorsed, whereas performance goals such as competition and social power are endorsed to a somewhat low extent. Sense of purpose and self-reliance are also strongly endorsed across all groups.

In multiple regression analyses using scales from the ISM and the FCQ, equivalent levels of variance in achievement outcomes, such as academic marks and school attendance, are explained across widely diverse groups, and key predictors are consistent across all groups. Furthermore, goals and values that are stereotypically used to distinguish between Western and other cultural groups (such as competition, affiliation, social concern, and social power) do not appear to be salient in the school contexts studied. In other words, they don't, in general, predict academic outcomes, and this finding is generalizable across groups. Factors that have been considered important by many as key determinants of indigenous minority student's poor achievement and dropping out of school, such as the supposed mismatch between the school's goals and values and the student's goals and values are, in general, not supported by findings from a range of studies. What clearly emerge as important predictors of academic achievement across all groups are:

1. the students' values, beliefs, and goals relating to a positive sense of self, in particular, the students' positive self-esteem at school (feeling good about themselves as students), sense of purpose (having a goal of doing well at school and getting ahead in life), and sense of self-reliance (I can do this work);
2. their level of mastery motivation, in particular, task and effort goal orientations;
3. perceived parental support, and
4. the degree to which students value education for its instrumental purpose

(see McInerney, 1988, 1989a, 1989b, 1990, 1991a, 1991b, 1992, 1994, 1995, 2003, 2007; McInerney & McInerney, 1996; McInerney et al., 1997; McInerney & Sinclair, 1991, 1992; McInerney & Swisher, 1995; Suliman & McInerney, 2006).

While there is considerable consistency indicated above in motivational patterns across groups, there were also significant variations. The relative importance of motivational predictors varied within groups and across groups, which provides culturally specific (emic) information with which to explore the motivational characteristics of particular groups. For example, in the McInerney (2003) study, social power is a strong predictor of further education, affect, and valuing education for the Asian group but not for the Aboriginal group. Token is a strong negative predictor of further education for Australian Anglo, Aboriginal, and Asian groups but not for the European, Navajo, and Middle Eastern groups. Social concern varies in its salience across the three outcomes and six groups in the study. Competition appears to be salient for all groups (except Middle Eastern) for valuing education, but not for affect towards school or desire for further education. Affiliation and praise appear to be relatively unimportant as predictors in the school setting across all outcomes and all groups (see McInerney, 1988, 1989a, 1989b, 1990, 1991a, 1991b, 1992, 1994, 1995, 2003, 2007; McInerney & McInerney, 1996; McInerney et al., 1997; McInerney & Sinclair, 1991, 1992; McInerney & Swisher, 1995; Suliman & McInerney, 2006).

As elucidated above, in accord with PI model which highlights the important role of perceived external factors (or at least externally referenced) forces in students' social environments in facilitating and inhibiting the translation of students' internal forces (motivational goal orientations and sense of self) into actual achievement behaviours, McInerney had devised the Facilitating Condition Questionnaire (FCQ; McInerney, 1988, 1989a, 1989b, 1991a, 1991b, 1992). These early studies had examined the validity of the FCQ using exploratory factor analysis (EFA). To provide stronger evidence for the validity of the measure, McInerney, Dowson, and Yeung (2005) examined the psychometric properties of the FCQ through a CFA approach. The study utilized 26 of the 39 original FCQ items which were discarded based on results of previous studies (e.g., McInerney, 1991b, 1992) due to their inability to form reliable components of the FCQ scales. Seven scales examined were Value of Schooling, Affect toward Schooling, Peer Positive Influence, Peer Negative Influence, Parent Positive Influence, Parent Negative Influence, and Teacher (Positive) Influence. As hypothesized, analysing responses to the FCQ indicated that the 26 items could be explained well by the seven-factor model, each of which represented one of the seven constructs described above. The five positive/facilitating conditions were correlated with each other, whereas the two negative/inhibiting conditions were positively correlated with each other and negatively with all the five facilitating conditions, demonstrating the convergent and discriminant validity of the seven factors. In addition, the seven factors were also found to be invariant across the elementary and high school sub-samples, providing evidence for the applicability of the 26-item FCQ for use with students in different levels of education. Equally important, the high school students' GPAs were found to be positively correlated with the positive FCQ factors but negatively with the negative FCQ factors, an array of findings that supported not only the relationships found in previous studies but also the proposition in PI theory emphasizing the critical role of (perceived) students' social environment in their motivated behaviours and, in turn, achievements.

### Personal Investment and Learning Strategies

A review of classroom and laboratory studies (Covington, 2000; Elliot, 2005) concluded that there was adequate empirical support for the theoretical propositions that mastery goals are associated with deeper, meaning-oriented learning strategies whereas performance goals tend to be associated with superficial, rote-level processing. Covington warned, however, that the bulk of the research he reviewed was based on mainstream American students and there is little evidence that the theory and these findings can be generalized to other cultural groups. This, of course, prevented the claim for cross-cultural validity of the goal constructs and their functional and conceptual equivalence for students in other educational and cultural contexts (Van de Vijver & Leung, 1997). These levels of equivalence need to be established with empirical investigations by examining not only within-construct validity and internal consistency reliability of goal orientations as measured by the ISM but also the nomological network of the goal orientations with other relevant external variables, including one of the most important ones, students' adoption of learning strategies.

In an extension of the McInerney research, Watkins, McInerney, and Lee (2002) not only tested using factor analysis the validity of the Chinese translation of the ISM with a sample of Hong Kong secondary school students, but also set out to examine the between-construct validity of the ISM dimensions by finding out if they correlated as predicted with independent measures of Intellectual Self-Esteem (10 items measuring the intellectual self from the Chinese Adolescent Self-Esteem Scale; see Cheng & Watkins, 2000), and Surface, Deep, and Achieving Learning Strategies (Biggs, 1987; Entwistle & Ramsden, 1983). Deep learning strategies are concerned with an intention to understand by means of interrelating ideas, reading widely, and thinking independently and critically. Surface learning strategies, on the other hand, are concerned with an intention to memorize or rote-learn study materials with minimal understanding. These strategies tend to be associated with fear of failure and an external locus of control, and a context characterized by boredom or fear, and assessment methods such as multiple-choice items, perceived as rewarding low quality learning. The third, achieving learning strategies, is said to be adopted by students when the students are driven to work hard and use whatever specific strategy they feel will maximize their chances of high marks, be it gaining mastery of what is to be learned. Adoption of the achieving strategy is thought to be dependent on both the students' need for success and their perception of the assessment task (Biggs, 1987).

In their studies Watkins, McInerney, and Lee (2002) tested the hypotheses that Intellectual Self-Esteem would correlate highly with the ISM Self-Reliance and Self-Esteem scales; that the Mastery-oriented scales would correlate significantly and positively with the Leaning Process Questionnaire's (LPQ; Biggs, 1987) Deep and Achieving Strategy scales but negatively, if anything with the Surface Strategy scale; and that performance-oriented scales, including extrinsic motivation, would be the only ISM scales to correlate significantly positively with the Surface Strategy scale. As expected, the mastery-oriented scales correlated most highly with the Deep and Achieving Strategy scales, although performance- and social-oriented scales also correlated positively with the Deep and Achieving scales, but not so strongly. The mastery oriented scales also correlated negatively and significantly with the Surface Strategy scale. Only the Extrinsic Motivation scale correlated positively with the Surface Strategy scale indicating that those engaging in surface strategies were more likely to say they value extrinsic rewards for their study. All other significant correlations with Surface Strategy were negative, although it is interesting to note that, in general, performance-oriented scales were unrelated to Surface Strategies. The three Sense-of-Self scales (Self-Reliance, Self-Esteem, and Sense of Purpose) all correlated as predicted quite highly and positively with the Deep and Achieving Strategy scales. The ISM Self-Reliance and Self-Esteem scales also negatively and significantly associated with the LPQ Surface Strategy scale. The Mastery-oriented scales were most strongly positively related to Intellectual Self, although the Performance and Social-oriented scales were also positively related to Intellectual Self. However, the two strongest correlations were, as expected, with Self-Reliance and Self-Esteem. Sense of Purpose was also positively related to Intellectual Self.

In summary, this study demonstrated the usefulness of the ISM and the PI model on which it is based for drawing a motivational profile on Chinese-speaking students in Hong Kong, and for examining the relationship of this profile to learning strategies. It provided some limited support for the contention that mastery but not performance goals would be related to deep learning strategies, as mastery-oriented goals were most strongly correlated with Deep Strategies. While the Mastery-oriented scales were clearly negatively related to Surface Strategies, which supports the researchers' hypothesis, there was, rather than a positive relationship, no relationship between the Performance oriented scales and Surface Strategies (except for extrinsic motivation discussed above).

The study with Chinese Hong Kong students was further extended to a range of other cultural groups including students from Malawi, Nepal, South Africa (Black and White samples), Zambia (Watkins, McInerney, Lee, Akande, & Regmi, 2002) and more recently to students in the Philippines (Watkins, McInerney, & Boholst, 2003). Initial factor analytic studies with these groups supported the validity of the ISM for use with these very diverse groups. The reliability estimates on each scale were also very similar across the groups, and in general, quite high, although there was some variability across groups with the Nepalese group recording lower reliabilities across most scales including the LPQ scales. While initially this might suggest that either there was a language difficulty (the ISM was administered in Nepalese) or that the ISM was less valid than for the other groups, the overall evidence is that on twelve of the seventeen scales utilized in the study the reliability estimates for the Nepalese were very similar to the other groups. It is interesting to note that the scales that seemed to be least reliable for the Nepalese group were those dealing with more collectivist values such as affiliation and social concern. The reliability for Self-Reliance scale was also low for this group. The reasons for these low reliabilities need to be further investigated.

In order to examine the relationship of the ISM scales to Deep, Surface and Achieving Learning Strategies a series of multiple regressions were conducted with the scales of the LPQ as dependent variables and the scales of the ISM as predictor variables. Across all samples the combination of ISM scales were able to predict Deep, Achieving, and Surface Strategies quite well, although least well for the Surface Strategy scale. Mastery-oriented scales, Sense of Purpose and Self-Reliance were consistently strong predictors for Deep and Achieving Strategies across most samples. Indeed, most of the other scales contributed little to the variance explained. The results for the Surface Strategy were not as clear-cut, with performance-oriented motivation, extrinsic motivation, Self-Reliance, and Self-Esteem providing the highest Beta weights across most samples.

While the authors had expected that students' adoption of different types of learning strategies might be triggered by different motivation impetus based not only on mastery but also on a mix of intense personal ambition, family face, peer support, and/or material reward, the findings suggested that the relationships between motivational goals and learning strategies were remarkably similar across cultural groups. Considering the diversity of the samples utilized in the study it does seem that motivational variables relate in similar ways to the learning strategies students adopt in a range of cultures. The results of this study are consistent with previous Western research showing that mastery goals tend to be associated with deeper, better-organized learning strategies (Covington, 2000). While there is some evidence that performance-oriented goals are associated with Surface Learning, the evidence is not as strong. Given the fact that the Surface Strategy scale had a lower reliability than either the Deep or Achieving Strategies across all groups, the lack of definitive results regarding the relationship of the motivational scales to Surface Learning might reflect the inadequacy of the Surface Strategy scale as an outcome measure. Using a more reliable measure of surface learning strategies, future studies need to confirm the relationships between motivational goals and surface learning.

### Multidimensionality and Hierarchical Model of Motivation

The early studies conducted by McInerney and his colleagues (e.g., McInerney, 1988; McInerney & Sinclair, 1991, 1992) were concerned with establishing the emic validity of multidimensional scales across a range of cultural groups and utilized explorative factor analyses (EFA). A more recent development of the program of research focuses not only on the multidimensional and hierarchical nature of student achievement motivation (McInerney, Marsh, & Yeung, 2003), but also on providing a validated standardized short form of the ISM for use in cross-cultural settings (McInerney & Ali, 2006; McInerney, Yeung, & McInerney, 2001), which might be considered an etic scale.

First, based on the proposition in PI theory that multiple goals, namely task, ego, social, and extrinsic related goals, are likely to drive and direct individuals' motivated behaviors in relation to the pursuit of desired ends in an achievement setting, McInerney, Marsh, & Yeung (2003) statistically tested the multidimensionality and the hierarchical nature of the eight goal orientations among 774 Australian Year-7 to Year-9 students. To this end, they utilized two motivational instruments. The first one was the original ISM (McInerney & Sinclair, 1991, 1992). The second one was a relatively new 14-item instrument called the General Achievement Goal Orientation Scale (GAGOS; McInerney, Marsh, & Yeung, 2003) which was designed to reflect general motivation in three general areas, namely General Mastery, (four items, e.g., *I am most motivated* when I see my work improving), General Performance (three items, e.g., *I am most motivated* when I am doing better than others), and General Social (three items, e.g., *I am most motivated* when I work with others). Thus, the nature of the items in the ISM and in the GAGOS is different in that the items in the ISM do not specifically directly refer to an individual's state of being motivated. Also included in the GAGOS is a Global Motivation scale which is comprised of "precision alternatives" of the question "I am motivated at school." In other words, four similarly phrased items are randomly presented to evaluate students' perceived level of what is called "global motivation."

To test the robustness of multidimensionality of achievement goal constructs, McInerney, Marsh, and Yeung (2003) performed a series of confirmatory factor analyses (CFAs) to test if the 35 items of the ISM designed a priori to measure 10 specific goals could be explained by 10 first-order factors called effort, task, sense of purpose, praise, competition, social power, token, social concern, social dependency, and affiliation. Second, to examine the hierarchical nature of achievement goals, they tested whether the 10 first-order factors could be explained by three a priori determined second-order factors called Mastery Goal (with effort, task, and sense of purpose as indicators), Performance Goal (with praise, competition, social power, and token as indicators), and Social Goal (with social concern, social dependency, and affiliation as indicators). These three second-order achievement goal factors were, in turn, hypothesized to be explained by a third-order factor called ISM General Motivation. These researchers also aimed to investigate if the 14 items of the GAGOS would load substantially on four first-order goal factors of General Mastery, General Performance, General Social, and Global Motivation. These four first-order factors were in turn hypothesized to be explained by a second-order factor called "GAGOS Higher-Order Motivation," empirical evidence of which would provide additional and stronger support to the hierarchical nature of achievement goals.

The CFA result indicated that, first the 35 ISM items could be nicely summarised by 10 first-order factors of goal orientations. The model was well-defined in that all items' factor loadings on their a priori factor were positive and significant (varying from .40 to .77) and the goodness of fit indices were appropriate. This finding provided evidence of the multidimensionality of achievement goals. The 10 specific goals were found to be positively associated as indicated by correlation coefficients ranging from close-to-zero to substantial. With some minor exceptions, the largest correlations were consistently found among first-order factors that were posited to reflect the same second-order factors. For example, effort, task, and sense of purpose were found to be highly correlated to each other and their intercorrelations were higher than each of their correlations with other first-order factors (e.g., praise, social concern). As hypothesized, the 10 first-order achievement goal factors could be summarized by three second-order goal orientations, Mastery Goal, Performance Goal, and Social Goal, each of which was well defined in that the 10 first-order factors' loadings were all positive and statistically significant (the smallest loading was .67), and equally important the fit indices reflected a good fit of the model to the data. This was the first evidence exhibiting the hierarchical nature of achievement goals. With regard to the GAGOS, the 14 items were found to load significantly and positively (the lowest loading being .54) on their a priori first-order factors, namely General Mastery, General Performance, General Social, and Global Motivation, respectively. These four first-order factors were, in turn, found to be appropriately explained by a GAGOS Higher-Order Motivation where each of the four first-order factors loaded significantly and positively on a general motivation construct (loadings ranging from .52 to .92, except General Social with a loading of .29). The GAGOS findings largely converged with the ISM-related findings, and both indicated the multidimensional and hierarchical nature of achievement goals, which means that the evidence for the multidimensional and hierarchical nature of students' achievement goals is not dependent on a single measure.

McInerney and his associates' study subsequently set out to test the invariance of the achievement goal constructs (scales) and their indicators (items) as measured by the ISM to students from various cultural backgrounds using a multi-group CFA. The impetus of this research was the heightened caution by cross-cultural methodologists (e.g., Van de Vijver & Leung, 1997) of the importance of not only utilizing cross-culturally appropriate measures and researching cross-culturally relevant constructs, but also of establishing:

1. conceptual equivalence which is the lowest level of equivalence,
2. functional equivalence,
3. scalar equivalence, and
4. metric or measurement unit equivalence which is the highest level of equivalence of participants' responses on the dependent variables of interest before comparisons of such variables' mean scores to be made across cultural groups, typically using t-tests or ANOVAs.

The abovementioned levels of equivalence are hierarchical, suggesting that the establishment of the highest level of equivalence (i.e., metric equivalence) presumes the fulfilment of requirements of the lower levels (scalar, functional, and conceptual equivalence). To compare the mean scores of a variable of interest among different groups (e.g., across gender, cultural groups, or other categorical variables), a researcher first needs to demonstrate metric equivalence which implies that participants across different cultural groups respond to measurement scales in the same way, or in other words, they construe the content of each item of an instrument in the same fashion (see Van de Vijver & Leung, 1997 for a further elaboration of equivalence issue in cross-cultural research). This evidence for equivalence of the meaning of each item across groups can be established by performing a multi-group CFA and evaluating the goodness of fit indices.

In the first study establishing metric equivalence of the ISM scales, Mc-Inerney, Yeung, and McInerney (2001) performed a series of multi-group CFA with Navajo ($n = 760$) and Anglo-American ($n = 1012$) students. The study set out to examine whether responses to the items within each of the scales in the ISM have the same meanings across different cultural groups (i.e., by showing invariance of each item's factor loadings across the two cultural groups) and whether cross-cultural generalizability of the factorial structure of goal orientations could be established. Using 39 items of the ISM which were hypothesized to be explained by eight motivational goal latent factors, McInerney et al. found that the eight goal factors were applicable and equivalent across the two groups. Next, to evaluate the invariance of meaning of each item, the researchers constrained factor loadings of all the items to be equal across the two groups. This procedure demonstrated that only 30 out of the 39 items used were invariant. In their subsequent analysis, they therefore used only the 30 items to form a basis for meaningful between-group mean comparison as these items were found to mean the same for both Navajo and Anglo-American groups of students.

In much of the earlier McInerney research, various numbers of items were used to define ISM scales, reflecting his earlier preoccupation with the emic dimension. His more recent work has attempted to establish a standardized set of scales based upon an expanded number of items drawn from the original ISM. In this context, McInerney and Ali (2006) examined the cross-cultural validity of the multidimensional and hierarchical structure of the eight achievement goal orientations measured by the 43-item version of the ISM. A database comprising seven culturally diverse samples ($n = 8963$) of Anglo-Australian, migrant Australian, Aboriginal Australian, Hong Kong Chinese, Navajo, Anglo-American, and African students was subjected to a multi-group CFA. Extending what had been found in the McInerney, Marsh, and Yeung (2003) study described earlier, McInerney and Ali aimed to evaluate

1.  whether the 43 items used could be explained by eight first-order factors (task, effort, competition, social power, affiliation, social concern, praise, and token),
2.  whether the eight first-order factors could be explained by four second-order factors (Mastery, Performance, Social, and Extrinsic), and
3.  whether the four second-order factors could be explained by a third-order factor called General Motivation (GMOT), and finally,
4.  whether the higher-order structures were invariant across the seven cultural groups included in this study.

The first key finding indicated that the 43 ISM items could be explained by the eight a priori determined factors across groups. All factor loadings were positive and significant ranging from .46 to .80 (median .68). This result provides evidence that students in the seven cultural groups under study recognized the multidimensional structure of goal orientations. The next key finding suggested that the eight goal orientations could be explained by four second-order factors of Mastery, Performance, Social, and Extrinsic Goals. Each of these four factors was well defined, that is, factor loadings are large, positive, and statistically significant, and the solution is completely proper and supported by appropriate values of goodness of fit indices. In the next model tested, the third-factor called GMOT was also found to be well defined, with the following factor loadings: Mastery (.63), Performance (.84), Social (.73), and Extrinsic (.88). The goodness-of-fit indices were also appropriate and the solution was proper. The last analysis aimed to test the invariance of the multidimensional and hierarchical model of motivational goal orientations across the seven cultural groups. The result demonstrated that the expected structure, suggesting that students in the seven cultural groups construed their motivation as comprising four major goal orientations, namely Mastery, Performance, Social, and Extrinsic Goals, each of which comprises two goal dimensions. The study demonstrated that the 43 items used in the analyses have the same meanings (i.e., measurement unit or metric equivalence) across diverse social and cultural groups. This finding provides a methodologically more defensible approach to making comparisons of the profiles of students' goal orientations across a range of cultures.

Taken together, the three studies reported above (McInerney & Ali, 2006; McInerney, Marsh, & Yeung, 2003; McInerney, Yeung, & McInerney, 2001) provided cross-cultural empirical support to consider achievement goals as multidimensional and hierarchical in nature. They pointed out that while information coming from examining the multidimensionality of achievement goals allows researchers and educators to examine in detail student motivation profiles and to relate these profiles to various achievement outcomes (see e.g., McInerney et al., 1997), the hierarchical nature of achievement goals provides a picture of the interrelationships among goals in addition to allowing the researchers and educators to examine students' motivational profiles in three broader, more general areas, namely their task motivation, their performance motivation, and their social motivation for doing well at school. The evidence showing that the three more general areas of goals can also be explained by a higher-order general motivation construct implies that when students use the term "motivation" they are subsuming notions of mastery, performance, and social goals, as well as a diverse range of sub-goals reflecting these (e.g., effort, task, praise, competition, and social concern).

*Qualitative Study of Motivation*

Accompanying the psychometric, quantitative research reported above is a series of large-scale qualitative interviews also based on PI model (McInerney, McInerney, Ardington, & De Rachewliltz, 1997; McInerney, McInerney, Bazeley, & Ardington, 1998). These interviews reveal the complex forces that operate in molding school motivation and in particular focus on the perceived options available to students and how these options moderate motivation in school settings. The interviews reveal the dilemmas and shifting value orientations that occur as children from a variety of cultural groups attempt to preserve cultural traditions on the one hand, while on the other, seek to modernize through education in which alternative and sometimes competing values are seen to have a place. Clearly emerging from the qualitative interviews is the importance of mastery goals and social concern, and to a lesser extent, affiliation, recognition, and praise, across all groups. In contrast, emerging from the interviews is the relative unimportance (and negative valuing) of competition, social power, rewards, and tokens, again across all groups. Parental and community support for education and learning is consistently mentioned as important, as are the norms and role beliefs held by the students. Students argue that in order to feel motivated it is important for them to believe that it is "appropriate" for them to be successful at school; that they like and value school; and that they have access to models of successful schooling (either students, parents, or community members who do well at school and influence the student) (McInerney et al., 1997, 1998). According to the students themselves, students who espouse these norms and role beliefs, and have access to successful models, are more likely to be successful at school.

A more recent qualitative strand of research conducted by McInerney and his colleague (Dowson & McInerney, 2001, 2003) focuses on the exploration and identification of multidimensionality of goals as viewed from students' own perspectives. Based on an observation that the goals students bring to a real-life situation in the classroom are both more complex and more dynamic than the uni- or bi-dimensional conceptualizations of mastery and performance goals (cf. Boekartz, de Koning, & Vedder, 2006; Ford, 1992; Urdan & Maehr, 1995), and spurred by a realization that past quantitative studies documented in the literature had typically used such a simplified a priori, preconceived categorizations of goals, Dowson and McInerney took an inductive, systematic, and contextual approach to the study of students' motivational goals. In this research, Dowson and McInerney conducted 114 interviews, which can be divided into conversational, semi-structured, and structured interviews, with 86 middle-school, 12–15 years old, Australian students. Questions asked during the interviews included, for example, "Do you want to do well in school? Why? What reasons do you have for wanting to do well in school? How do you know when you are motivated to do well at school?" In addition, to enhance the validity of the findings revealed in the interviews, Dowson and McInerney also conducted 24 sessions of structured classroom observations including structured classroom schedules and unstructured field notes.

The analysis of these qualitative data resulted in a number of interesting findings that indicated the presence of eight categories of goal orientations which could be hierarchically structured into two major meta-categories: academic goals and social goals. The former comprised goal orientations that had been widely studied, namely mastery, performance, and work-avoidance goals, whereas the latter consisted of social affiliation, social approval, social responsibility, social status, and social-concern goals. Equally important, the study also uncovered the affective and behavioral concomitants of each of these eight goal orientations in addition to the cognitive component of goal orientation that had been more widely investigated. This study was important for a number of reasons. First, it confirmed that it is possible for a student to hold multiple motivational academic and social goals. Second, the study also shed some light on how these multiple goals could interact to differentially influence students' general motivation and academic performance. Specifically, a student's multiple goals may either conflict with, converge upon, or compensate for, each other with respect to their combined effects on students' engagement in learning. In summary, the study provided evidence for a more complex and dynamic understanding of student motivation and suggests that future research and teaching practice should more carefully assess both the complexity and interactivity of students' motivational goals, echoing what had been articulated by other goal theorists (e.g., Baron & Harackiewic, 2001; Pintrich, 2000), and particularly in the work of Maehr.

Based upon the categorization of academic and social goals found in the qualitative research reported above, Dowson and McInerney (2004) developed an 84-item self-report survey to measure middle and senior high school students' motivational goal orientations and their cognitive and metacognitive strategies. The measure, called the Goal Orientation and Learning Strategies Survey (GOALS-S), comprises 14 scales which can be divided into three academic goals scales (Mastery, Performance, Work Avoidance), five social goals scales (Social Affiliation, Social Approval, Social Concern, Social Responsibility, Social Status), three cognitive strategies scales (Elaboration, Organization, Rehearsal), and three metacognitive strategies scales (Monitoring, Planning, Regulating). Cronbach's alpha coefficients of the scales ranged between .72 and .87 for the Academic Goal scales, between .74 and .84 for the Social Goal scales, between .73 and .82 for the Cognitive Strategies scales, and between .79 and .83 for the Metacognitive Strategies scales. These high ranges of internal consistency reliability were made possible because the GOALS-S items were developed based on students' own words or responses in a qualitative study; a method that enhances the content validity of the measure. A series of CFAs performed on responses to the GOALS-S supported not only a conceptual distinction between students' goal orientations (academic and social goals) and their learning strategies (cognitive and metacognitive strategies) but also suggested a multidimensional and hierarchical structure of the goal orientations and the learning strategies. The development and validation of the GOALS-S contribute to the body of literature on student motivation and learning in that it allows researchers to use a single comprehensive, reliable, and valid instrument measuring a broad range of goal orientations and learning strategies.

## A COMPLEX PERSPECTIVE: IS IT JUSTIFIED, USEFUL, AND PRACTICAL?

In general, social-cognitive theories of motivation, in particular PI theory, have alerted researchers to the ways in which motivation and achievement may be differentially constructed across cultural (and other) contexts. However, significant issues and questions from PI perspective in relation to understanding how culture and individual differences interact in generating achievement motivation remain. Does a multiple goal, sense of self and facilitating conditions perspective add anything to our understanding of student motivation and achievement, and second, does cultural background make a difference?

Clearly a complex model such as Personal Investment does add considerable depth to our understanding of student motivation in school settings. Using such an approach enables us to see the relative importance of a complex set of motivational goals to students, and how they interact with sense of self and the action possibilities available to students in their real life settings. All of the variables considered in the research reported in this chapter help explain, to varying degrees, variance in academic outcomes. It is more than likely that in non-educational settings, such as sporting, social and familial settings, the relative salience of the variables may vary, and this is worth study.

The consistency in the salience of mastery oriented motivation, sense of self variables, as well as the importance of future perspective and parents to students' engagement in schooling across widely divergent cultural groups provides evidence that these factors may be universal (etic) in their salience. On the other hand, the different patterning of significant predictors across cultural groupings provides culturally specific (emic) information with which to explore the unique motivational characteristics of particular groups.

These patterns of predictors across cultural groupings in which there is both consistency (perhaps universality) and variability, give the researcher much rich information with which to explore the emics and etics of student motivation in school settings. This would not be possible unless a complex perspective was taken. In other words, the nature of the outcome measured is differentially related to the range of variables considered and this varies across cultures. While evidence suggests few mean differences between groups on many of the dimensions it appears that culture does matter when these dimensions are used to predict outcomes. The possibilities for understanding motivation uncovered in these analyses would not have been possible if only mastery and performance goals, for example, had been considered.

## PERSONAL FINALE

It is not an exaggeration to state that the programmatic research described above developed out of the profound effect Marty Maehr had on my (the first author, Dennis M. McInerney) research. I first met Marty in 1982 at Sydney University. I spent a study leave with him in Illinois at the University of Illinois in Urbana Champagne during what was a very cold winter in 1984 when I was developing the theoretical framework for my doctoral thesis on the psychological determinants of school motivation for non-traditional Aboriginal students. This was an exciting time for me, and apart from fending off frost bite, trying not to slip too heavily on the black ice that covered the walkways in Urbana, and trying to keep a young wife and even younger daughter occupied in a student apartment blockaded regularly by snow drifts, I learned an enormous amount about cross-cultural research from both Marty and Harry Triandis.

Marty was, at the time, working on the text on Personal Investment Theory with Larry Braskamp and was very excited about the contribution it would make. I was also very excited because I saw in the motivation model outlined enormous possibilities for exploring learning and motivation in cross-cultural settings. I have persisted with this model for more than twenty years and I am not sure why. It has never become mainstream, and indeed, Marty himself seemed to have abandoned it at times in favour of the constricted view of motivation provided by goal theory. In persisting with this theoretical model I think I also limited my ability to become mainstream, particularly when I was compounding the complexity of the model with my emic/etic incursions and excursions with people often querying me about the number of items defining the ISM scales for different cultural groups in articles that eventually got published. Then again my limited exposure in the research literature and citations may reflect that I have simply done a bad job of both articulating and operationalizing the theory.

I strongly believe, however, that other researchers should have adopted this model as a holistic approach to examining student motivation in all its complexity and developed better tools for its operationalisation, and better research and analytic designs than I have been capable of. But at the end of the day I have to thank Marty heartily. He has been a great mentor in both style and substance, and I have always enjoyed every interaction I have had with him: scholarly and academic. I hope his legacy of the Personal Investment theory and his sensitivity to cross-cultural issues lives on. And maybe, someone out there reading this might have another look at the theoretical perspective presented in *The motivation factor: A theory of personal investment* and breathe new life into it through research and practice.

## REFERENCES

Ames, C. (1992). Classrooms: Goals, structures, and student motivation. *Journal of Educational Psychology, 84,* 261–271.

Atkinson, J. W. (1958). *Motives in fantasy, action, and society.* Princeton, NJ: Van Nostrand.

Atkinson, J. W., & Feather, N. T. (Eds.). (1966). *A theory of achievement motivation.* London: Wiley.

Atkinson, J. W., & Raynor, J. O. (1974). *Motivation and achievement.* Washington, DC: V. H. Winston.

Barron, K. E., & Harackiewicz, J. M. (2001). Achievement goals and optimal motivation: Testing multiple goal models. *Journal of Personality and Social Psychology, 80,* 706–722;

Berry, J. W. (1989). Imposed etics-emics-derived etics: The operationalization of a compelling idea. *International Journal of Psychology, 24,* 721–735.

Biggs, J. B. (1987). *Student approaches to learning and studying.* Melbourne: Australian Council for Educational Research.

Boekaerts, M., de Koning, E., & Vedder, P. (2006) Goal-directed behavior and contextual factors in the classroom: An innovative approach to the study of multiple goals. *Educational Psychologist, 41,* 33–51.

Braskamp, L. A., & Maehr, M. L. (1983). *Personal investment: Theory, assessment and application.* Revision of a paper presented at AERA, Montreal, Canada.

Cheng, C., & Watkins, D. A. (2000). Age and gender invariance of self-concept factor structure: An Investigation of a newly developed Chinese self-concept instrument. *International Journal of Psychology, 35,* 186–193.

Covington, M. V. (2000). Goal theory, motivation, and school achievement: An integrative review. *Annual Review of Psychology, 51,* 171–200.

Dowson, M., & McInerney, D. M. (2001). Psychological parameters of students' social and work avoidance goals: A qualitative investigation. *Journal of Educational Psychology, 93,* 35–42.

Dowson, M., & McInerney, D. M. (2003). What do students say about their motivational goals? Towards a more complex and dynamic perspective on student motivation. *Contemporary Educational Psychology, 28,* 91–113.

Dowson, M., & McInerney, D. M. (2004). The development and validation of the Goal Orientation and Learning Strategies Survey (GOALS-S). *Educational and Psychological Measurement, 64,* 290–310.

Draguns, J. G. (1979). Culture and personality. In A. J. Marsella, R. G. Tharp, & T. J. Ciborowski (Eds.), *Perspectives on cross-cultural psychology.* New York: Academic Press.

Duda, J. L. (1989). Goal perspective and behavior in sport and exercise settings. In C. Ames & M. L. Maehr (Eds.), *Advances in motivation and achievement* (Vol. 6) (pp. 81–115). Greenwich, CT: JAI Press.

Duda, J. L., & Hall, H. (2001). Achievement goal theory in sport: Recent extension and future directions. In R. N. Singer, H. A., Hausenblas, & C. M. Janelle (Eds.), *Handbook of Sport Psychology* (pp. 417–443). New York: Wiley.

Duda, J. L., Smart, A. E., & Tappe, M. K. (1989). Predictors of adherence in the rehabilitation of athletic injuries: An application of personal investment theory. *Journal of Sport and Exercise Psychology, 11,* 367–381.

Duda, J. L., & Tappe, M. K. (1989). Personal investment in exercise among middle-aged and older adults. In A. Ostrow (Ed.), *Aging and motor behavior* (pp. 219–238). Indianapolis: Benchmark Press.

Dweck, C. S. (1986). Motivational process affecting learning. *American Psychologist, 41,* 1040–1048.

Elliot, A. J. (2005). A conceptual history of the achievement goal structure. In A. J. Elliot, & C. S. Dweck (Eds.), *Handbook of competence and motivation* (pp. 52–72). New York: The Guilford Press.

Entwistle, N., & Ramsden, R. (1983). *Understanding student learning.* London: Croom Helm.

Flowerday, T., & Shaughnessy, M. (2005). An interview with Dennis McInerney. *Educational Psychology Review, 17,* 83–97.

Ford, M. E. (1992). *Motivating humans: Goals, emotions, and personal agency beliefs.* Newbury Park, CA: Sage.

Fyans Jr., L. J. Salili, F., Maehr, M. L., & Desai, K. A. (1983). A cross-cultural exploration into the meaning of achievement. *Journal of Personality and Social Psychology, 44,* 1000–1013.

Granzin, K. L., & Mason, M. J. (1999). Motivating participation in exercise: Using personal investment theory. *Advances in Consumer Research, 26,* 101–106.

Gray-Lee, J. W., & Granzin, K. L. (1997). Understanding participation in exercise and sport: An extended application of personal investment theory. *Journal of Sport Behavior, 20,* 37–53.

Hicks, G. L., & Reddings, S. G. (1983). The story of the East Asian "economic miracle": Part one. Economic theory be damned! *Euro-Asia Business Review, 2,* 24–32.

Jahoda, G., & Krewer, B. (1997). History of cross-cultural and cultural psychology. In J. W. Berry, Y. H. Poortinga, & J. Pandey (Eds.), *Handbook of cross-cultural psychology* (Vol. 1, pp. 1–42). Needham Heights, MA: Allyn & Bacon.

Juvonen, J., & Wentzel, K. R. (1996). *Social motivation: Understanding children's school adjustment.* Cambridge: Cambridge University Press.

Maehr, M. L. (1974a). *Sociocultural origins of achievement.* Monterey, CA: Brooks-Cole.

Maehr, M. L. (1974b). Culture and achievement motivation. *American Psychologist, 29,* 887–896.

Maehr, M. L. (1984). Meaning and motivation: Toward a theory of personal investment. In C. Ames & R. Ames (Eds.), *Research on motivation in education* (Vol. 1, pp. 115–144). Orlando, FL: Academic Press.

Maehr, M. L., & Braskamp, L. A. (1986). *The motivation factor: A theory of personal investment.* Lexington, MA: Lexington Books.

Maehr, M. L., & McInerney, D. M. (2004). Motivation as personal investment. In D. M. McInerney & S. Van Etten (Eds.), *Big theories revisited* (pp. 61–90). Greenwich, CT: Information Age.

Maehr, M. L., & Nicholls, J. C. (1980). Culture and achievement motivation: A second look. In N. Warren (Ed.), *Studies in cross-cultural psychology* (Vol. 2). London: Academic Press.

McClelland, D. C. (1961). *The achieving society.* New York: The Free Press.

McClelland, D. C., Atkinson, J. W., Clark, R. A., & Lowell, E. L. (1953). *The achievement motive.* New York: Appleton-Century-Crofts.

McClelland, D. C., Baldwin, A. L., Bronfenbrenner, U., & Strodtbeck, F. L. (1958). *Talent and society: New perspectives in the identification of talent.* Princeton, NJ: Van Nostrand.

McInerney, D. M. (1988). *The psychological determinants of motivation of urban and rural non-traditional Aboriginal students in school settings: A cross-cultural study.* Unpublished doctoral dissertation, Sydney University, Sydney.

McInerney, D. M. (1989a). Urban Aboriginals parents' views on education: A comparative analysis. *Journal of Intercultural Studies, 10,* 43–65.

McInerney, D. M. (1989b). A cross-cultural analysis of students' motivation. In D. M. Keats, D. Munro, & L. Mann (Eds.), *Heterogeneity in cross-cultural psychology.* Lisse: Zwets & Zeitlinger.

McInerney, D. M. (1990). The determinants of motivation for urban Aboriginal students in school settings: A cross-cultural analysis. *Journal of Cross-Cultural Psychology, 21,* 474–495.

McInerney, D. M. (1991a). The behavioral intentions questionnaire. An examination of construct and etic validity in an educational setting. *Journal of Cross-Cultural Psychology, 22,* 293–306.

McInerney, D. M. (1991b). Key determinants of motivation of urban and rural non-traditional Aboriginal students in school settings: Recommendations for educational change. *Australian Journal of Education, 35,* 154–174.

McInerney, D. M. (1992). Cross-cultural insights into school motivation and decision making. *Journal of Intercultural Studies, 13,* 53–74.

McInerney, D. M. (1994). Psychometric perspectives on school motivation and culture. In E. Thomas (Ed.), *International Perspectives on Culture and Schooling* (pp. 327–353). London: Institute of Education, London University.

McInerney, D. M. (1995). Achievement motivation research and indigenous minorities: Can research be psychometric? *Cross-Cultural Research, 29,* 211–239.

McInerney, D. M. (2003). Motivational goals, self-concept and sense of self—What predicts academic achievement? Similarities and differences between Aboriginal and Anglo Australians in high school settings. In H. W. Marsh, R. G. Craven, & D. M. McInerney (Eds.), *International Advances in Self Research* (Vol. 1, pp. 315–346). Greenwich, CT: Information Age.

McInerney, D. M. (2007). Personal investment, culture, and learning: Insight into the most salient influence on school achievement across cultural groups. In F. Salili & R. Hoosain (Eds.), *Culture, Motivation and Learning: A Multicultural Perspective* (Vol. 6, pp. 169–191). Greenwich, CT: Information Age.

McInerney, D. M., & Ali, J. (2006). Multidimensional and hierarchical assessment of school motivation: Cross-cultural validation. *Educational Psychology, 26,* 595–612.

McInerney, D. M., Dowson, M., & Yeung, A. S. (2005). Facilitating conditions for school motivation: Construct validity and applicability. *Educational and Psychological Measurement, 65,* 1–21.

McInerney, D. M., Hinkley, J., Dowson, M., & Van Etten, S. (1998). Aboriginal, Anglo, and Immigrant Australian Students' motivational beliefs about personal academic success: Are there cultural differences? *Journal of Educational Psychology, 90,* 621–629.

McInerney, D. M., Marsh, H. W., & Yeung, A. S. (2003). Toward a hierarchical model of school motivation. *Journal of Applied Measurement, 4*(4), 335–357.

McInerney, D. M., & McInerney, V. (1996). Goals and school motivation: Aboriginal and Navajo Perspectives. *SET Research Information for Teachers, SET 1,* 1–4.

McInerney, D. M., McInerney, V., Ardington, A., & De Rachewiltz, C. (1997). *School success in cultural context: Conversations at Window Rock. Preliminary Report.* Paper presented at the annual meeting of the American Educational Research Association, Chicago, March 24–28. ERIC Doc ED407202.

McInerney, D. M., McInerney, V., Bazeley, P., & Ardington, A. (1998). *Parents, peers, cultural values and school processes: What has most influence on motivating indigenous minority students' school achievement? A qualitative study.* Paper presented at the annual meeting of the American Educational Research Association, San Diego, April 13–17. ERIC Doc ED420706.

McInerney, D. M., Roche, L., McInerney, V., & Marsh, H. W. (1997). Cultural perspectives on school motivation: The relevance and application of goal theory. *American Educational Research Journal, 34,* 207–236.

McInerney, D. M., & Sinclair, K. E. (1991). Cross-cultural model testing: Inventory of school motivation. *Educational and Psychological Measurement, 51,* 123–133.

McInerney, D. M., & Sinclair, K. E. (1992). Dimensions of school motivation: A cross-cultural validation study. *Journal of Cross-Cultural Psychology, 23,* 389–406.

McInerney, D. M., & Swisher, K. (1995). Exploring Navajo motivation in school settings. *Journal of American Indian Education, 33,* 28–51.

McInerney, D. M., Yeung, S. Y., & McInerney, V. (2001) Cross-cultural validation of the Inventory of School Motivation (ISM). *Journal of Applied Measurement, 2,* 134–152.

Nelson, G. F., O'Mara, A. J., McInerney, D. M., & Dowson, M. (2006) Motivation in cross-cultural settings: A Papua, New Guinea Psychometric Study. *International Education Journal, 7,* 400–409. (http://iej.cjb.net)

Murray. H. A. (1938). *Explorations in personality.* New York: Oxford University Press.

Nicholls, J. G. (1989). *The competitive ethos and democratic education.* Cambridge, MA: Harvard University Press.

Osgood, C. E., Miron, M., & May, W. (1975). *Cross-cultural universals of affective meaning.* Urbana: University of Illinois Press.

Pederson, P. (1979). Non-western psychology: The search for alternatives. In A. J. Marsella, R. G. Tharp, & T. J. Ciborowski (Eds.), *Perspectives on cross-cultural psychology.* New York: Academic Press.

Perrot, L. J., Deloney, L., Hastings, J., Savell, S., & Savidge, M. (2001). Measuring student motivation in health professions' colleges. *Advances in Health Science Education, 6,* 193–203.

Pintrich, P. R. (2000). Multiple goals, multiple pathways: The role of goal orientation in learning and achievement. *Journal of Educational Psychology, 92,* 544–555.

Ryan, A. M., & Shim, S. S. (2006). Social achievement goals: The nature and consequences of different orientations towards social competence. *Personality and Social Psychology Bulletin, 32,* 1246–1263.

Spence, J. (1985). Achievement American style: The rewards and costs of individualism. *American Psychologist, 40,* 1285–1295.

Suliman, R., & McInerney, D. M (2006). Motivational goals and school achievement: Lebanese-background students in south western Sydney. *Australian Journal of Education, 50,* 242–264.

Triandis, H. C. (1972). *The analysis of subjective culture.* New York: John Wiley.

Triandis, H. C. (1980). Introduction. In H. C. Triandis & W. W. Lambert (Eds.), *Handbook of cross-cultural psychology* (Vol. 1). Boston: Allyn & Bacon.

Urdan, T. C., & Maehr, M. L. (1995). Beyond a two-goal theory of motivation and achievement: A case for social goals. *Review of Educational Research, 65,* 213–243.

Van de Vijver, F., & Leung, K. (1997). *Method and data analysis for cross-cultural research.* Thousand Oaks, CA: Sage.

Watkins, D., McInerney, D. M. & Boholst, F. (2003). The reliability and validity of the Inventory of School Motivation: A Filipino investigation. *Asian-Pacific Education Researcher, 12,* 87–100.

Watkins, D., McInerney, D. M., Akande, A., & Lee, C. (2003). An investigation of ethnic differences in the motivation strategies for learning of students in desegregated South African schools. *Journal of Cross-Cultural Psychology, 34,* 189–194.

Watkins, D., McInerney, D. M., & Lee, C. (2002). Assessing the school motivation of Hong Kong students. *Psychologia, 45,* 144–154.

Watkins, D., McInerney, D. M., Lee, C., Akande, A., & Regmi, M. (2002). Motivation and learning strategies. A cross-cultural perspective. In D. M. McInerney & S. Van Etten (Eds.), *Research on Sociocultural Influences on Motivation and Learning* (Vol. 2, pp. 329–343). Greenwich, CT: Information Age.

Wentzel, K. R. (2005). Peer relationships, motivation, and academic performance at school. In A. J. Elliot & C. S. Dweck (Eds.), *Handbook of Competence and Motivation* (pp. 279–296). New York: The Guildford Press.

Yang, K. S. (1986). Chinese personality and its change. In M. H. Bond (Ed.), *The psychology of the Chinese people* (pp. 106–170). Hong Kong: Oxford University Press.

Yeung, A. S., & McInerney, D. M. (2005). Students' school motivation and aspiration over high school years. *Educational Psychology: An International Journal of Experimental Educational Psychology, 25,* 537–554.

Yu, A. B., & Yang, K. S. (1994). The nature of achievement motivation in collectivist societies. In U. Kim, H. C. Triandis, C. Kagitcibasi, S. C. Choi, & G. Yoon. (Eds.), *Individualism and collectivism: Theory, methods, and applications* (pp. 239–250). London: Sage Publications.

CHAPTER 10

# THE CULTURAL SITUATEDNESS OF MOTIVATION

**Julianne C. Turner and Helen Patrick**

During the academic year 2000–01, Marty spent a sabbatical year at Notre Dame, writing about his interests in psychology, religion, and motivation. This was a happy coincidence for Julie, because it provided a wonderful opportunity to reflect on their mutual interests in motivation. Every Wednesday afternoon we met to talk about motivation theory and research. It was a luxury for both of us to leave our daily concerns behind and to talk about big ideas. Both of us had a history of commitment to understanding and fostering motivation to learn in schools, not just because of our research enterprises (Maehr & Midgley, 1996), but also because of its importance for education and achievement. We came to the conclusion that motivation research had not fulfilled its promise—it was ill-suited to meeting the needs of those who were at the center of our concerns as researchers—that is, teachers and children.

We began to plan and write a paper that would address those issues. Marty drew on his extensive research career, including his writing on sociocultural origins of achievement (e.g., Maehr, 1974a, 1974b, 1984) and expertise in social psychology, while Julie continued to develop her growing interest in situated and sociocultural approaches to psychological and educational research (e.g., Turner, 2001). Sadly, the article we planned was never completed. Happily, however, the ideas continued to percolate. For Julie, they contributed to later discussions with Helen while collaborating

*Culture, Self, and Motivation: Essays in Honor of Martin L. Maehr,* pages 243–265

on research, as we both struggled with the question of how we could represent both the person and the context as integral to each other. These discussions led to a study (Turner & Patrick, 2004) in which we found that self-reports of motivational beliefs (goal orientations, classroom goal structures, perceived teacher support) were poor correlates and predictors of two students' motivated behaviors and interactions in their mathematics classes, both in sixth and seventh grades. Although the students' self-reports changed little from one year to the next, their behavior and engagement changed dramatically. Clearly, it was more than beliefs that explained or predicted their behavior. Our classroom recordings and field notes, however, showed that the classroom context, including social interactions and classroom norms, was crucial in explaining the students' observed motivation to learn. This experience led to our conclusion that our previous research, and most motivation research in general, did not describe how motivation develops and changes. And we came to believe that if motivation researchers are to understand how motivation develops and changes, our research needs to be reconceptualized or reframed (see Turner & Patrick, 2008, for a suggested framework). Our current thinking and research, reflected in this chapter, is a tribute to Marty's intellectual collegiality, to his generative thinking and to his lifelong scholarship on the social, cultural, and situated nature of achievement motivation.

In this chapter, we argue that motivation research has been of limited value because it has focused too little on the problems and issues of motivation where they occur—in schools, workplaces, and families. Instead, the research has focused mostly on individuals and their psychological states, portrayed largely as both relatively stable and isolated from the very social and cultural contexts in which they exist. We note further that the predominant methods, measuring mostly "beliefs and cognitions, [and] emphasizing psychological and interpretational process" (Eccles, Wigfield, & Schiefele, 1998, p. 1022), have not adequately captured how motivation develops and changes. We critique these interpretations, and briefly refer to a history of psychological theory and research that supports the situated nature of motivation and behavior. Finally, we illustrate these approaches with some of our current research that demonstrates the social situativity of beliefs, motivation and behavior. Our thinking is reflected well by Gergen's (1985) comment: "The question 'why' is not answered with a psychological state, but with consideration of person in relationship" (p. 271).

We see three issues that hinder the instructional application of most motivation research over the past fifty years or so:

1. the separation of person and context, with each being examined separately;

2. the predominant emphasis on people's beliefs and internal psychological representations; and,
3. the use of research methods and designs that assume, and thus over-generalize, the consistency of people's behavior across contexts.

We believe that in order for motivation research to be of more practical benefit to educators—that is, to concentrate on how motivation develops and why it changes—researchers need to address these issues explicitly.

## Separating Person and Context

Motivation research, in our view, tends to be framed dualistically—focused on either individuals' beliefs or, less often, on the context, either singly or consecutively. Noting dualisms within psychology is not new, we recognize. Psychology in the United States has struggled with dualistic views since its early beginnings (Dewey & Bentley, 1949). Should measures be objective or subjective? Was psychology to focus on science or practice? Was our concern with human behavior to be located in the study of individuals or in their social interactions? Questions about the goal of psychology, as well as the relationship between the social and the cognitive, were central concerns of Dewey's personality-social psychology in the early 20ᵗʰ century, and they endure to this day (Barone, Maddux, & Snyder, 1997). We believe that current motivation research is enmeshed in these same dilemmas. Perhaps re-visiting Dewey's writing, in which he advocated for moving beyond simple dichotomies to taking a holistic view, can inform our present situation.

Dewey's response to the dualisms of his day was to call for a psychology that linked science and practice, and that integrated the social and the cognitive. He reacted to the dominant psychology of consciousness with the theoretical formulation of a "social" psychology in which the "social" was not an add-on to a psychology of behavior or cognition, but a concept that should be considered throughout the inquiry (Barone et al., 1997). Cognition and social activity could not be separated as objects of study. Dewey expressed it this way:

> The subjectmatter [sic] of behavioral inquiries involves organism and environmental objects jointly at every instance of their occurrence, and in every portion of space they occupy.... The organism, of course, seems in everyday life and language to stand out strongly apart from the transactions in which it is engaged. This is superficial observation (Dewey & Bentley, 1949, pp. 122, 129).

Thus, psychologists must examine the transactions between the person and context.

Dewey's (1922) "social-cognitive" (i.e., integrating the social and the cognitive) theory spawned different lineages, including Lewin, Vygotsky, and Bandura, all of whom considered the person and context holistically (Barone et al., 1997). Bruner (1990), an intellectual descendent of both Dewey and Vygotsky, also advocated for a holistic perspective:

> It is man's (sic) participation in culture and the realization of his mental powers through culture that make it impossible to construct a human psychology on the basis of the individual alone. . . . Human beings do not terminate at their own skins; they are expressions of a culture . . . . Meaning achieves a form that is public and communal rather than private and autistic. (pp. 12, 33-34)

We contend that, despite the history of holism within social cognitive theories, a great deal of contemporary motivation research has come to emphasize the cognitive, and regard social settings as either psychological phenomena or additional variables. Furthermore, we believe that motivation researchers have over-generalized the power of individuals' beliefs by neglecting to study them as they constitute and are constituted by the situations in which they function (Turner, 2001; Turner & Patrick, 2005, 2008).

We believe that Dewey's notion of transaction provides both a profitable theoretical and practical direction for motivation research today. By attending to the holistic nature of thinking and acting as social processes we think researchers can formulate better explanations for behavior[1]—explanations that are both useful for educators, and that can test our theories' ecological validity. In the next section we discuss some limitations of current motivational research, limitations that we believe can be addressed with the fruitful theorizing of our social cognitive and sociocultural ancestors, including Dewey, Vygotsky, and Bruner, among others.

### A Focus on the Individual

Most motivation research (including ours) has focused on the person—notably individuals' construals and beliefs (Eccles et al., 1998). It seems that motivation researchers have continued in the psychological tradition of separating person and context, thus "reinforce[ing] our conception of motivation as an individual difference variable." (Maehr & Turner, 2001)

A number of researchers have referred to the domination—within motivation research and educational psychology in general—of self-constructs, at the expense of attention to the context and understanding of the transaction. In his 1990 summary of the then most recent motivation research,

Weiner noted a marked increase over the previous eight years in the range of cognitive variables invoked. In his opinion, there was a "current dominance of issues related to the self, self-directed emotions, and what may be called a psychology of the individual" (p. 621). To redress the balance, Weiner argued, "we have to consider frameworks larger than the self . . . . [because] school motivation cannot be divorced from the social fabric in which it is embedded" (p. 621).

Sivan (1986) also warned of an over-emphasis on the individual in motivation research:

> Motivation has traditionally been seen as a product of the intrapsychological functioning of the individual. . . . Studies of student motivation place the student as the agent who *alone* processes environmental, cognitive and affective information (p. 209).

More recently, Martin (2006) noted that despite educational psychology's seeming recognition of the "individual and contextual differences in learners and educational settings, .... at a deeper level, the basic assumptions and image of the strategic, self-regulated learner remain intact" (p 595). He portrayed educational psychology as treating social contexts merely as potential sources for individual information processing. In this view, people are individuals first, who "enter into relationships" rather than as "social participants from the beginning" (Barone et al., 1997, p. 12).

Even attempts (ours included) to acknowledge the importance of classroom contexts (e.g., goal structures) for motivation is mostly devoted to measuring, and then aggregating, individuals' beliefs to approximate situated motivation. But, we argue, aggregated beliefs are not a good representation of the complexity of students' classroom experiences. Aggregation erases the typically sizable differences within classes among people, activities, and experiences. In this case, "classroom" research refers more to a site for data collection than to the study of motivation situated in classroom activity. Another method of representing the classroom context has been to report what the teacher does or says while instructing the class as a whole; here, the focus is on the individual teacher as constructing the context. This approach is also problematic; it assumes implicitly the teacher's messages are interpreted and experienced uniformly by students—another assumption that our data do not support (Turner & Patrick, 2004).

*Research Methods and Designs That Over-Generalize the Consistency of Behavior Across Contexts*

Much motivation research, particularly in the last fifteen years or so, has been carried out with survey methods—asking students at a point in time (sometimes more than once) to report on their construals of themselves, the task or domain, and their context, and then conducting correlations among constructs. A consequence of much of this research has been that the results are abstracted generalizations (e.g., "goal orientations" or "perceived goal structures," in the case of achievement goal theory), specific to no particular person or situation. The view of individuals, contexts, and transactions across individuals and contexts is thus obscured. The popularity of statistical techniques like structural equation modeling and path analysis attest to our predilection for identifying and predicting relations among constructs, rather than relationships of people acting together in learning and achievement situations (Brophy, 2007). Consequently, in Brophy's words,

> we know a great deal about how to predict students' learning-related behavior from measures of their motivational patterns, but much less about how to shape undesirable motivational patterns toward more optimal patterns. Given that teachers are change agents charged with optimizing their students' functioning, this imbalance needs attention.

Another methods-related issue is that the survey items in motivation measures often ask students to rate their beliefs across multiple situations, such as "in math class" or "at school." Doing so, however, treats situations as homogeneous. It implies that there is constancy as to how students experience math classes during a semester, or experience school with different subjects and teachers, or that differences in context are minor and not important. Research indicates otherwise, however.

A good deal of psychological research has demonstrated that neither behavior nor situations are stable. Following in Dewey's tradition, Lewin illustrated the power of contextual variations with a series of studies in which he investigated differences in group dynamics. Lewin examined children's behavior within a mask-making club under one of three different leadership styles—democratic, authoritarian, and laissez-faire (Lewin, 1948; Lewin, Lippitt, & White, 1939). The children in the authoritarian-led group exhibited more hostile domination and criticism, and less co-operation and praise, than those in the democratic-led group. When children were transferred to other groups with different leadership styles, their behavior also changed markedly.

Ross and Nisbett (1991) noted that contemporary social (cognitive) psychology attests to the power and subtlety of situational influences on behavior, even when situations differ in seemingly trivial ways. Darley and Bateson (1973, cited in Ross & Nisbett, 1991, pp. 48-49) designed an experiment in which young Princeton Theological seminarians were told to prepare a brief extemporaneous talk to be recorded in a building nearby (for half of them it was on the Good Samaritan parable). The seminarians in the "late" condition were told "you're late; they were expecting you a few minutes ago, so you'd better hurry." Seminarians in the "early" condition were told "it will be a few minutes before they they're ready for you, but you might as well head on over." As they walked to their destination, participants in both conditions passed by a man slumped in a doorway, coughing and moaning. Only 10 percent of the "late" seminarians stopped to help, whereas 63 percent of those with ample time did so. Even though one might predict that seminarians would be "altruistic people," situational constraints altered the predictability of their behavior.

In a research career spanning 40 years, Mischel and his colleagues (Mischel, 2004; Mischel & Schoda, 1985) have investigated the consistency of personality and behavior across situations. They have concluded that although people's behavior may be somewhat consistent in the same context, they are likely to behave quite differently in different contexts—even ones that share many similar features, like "history class." That is, stability of behavior in the same context is confused with consistency of behavior across (even slightly) different situations. In a recent article, McAdams and Pals (2006) presented a model describing how

> self-defining features of psychological individuality [are] constructed in response to situated social tasks and the human need to make meaning in culture. (p. 204)

Therefore, even those psychologists who have devoted themselves to the study of personality acknowledge the power of situational influences and suggest that it must be taken into account to understand human behavior.

Just as people change, so, too, do situations. Yet Kindermann and Valsiner (1995) have observed: "Typically, context change across time is considered either irrelevant or is explicitly controlled" (p. 238). To understand the mutuality of people and contexts one must attend to:

> processes of individuals' adaptation to changing contexts, . . . processes of context adaptation to changing individuals, and [to] individuals' potential to instigate and shape the development of their contexts, as well as [to] contexts' potential to instigate and shape the developmental pathways of individuals (p. 230).

Motivational research that does this, though, is rare. However, there is ample evidence that both people and situations are changeable, even malleable, and this is good news for teachers. Although teachers believe that motivation is crucial, they often view motivation as a personality trait, as stable and largely immune to classroom influences. We believe that motivation research can and should address these issues.

## LINKS WITH MARTY MAEHR'S SCHOLARSHIP

Throughout his career, Marty has advocated many of the suggestions for motivation research that we have presented in this chapter. He has argued for the importance of taking a situated perspective in order to understand motivation: "The important principle is that achievement and achievement motivation must be understood in terms of the sociocultural context in which they are found" (Maehr, 1974a, p. 894). Even during the heyday of the cognitive revolution, Marty remained true to his social cognitive roots and attentive to the importance of social and cultural contexts to motivation.

Nevertheless, Marty noted (Maehr & Turner, 2001) a long-standing emphasis in motivation research on individual differences—those formed early, and not particularly amenable to change. He attributed this emphasis to the work of McClelland (e.g., McClelland, Atkinson, Clark & Lowell, 1953). Although McClelland's work has been credited as being very influential in Marty's intellectual development (Maehr & Braskamp, 1986), it is clear that Marty did not follow the same path. More than thirty years ago, he contended:

> A focus on the inner state of the person . . . has typically eventuated in an ethnocentric construction of the nature of things. . . .What is needed is a framework within which culturally based conceptions of achievement motivation can arise . . . [and] a clearer specification of the object of study and more serious devotion to the analysis of situations, contexts, places, and events in which this object of study is to be found (Maehr, 1974a, p. 894).

And the framework Marty and his colleagues developed to conceptualize motivated behavior was achievement goal theory. For Marty's part, at least, achievement goal theory grew from "work on the role of social and cultural context in determining motivational patterns in performing achievement tasks" (Maehr, 1984, p. 117).

Echoing his much-earlier concerns (e.g., Maehr, 1974a), Marty noted recently that

> motivation theories have typically portrayed achievement motivation as an enduring characteristic of an individual rather than as a response that is tied to, and varies with, situations and circumstances. (Maehr & Turner, 2001)

He expressed concern that motivation research has not been as helpful to educators as it might be: "survey research has typically underestimated the focal issue for practitioners: the role that the achievement context plays in co-constructing meanings (McCaslin & Good, 1996) and taking action" (Maehr & Turner, 2001). Thus, "the very paradigms that guide the research are unlikely to yield truly useful results" (Maehr & Turner).

## APPROACHES TO MOTIVATION RESEARCH THAT REFLECT A HOLISTIC CONCEPTUALIZATION

In the following sections we—Helen, then Julie—describe some of our recent research in which our objective is to understand development and change of motivation through examining transactions of people and their situations. The research projects are at different stages, and so we have taken different approaches to our contributions.

### The Development of Children's Motivation for Learning Science

Young children are tremendously interested in science. Their spontaneous, sometimes incessant, questions are frequently about the natural world: Why does winter happen? Where does the sun go at night? What are people made of? How do the clouds get in the sky? What color is rain? Do bugs have bones? How fast does hair grow? What does a worm look like in the inside? This seemingly inherent curiosity would seem to bode well for studying science—if people are naturally interested in finding out about the world and how things in it work, then science classes in a range of areas should be popular in school and beyond. Unfortunately, though, that isn't usually the case. Children in kindergarten through sixth grade report liking science less than they do other academic subjects (Andre, Whigham, Hendrickson, & Chambers, 1999). And, in general, their interest in science declines across the years between upper elementary and high school (Greenfield, 1997). Children typically express beliefs that science is more difficult than many other school subjects, and that they are better at language arts and math than at science (Andre et al., 1999; Cleaves, 2005; Licht, Stader, & Swenson, 1989).

How can we explain the normative decline in motivation for science? How does motivation for school science develop? And what is different for that small proportion of children who remain curious and want to learn about science-related phenomena? These are questions that intrigue us— my colleagues Youli Mantzicopoulos, Ala Samarapungavan, and myself— and are a central focus of our Scientific Literacy Project (SLP: Mantzicopoulos, Patrick, & Samarapungavan, 2005), a three-year investigation of kindergarten children's science learning.

Thirty-five years ago Marty wrote: "Complex human behavior is seldom if ever solely a function of the person . . . situations and contexts are critical in eliciting or maximizing any predisposition to achieve" (Maehr, 1974b, p. 64). We agree. Therefore, in setting out to learn more about the development of children's motivation for science in the early school years, we drew from Bronfenbrenner's (1989) model and are considering different spheres within which children interact, directly and indirectly. Accordingly, throughout each year we have collected data about children in kindergarten, their science lessons, their science teachers, classroom norms, school norms and requirements, and the children's home environments. With respect to the children, we are examining what they do and say during science lessons, what they think about science as a discipline, how good they think they are at science and how much they like it, and what kinds of questions they ask, books they read and television shows they watch at home. During science lessons we are attending to aspects such as the content, activities, norms and routines, participation structures. We are interested in the teachers' instructional and management practices during science lessons, how and why teachers structure their lessons the way they do, what they think kindergarten children should learn in science, their science knowledge and conceptions of what science involves, and how confident they feel teaching science. We are examining teachers' differences and similarities (both intra- and inter-individual) throughout each year, in terms of different topics, activity structures, and child compositions, and also across the three years. We record school norms and requirements, such as formal policies and informal understandings about time spent in different subjects, and what teachers are held accountable for. And finally, we have collected a variety of data about the children's home environments, including details about parents' expectations for how well their child will do at school in general and in different subjects, what kinds of questions their child asks about and how they answer science-related questions, parents' backgrounds and current interests in areas of science, beliefs about what young children should know about different science topics, and provision of science-related books, visits, and activities). To examine these different spheres we have asked children and parents open-ended and forced-response questions, videotaped parents and children reading science books together at home, interviewed teachers, and videotaped whole class and small group science lessons over the course of three years.

The amount and variety of data is considerable—daunting at times, and requires many different procedures for synthesizing and representing the confluence of data. Nevertheless, I believe this approach will yield worthwhile results—it should help us understand how different motivational trajectories play out for different children within different configurations of contexts and transactions. My thinking about how to frame analyses has been influenced considerably by the writings of many psychologists that Julie and I read as part of preparing our recent paper on reframing motivational research (Turner & Patrick, 2008).

Developmental psychologists such as Magnusson (1992), Rogoff (1997), and Valsiner (1994) have been helpful in assuaging concerns that we will produce seemingly endless cases that do not generalize to other people and cannot be used for prediction. Like with all research, our objective is to identify and explain patterns—similarities, differences, and regularities—in behavior. Therefore, Rogoff (1997) contended,

> Those who become concerned that the study of contextual issues leads towards chaos are likely to be considering those infinite interactions rather than to be aware of the regularities and simplifications of patterns. (p. 276)

Thus, we must reduce our records of events and details systematically so that meaningful patterns become evident. In other words, we can examine data for general models that might still differ in particulars (Valsiner, 1994). Generalization, in this framework, involves the extent to which similar patterns are apparent in different contexts. Therefore, "the question of how people's efforts in one activity relate to those in another is an empirical question" (Rogoff, Radziszewska, & Masiello, 1995, p. 128), rather than an assumption that processes generalize automatically.

I am sympathetic with Magnusson's (1992, 2003) arguments that there has been too little attention to systematic observations and descriptions as part of the search for basic principles, and that researchers have over-privileged the importance of prediction. He contended that

> the overriding goal [within developmental psychology] is not to arrive at strong predictions of individuals' life courses but to understand and explain principles underlying developmental processes and mechanisms operating in these processes (2003, p. 5).

Predictions do not tell us *how* something happens, but just the likelihood that it will. For people concerned with children developing adaptive patterns of adjustment, motivation, and achievement, predicting relative success for different children is not sufficient. We need to understand better the processes by which different developmental courses unfold and the processes by which adaptive outcomes can be facilitated for different children in different situations, including those for whom initial predictions are less than positive.

Walker and Pressick-Kilborn's (Pressick-Kilborn & Walker, 2002; Walker, Pressick-Kilborn, Arnold, & Sainsbury, 2004) use of the constructs 'canalization' and 'self-canalization,' taken from Valsiner, seems useful for considering the development of children's motivation in our research. These constructs

> explain how the structuring of the social world, as well as the actions and choices of the individuals involved, create the context in which interest may emerge and be maintained (Walker et al., p. 247).

Thus, different affordances and constraints which are present in different contexts, including those that the individual may create for him- or herself, help to channel different patterns of behavior—toward some options and away from others.

In the case of the kindergarten children in our research, this would include the teachers' structuring of the lessons. For example, one teacher had children sit in groups around small tables, with their science equipment and notebooks in the middle, and she typically spent about 20–30 minutes talking about the upcoming lesson. Although most children appeared to grow tired of listening without some action happening, a small number of children found it especially difficult to sit still and not fiddle. They gravitated to playing with the materials or flipping through their notebook, looking at the pages, despite frequent reprimands for doing so. These children may be particularly restless, or have little experience sitting still for relatively long periods of time, or—a supposedly positive occurrence—be especially excited about doing science. Over time, the interaction between teacher and these few children became quite negative. One would not expect these experiences to elicit positive views of learning science for these children. However, as noted, many other children in that class appeared enthralled and did not receive frequent reprimands. One wonders how the former children would have fared in the classroom next door, where the teacher talked with the children seated on the carpet at her feet, gave much shorter instructions for activities, and passed out notebooks and materials when the children were ready to begin. In that class, children's differential engagement was evidenced in other ways, though. Some children were called on very infrequently, despite their hand-raising, to participate in lessons, and were given little time to speak if they seemed to be collecting their thoughts, whereas other children were frequent contributors. One wonders, again, how children's out-of-school experiences counter or confirm their developing views of themselves as learners, and learners of science.

Teachers had different opportunities and constraints on their lessons. In classes where children attend kindergarten for 2.5 hours a day, and teachers have to "fit in" 90 minutes of literacy and 60 minutes of math each day, in addition to music, art, library, physical education, snack time, and bathroom breaks, there isn't a lot of time left for science. In two classrooms children were in kindergarten for the entire school day; not surprisingly, those teachers were less pressured about including science in their weeks. Teachers reported they were never asked by administrators about science in their classrooms, although they were required to complete sheets recording time spent on reading and math each day. One teacher explained, "There are science standards, but ... they're just there and they're not on their report card and so they're not really something that's a focus." Therefore, for teachers who did not participate in the SLP activities, what they presented in the way of science, and how often, was influenced in large part by their interests, efficacy, knowledge, and beliefs about its importance.

Baseline classroom data showed great variety in the content of science lessons. Activities we observed or were described by teachers included comparing two plants (one placed in the light and one in the dark), using cookies and twizzlers to make insects (showing insects have 3 body parts and 6 legs), using one's hands to make shadow patterns from a light source, and pasting mini marshmallows onto paper to make a mouth of teeth. Interestingly, although the teachers not using SLP activities identified lessons as science to us, they did not label it as "science" to the children. Accordingly, most of these children did not recognize they learned science in kindergarten, although they knew they were learning reading and math (Mantzicopoulos, Patrick, & Samarapungavan, 2008). Nevertheless, many of them told us they "knew" that science involves potions, robots, or computers, and significantly fewer girls than boys said they like science (Patrick, Mantzicopoulos, & Samarapungavan, 2009). Clearly, early motivational trajectories are influenced by children's multiple spheres of participation.

As expected, there was also considerable variability in children's home environments. This variability extended to reading with their children the non-fiction, kindergarten-level science books that were provided as part of SLP, or looking at the completed science notebooks that children brought home when each unit was finished.

Within each sphere there were differences in the amount and quality of opportunities to learn about science, and to construct an accurate base of science knowledge and understanding that can be added to in the future. There were also differences in the affect generated, and in the importance of science conveyed through words and behaviors. The confluence of transactions within numerous spheres is posited to enhance or constrain children's early development of motivation for school science. The challenge is for us to identify how children's motivation is channeled one way rather than another.

In this section, Helen chose to reflect mostly on the theoretical influences on her current research about science in kindergarten. In the next section, Julie illustrates how she has made use of one approach to capturing the holistic nature of the cognitive and the social in her empirical research on the development of teachers' motivation practices in mathematics in intermediate school.

### The Development of One Teacher's Motivational Practices in Mathematics; "This Is a Big Drag, and I Hate It."

The analyses that I present below come from an ongoing collaborative project with intermediate grade teachers. The goal is to introduce teachers to theory-based motivational principles that they can integrate into mathematics instruction. The principles include fostering student competence, autonomy, belongingness, and making mathematics meaningful. Data include transcripts of monthly collaborative meetings in which we discussed the principles, how to enact them, as well as "problems" and "solutions;" fall and spring teacher interviews about motivation and mathematics; observations of teachers' lessons over the year; post-observation interviews, and unsolicited teacher emails. We also collect student surveys and interviews.

The framework that I use is an adaptation of Rogoff's (1995) "three planes" of analysis. The *personal plane* focuses on how individuals change through their participation in an activity. The *interpersonal plane* focuses on the ways in which activities (and materials) are communicated and coordinated among individuals and how they facilitate or hinder certain types of participation. The *community plane* focuses on institutional practices and cultural values which have developed over time. Rogoff (1995) stresses that while the analysis may focus on one plane, all the others must be represented "in the background" in order to understand development.

In this analysis, I use Ms. McNamara's (all names are pseudonyms) interviews and emails as reports of her changing beliefs and practices (personal plane) over the school year. I use transcripts from teacher meetings and from her classroom instruction to demonstrate how the interpersonal events with students and with other teachers facilitated or hindered her practices. Third, I introduce standardized testing as one facet of the community plane that greatly influenced the teacher's thinking, creating an important conflict for her.

Of course, it is challenging to try to understand and represent how these events converged to explain Ms. McNamara's development, but I believe it offers a promising approach to interpreting the holistic nature of the process. I also try to convey the interrelatedness of the teacher's views about motivation, mathematics, and instruction. Although the collaboration focused on principles of motivation, to be effective, they had to be integrated into mathematics instruction. Therefore, a major goal of the project was for teachers to understand the integral nature of all three; that is, motivation is only as "good" as the mathematics instruction in which it inheres.

Ms. McNamara had been teaching 5th grade for 7 years in an urban school district in the Midwest. In the fall, we asked teachers to discuss motivation in their classrooms. Ms. McNamara described both herself and her fifth grade students as "bored." During her first interview, she implicated her instruction in her students' motivation: "The common denominator is me going up to the board and doing example after example after example and then losing interest… [It is] so stinkin' borin' that they don't care about it anymore." She noted that her attempts to convince her students that math was "important," (albeit boring) were futile. "They just weren't buying it. They were like, 'No, this is a big drag and I hate it.'" To this she added her own view: "I still don't think of math as an enjoyable subject, necessarily" and "What is interesting about the hundredths place?" Both teacher and students appeared to view mathematics negatively.

Ms. McNamara also attributed her students' low achievement to motivation. She described her fifth grade students as "struggling learners," who considered themselves "dumb," who were used to failure, and intent on "saving face." Many had just rejoined regular education from special education, and many believed that they were now in a class where they "didn't belong." She believed that the "stigma" of special education followed them, contributing a "huge intimidation factor" in math. The teacher described her students' typical behavior as saying, "I don't get it," to "panic" and to ask "three million questions." She wished she could give them a "dose of whatever that is" that motivated students have, an attitude that "even if I don't get it right all the time, I have been able to do this successfully in the past."

Interestingly, Ms. McNamara shared some of her students' beliefs. During the first collaborative meeting in September, she acknowledged that she believed that "good" math students were fast and accurate, at the same time lamenting that her students were fixated on "right answers" and afraid of making mistakes. Calling herself a "control freak," she indicated her belief that she needed to be "in charge," both for students to learn, and also so that she could "save [the] kid" who makes mistakes. While viewing a video of Japanese students engaged in group work (TIMSS, 1997), she noted her assumption that when math became too "social" in her class she needed to "take control again" fearing that "the math is lost" and that such activities might not be worth "the time spent."

Nevertheless, Ms. McNamara believed that motivation was malleable, and this probably explained her desire to join the collaboration. During the same meeting in September, I asked teachers where motivation came from. One participant replied quickly that motivation came "from within and from home" implying its stable nature. Ms. McNamara disagreed, countering that motivation can come "from having an interest in whatever the desired outcome is … like … getting to the next level in a video game." In this situation, she noted that students "will play and play and play." She reasoned that the desired outcomes are not clear in math because "a lot of them … don't really see themselves as mathematicians or having a future in math."

Even in this first meeting, Ms. McNamara revealed her penchant for reflecting on her beliefs and practices (her reflections constituted 66% of the total from all meetings). She worried that if she used more discussion-based practices, students might not connect this kind of learning to the "paper and pencil" questions asked on standardized tests. Seconds later, though, she acknowledged her conflict. She noted that such instructional practices would be a "bigger confidence builder than just sitting alone at your desk and continuously having no clue." She concluded that even if the mode of instruction did not "match" the test, "it's definitely worth it anyway." This conflict, between enacting engaging activities that fostered learning and the pressures of preparing students for standardized tests, proved to be a dilemma that Ms. McNamara (and her colleagues) struggled to resolve throughout the year-long collaboration.

By spring, most of Ms. McNamara's beliefs about mathematics and instruction had changed dramatically. Her conviction that her students could engage willingly and meaningfully in mathematics was ratified by their classroom experience. She had constructed an understanding of the relation between the motivational principles and mathematics instruction. As one reads her reflections, written as part of an AERA proposal, her attention to students' competence, autonomy, and belongingness, as well as the central role of making mathematics meaningful, emerge. She wrote:

> I now realize that [the principles] are purposely interconnected, so that when you are focusing on one principle, it is really very natural to end up focusing on all of them. In the end, I felt I was not only learning a new way to teach math, but also changing my existing philosophy of teaching . . . . It's like riding a bike: I learned how by getting on the bike and trying over and over. I didn't spend a week practicing pedaling, another practicing braking, another memorizing the parts of the bike.
>
> In day-to-day teaching, use of these motivational principles moved a class of struggling, apathetic, negative students with no mathematical confidence to a group of eager, confident mathematicians. I created situations where the students were honored for what mathematical knowledge they *did* have, instead of emphasizing what knowledge they didn't have. In some of my most powerful lessons, we started with what the students were great at, with knowledge they truly *owned*. We spent a lot of time discussing what they already knew. Some may see this as a waste of time, going over what they know again and again. But it never failed; when most of the students in the class were close to tuning out, someone would ask a question that made everyone take a step deeper. Instantly, everyone was hooked, trying to develop a solution to the problem.
>
> I now believe that learning is deeper when it is firmly planted in knowledge of broader ideas or concepts. [Now I] identify one or two key ideas from each mathematical concept. I identified equivalence as the essential idea upon which I based all my fraction instruction. We did problem after problem and always came back to the issue of equivalence. That attention to a central idea was *the lifeline* for my students. When planning for the upcoming year, I look at each major concept and pull out a couple of central ideas. I then dig for thought-provoking, meaningful problems that we may work on for several days at a time.

Ms. McNamara's process of change over the year was not linear. It was fitful, frustrating, and fraught with conflicts, and it was punctuated with moments of self-discovery, success, and pure joy in her students' accomplishments. Her willingness to take risks with her classroom instruction was clearly a major source of her changing beliefs and practices. One of her major innovations, *discussing* mathematics with her students, came about because she became "desperate" trying to walk students through meaningless exercises. I will briefly describe three classroom observations and subsequent interviews which help to explain Ms. McNamara's development.

In October, the teacher had begun using one of the competence strategies, which was to ask students to lead homework review. She struggled to relinquish "control" by purposely standing in the back of the classroom while students led the discussion from the front. Almost immediately she noted, "I have seen some more motivation ... [from] giving them the liberty to go over the problem ... and they LOOOVE that, they can't get enough of it." She described one exhilarating lesson where "I had students just looking at me with those gaga eyes, more excited about at least trying to answer." She recounted that one of her most math-avoidant students had led a successful discussion and that "she would never have done that, even a week ago." She connected the student's growing sense of competence to belongingness in the classroom: "I think that she finally thought 'Ok I do belong in this group of people! I am here ... and I can handle it.'" How did the teacher feel? "I felt like singing out the window."

One of the most interesting and intriguing aspects of teacher change was how implementation of motivational strategies in mathematics instruction led teachers to begin to question instructional practices. For example, when Ms. McNamara altered her teacher-centered and procedural practices to create opportunities for students to develop autonomy as thinkers, there were unanticipated consequences. On the one hand, she discovered that her students could do sophisticated mathematical thinking. On the other hand, she uncovered some alarming misconceptions. Both kinds of events led her to conclude that she needed to focus on fundamental concepts, such as place value, rather than on merely "covering" the curriculum objectives. And she began to believe that her students could become mathematical thinkers.

In February, in an attempt to foster autonomy and conceptual thinking, Ms. McNamara designed an activity in which student partners were to create line graphs showing the relative frequency at different times of day of people "at a football game on Saturday" or "at McDonalds during the day." In brief, students had great difficulty with the lesson, and the teacher wanted to abandon it as a bad idea. With encouragement, she extended the lesson to three days, each day reflecting on and redesigning the instruction. This experience challenged her previous practice of "moving on" if something was not working and also her initial skepticism that her students could master the topic. In the end, her students displayed a deeper conceptual understanding of graphic representations than any previous group, and some of her lowest achieving students excelled.

In her final unit of the year, Ms. McNamara applied the lessons she had learned by dint of experimentation and reflection. She selected a central mathematical concept, equivalence of fractions, and taught it through partner work with manipulatives, group discussion, and student explanation. As she observed in her May reflection, the motivation principles were "natural" by now, and she seamlessly interwove instructional strategies that fostered competence, autonomy, belongingness and meaningfulness. She discovered that once students understood the big idea, they somewhat quickly and effortlessly learned the procedures: "Today in Math we were talking about adding/subtracting mixed numbers … we have been barreling through this add/subtract stuff because they have such a clear understanding of equivalence, which I feel is the key." Then she related some conceptual "discoveries" her students had made. She asked how they could rename 10 in order to subtract 5 4/7. "Finally, Tara says, can't we call ten 70/7? It was fantastic. Their understanding is so rich! So we did the problem using 70/7 AND 9 7/7 to show how they got the same answer. It was great. Tara was beaming." And so was her teacher, right through the email.

In addition to her classroom experiences, Ms. McNamara used the monthly collaborative meetings as an opportunity to reflect on motivation and instruction, reflections that appeared to both nurture and challenge her changing beliefs and practices. These ranged from confidently reporting classroom successes to anxieties about whether such changes adequately prepared her students for the mandated quarterly assessments in mathematics. Over the year she articulated this conflict, which tended to recur in the months when assessments were scheduled. As of March, she had still not resolved it, despite her notable successes in the classroom. On the one hand, she wanted to

> take the topic of place value and discuss how to integrate meaningfulness into it. Place value is integral to nearly every other mathematical concept, yet it's the concept I feel like most of my students struggle with the most.

On the other hand, she questioned whether she could devote the time to such a luxury. Her concern dominated the first half of the collaborative meeting, resulting in a revelation that better planning was a key to both teaching conceptually and having adequate time to address the test objectives. Both her decision to plan carefully and her commitment to making learning meaningful led to Ms. McNamara's decision to base her fractions unit around the central idea of equivalence, which she referred to in her comment written in May.

Ms. McNamara's reflections also appeared to help other teachers make connections between the motivational principles and mathematics and instruction. The teachers routinely took up the topics raised by their colleagues. Ms. McNamara also was one of the teachers most likely to challenge an assertion or idea expressed by another teacher. Most often, the challenges were made in response to negative beliefs about students expressed by one teacher. Ms. McNamara frequently offered counter evidence from her own classes, reframing problems, and offering suggestions. These comments legitimated others' views that this teacher's negative views were hindering group progress.

In summary, at the beginning of the year Ms. McNamara expressed a conviction that her students could be motivated to learn mathematics, even though they were not at that time. She believed that lack of efficacy, disinterest, and conceptions of good mathematics students as fast and accurate hindered the students' motivation to learn. The teacher's instructional practices reinforced, rather than challenged, such conceptions. In the fall, she believed that math instruction could not be "social," that it wasn't meaningful, and that she had to be in full control for students to focus and learn. By the end of the year, she had changed most of these beliefs and practices. She commented.

> You know, we talked at the very beginning of this study about how you know when the teacher has full control—she does all the talking, and it's got to be incredibly tiresome to just listen to the same person's voice, the same inflections ... all of the time.... [Now] I feel like they're doing as much teaching, if not more, than I am.

She noted that her formerly avoidant students could accept making mistakes as part of learning; they weren't "bothered at all." Very important for her, Ms. McNamara had resolved her major conflict between teaching for understanding and preparing students for standardized tests:

> If I spend whatever amount of time necessary to get a really firm foundation laid with a lot of high press questions and activities then... it's so much easier to get through that [paper/pencil computation similar to test questions] quickly and not necessarily have to spend weeks on going through the steps ... so we'll sort of make up for lost time. And I'm trying to not think about lost time anymore because it's not lost time.

Perhaps one of her (formerly "struggling") students expresses the outcomes best. When asked in May, "How do you think of yourself as a math student?" a male student thought for a long time, and then replied, "I feel like a mathematician in math."

## CONCLUSION

In this chapter we have argued that motivation research should be focused on how motivation develops and changes. We suggest that research on the situated nature of motivation will help to address the practical and important questions of educators as well as to advance motivational theory. We have illustrated our current thinking by describing our research in progress. Our unfolding results—examining changes in children's and teachers' motivation—reinforce our beliefs in the utility of this approach. Our emerging research programs stand in fitting tribute to the seminal thinking and example of Marty Maehr, our friend and mentor. We hope to demonstrate to all the readers of this volume how the overriding concerns that Marty addressed throughout his career continue to be relevant, even prescient, today. The fact that motivation can and does change in response to affordances and constraints of classrooms, offices, and home, offers hope to teachers and to all those who want to foster the development and direction of motivation. We need to believe *that* people can change and we need to know *how* to do it. We thank Marty for keeping our eyes on the prize.

## ENDNOTE

1.  Interestingly, Dewey's basic unit of study was "conduct" not [Watson's] "behavior," because conduct is always shared (Barone et al., 1997, p. 11).

## REFERENCES

Andre, T., Whigham, M., Hendrickson, A., & Chambers, S. (1999). Competency beliefs, positive affect, and gender stereotypes of elementary students and their parents about science versus other school subjects. *Journal of Research in Science Teaching, 36*, 719–747.

Barone, D. F., Maddux, J. E., & Snyder, C. R. (1997). *Social cognitive psychology: History and current domains.* New York: Plenum Press.

Bronfenbrenner, U. (1989). Ecological systems theory. In R. Vasta (Ed.), *Annals of child development* (pp. 187–249). Greenwich, CT: JAI Press.

Brophy, J. (2007, April). *Future directions in motivation theory and research.* Presented in symposium at the annual meeting of the American Educational Research Association conference in Chicago.

Bruner, J. (1990). *Acts of meaning.* Cambridge, MA: Harvard University Press.

Cleaves, A. (2005). The formation of science choices in secondary school. *International Journal of Science Education, 27*, 471–486.

Dewey, J. (1922). *Human nature and conduct: An introduction to social psychology.* New York: Henry Holt. Republished as Boydston, J. A. (Ed.), *John Dewey: The middle works, 1899–1924. Volume 14: 1922.* Carbondale, IL: Southern Illinois University Press.

Dewey, J., & Bentley, A. F. (1949). *Knowing and the known.* Boston: Beacon Press.

Eccles, J. S., Wigfield, A., & Schiefele, U. (1998). Motivation to succeed. In W. Damon (Series Ed.) & N. Eisenberg (Vol. Ed.). *Handbook of child psychology: Vol.*

*3. Social, emotional, and personality development* (5th Ed., pp. 1017–1095). New York: Wiley.

Gergen, K. J. (1985). The social constructivist movement in modern psychology. *American Psychologist, 40*, 266–275

Greenfield, T. A. (1997). Gender- and grade-level differences in science interest and participation. *Science Education, 81*, 259–276.

Kindermann, T. A., & Valsiner, J. (1995). Directions for the study of developing person-context relations. In T. A. Kindermann & J. Valsiner (Eds.), *Development of person-context relations* (pp. 227–240). Hillsdale, NJ: Lawrence Erlbaum.

Lewin, K. (1948). Experiments in social space. In K. Lewin & G. W. Lewin (Eds.), *Resolving social conflicts: Selected papers on group dynamics* (pp. 71–83). New York: Harper & Row.

Lewin, K., Lippitt, R., & White, R. K. (1939). Patterns of aggressive behavior in experimentally created "social climates." *Journal of Social Psychology, 10*, 271–299.

Licht, B. G., Stader, S. R., & Swenson, C. C. (1989). Children's achievement-related beliefs: Effects of academic area, sex, and achievement level. *Journal of Educational Research, 82*, 253–260.

Maehr, M. L. (1974a). Culture and achievement motivation. *American Psychologist, 29*, 887–896.

Maehr, M. L. (1974b). *Sociocultural origins of achievement.* Monterey, CA: Brooks/ Cole.

Maehr, M. L. (1984). Meaning and motivation: Toward a theory of personal investment. In R. Ames & C. Ames (Eds.), *Research on motivation in education: Student motivation* (Vol. 1, pp. 115–143). New York: Academic Press.

Maehr, M. L., & Braskamp, L. A. (1986). *The motivation factor: A theory of personal investment.* Lexington, MA: Lexington Books.

Maehr, M. L., & Midgley, C. (1996). *Transforming school cultures.* Boulder, CO: Westview Press.

Maehr, M. L., & Turner, J. C. (2001). *Situating achievement motivation: Putting an old wine into a new bottle.* Unpublished manuscript.

Magnusson, D. (1992). Back to the phenomena: Theory, methods and statistics in psychological research. *European Journal of Personality, 6*, 1–14.

Magnusson, D. (2003). The person approach: Concepts, measurement models, and research strategy. *New Directions for Child and Adolescent Development, 101*, 3–23.

Mantzicopoulos, P., Patrick, H., & Samarapungavan, A. (2005). *The Scientific Literacy Project: Enhancing young children's scientific literacy through reading and inquiry-centered adult-child dialog.* Grant proposal to the Institute of Education Sciences.

Mantzicopoulos, P., Patrick, H., & Samarapungavan, A. (2008). "We learn how to predict and be a scientist:" Early science experiences and kindergarten children's ideas about science. Manuscript submitted for publication.

Martin, J. (2006). Social cultural perspectives in educational psychology. In P. Alexander & P. Winne (Eds.), *Handbook of educational psychology* (2nd Ed., pp. 595–614). Mahwah, NJ: Erlbaum.

McAdams, D., & Pals, J. (2006). A new big five: Fundamental principles for an integrative science of personality. *American Psychologist, 61*, 204–217.

McCaslin, M., & Good, T. L. (1996). *Listening in classrooms.* New York: Harper-Collins.

McClelland, D. C., Atkinson, J. W., Clark, R. A., & Lowell, E. L. (1953). *The achievement motive.* New York: Appleton-Century-Crofts.

Mischel, W. (2004). Toward an integrative science of the person. *Annual Review of Psychology, 55,* 1–22.

Mischel, W., & Schoda, Y. (1985). A cognitive-affective system theory of personality: Reconceptualizing situations, dispositions, dynamics, and invariance in personality structure. *Psychological Review, 49,* 229–258.

Patrick, H., Mantzicopoulos, P., & Samarapungavan, A. (2009). Motivation for learning science in kindergarten: Is there a gender gap and does integrated inquiry and literacy instruction make a difference? *Journal of Research in Science Teaching, 46,* 166–191.

Pressick-Kilborn, K., & Walker, R. (2002). The social construction of interest in a learning community. In D. McInerney & S. Van Etten (Eds.). *Research on sociocultural influences on motivation and learning* (pp. 153–182). Greenwich, CT: Information Age.

Rogoff, B. (1995). Observing socio-cultural activity on three planes: Participatory appropriation, guided participation, and apprenticeship. In J. V. Wertsch, P. D. Rio, & A. Alvarez (Eds.), *Socio-cultural studies of mind* (pp. 139–164). Cambridge, UK: Cambridge University Press.

Rogoff, B. (1997). Evaluating development in the process of participation: Theory, methods, and practice building on each other. In E. Amsel & K. A. Renninger (Eds.), *Change and development: Issues of theory, method, and application* (pp. 265–285). Mahwah, NJ: Erlbaum.

Rogoff, B., Radziszewska, B., & Masiello, T. (1995). Analysis of developmental processes in sociocultural activity. In L. M. W. Martin, K. Nelson, & E. Tobach (Eds.), *Sociocultural psychology: Theory and practice of doing and knowing* (pp. 125–149). New York: Cambridge University Press.

Ross, L. & Nisbett, R. E. (1991). *The person and the situation: Perspectives of social psychology.* New York: McGraw-Hill.

Sivan, E. (1986). Motivation in social constructivist theory. *Educational Psychologist, 21,* 209–233.

Third International Mathematics & Science Study: Eighth-grade mathematics lessons [TIMSS] (1997). Washington, D.C.: U.S. G.P.O.[videorecording] :

Turner, J. C. (2001). Using context to enrich and challenge our understanding of motivational theory. In S. Volet, & S. Järvelä (Eds.), *Motivation in learning contexts: Theoretical advances and methodological implications* (pp. 85–104). Elmsford, NY: Pergamon Press.

Turner, J. C., & Patrick, H. (2004). Motivational influences on student participation in classroom learning activities. *Teachers College Record, 106,* 1759–1785.

Turner, J., & Patrick, H. (2005, August). Mixed messages: The difficulty and challenge of defining and measuring situated classroom motivation. In *How to conceptualise and measure the situated nature of motivation in context-oriented research.* Symposium presented at the biennial meeting of the European Association for Research on Learning and Instruction, Nicosia, Cyprus.

Turner, J. C., & Patrick, H. (2008). How does motivation develop and why does it change? Reframing motivation research. *Educational Psychologist, 43,* 119–131.

Valsiner, J. (1994). Replicability in context: The problem of generalization. In R. van der Veer, M. van IJzendoorn, & J. Valsiner (Eds.), *Reconstructing the mind: Replicability in research on human development* (pp. 173–181). Norwood, NJ: Ablex Publishing.

Walker, R. A., Pressick-Kilborn, K., Arnold, L. S., & Sainsbury. E. J. (2004). Investigating motivation in context: Developing sociocultural perspectives. *European Psychologist, 9*, 245–256.

Weiner, B. (1990). History of motivational research in education. *Journal of Educational Psychology, 82*, 616–622.

CHAPTER 11

# THE CONTRIBUTIONS OF MARTIN L. MAEHR TO THE STUDY OF CULTURAL INFLUENCES ON ACHIEVEMENT MOTIVATION

**Tim Urdan**

Because personal experience so strongly influences one's perceptions, it can be difficult for younger people to develop the same sort of appreciation for change that their elders have. My parents and grandparents used to talk about how different their childhood experiences were without television or airplane travel. They would wax poetic about sitting together and staring at the radio as their favorite programs played. My siblings and I usually responded with half-interested responses: "That sounds weird," we'd say with little appreciation for how enormous the change really was from pre-to-post television. We had never known a world without television, so we could not fully understand the effects of its introduction to society.

In the current era of motivation research, a similar generation gap exists. The social-cognitive perspectives that have dominated the field since the late 1970s have been around so long that it is difficult for many younger motivation researchers to conceive of a time when less cognitively-oriented motivation theories held sway. We all know that Psychoanalytic, Behaviorist, and Achievement Motivation theories had their day, but most of us were

*Culture, Self, and Motivation: Essays in Honor of Martin L. Maehr,* pages 267–284
Copyright © 2009 by Information Age Publishing
**267**

not active researchers when any of these theories dominated. Given what we know today about the shortcomings of these perspectives, it is often difficult for motivation researchers younger than 50 years old to understand why these theoretical perspectives became as prominent as they did. Indeed, it is often hard to remember that current social-cognitive theories of motivation will soon be viewed by a new generation of researchers as relics, dinosaurs of a previous, less enlightened generation of motivation researchers.

Today, motivation researchers readily acknowledge that behavior is situated, and that a combination of personal characteristics and situational factors influence the motivated behavior of individuals. The person-in-context perspective underscores most currently prominent perspectives on motivation, from self-efficacy to achievement goal theory to self-determination theory. Similarly, although it remains understudied, culture is accepted as an important contributor to motivated behavior. Cognitions about the self and various achievement situations are influenced by cultural norms as well as by ethnic and gender identity, and these cognitions influence motivation and achievement, according to social-cognitive theories of motivation. Such beliefs about the role of culture are widely accepted, and it is difficult to imagine a time when they were not.

Of the many contributions that Martin L. Maehr has made to the field of motivation research, perhaps none are more important than his focus on the role of culture. As a graduate student at the University of Michigan, I had the good fortune to work with Professor Maehr and he served as the chairman of my dissertation committee. Under his direction, I became deeply interested in the role that culture plays in shaping achievement motivation, an interest that persists today. This interest led me to read Maehr's work on this issue from the 1970s and early 1980s. In this work, Maehr makes his mark as one of the leaders of the next generation of motivation researchers, breaking from the tradition built by McClelland, Atkinson, and others. In this chapter, I summarize Maehr's major arguments regarding the influence of culture on motivation, beginning with his seminal 1974 article in *The American Psychologist*. Focusing on three of these arguments, I then critique the value and practical utility of these ideas. The chapter ends with a consideration of the current state of research on culture, motivation, and education vis-à-vis Maehr's arguments. As this critique of Maehr's work indicates, my own view of this issue, as a member of a subsequent generation of motivation researchers, is appreciative of the work of Maehr and his colleagues while also challenging some of the assumptions.

### Maehr's Major Arguments

In 1974 Maehr published two works, one in the *American Psychologist* article and the other an elaboration of the ideas regarding the cultural influences of motivation in a monograph entitled *Sociocultural Origins of Achievement.* In these two pieces, he presented his argument against the dominant motivation theory of the day, the Achievement Motivation model espoused by David McClelland, John Atkinson, and colleagues (e.g., Atkinson & Feather, 1966; McClelland, 1961). In this chapter, I refer to this as the McClelland-Atkinson model. According to this model, one's motivation to achieve is determined, in large part, by a stable personality trait called the Need for Achievement (abbreviated as nAch or *n* Achievement). The McClelland-Atkinson model posits that some people are higher than others in their need for achievement and therefore more motivated to achieve across a variety of situations and tasks. Although the McClelland-Atkinson model also includes a consideration of incentive value (i.e., whether an individual values success at the activity) and perceived probability of success at the task, the dominant factor in this model is the level of nAch. Maehr proposed a model of motivation that emphasized social-cognitive factors over stable personality traits and emphasized three points marking the distinction between his view and the McClelland-Atkinson model. First, Maehr argued that it was a mistake to conceive of motivation as a global, stable personality trait. Achievement motivation, according to Maehr, was not an individual difference variable that some people possessed in great amounts whereas others were bereft of it. Rather, motivated behavior was the result of a decision-making process about where to invest one's efforts and energies, and these decisions were informed, in part, by the perceived options and affordances available in the social-cultural context that one lived in. To illustrate this point, Maehr offered the example of a poor African American child who, perceiving few opportunities to succeed academically, chose to express his motivation on the basketball court. According to Maehr, the middle-class White child who excels academically and the impoverished Black child who excels on the basketball court may have equal levels of achievement motivation but differ in their beliefs about the appropriate motivated behaviors to engage in.

A second important theme in Maehr's early work on cultural influences on motivation was that it is empowering to educators to realize that motivation is at least partly situationally determined and not entirely determined by the students' personality traits (Maehr, 1974a, 1974b, 1978). In his 1978 chapter, Maehr phrased his argument thusly:

> Educators have yet another reason for not focusing exclusively on the role of personality in achievement. Such a focus may suggest that there is little or nothing that can be done by the teacher to foster an interest in achievement: If the child happens to possess it—of course, make the most of it—but what teacher can presume to initiate basic changes in personality? …[T]he teacher is left hanging with the question: But what do *I* do? (p. 210).

Because teachers cannot reasonably be expected to change a student's personality to increase her achievement motivation, and any attempt to alter the motivation of students will require an expensive, intensive, and time-consuming effort, a personality theory of motivation is disempowering to teachers.

The third theme found in Maehr's early work on this topic is his contention that the McClelland-Atkinson view of motivation is, at best, Western-centric and, at worst, racist. "Most disturbing is the question of whether the whole theory of achievement motivation is hopelessly ethnocentric in nature." (Maehr, 1978, p. 208). Maehr argued that McClelland's work fits in a larger context of social scientific research that was quick to assume some sort of cultural deficiency among groups of children who underperformed in school. For example, in their research on the racial achievement gap in the 1960s and early 1970s, Coleman, Moynihan, and colleagues argued that Black children lacked linguistic abilities, and this explained their low achievement in school (Coleman et al., 1966; Mosteller & Moynihan, 1972). But other research indicated that Black children often exhibited strong linguistic abilities once outside of the school context (Delpit, 1995). Similarly, according to Maehr, McClelland (1961) defined achievement motivation as the Protestant work ethic, and other definitions of motivation found in other cultures were devalued. Through parenting practices that did not emphasize this work ethic, at least in the academic arena, children in some cultures developed little achievement motivation (McClelland, 1961). Maehr argued that this definition of motivation was culturally myopic and did not account for intra-individual variations in motivated behavior. Although poor Black children may not have appeared motivated in school, they often demonstrated intense achievement motivation in athletics (Maehr, 1974a; 1978).

*Stability of Maehr's Perspective Over Time*

To summarize, Maehr's primary argument is that it was a mistake to conceive of motivation is a stable trait that some people possess in greater amounts than others. Cross-cultural research, in particular, is difficult to conduct validly if the particular values, meanings of motivation, and achievement opportunities of specific contexts are not fully considered. "The point, of course, is that, in the study of culture and achievement motivation, one dare not focus on the person to the exclusion of the context." (Maehr, 1978, p. 10)

Most of Maehr's publications regarding cultural influences on achievement motivation since his seminal work in 1974 (and even some before, cf: Rubovits & Maehr, 1973) focused on illustrating and identifying the contextual influences on achievement motivation. His basic argument regarding the importance of attending to specific situational influences and cultural definitions of motivation has remained remarkably stable (e.g., Kaplan & Maehr, 2002). For 30 years, he has continued to rely on decision-making theory as a lens through which to understand cultural differences in motivated behavior (Maehr, 1984). According to this model, all people share an internal wellspring of motivation, but where they choose to express that motivation depends largely on perceived opportunities within specific settings. These perceived opportunities are influenced by a number of factors including perceptions of competence in a domain, cultural and individual values, and messages in the environment about the definitions of success and the opportunities for people with various characteristics (e.g., gender, social class, race) to achieve in that domain. For a female college student to choose to pursue a major in mathematics, for example, she must believe herself capable, must perceive that she will not be ostracized by her friends, family, and society for pursuing a mathematics major, and must perceive that her sense of self is not at odds with the culture promoted in her mathematics classrooms or a future work environment.

Decision-making theory is based largely on cognitive factors (i.e., perceptions about affordances, values, goals, attributions). Consequently, much of Maehr's work on culture and motivation over the last three decades has focused on the variables that influence such cognitions. Early in his career, even before the publication of the *American Psychologist* article in 1974, Rubovits and Maehr (1973) conducted research examining teacher expectancies and their effects on the motivation of black and white students.

This early work on teacher expectancies was followed by a period of research examining cultural variations in the definition of achievement. For example, Maehr and Nicholls (1980) considered, among other issues, the association between achievement and affiliation motives across cultures. Whereas McClelland and others had argued that the need for achievement was often in conflict with the need for affiliation (e.g., wanting to be popular undermined the desire to achieve academically—cf. Coleman, 1961), in collectivist cultures social and achievement motives are often positively correlated. Indeed, a desire to bring honor and respect to one's family can activate the goal of succeeding academically, and this complementary relationship is readily observed in collectivist cultures like Japan.

In a later study of cross-cultural variations and similarities in the meaning of achievement, Maehr and his colleagues performed a secondary analysis of data collected across 30 cultures regarding the meaning of achievement (Fyans, Salili, Maehr, & Desai, 1983). They found that all cultures consider hard work, freedom, and success as components of achievement. However, cultures differed in whether they associated achievement with future-oriented concepts (e.g., saving money, schooling) or more immediate (lotteries) or past-oriented concepts (e.g., tradition). These data suggest that although cultures share the belief that hard work is required for achievement, the outcomes associated with achievement differ across cultures.

Following his work examining cultural variations in the definition of achievement, Maehr turned his attention to the contextual influences of motivation across different cultural groups. As Maehr (1984) developed his own theory of achievement motivation and built it around decision making and personal investment, he increasingly focused on the influence of messages in classrooms and schools regarding the purposes and definitions of success and achievement in those settings. Two book chapters from the 1980s represent this new focus well. First, Hartman and Maehr (1984) considered some of the ways that classroom organization, structure, and practices can influence the expectancies, perceptions of ability, and values of students. The purpose of the chapter was to discuss ways that motivation theory and research might relieve some of the problems associated with school desegregation. In this chapter, the authors began discussing the various components of achievement goal theory (e.g., the task and evaluation structures of the classroom, messages about the purposes of achievement). Two years later, Baden and Maehr (1986) wrote a chapter in which they discussed methods for confronting unequal academic motivation and achievement between sub-cultures of American students by altering school practices. In this chapter the authors began linking early work related to achievement goal theory to the concept of ethnic and cultural factors. For example, they discuss Ames (1984) early work on goal and reward structures and the association between these classroom variables and students' concerns about appearing more able than their peers (what Ames called "Ego goals") and attributing success and failure to academic ability rather than to effort. An emphasis on ego goals and ability attributions in the classroom will lead to race-based labeling if ability differences between students occur along racial lines (i.e., if Black students are lower achieving than white students and these differences are made salient through instructional practices).

The connection between culture and achievement goal theory that was beginning to take shape in Maehr's work in the 1980s has taken fuller form since then. For example, Kaplan and Maehr (1999) argued that the benefits of an emphasis on learning and improvement of skills (mastery goals) in classrooms and schools may hold particular benefits for African American students in majority-Caucasian schools. Later, Maehr and Yamaguchi (2001) argued that transforming the school culture toward an emphasis on mastery goals will create an environment that makes students of various cultures feel a sense of belonging and enhanced motivation. Arunkumar and Maehr (in press) extend this line of reasoning a bit further. They suggest that the boundaries that make it difficult for students of some cultural backgrounds to navigate the transitions across school, home, and peer contexts are lessened when classrooms and schools emphasize mastery goals rather than performance goals (i.e., competition among students and defining success in normative terms). The common theme in this work is that when performance goals are emphasized in classrooms and schools, differences between students in achievement levels, culture, and ethnicity become salient. In contrast, when the emphasis is placed on mastering new material and developing new competencies (i.e., mastery goals), the definition of success switches from social-comparative to intra-individual, and issues of cultural and ethnic differences take a back seat to individual development.

Over the last 30 years, Maehr's work examining the link between culture and motivation has revealed both consistency and evolution. Since his early attempt to move motivation research away from strict personality interpretations and toward a more cognitive-contextual model, Maehr remained focused on examining the ways that students' beliefs, cultural background, and situational factors combined to influence motivation and achievement. Over time, his examinations of the factors that influence motivation shifted from specific teacher beliefs to broad cultural variations and back to school- and classroom-level motivational messages. Through the changes, his belief that motivated behavior is the result of a decision-making process that is informed by culturally influenced values and affordances has remained consistent.

## CRITICAL ANALYSIS OF MAEHR'S EARLY ARGUMENTS

As described earlier, Maehr's critique of the McClelland-Atkinson model of achievement motivation theory focused on three issues:

1. the McClelland-Atkinson model conceived of motivation as a stable personality trait and underemphasized situational influences;
2. the model was disempowering to educators; and
3. the model was ethnocentric.[1]

In this section of the chapter I consider both the veracity and practical utility of Maehr's arguments.

### Argument 1: Importance of Cognitive and Contextual Factors

Thirty years of research and hundreds of studies in the social-cognitive tradition have left little doubt that students' cognitions and contextual factors influence motivated behavior. Experimental manipulations of students' beliefs about their own abilities (Schunk, 1984), the definition of achievement on the task (Dweck & Leggett, 1988; Elliot & Harackiewicz, 1996), and reasons for success and failure at the task (Weiner, 1986) all demonstrate that even subtle cues in the environment can alter students' cognitions thereby altering their motivation and performance. Correlational research has also consistently demonstrated that such cognitions as beliefs about one's abilities (Pajares, 1996), perceptions of the goal related messages in the classroom (Ames, 1992; Urdan, Midgley, & Anderman, 1998), and valuing of the work (Wigfield & Eccles, 1992) are related to student motivation and achievement.

The pertinent question here is not *whether* cognitions and contextual cues influence student motivation. Rather, the important questions to consider may be *how* and *how much* these factors influence motivation. In an article that included a response to Maehr's (1974a) criticisms, McClelland argued that social-cognitive theories of motivation only deal with the value-related attitudes of students, not their core motivational drives.

> A generation ago, deCharms, Morrison, Reitman, and McClelland (1955) demonstrated that the behavioral correlates of such a measure of achievement goals (i.e., attitudinal measures of incentive value) were quite different from the behavioral correlates of the TAT *n* Achievement variable. For instance, *n* Achievement was significantly related to better performance in an anagrams test and to better recall of the achievement content of stories, whereas *v* Achievement was not...In other words, strong achievement values affected cognitive judgments, as they should if they are tapping INs. (McClelland, 1985, p. 814).

McClelland went on to summarize empirical evidence indicating that Thematic Apperception Test (TAT) measures of achievement motivation were better at predicting long-term trends in behavior whereas "value attitude measures" were better at predicting short-term choices, attributions, and "other cognitively guided behavior." Although McClelland admitted that Maehr (1974a) was right when he argued that incentive value should be more broadly defined than simply a preference for moderate challenge to include such culturally-influenced values as opportunities for cooperation and to build social bonds, he downplayed the importance of Maehr's argument when he wrote that incentive values only predict short-term, cognitively related motivational variables. Moreover, according to McClelland (1985), values predict choices of which behaviors to engage in, but do not predict performance. "It is not yet clear that they (values) energize behavior and lead to faster learning of related activities in the ways that motives do." (p. 815)

McClelland used the distinction between values and motives to counter another of Maehr's criticisms. According to Maehr, two children may be equally motivated but choose to express their motivation in different domains, in part due to different perceived affordances of those domains. Maehr argued that McClelland would have identified the child who achieved in school to be highly achievement motivated (i.e., have high $n$ Achievement) but would have determined that the child who achieved well on the basketball court would not be high in $n$ Achievement. McClelland responded by writing that Maehr and others (e.g., Parsons & Goff, 1978) missed the point. Although he conceded that a number of cultural and contextual factors influence the value component of motivation, this does not invalidate his argument that the *energization* of motivated behavior wells from a deeper, more stable place. In short, whereas values influence the direction of motivated behavior, deep-seeded *needs* are what drive the behavior in the first place. Even if a person decides that the basketball court is the best place to express motivated behavior, some will be more energetic and motivated to win than others.

In his later writing, Maehr acknowledged that the McClelland-Atkinson model did build in a value component (Hartman & Maehr, 1984). Even in his earlier writings on the topic, Maehr (1974a) did not dismiss the idea of a personality component of motivation. Rather, he argued that decisions about which behaviors to engage in were influenced by a number of factors, including personality traits, cognitions, situational demands, and cultural values. In the end, Maehr and McClelland seemed to agree that these factors all influenced motivated behavior. The extent to which they agreed regarding the relative influence of each of these factors, however, is not entirely clear. It appears that McClelland and Atkinson continued to emphasize the importance of enduring personality traits whereas Maehr tended to focus more on the cognitive, situational, and cultural contributors to motivation (Maehr & Midgley, 1991; 1996; Maehr & Nicholls, 1980).

## Argument 2: Empowerment of Teachers

The second of Maehr's major arguments was that it is disempowering for teachers to conceive of motivation as a stable personality trait that is set relatively early in childhood. After all, if early socialization experiences with parents are the primary source of the $n$ Achievement and fear of failure, as McClelland argued, teachers have little influence over the motivation of their students. This is especially true for teachers of older children and adolescents.

But empowering teachers to enhance the motivation of their students is not as simple as merely telling them that situational factors influence motivation. Indeed, telling teachers that social-contextual factors can influence student motivation may have a number of unintended consequences. The first such consequence may be active resistance from teachers, and this resistance can be informed by several sources of information. For example, teachers can readily see that the same class assignment will be met with enthusiasm by some students and indifference or resistance by others. To many teachers, these different students' responses point to pre-existing and stable differences between students rather than the malleability of motivation. Of course, those with knowledge of motivation theory and research will note that this example does not account for a number of factors, such as students' beliefs about their abilities to complete the task, the interest or relevance of the task to different students, and the students' different goals for completing the task. But that is the point: Motivation theory and research adds a layer of complexity to teaching that is difficult for most teachers to effectively incorporate into their curriculum and pedagogy.

What is a teacher supposed to do with the knowledge that cultural factors influence the motivation of students in her classroom? Should she take a look at her students and conclude that students of different races probably have different beliefs about the value of the work in her classroom? Such stereotyped thinking would be discouraged by most motivation researchers. Instead, should the teacher use her awareness of the importance of culture to learn more about the cultural values of her students and try to design or present tasks in a manner that is consonant with these different cultural values? That would be fantastic, but would require a great deal more work for the teacher and may be very difficult to execute, especially in classrooms with students of various cultural backgrounds.

Even if we move away from the complexity of cultural variation to the seemingly less complicated world of motivation theory, the gap from theory to practice is a difficult one to bridge. For example, research has consistently demonstrated that students with higher self-efficacy are generally more motivated (i.e., exert more effort, persist longer) than are students with low self-efficacy (Bandura, 1993). The message to teachers is clear: Boost your students' self-efficacy. But how should they do this? Bandura (1986) argues that past successes on similar tasks (i.e., mastery experiences) are the strongest contributor to self-efficacy. Teachers are encouraged to provide ample opportunities for their students to experience genuine success in the classroom, and genuine success means success on moderately challenging tasks. Success on overly easy tasks does little to promote feelings of efficacy. But for teachers of students who vary in ability, providing frequent opportunities for genuine success involves developing tasks of various difficulty levels and determining what the appropriate level of challenge is for each of her students. Teachers are not particularly good at designing tasks of appropriate challenge levels for students of differing abilities, and even if they were able to there is evidence that students often resist challenging tasks (Blumenfeld, 1992). Even if teachers could design such tasks and students willingly engaged in them, the extra work required of the teacher and the stratification of students within the same classroom into different levels of academic work would prove problematic.

In addition to the complexity and increased workload, teachers may resist the idea that they can strongly influence the motivation of their students because of the psychological burden it places on them. When teachers believe that their job is primarily to clearly present information and to provide feedback to students about their progress, they can do their job effectively and still not hold themselves accountable if some students fail. But if teachers are also responsible for motivating their students, then student failure is evidence of the teachers' failure. Teaching is a profession that involves a tremendous amount of vulnerability. It is difficult not to take it personally when students skip class, doze off, or fail to take the work seriously. It may be helpful for teachers not to feel entirely responsible for the motivation of their students, for to take responsibility for motivating students requires one to take blame for failing to motivate them.

A third reason that teachers may resist feeling empowered by the knowledge that situational and contextual variables influence motivation is their awareness that their students operate in numerous contexts, and many of these contexts de-value academic achievement. In fact, many teachers readily acknowledge that contextual variables influence student motivation and use this knowledge to explain why they have *less* influence than they would like. Teachers often point to troubled home lives, unsafe neighborhoods, materialistic, get-rich-quick values promoted in popular culture media, and negative peer pressure as stronger influences than their own on their students' motivation. In short, opening up the Pandora's box of situational, contextual, and cultural influences on motivation can be a double-edged sword. While it suggests that motivation is malleable and can be influenced by the teacher, it also suggests that the myriad other contextual, cultural, and situational factors have influence as well. One cannot open the door to one situational influence without opening the door wide to all.

If one believes that cultural and contextual factors are equally, or more strongly, related to student motivation than are enduring personality traits, a troubling question arises: Which of these is easier to change? The problems of racism, poverty, and social-class division appear to be at least as resistant to change as personality. Of course, there is ample evidence of gifted and dedicated teachers overcoming these societal problems and motivating their students to achieve (e.g., Esquith, 2004; Meier, 1995). Yet these examples rarely come from motivation research. Most motivation research has not been conducted in actual classrooms, and when it has the research has rarely focused on the processes through which instructional practices influence student motivation (Urdan & Turner, 2005).

Ideally, teachers would realize that they can influence the motivation of their students and take responsibility for promoting student motivation without becoming so emotionally invested that they develop self-loathing when some of their students fail. Teachers who are able to do this can feel empowered to enhance student motivation. But we must also realize that there are powerful grounds for teachers not to adopt this perspective, and these reasons are reasonable.

### Argument 3: Ethnocentrism of Achievement Motivation Theory

When Maehr criticized the ethnocentrism of McClelland's theory in 1974, many in the fields of psychology and education were mired in a heated argument about the possible influence of genetics in racial differences in IQ scores. Jensen (1969) had published his (in)famous article five years earlier, and the psychological community of scholars was particularly sensitive to any suggestions that racial or cultural differences in psychological functioning may be explained by intra-individual factors rather than contextual factors.

Maehr was certainly correct in noting that cultural factors influence motivation, by framing the possible choices for behavior, not by developing or thwarting the development of motivation individuals possess. In this regard, Maehr's contribution to the field was immense. Yet Maehr's proposition raises difficult questions. Once we understand that life success through academic achievement is perceived as valuable and attainable for some cultures more than others, the questions that remain are "Why?" and "What can be done about it?" Scholars from a variety of fields including sociology (Coleman et al., 1966), anthropology (Ogbu, 1992), education (Delpit, 1995; Irvine, 1990) and psychology (Steele, 1992) have taken turns trying to answer these questions. But decades after Maehr presented his criticism of the McClelland-Atkinson model, and with the tailwind of 30 years of social-cognitive theory and research on motivation, it is not clear that we have made much progress in answering these two lingering questions.

In one regard, Maehr's exhortation to consider the cultural meanings of achievement has greatly helped us understand differences in motivated behavior without casting the same sort of ethnocentric judgments that once held sway. The achievement motivation definition of achievement of McClelland (1961) did appear to emphasize competition and individual accomplishment at the expense of cooperation and group goals. By noting the cultural myopia of such a definition, Maehr (1974b) helped researchers recognize that although people in other cultures may not discuss motivation in terms of competition and individual accomplishment, this does not necessarily indicate lower levels of motivation.

On the other hand, when considering variations among the sub-cultures in the United States, Maehr's argument about McClelland's ethnocentrism is somewhat less satisfying. In several of his early writings on the subject, Maehr tried to illustrate his point about cultural differences by noting that although middle class white kids may express their motivation in the classroom, poor black children may express similar levels of motivation on the basketball court. Leaving aside the question of the veracity of this statement for a moment, let us consider the implications. If Maehr was right, what does this imply for how educators should try to motivate black and white students? And are these implications for teacher behavior any more realistic than the implications of a personality theory of motivation?

The answers to these questions depend in large part on how one answers an earlier question: "Where do these differences come from?" There are several possible answers. One is that poor, black students, as members of a caste-like minority, devalue academic achievement because it is too closely associated with the values of the white majority, and to succeed in an academic environment would require a psychological (and perhaps social) distancing of one's self from the black community (Ogbu, 1992). If this explanation is true, such perceptions of poor, black students are developed over several years and become engrained as elements of the identity and personality of the individuals who hold the beliefs. These may be no easier to change than the need for achievement described by McClelland.

Others have argued that the life circumstances of the poor, which often include persistent racism, frequent exposure to violence and drugs, few academically successful role models who display the benefits of their academic success, lower-quality schools staffed by less qualified teachers and marked by more frequent teacher turnover, and, of course, the constant stress of being chronically poor, conspire to reduce academic motivation. It is undoubtedly true that shortages of human and financial capital in poor neighborhoods make the benefits of academic achievement less visible, and thereby reduce the academic motivation of many students in those neighborhoods. Unfortunately, it is also true that for most students who are poor, their poverty is a chronic, rather than a temporary, condition. So if it is the multiple factors associated with poverty that reduce student motivation, there is little reason to suspect that radical improvements in the academic motivation of most of these students are on the way.

My point here is that although I believe Maehr was right when he argued that cultural and situational factors influence motivation, it is not clear that this insight provided any easy solutions for educators working with students from underprivileged or socially marginalized groups. As a practical matter, it may make little difference to say that a student lacks the motivation to achieve in school because he is poor and does not perceive academic success as a viable behavioral option rather than to say his parents did not instill a need for achievement at an early age. In the end, both explanations point to belief systems (or needs) within the individual that are resistant to change and to sources of these belief systems (or needs) that are equally en-during. One need only to consult the data on the racial achievement gap, re-segregation of schools, and widening income gap between the wealthy and the poor in the U.S. to observe the persistence of the economic and racial inequities that perhaps give rise to some of the cultural variations in academic motivation that Maehr discussed 30 years ago.

## WHERE ARE WE NOW? CURRENT CONCEPTIONS OF CULTURAL INFLUENCES ON MOTIVATION

When Maehr (1974a, b) argued that the prevailing theory of achievement motivation was not appropriately sensitive to cultural influences, his ideas were novel. Today, considerable bodies of work exist examining cross-cultural variations in motivation and ethnic differences in motivation. Although some of this research indicates differences across cultures (e.g., Markus & Kitayama, 1991; Volet, 1997) and across cultural and ethnic sub-groups in the U.S. (e.g., Fuligni, 1997; Suarez-Orozco, 1995; Urdan, 2004), the similarities are often more striking than the differences. For example, in a review of the literature on motivation among African American students, Graham (1994) found that African American students did not have lower personal control beliefs, self-concept of ability, or valuing of academic achievement than other students.

Although cultural factors are widely acknowledged to be important contributors to academic motivation, the research to date has not revealed clear patterns of differences between cultures or ethnic groups in motivational orientations. The achievement gap that has existed between Asian American and Caucasian Americans on the one hand and African American and Latino students on the other has not been explained adequately by motivational variables. Because most of the motivation research has focused on social-cognitive variables such as values, attributions, goals, and self-efficacy, and students of different ethnicities usually differ little on these variables, current motivational theories have done little to help us understand, or ameliorate, the persistent achievement gap. It may be that the achievement gap owes more to societal inequities in income, housing, and education quality than to motivational beliefs. Or perhaps current social-cognitive theories of motivation are not quite sensitive enough to reveal the underlying motivational processes that contribute to the achievement gap.

A few years ago, in a special issue of *Educational Researcher* (2003, Volume 32), a number of articles were published on the topic of culture and education. All of the articles in the special issue, together, built an argument for the need to move beyond static conceptualizations of race, and race-based differences in learning and achievement, to a more nuanced and dynamic view of race. Global statements about the learning styles of Latino students or the motivation of African American students were of little use because of wide variation within ethnic groups and because of the individual educational histories of individual students (e.g., Gutierrez & Rogoff, 2003; Orellana & Bowman, 2003). Similarly, broad statements about the motivational differences between ethnic groups hold little explanatory power because the ethnic groups being compared are not monolithic. To be sure, culture and ethnicity are important factors in the lives of many students. But these factors must be considered in the context of other important factors (e.g., family economic status, prior achievement history in the domain, the classroom context, the interpersonal relationship between the student and the teacher, peer group affiliations, etc.) when trying to understand the motivation and achievement of individual students in specific situations.

Maehr was at the front end of a paradigm shift in motivation research. Decades of achievement motivation research that focused on internal needs and stable personality traits gave way to a slew of social-cognitive theories that took situational, cognitive, and cultural factors into account. This new approach to motivation has yielded important insights into the cultural and contextual contributors to academic motivation, and for this all of us in the field of motivation research owe Maehr an enormous debt of gratitude. Yet these insights have, for the most part, not been translated into meaningful action to reduce the inequalities either in student achievement or in access to educational opportunities. To take full advantage of the opportunities raised by Maehr's attention to sociocultural influences of motivation, researchers in the field must continue to hone our understanding of these influences and use this knowledge to promote enhanced motivation and achievement of marginalized students.

## ENDNOTE

1. A fourth criticism from Maehr was that the methods used to study achievement motivation, particularly the Thematic Apperception Test, were not valid. Although there is support for such criticism, I do not address it in this chapter because it opens up a nasty can of worms regarding survey and experimental methods employed by more cognitive theorists, and such a debate about methods is beyond the scope of this chapter.

## REFERENCES

Ames, C. A. (1984). Competitive, cooperative, and individualistic goal structures: A motivational analysis. In R. E. Ames & C. Ames, (Eds.), *Research on motivation in education*, (Vol. 1, pp. 177–207). New York: Academic Press.

Ames, C. A.(1992). Classrooms: Goals, structures, and student motivation. *Journal of Educational Psychology, 84,* 261–271.

Atkinson, J. W., & Feather, N. T. (1966). *A theory of achievement motivation.* New York: Wiley.

Baden, B., & Maehr, M. L. (1986). Confronting culture with culture: A perspective for designing schools for children of diverse sociocultural backgrounds. In R. Feldman (Ed.), *Social Psychology Applied to Education.* New York: Academic Press.

Bandura, A. (1986). *Social foundations of thought and action: A social cognitive theory.* Englewood Cliffs, NJ: Prentice Hall.

Bandura, A. (1993). Perceived self-efficacy in cognitive development and functioning. *Educational Psychologist, 28,* 117–148.

Blumenfeld, P. C. (1992). Classroom learning and motivation: Clarifying and expanding goal theory. *Journal of Educational Psychology, 84,* 272–281.

Coleman, J. S. (1961). *The adolescent society.* Glencoe, IL: Free Press.

Coleman, J. S. et al. (1966). *Equality of educational opportunity.* US Department of Health, Education, and Welfare, Washington, DC: US Government Printing Office.

Delpit, L. (1995). *Other people's children: Cultural conflict in the classroom.* New York: New Press.

Dweck, C. S., & Leggett, E. L.. (1988). A social-cognitive approach to motivation and personality. *Psychological Review, 95,* 256–273.

Elliot, A. J., & Harackiewicz, J. M. (1996). Approach and avoidance achievement goals and intrinsic motivation: A mediational analysis. *Journal of Personality and Social Psychology, 70,* 461–475.

Esquith, R. (2004). *There are no shortcuts.* New York: Random House.

Fuligni, A. J. (1997). The academic achievement of adolescents from immigrant families: The roles of family background, attitudes, and behavior. *Child Development, 68,* 261–273.

Fyans, L. J., Jr., Salili, F., Maehr, M. L., & Desai, K. (1983). A cross-cultural exploration into the meaning of achievement. *Journal of Personality and Social Psychology, 44,* 1000–1013.

Graham, S. (1994). Motivation in African Americans. *Review of Educational Research, 64,* 55–117.

Guitierrez, K. D., & Rogoff, B. (2003). Cultural ways of learning: Individual traits or repertoires of practice. *Educational Researcher, 32,* 19–25.

Hartman, A., & Maehr, M. L. (1984). In search of a remedy: Desegregation and achievement motivation. In D. E. Bartz (Ed.), *Advances in motivation and achievement, Vol. 1: School desegregation, motivation and achievement.* Greenwich, CT: JAI Press.

Irvine, J. J. (1990). *Black students and school failure.* Westport, CT: Greenwood Press.

Jensen, A. R. (1969). How much can we boost I.Q. and academic achievement? *Harvard Educational Review, 33,* 1–123.

Kaplan, A., & Maehr, M. L. (1999). Enhancing the motivation of African American students: An achievement goal theory perspective. *Journal of Negro Education, 68,* 23–41.

Kaplan, A., & Maehr, M. L. (2002). Adolescents' achievement goals: Situating motivation in sociocultural contexts. In F. Pajares & T. Urdan (Eds.), *Academic motivation of adolescents* (pp. 125–167). Greenwich, CT: Information Age.

Kumar, R., & Maehr, M. L. (accepted). Cultural diversity and student motivation: A problem for schools, a challenge for teachers. In J. L. Meece & J. Eccles (Eds.), *Handbook of schools, schooling and human development*. Hillsdale, NJ: Lawrence Erlbaum Associates Publishers.

Maehr, M. L. (1974a). Culture and achievement motivation. *American Psychologist, 29,* 887–896.

Maehr, M. L. (1978). Sociocultural origins of achievement. In D. Bar-Tal & L. Saxe (Eds.), *Social psychology of education: Theory and research.* New York: Wiley.

Maehr, M. L. (1984). Meaning and motivation: Toward a theory of personal investment. In R. Ames & C. Ames (Eds.), *Research on Motivation in Education, Vol. 1: Student Motivation* (pp. 115–144). New York: Academic Press.

Maehr, M. L., & Midgley, C. (1991). Enhancing student motivation: A school-wide approach. *Educational Psychologist, 26,* 399–427.

Maehr, M. L., & Midgley, C. (1996). *Transforming school cultures.* Boulder, CO: Westview Press.

Maehr, M. L., & Nicholls, J. G. (1980). Culture and achievement motivation: A second look. In N. Warren (Ed.), *Studies in cross-cultural psychology,* (Vol. 2, pp. 221–267). New York: Academic Press.

Maehr, M. L., & Yamaguchi, R. (2001). Cultural diversity, student motivation and achievement. In F. Salili, C. Chiu, & Y. Hong (Eds.), *Student motivation: The culture and context of learning* (pp. 121–148). New York: Kluwer Academic/Plenum.

Maehr, M.L. (1974b). *Sociocultural origins of achievement.* Monterey, CA: Brooks-Cole.

Markus, H., & Kitayama, S. (1991). Culture and the self: Implications for cognition, emotion, and motivation. *Psychological Review, 98,* 224–253.

McClelland, D. C. (1961). *The achieving society.* New York: The Free Press.

McClelland, D. C. (1985). How motives, skills, and values determine what people do. *American Psychologist, 40,* 812–825.

Meier, D. (1995). *The power of their ideas: Lessons for America from a small school in Harlem.* Boston: Beacon Press.

Mosteller, F., & Moynihan, D. (Eds.) (1972). *On equality of educational opportunity.* New York: Vintage (Random House).

Ogbu, J. (1992). Understanding cultural diversity and learning. *Educational Researcher, 21,* 5–14.

Orellana, M. F., & Bowman, P. (2003). Cultural diversity research on learning and development: Conceptual, methodological, and strategic considerations. *Educational Researcher, 32,* 26–32.

Pajares, F. (1996). Self-efficacy beliefs in achievement settings. *Review of Educational Research, 66,* 543–578.

Parsons, J. E. & Goff, S. B. (1978). Achievement motivation: a dual modality. *Educational Psychologist, 13,* 93–96.

Rubovits, P. C., & Maehr, M. L. (1973). Pygmalion black and white. *Journal of Personality and Social Psychology, 25,* 210–218.

Schunk, D. H. (1984). Enhancing self-efficacy and achievement through rewards and goals: Motivational and informational effects. *Journal of Educational Research, 78,* 29–34.

Steele, C. (1992). Race and the schooling of Black Americans. *The Atlantic Monthly, 269,* 68–78.

Suarez-Orozco, C., & Suarez-Orozco, M. M. (1995). *Transformations: Immigration, family life, and achievement motivation among Latino students.* Stanford, CA: Stanford University Press.

Urdan, T. (2004). Predictors of academic self-handicapping and achievement: Examining achievement goals, classroom goal structures, and culture. *Journal of Educational Psychology, 96,* 251–264.

Urdan, T., & Turner, J. C. (2005). Competence motivation in the classroom. In A. E. Elliot and C. Dweck (Eds.) *Handbook of Competence Motivation* (pp. 297–317). New York: Guilford.

Urdan, T., Midgley, C., & Anderman, E. (1998). The role of classroom goal structure in students' use of self-handicapping strategies. *American Educational Research Journal, 35,* 101–122.

Volet, S. (1997). Motivation within and across cultural-educational contexts: A multi-dimensional perspective. In T. Urdan (Ed.) *Advances in Motivation and Achievement, Vol. 11: The Role of Context.* Greenwich, CT: JAI Press.

Weiner, B. (1986). *An attributional theory of motivation and emotion.* New York: Springer-Verlag.

Wigfield, A., & Eccles, J. (1992). The development of achievement task values: A theoretical analysis. *Developmental Review, 12,* 265–310.

CHAPTER 12

# VITA: MARTIN L. MAEHR

*Office Address:*
Combined Program in Education
  and Psychology
The University of Michigan
1400 E School of Education
  Building
Ann Arbor, Michigan 48109-1259
Telephone: (734) 647-0627
E-mail: mlmaehr@umich.edu

*Home Address:*
15 Haverhill Court
Ann Arbor, MI 48105
Telephone: (734) 994-8904

## EDUCATION/PROFESSIONAL DEVELOPMENT

Washington University, St. Louis, MO (1955-1956)
Concordia Seminary, St. Louis, MO (B.A., 1955; M. Div., 1958)
University of Nebraska-Lincoln (M.A., 1959; Ph.D., 1960)
  Areas: Education, Psychology, Sociology
  Major Advisor: Warren R. Baller, Ph.D.

*Culture, Self, and Motivation: Essays in Honor of Martin L. Maehr*, pages 285–299
Copyright © 2009 by Information Age Publishing
All rights of reproduction in any form reserved.

National Institute of Mental Health, Special post-doctoral Research
   Fellow, Syracuse University (1965–1966)
Fellow, American Psychological Association
Fellow, American Psychological Society
Arnold O. Beckman Research Award, University of Illinois, 1984
Research Fellowship, Katholieke Universiteit Leuven, Belgium, 1995
Pew Foundation Senior Research Fellow, The Erasmus Institute, Notre
   Dame University, South Bend, Indiana, 2002–2003

## PROFESSIONAL POSITIONS HELD

| | |
|---|---|
| 2005–present | Emeritus Professor of Education and Psychology |
| 2007–present | PI/CO-PI NSF Motivation Assessment Program |
| 2007–continuing | Co-PI A Study of Middle Eastern Students in Public Schools in the U.S. (A Project funded by the Spencer Foundation) |
| 1988–2005 | Professor of Education and Psychology, The University of Michigan, Ann Arbor |
| 1989–1993 | Senior Investigator, The National Center for School Leadership |
| 1989–1992 | Director, Combined Program in Education and Psychology, The University of Michigan, Ann Arbor |
| 1989–1991 | Co-Director, The National Center for School Leadership |
| 1975–1988 | Professor of Educational Psychology, University of Illinois at Urbana-Champaign |
| 1986–1988 | Director and Research Professor, Institute for Research on Human Development; Affiliate, Rehabilitation Education Center |
| 1980 (January–July) | Acting Director, Office of Gerontology and Aging Studies |
| 1977–1986 | Research Professor, Associate Director, and Director, Institute for Child Behavior and Development, University of Illinois at Urbana-Champaign; |
| 1975–1977 | Associate Dean for Graduate and International Programs; College of Education, University of Illinois at Urbana-Champaign |

| 1967–1975 | Associate Professor, University of Illinois, Urbana-Champaign; |
|---|---|
| 1970–1975 | Chairman, Department of Educational Psychology |
| 1960–1967 | Assistant-Associate Professor, Concordia Senior College, Ft. Wayne, Indiana |
| 1959–1960 | Counselor, University of Nebraska-Lincoln, Counseling Service |

## GUEST LECTURESHIPS/PROFESSORSHIPS/MAJOR ADDRESSES (SELECTED LISTING)

Toledo University (Summer 1962)
Valparaiso University (Part-time 1963–64)
University of Nebraska (Summer 1964)
Purdue University-Ft. Wayne Regional Campus
Concordia Seminary-St. Louis (July 1969)
Visiting Professor, Faculty of Education, University of Tehran, Tehran, Iran, 1973–1974
Visiting Professor, University of Queensland, Brisbane, Australia, September 1981; February–April 1983
Visiting Professor, Newcomb College (Tulane University), February 1986
Distinguished Visiting Professor, Chico State University, March 1987
Guest lectureship, University of Chicago, Management Development Seminar, Summer, 1989
Visiting Lectureship at selected Universities, in Taiwan under sponsorship of National Research Council, March 1993
Visiting Professor, Peking University, Summer 1994
Visiting Professor, Multiple Colleges and Universities in Norway, Spring/ Summer 1997
Visiting Lecturer, China Academy of Science, Beijing, 1994, 1998
Keynote Address and selected seminars, National Conference on Education, Malaysia, 1996
Invited Address, North American Society for Psychology of Sport and Physical Activity, Florida, June 1999
Keynote Address (and related talks), International Conference on Motivation, Leuven, Belgium, EARLI-WATM, May 2001
Fellow, Self-concept Enhancement and Learning Facilitation Research Centre (SELF), University of Western Sydney, Australia, 2002
Invitational Conference, Social Inequalities, University of Michigan, September, 2002

Speaker, Northern Illinois University, March, 2003

Keynote Address, Self Conference, Max Planck University, Berlin,
Germany, July 2004

Invited Lecture, Diamond Anniversary Lecture Series, University of
Oklahoma, Norman, Oklahoma, February 2005

Invited Lecture, Leuven University, Belgium, October 2005

Visiting Scholar, Ben Gurion University, Israel, 2006

## CONSULTANT (SELECTED LISTING)

Fort Wayne State School

United States Office of Education

Illinois State Board of Education

Faculty of Education, University of Tehran, Tehran, Iran

Consortium of Schools and State of Michigan (School Desegregation
Plans and Litigation)

Norfolk, Virginia Public Schools (School Desegregation Plans and
Litigation)

State of Virginia-Office of the Attorney General (School Desegregation
Plans and Litigation)

State of New Jersey-Office of the Attorney General (School Organization
Financing Plans and Litigation)

Consortium of Schools and State of Wisconsin (School Desegregation
Plans and Litigation)

Metritech Inc., Champaign, Illinois (Test Development and Research)

Selection Research Inc., Lincoln, Nebraska (Personnel Selection,
Organization Design, Assessment)

JAI Press, Inc., Greenwich, Connecticut (Consulting Editor, Behavioral
Science and Education Series)

SUNY Press, Albany, New York (Consulting Editor, Motivation and
Achievement in Education Series)

Life-long Learning Systems, Inc.

University of Illinois (Urbana-Champaign), Home and School
Cooperation in Social and Motivational Development Project

## JOURNAL ARTICLES AND BOOK CHAPTERS[1]

Maehr, M.L. and B. Ammon, B. (Submitted/in Revision) Employing motivation
theory in the design and carrying out of instruction.

---

[1]    *Articles/chapters that have been republished at the request of editors, sometimes with adaptations. **Invited chapters/papers

Zusho, A., & Maehr, M. L. (In press) Achievement Goal Theory: The past, present and the future. In K. Wentzel & A. Wigfield, (Eds.), *Handbook of motivation at school.* NY: Erlbaum.

Kumar. R., & Maehr, M. L. (In press). Cultural interpretations of achievement motivation: A situated perspective. In F. Salili & R. Hoosain (Eds.), *Culture, motivation, and learning: A multicultural perspective.* Greenwich, CT: Information Age.

Kumar, R., & Maehr, M. L. (In press). Cultural diversity and student motivation: A problem for schools, a challenge for teachers. In J. L. Meece & J. Eccles (Eds.), *Schools, schooling and human development.* Hillsdale, NJ: Erlbaum.

Kaplan, A., & Maehr, M. L. (2007). The contributions and prospects of goal orientation theory. *Educational Psychology Review, 19,* 141–184.

Maehr, M. L. (2005). Paul Pintrich: A once and continuing influence. *Educational Psychologist, 40,* 129–133.

Maehr, M. L., & Simmonds, P. (2004) Achievement motivation: It may be all about self after all. In Marsh, H. (Ed.), *Proceedings of the SELF conference.* Berlin, Germany: Max Planck Institute and Sydney, Australia: Self Research Centre, University of Western Sydney.

Yamaguchi, R., & Maehr, M. L. (2004). Children's emergent leadership: The relationships with group characteristics and outcomes. *Small Group Research, 35,* 388–406

Maehr, M. L. (2004). The meaning that religion offers—and the motivation that may result. In W. R. Miller & H. D. Delaney (Eds.), *Human nature, motivation and change: Judeo-Christian perspectives on psychology.* American Psychological Association.

Maehr, M. L., & McInerney, D. M. (2004). Motivation as personal investment. In D. M. McInerney & S. Van Etten (Eds.), *Research on sociocultural influences on motivation and learning. Big theories revisited* (Vol. 4). Greenwich, CT: Information Age.

McInerney, D. M., Maehr, M. L., & Dowson, M. (2004) Motivation and Culture. In *Encyclopedia of applied psychology* (Vol. 2). Elsevier Press.

Kaplan, A., & Maehr, M. L. (2002). Adolescents' achievement goals: Situating motivation in sociocultural contexts. In F. Pajares & T. Urdan (Eds.), *Academic motivation of adolescents* (pp. 125–167). Greenwich, CT: Information Age.

**Maehr, M. L., Pintrich, P. R., & Linnenbrink, E. A. (2002/2007). Motivation and achievement. In R. Colwell & C. Richardson (Eds.), *The new handbook of research on music teaching and learning* (pp. 348–372). New York: Oxford University Press.

Maehr, M. L. (2001). Goal theory is *not* dead—not yet, anyway: A reflection on the special issue. *Educational Psychology Review, 13,* 177–185.

Maehr, M. L., & Yamaguchi, R. (2001). Cultural diversity, student motivation and achievement. In F. Salili, C. Chiu, & Y. Hong (Eds.), *Student motivation: The culture and context of learning* (pp. 121–148). New York: Kluwer Academic/Plenum.

Treasure, D. C., Duda, J. L., Hall, H. K., Roberts, G. C., Ames, C., & Maehr, M. L. (2001). Clarifying misconceptions and misrepresentations in achievement goal research in sport: A response to Harwood, Hardy, and Swain. *Journal of Sport & Exercise Psychology, 23,* 317–329.

Kaplan, A., & Maehr, M. L. (1999a). Achievement goals and student well being. *Contemporary Educational Psychology, 24,* 330–358.

Kaplan, A., & Maehr, M. L. (1999b). Enhancing the motivation of African American students: An achievement goal theory perspective. *Journal of Negro Education, 68,* 23–41.

Maehr, M. L., & Midgley, C. (1999). Creating optimum environments for students of diverse sociocultural backgrounds. In J. Block, S. T. Everson, & T. R. Guskey (Eds.), *Comprehensive school reform: A program perspective* (pp. 355–375). Dubuque, IA: Kendall/Hunt.

Midgley, C., & Maehr, M. L. (1999). Using motivational theory to guide school reform. In A. J. Reynolds, H. J. Walberg, & R. P. Weissberg (Eds.), *Promoting positive outcomes: Issues in children's and families' lives* (pp. 129–159). Washington D.C.: CWLA Press/Child Welfare League of America.

Anderman, E., Maehr, M. L., & Midgley, C. (1999). Declining motivation after the transition to middle school: Schools can make a difference. *Journal of Research and Development in Education, 32,* 131–147.

Maehr, M. L., Shi, K., Kaplan, A., & Wang, P. (1999). Culture, motivation and achievement: Toward meeting the new challenge. *Asia Pacific Journal of Education, 19,* 15–29.

Anderman, E. & Maehr, M. L. (1994). Motivation and schooling in the middle grades. *Review of Educational Research, 64,* 287–309. Republished in Hittleman, D. R., & Simon, A. J. (1997). *Interpreting educational research: An introduction for consumers of research.*. Upper Saddle River, NJ: Merrill.

Midgley, C., Kaplan, A., Middleton, M., Maehr, M. L., Urdan, T., Hicks Anderman, L., Anderman, A., & Roeser, R. (1998). The development and validation of scales assessing students' achievement goal orientations. *Contemporary Educational Psychology, 23,* 113–131.

Maehr, M. L., & Meyer, H. (1997). Understanding motivation and schooling: Where we've been, where we are, where we need to go. *Educational Psychology Review, 9,* 371–409.

Kaplan, A., & Maehr, M. L. (1997). School cultures. In Walberg, H. J., & Haertel, G. D. (Eds.), *Educational Psychology: Effective Practices and Policies.* NSSE's Series on Contemporary Issues. Berkeley, CA: McCutchan.

Maehr, M. L., & Maehr, J. (1996). Schools aren't what they used to be: They never were. *Educational Researcher, 25,* 21–24.

Leung, J. J., Maehr, M. L., & Harnisch, D. L. (1996). Some gender differences in academic motivational orientations among secondary school students. *Educational Research Quarterly, 20,* 17–32.

Urdan, T. C., & Maehr, M. L. (1995). Beyond a two-goal theory of motivation and achievement: A case for social goals. *Review of Educational Research, 65,* 213–243.

Anderman, E., & Maehr, M. L. (1994). Motivation and schooling in the middle grades. *Review of Educational Research, 64,* 287–309.

*Maehr, M. L., & Midgley, C. (1994). Enhancing students' motivation: A school-wide approach. In H. F. Clarizio, W. A. Mehrens, & W. G. Hapkiewicz (Eds.), *Contemporary issues in educational psychology* (6th Ed., pp. 334–341). New York: McGraw-Hill.

\*\*Maehr, M. L., & Anderman, E. (1993). Reinventing schools for early adolescents. *The Elementary School Journal, 93,* 593–610.

\*\*Maehr, M. L., & Buck, R. (1993). Transforming school culture. In H. Walberg and M. Sashkin (Eds.), *Educational leadership and school culture: Current research and practice* (pp. 40–57). Berkeley, CA: McCutchan.

Maehr, M. L., & Parker, S. (1993). A tale of two schools—and the primary task of leadership. *Phi Delta Kappan, 75,* 233–239.

Smith, J., Maehr, M. L., & Midgley, C. (1992). Relationship between personal and contextual characteristics and principals' administrative behaviors. *Journal of Educational Research, 86,* 111–119.

Maehr, M. L., Midgley, C., & Urdan, T. (1992). School leader as motivator. *Educational Administration Quarterly, 18,* 412–431.

Shwalb, D. W., Shwalb, B. J., Harnisch, D. L., Maehr, M. L., & Akabane, K. (1992). Personal investment in Japan and the USA: A study of worker motivation. *International Journal of Intercultural Relations, 16,* 107–123.

Maehr, M. L. (1991). The "psychological environment" of the school: A focus for school leadership. In P. Thurston & P. Zodhiatas (Eds.), *Advances in Educational Administration* (Vol. 2). Greenwich, CT: JAI Press.

Maehr, M. L. (1991). Environments affect teachers and students. *Instructional Leader, 4,* 8–9.

Maehr, M. L., & Midgley, C. (1991). Enhancing student motivation: A school-wide approach. *Educational Psychologist, 26,* 399–427.

Farmer, N., Vispoel, W., & Maehr, M. L. (1991). Achievement contexts: Effects on achievement values and causal attributions. *Journal of Educational Research, 85,* 26–38.

Maehr, M. L. (1989). Thoughts about motivation. In C. Ames & R. Ames (Eds.), *Research on Motivation in Education* (Vol. 3). New York: Academic Press.

Maehr, M. L. (1989). Building job commitment among employees. In R. Rubin (Ed.), *Critical issues in library personnel management.* Urbana-Champaign, IL: Graduate School of Library and Information Science.

Maehr, M. L., & Fyans, L. J., Jr. (1989). School culture, motivation and achievement. In M. L. Maehr & C. Ames (Eds.), *Advances in Motivation and Achievement, Vol. 6: Motivation Enhancing Environments,* Greenwich, CT: JAI Press.

Maehr, M. L. (1987). Managing organizational culture to enhance motivation. In M. L. Maehr & D. A. Kleiber (Eds.), *Advances in Motivation and Achievement, Vol. 5: Enhancing Motivation.* Greenwich, CT: JAI Press.

Maehr, M. L., & Archer, J. (1987). Motivational factors in school achievement. In L. Katz (Ed.), *Current Topics in Early Childhood Education.* Norwood, NJ: Ablex.

Baden, B., & Maehr, M. L. (1986). Confronting culture with culture: A perspective for designing schools for children of diverse sociocultural backgrounds. In R. Feldman (Ed.), *Social Psychology Applied to Education.* New York: Academic Press. (Republished in 1990.)

Spink, K. S., & Maehr, M. L. (1986). Contingent and non-contingent conditions, task meaning and continuing motivation. *Australian Journal of Science and Medicine in Sport, 18,* 22–26.

Maehr, M. L. (1984). Meaning and motivation: Toward a theory of personal investment. In R. Ames & C. Ames (Eds.), *Research on Motivation in Education, Vol. 1: Student Motivation* (pp. 115–144). New York: Academic Press.

Maehr, M. L., Hartman, A., & Bartz, D. E. (1984). Metropolitan solutions to desegregation problems: The social psychological harm of an administrative remedy. In D. E. Bartz & M. L. Maehr (Eds.), *Advances in Motivation and Achievement, Vol. 1: School Desegregation, Motivation and Achievement.* Greenwich CT: JAI Press.

Hartman, A., & Maehr, M. L. (1984). In search of a remedy: Desegregation and achievement motivation. In D. E. Bartz (Ed.), *Advances in Motivation and Achievement, Vol. 1: School Desegregation, Motivation and Achievement.* Greenwich, CT: JAI Press.

Steinkamp, M., & Maehr, M. L. (1984). Gender differences in motivational orientations toward achievement in school sciences: A quantitative synthesis. *American Educational Research Journal, 21,* 39–59.

Maehr, M. L. (1983). *The development of continuing interests in music: Motivation and creativity.* (Documentary report of the Ann Arbor Symposium on the applications of psychology to the teaching and learning of music: Session III). Reston, VA: Music Educators National Conference.

Maehr, M. L. (1983). On doing well in science: Why Johnny no longer excels—Why Sarah never did. In S. Paris (Ed.), *Learning and motivation in the classroom.* Hillsdale, NJ: Lawrence Erlbaum.

Willig, A., Harnisch, D., Hill, K. T., & Maehr, M. L. (1983). Sociocultural and educational correlates of success-failure attributions and evaluation anxiety in the school setting. *American Educational Research Journal, 20,* 385–410.

Fyans, L. J., Jr., Salili, F., Maehr, M. L., & Desai, K. (1983). A cross-cultural exploration into the meaning of achievement. *Journal of Personality and Social Psychology, 44,* 1000–1013.

Steinkamp, M., & Maehr, M. L. (1983). Affect, ability and science achievement: A quantitative synthesis of correlational research. *Review of Educational Research, 53,* 369–396.

Fyans, L. J., Jr., & Maehr, M. L. (1982). A comparison of sex differences in career and achievement motivation in Iran and the US. *International Journal of Intercultural Relations, 6,* 355–367.

Maehr, M. L., & Willig, A. C. (1982). Expecting too much or too little: Student freedom and responsibility in the classroom. In H. Walberg & R. Luckie (Eds.), *Improving Educational Productivity: The Research Basis of School Standards.* Chicago: NSSE Series in Contemporary Issues in Education.

Fyans, L. J., Jr., Kremer, B., Salili, F., & Maehr, M. L. (1981). The effects of evaluation conditions on "Continuing Motivation": A study of the cultural, personological and situational antecedents of a motivational pattern. *International Journal of Intercultural Relations, 5,* 1–22.

Maehr, M. L., & Kleiber, D. A. (1981). The graying of achievement motivation. *American Psychologist, 36,* 787–799.

Salili, F., Maehr, M. L., & Fyans, L. J., Jr. (1981). Evaluating morality and achievement: A study of the interaction of social, cultural and developmental trends. *International Journal of Intercultural Relations, 5,* 147–163.

*Fyans, L. J., Jr., & Maehr, M. L. (1980). Attributional style, task selection and achievement. In L. J. Fyans, Jr. (Ed.), *Achievement motivation*. New York: Plenum Press.

Maehr, M. L., & Kleiber, D. (1980). The graying of America: Implications for achievement motivation theory and research. In L. J. Fyans, Jr. (Ed.), *Achievement motivation*. New York: Plenum Press.

Maehr, M. L., & Nicholls, J. (1980). Culture and achievement motivation: A second look. In N. Warren (Ed.), *Studies in Cross-Cultural Psychology* (Vol. 3, pp. 221–267). New York: Academic Press.

*Rubovits, P. C., & Maehr, M. L. (1980). Pygmalion black and white. In M. Bloom (Ed.), *Life Span Development*. New York: Macmillan.

*Rubovits, P. C., & Maehr, M. L. (1980). Pygmalion black and white. In R. D. Parke & E. M. Heatherington (Eds.), *Child Psychology: Contemporary Readings* (2nd Ed.). New York: McGraw-Hill.

Maehr, M. L. (1978). Sociocultural origins of achievement. In D. Bar-Tal & L. Saxe (Eds.), *Social Psychology of Education: Theory and Research*. New York: Wiley.

Maehr, M. L., & Lysy, A. (1978). Motivating students of diverse sociocultural backgrounds to achieve. *International Journal of Intercultural Relations, 2*, 38–69.

Fyans, L. J., Jr., & Maehr, M. L. (1978). Attributional style, task selection and achievement. *Journal of Educational Psychology, 71*, 499–507.

Maehr, M. L. (1977). Turning the fun of school into the drudgery of work: The negative effects of certain grading practices on motivation. *UCLA Educator, 19*, 10–14.

Maehr, M. L. (1977). Motivation and the use of awards. *Interaction, 18*, 4–7.

Sorensen, R. L., & Maehr, M. L. (1977). A comparison of achieving orientations of preschool and school-age children. *Child Study Journal, 7*, 7–16.

Maehr, M. L. (1976). Continuing motivation: An analysis of a seldom considered educational outcome. *Review of Educational Research, 46*, 443–462.

Maehr, M. L., & Haas, H. I. (1976). Physical self-test. In O. G. Johnson & J. W. Bommarito (Eds.), *Tests and Measurements in Child Development: A Handbook*. San Francisco: Jossey-Bass, Inc.

Maehr, J. M., & Maehr, M. L. (1976). . . . and throw away the box of gold stars. *Lutheran Education, 111*, 242–249.

*Rubovits, P. C., & Maehr, M. L. (1976). Pygmalion black and white. In N. Kalt, & S. Zahlkind (Eds.), *Urban Problems: A Psychological Approach*. New York: Oxford University Press.

Salili, F., Maehr, M. L., & Gillmore, G. (1976). Achievement and morality: A cross-cultural analysis of causal attribution and evaluation. *Journal of Personality and Social Psychology, 33*, 327–337.

Salili, F., Maehr, M. L., Sorensen, R. L., & Fyans, L. J., Jr. (1976). A further consideration of the effects of evaluation on motivation. *American Educational Research Journal, 13*, 85–102.

Sorensen, R. L., & Maehr, M. L. (1976). Toward the experimental analysis of "continuing motivation." *The Journal of Educational Research, 69*, 319–322.

Rubovits, P. C., & Maehr, M. L. (1975). Teacher expectations: A special problem for black children with white teachers? In M. L. Maehr & W. M. Stallings (Eds.), *Culture, child and school*. Monterey, CA: Brooks/Cole.

Maehr, M. L. (1974). Toward a framework for the cross-cultural study of achievement motivation: McClelland considered and redirected. In M. G. Wade & R. M. Martens (Eds.), *Psychology of motor behavior and sport. Proceedings of the Annual Conference of the North American Society for the Psychology of Sport and Physical Activity,* Urbana, IL: Human Kinetics Publishers, 146–163.

Maehr, M. L. (1974). Culture and achievement motivation. *American Psychologist, 29,* 887–896.

Maehr, M. L. (1973). Experience-based education. *Journal of the Faculty of Education-University of Tehran, 3,* 1–14.

*Maehr, M. L., & Sjogren, D. (1973). Atkinson's theory of achievement motivation: First step toward a theory of academic motivation? In H. Thornburg (Ed.), *Readings in Educational Psychology.* Monterey, CA: Brooks/Cole.

*Rubovits, P. C., & Maehr, M. L. (1973). Pygmalion black and white. In F. Rebelsky & L. Dorman (Eds.), *Child Development and Behavior.* New York: Alfred A. Knopf.

Rubovits, P. C., & Maehr, M. L. (1973). Pygmalion black and white. *Journal of Personality and Social Psychology, 25,* 210–218.

Maehr, M. L., & Stallings, W. M. (1972). Freedom from external evaluation. *Child Development, 43,* 177–185.

Maehr, M. L., & Sjogren, D. (1971). Atkinson's theory of achievement motivation: First step toward a theory of academic motivation? *Review of Educational Research, 41,* 143–161.

*Ludwig, D. J., & Maehr, M. L. (1971). Changes in self-concept and stated behavioral preferences. In J. P. Hill & J. Shelton (Eds.), *Readings in adolescent development and behavior.* Englewood Cliffs, NJ: Prentice-Hall.

Rubovits, P. C., & Maehr, M. L. (1971). Pygmalion analyzed: Toward an explanation of the Rosenthal-Jacobson findings. *Journal of Personality and Social Psychology, 19,* 197–203.

**Maehr, M. L. (1970). First Communion and Confirmation in the Lutheran Church: Some psychological and educational considerations. *Lutheran Quarterly, 22,* 111–120.

Stuempfig, D. W., & Maehr, M. L. (1970). Persistence as a function of conceptual structure and quality of feedback. *Child Development, 41,* 1183–1190.

Maehr, M. L. (1969). Self-concept, challenge and achievement. *Lutheran Education, 105,* 50–57.

Maehr, M. L. (1969). First communion and confirmation in the Lutheran church: Some psychological and educational considerations. *Issues in Christian Education, 5–9.*

**Maehr, M. L. (1969). The construct of self in contemporary psychological theory. *The Lutheran Scholar, 26,* 2–16.

Stallings, W. M., Wolff, J. L., & Maehr, M. L. (1969). Fear of failure and the pass-fail grading option. *The Journal of Experimental Education, 38,* 87–91.

*Maehr, M. L., Mensing, J., & Nafzger, S. (1969). Concept of self and the reaction of others. In D. G. Dean (Ed.), *Dynamic Social Psychology.* New York: Random House.

*Maehr, M. L. (1968). Some limitations of the application of reinforcement theory to education. *School and Society, 96,* 108–110.

Maehr, M. L., & Videbeck, R. (1968). Predisposition to risk and persistence under varying reinforcement-success schedules. *Journal of Personality and Social Psychology, 9,* 96–100.

Maehr, M. L. (1968). Some limitations of the application of reinforcement theory to education. *The Education Digest, 34,* 23–25.

Ludwig, D. J., & Maehr, M. L. (1967). Changes in self-concept and stated behavioral preferences. *Child Development, 38,* 452–467.

Haas, H. I., & Maehr, M. L. (1965). Two experiments on the concept of self and the reaction of others. *Journal of Personality and Social Psychology, 1,* 100–105.

Maehr, M. L. (1964). Programmed learning and the role of the teacher. *Journal of Educational Research, 57,* 554–556.

Maehr, M. L., & Stake, R. E. (1962). The value patterns of men who voluntarily quit seminary training. *Personnel and Guidance Journal, 40,* 537–540.

Maehr, M. L., Mensing, J., & Nafzger, S. (1962). Concept of self and the reaction of others. *Sociometry, 25,* 353–357.

Maehr, M. L. (1962). The return of the Psyche to psychology. *Lutheran Scholar, 19,* 1–10.

Maehr, M. L. (1960). *The effect of food deprivation in binocular conflict.* Unpublished doctoral dissertation, University of Nebraska.

Maehr, M. L. (1959). *The value patterns of persisting and non-persisting seminary students.* Unpublished M.A. thesis, University of Nebraska.

## SELECTED CONFERENCE PRESENTATIONS AND LISTING OF UNPUBLISHED PAPERS

*Enhancing Human Development: An Emerging Theoretical Perspective.* Invited address. Taiwan National University, Taipei, Taiwan, March, 1993.

*Enhancing Student Motivation for Learning.* Invited address. National Kaohsiung Normal University, March, 1993.

*Transforming School Culture to Enhance Motivation.* Paper presented at the annual meeting of the American Educational Research Association, San Francisco, April, 1992.

*A Theory-Based Approach to Restructuring Middle Level Schools.* Paper presented at the annual meeting of the American Educational Research Association, Chicago, April, 1991. (With Carol Midgley).

*Changing the Schools: A Word to School Leaders about Enhancing Student Investment in Learning.* Paper presented at the annual meeting of the American Educational Research Association, Chicago, April, 1991.

*Restructuring the School Environment to Enhance Student Motivation and Learning.* Paper presented at the annual meeting of the American Educational Research Association, Chicago, April, 1991.

*Leadership and Culture: Quantitative Research Directions and Results.* Paper presented at the annual meeting of the American Educational Research Association, Boston, April, 1990.

*School "Culture," Motivation and Achievement.* Paper presented at the annual meeting of the American Educational Research Association, Boston, April, 1990.

*It's Not What You Know, But Also What You Want to Know that Counts.* Invited address, National Association of Research on Science Teaching, San Francisco, April, 1989.

*The Role of Organizational Goals in Enhancing Motivation.* Paper presented at the annual meeting of the American Educational Research Association, Washington, April, 1987.

*Leadership and Motivation.* Paper presented to the annual Phi Delta Kappa Research Symposium, Northwestern University, Evanston, IL, March, 1987.

*Social Psychological Perspectives on Management and Governance.* Paper presented at the annual meeting of the American Educational Research Association, Washington, April, 1987.

*Building Job Commitment Among Employees.* Keynote address, 19th Allerton Institute, Library Personnel Management, November, 1987.

*Setting the Organization's Mission: Problems and Possibilities for Alternative Leaders.* Paper presented at American Psychological Association Symposium, Los Angeles, August, 1985.

*Personal Investment: Theory Assessment and Application.* Paper presented at annual meeting of the American Educational Research Association, Montreal, April, 1983. (With L. Braskamp).

*The Development of Continuing Interest in Music.* Invited address. National Symposium on the Application of Psychology to the Teaching and Learning of Music, Ann Arbor, MI, August 2–6, 1982.

*Motivational Factors in School Achievement.* Paper commissioned by the National Commission on Excellence in Education (Department of Education, NIE), November, 1982.

*On doing well in science: Why Johnny no longer excels: Why Sarah never did.* Invited presentation. University of Michigan Summer Institute on Learning and Motivation in the Classroom, Ann Arbor, MI, June, 1981.

*Culture and achievement motivation: Beyond Weber and McClelland.* Paper presented at the annual meeting of the American Educational Research Association, Boston, April, 1980.

*Cultural differences do not have to mean motivational inequality.* Paper presented at the annual meeting of the American Educational Research Association, Boston, April, 1980.

*Exploring the subjective meaning of achievement.* Invited address, Canadian Society for Psychomotor Learning and Sport Psychology, Victoria, B.C., October, 1980.

*Attribution and values for personal success, failures and future goals.* (with H. S. Farmer & G. Rooney.) Department of Educational Psychology, University of Illinois, U-C, 1980.

*Student expectations, rights, and privileges.* Paper prepared for the State of Georgia, Department of Education, relative to the development of Standards for Public Schools of Georgia, September, 1979.

*Theoretical overview of the IOE/UIUC project on motivation and behavior.* Paper presented at the annual meeting of the American Educational Research Association, San Francisco, April, 1979.

*Sociocultural and motivational considerations in the assessment of educational achievement: A theoretical overview.* Paper presented at the annual meeting of the American Psychological Association, New York, September, 1979.

*Social, cultural, and contextual influences on achievement motivation behavior.* Paper presented at the annual meeting of the American Educational Research Association, Toronto, March, 1978.

*Expectations in the classroom: Status effects.* Discussant's comments in a symposium at the meeting of the American Psychological Association, Chicago, September, 1975.

*Toward culture-based educational development.* A programmatic statement for intercultural work, 1973. (With various members of the Committee on Culture and Education.)

*An evaluation of the Reading-Review-Award Process employed in rating and recommending EPD Proposals.* Final Report to the Consortium of Professional Associations (CONPASS), 1969. (With J. T. Hastings)

*Competence revisited.* Paper presented at the meeting of the American Educational Research Association, New York, February, 1967.

*The influence of need on binocular resolution and size judgment.* Research report pursuant to Contract M-3599(a), USPHS and the University of Nebraska, 1960. (With R. E. Stake)

## BOOKS

Urdan, T., Karabenick, S., & Maehr, M. L. (Eds.) (2007). *Advances in motivation and achievement: Volume 15.* Oxford, UK: Elsevier Press.

Maehr, M.L., & Karabenick, S.(Eds.) (2005) *Advances in motivation and achievement: Vol. 14, Religion and Motivation.* Oxford, UK: Elsevier Press.

Pintrich, P. R., & Maehr, M. L. (Eds.). (2004). *Advances in motivation and achievement: Vol. 13. Motivating students, improving schools: The legacy of Carol Midgley.* Oxford, UK: JAI, An Imprint of Elsevier Science.

Pintrich, P. R., & Maehr, M. L. (Eds.). (2002). *Advances in motivation and achievement: Vol. 12. New directions in measures and methods.* Oxford, UK: JAI, An Imprint of Elsevier Science.

Urdan, T., Maehr, M. L., & Pintrich, P. R. (Eds.). (1999). *Advances in motivation and achievement: Vol. 11. The role of context in motivational processes.* Greenwich, CT: JAI.

Maehr, M. L., & Pintrich, P. R. (Eds.). (1997). *Advances in motivation and achievement: Vol. 10. Current directions in motivation research.* Greenwich, CT: JAI Press.

Maehr, M. L., & Midgley, C. (1996). *Transforming School Cultures.* Boulder: Westview Press/Harper& Collins.

Maehr, M. L., & Pintrich, P. R. (Eds.). (1995). *Advances in motivation and achievement: Vol. 9. Motivation and culture.* Greenwich, CT: JAI Press.

Maehr, M. L., & Pintrich, P. R. (Eds.). (1993). *Advances in motivation and achievement: Vol. 8. Motivation and adolescent development.* Greenwich, CT: JAI Press.

Maehr, M. L., & Pintrich, P. R. (Eds.). (1991). *Advances in motivation and achievement: Vol. 7. Goals and self-regulation.* Greenwich, CT: JAI Press.

Maehr, M. L., & Ames, C. A. (Eds.). (1989). *Motivation Enhancing Environments* (Vol. 6).

Maehr, M. L., & Kleiber, D. (Eds.). (1987). *Enhancing Motivation and Achievement,* (Vol. 5).

Maehr, M. L., & Braskamp, L. (1986). *The Motivation Factor: A Theory of Personal Investment.* Lexington, MA: D. C. Heath.

Kleiber, D., & Maehr, M. L. (Eds.). (1985). *Motivation and Adult Development* (Vol. 4).

Bartz, D. E., & Maehr, M. L. (Eds.). (1984). *School Desegregation, Motivation and Achievement* (Vol. 1).

Nicholls, J. & Maehr, M. L. (Eds.). (1984). *Development of Achievement Motivation,* (Vol. 3).

Steinkamp, M., & Maehr, M. L. (Eds.). (1984). *Women in Science* (Vol. 2).

Maehr, M. L., & Maehr, J. M. (1980). *Being a Parent in Today's World.* St. Louis: Concordia.

Maehr, M. L., & Stallings, W. M. (Eds.). (1975). *Culture, Child and School.* Monterey, CA: Brooks/Cole.

Maehr, M. L. (1974). *Sociocultural Origins of Achievement.* Monterey, CA: Brooks/Cole.

Maehr, M. L. (Ser. Ed.). *Advances in Motivation and Achievement.* Greenwich, CT: JAI Press.

## BOOK REVIEWS (SELECTED LISTING)

Maehr, M. L. (1988). *The school achievement of minority children: New perspectives* (U. Neisser, Ed.). *Contemporary Psychology, 33,* 229–230.

Maehr, M. L. (1979). *Success and understanding* (Jean-Piaget). *Journal of Educational Research, 72,* 178.

Maehr, M. L. (1978). *Education, values, and society* (John Raven). *Journal of Curriculum Studies, 10,* 277–278.

Maehr, M. L. (1976). Cross-cultural perspectives on learning (R. W. Brislin, S. Bochner, & W. J. Lonner, Eds.). *Journal of Cross-Cultural Psychology, 7,* 247–250.

Maehr, M. L. (1975). *Motivation and achievement* (J. W. Atkinson, & J. O. Raynor). *Educational and Psychological Measurement, 35,* 201–204.

Maehr, M. L. (1971). *The culture of childhood* (Mary Goodman). *Young Children, 26,* 191–192.

## TESTS

Midgley, C., Maehr, M. L., Hruda, L. Z., Anderman, E., Anderman, L., Freeman, K. E., Gheen, M., Kaplan, A., Kumar, R., Middleton, M. J., Nelson, J., Roeser, R., & Urdan, T. (2000). *Manual for the patterns of adaptive learning scales (PALS).* University of Michigan, Ann Arbor, MI.

Maehr, M. L., & Ames, R. (1988). *Instructional Leadership Inventory.* Champaign, IL: MetriTech, Inc.

Braskamp, L. A., & Maehr, M. L. (1988). *Instructional Climate Inventory*. Champaign, IL: MetriTech, Inc.

Braskamp, L. A. & Maehr, M. L. (1988) *School Administrator Assessment Survey*. Champaign, IL: MetriTech, Inc.

Braskamp, L. A., & Maehr, M. L. (1985). *Spectrum: An Organizational Development Tool*. Champaign, IL: MetriTech, Inc.

LaVergne, TN USA
10 November 2009
163585LV00002B/4/P